The Survival Guide to Cooking in the Student Kitchen

by

Susan Crook

Edited by Carolyn Humphries

foulsham

LONDON • NEW YORK • TORONTO • SYDNEY

For my parents, with love

• • • • • • • •

foulsham

The Publishing House
Bennetts Close, Cippenham, Berkshire, SL1 5AP

ISBN 0-572-02455-X

Designed and phototypeset in Great Britain by Picturesque, Marlow, Bucks.
Printed in Great Britain by Cox & Wyman Ltd, Reading, Berks.

The Survival Guide to Cooking in the Student Kitchen

LEAN
MEAN
KITCHEN
MACHINE

Contents

Introduction

Kitchen survival isn't likely to be top of most people's anxiety list when they leave home for the first time. I'd put it well below concerns about making new friends, impressing them with your music collection, carrying condoms and holding your booze. But eventually gnawing hunger will take over. Man (not to mention woman) can't live by lager and crisps alone.

Moving away from home either to college or work may be your first experience of cooking since you last followed the *Blue Peter* recipe for peppermint creams ten years ago. Mum was probably around to help you then, but now it's just you and your housemates, struggling to survive in a hostile kitchen, deep within enemy territory.

For the first time you're responsible for a home and a budget. How you handle them will make a huge difference to your experience of student life. All you need is a manual to help you through the initial assault course. This book has been designed so that you can get the most out of shared living. It will help you stick to a budget, organise the cleaning, feed yourself instantly, impress your mates with sumptuous dinners and stun the world with wild parties.

A few words of warning through. It isn't easy. Don't be afraid to ask your mum or an older sibling who's already been there and done that for advice. And most importantly, don't go mad on spending at the beginning of term when your purse is full. You can always splash out on a binge at the end of term if you are able to save any money. But the other way round and you could be in dire straits.

Notes on Recipes

- All ingredients are given in metric and imperial measures. Use only one set per recipe, do not swop around.
- Wash all fresh produce before using and peel where appropriate.
- All eggs are size 3 unless otherwise stated.
- All spoon measures are level unless otherwise stated.
- When a handful is called for, use as much of the ingredient as you can comfortably hold in your hand without dropping it all over the floor.
- Washing up guide: at each recipe you will see the following symbol with a number beside it. The number is rated from 1-5 according to how much washing up that recipes makes. 1 is a minimal amount and so on.

HOME SWEET HOME
SLACKER
WILT
PAMELA
ELDERLY MILK
ROTA
FREDS FOOD
BEANS
MY KINDA PLACE
EXIDE BATTERY
KITTY
IOU
DICTIONARY
MATHS
ART
HONK
ALIEN LIFEFORMS

A CARING, SHARING HOUSEHOLD

It all seems desperately exciting as you pack up your posters, pots and pans, wave goodbye to a tearful mum and head for a home where you and a bunch of like-minded friends can do anything. But all too often those rosy dreams of shared living disappear under a pile of dirty dishes and rows about who finished the milk. So be realistic, plan ahead and don't be afraid to compromise – this is about sharing, after all.

Planning

Once you've decided who you're going to live with and where, start to sort out the details of HOW you're going to live. Do this simple multiple choice test together and don't fight – it's just for fun. (Take a majority decision on ♥, ✲ or ● and then see below for how to put each one into practice.)

How do you want to organise the cooking?

♥ All cook as a group.
✲ Take turns to cook for each other.
● All cook separately.

Your choice

- ♥ You've picked the cheapest and most fun way of getting fed, but it does involve everyone being prepared to pull their weight and come up with recipes to suit all tastes and an agreed household budget.
- ✳ You're giving yourselves more freedom to experiment and there won't be other cooks trying to spoil your broth. This system is also fairly flexible as not every member of the household needs to join in.
- ● You could end up with a rather unfriendly fridge full of individually named milk bottles and initialled eggs. There also tends to be a lot of waste – so it's more expensive. But it does give you total freedom.

How do you want to organise the shopping?

- ♥ All shop together.
- ✳ Buy the basics communally and buy food for the evening meal if it's your turn to cook it.
- ● Buy the basics communally and food separately.

(NOTE: if you seriously think you should each buy your own basics like loo rolls, then you shouldn't be living together.)

Your choice

- ♥ You're unlikely to be able to go shopping together so you'll have to rely on one or two people getting enough food for the week. You'll need to have a VERY good idea of what you all like.

- ✻ This is more practical. There will be problems if one person wants to cook steak while someone else is churning out variations on lentil spaghetti, but it will even out in the end. It allows for some people not to get involved in communal food at all.
- ● It is worth having a common fund for household necessities like loo rolls and bills (see Chapter 3 for hints on budgets and kitties).

Who's going to wash up?

- ♥ We'll have a rota.
- ✻ Whoever cooks that night.
- ● We'll all do our own as we go along.

Your choice

Washing up (or lack of it) causes more tension in shared households than almost any other issue. Nothing is more frustrating than rushing home for a hot cup of tea before *Neighbours* to discover that there isn't a clean mug in the house.To make things a little easier all the recipes in this book have a washing up graphic guide –number one for the do-it-yourself-under-the-cold-tap wash up through to number five for the friendship-busting baked-on grease.

- ♥ The rota. Photocopy this one, stick it on the wall and stick to it. Work out how many weeks there are in the term and allocate accordingly in strict rotation.

NAME	MON	TUES	WED	THURS	FRI	SAT	SUN

Be reasonable with each other – if you all have a quick meal then go out for a night on the town, you can't expect one person to stay behind being sad and doing the washing up. But it should be done by the time someone starts cooking the next day. Everyone will have to be helpful about swopping too if someone's away for the night, weekend or going out.

- ✲ This is quite harsh and you may feel that once you've cooked for the night then the last thing you want to do is go back into the kitchen to wash up. In that case follow the rota above.
- ● If you're cooking separately then you must do your own washing up too. And no trying to sneak your pile under someone else's – it won't win you any friends.

How are you going to get the cleaning done?

- ♥ We'll have a rota.
- ✲ We'll draw straws on who gets what clean and swap round each term.
- ● We'll all feel so guilty about the mess that we'll spontaneously burst into an energetic round of cleaning.

Your choice

- ♥ Another rota. Well, if you're going to have a go at one you may as well have another one. Decide what needs cleaning (nothing should need cleaning more than once a week and if you're thorough once a fortnight will be enough) and build your rota around that. The main areas are –

kitchen, bathroom, vacuuming, tidying and dusting.

- ✳ Less complicated to organise than a rota but it does mean that one person gets stuck with scrubbing the loo for a term/month – give them a nicer job next time.
- ● Dream on!

What are you going to do if one person doesn't pull their weight?

- ♥ It won't happen.
- ✳ Ignore them and hope they go away.
- ● Face the problem head on.

Your choice

The problem with all these plans is that one person will be the slacker. You will know who it is – their bedroom carpet has disappeared under a layer of grimy socks and congealed cereal bowls and it's only the second week of term. The problem is that they don't know who they are. They won't notice the ring of blackened grime round the bath or mould-encrusted mugs. Drastic action is called for.

- ♥ Believe me, it will.
- ✳ It may work, but pointing out to them that they are becoming very unpopular is better.
- ● Try these methods:

- ✔ Communal shouting – if you all shout at them then it doesn't turn into a personal argument.
- ✔ Dump all the washing up they should have done under their duvet.
- ✔ Phone their parents.
- ✔ Don't cook for them – even if they're sitting at the table with everyone else.
- ✔ If they are causing real tension, ask them to leave.

(But do remember these are drastic measures – hopefully it won't get this far.)

Basic equipment

If, like the majority of students, you rent furnished accommodation privately then your landlord is legally bound to supply some household necessities. However, what he gives you and what you'd like to have will probably be poles apart. You'll also find that three people in the house have kettles and no one has a toaster. Tick off what you've got from the list below then fill in gaps by:

- ✔ Dropping hints to your parents.
- ✔ Swapping with friends who have all toasters and no kettles etc.
- ✔ Tracking down the nearest knockdown household goods shop.
- ✔ Checking ads in the local papers.
- ✔ Rooting around in second-hand shops.

A well-equipped kitchen needs . . .

	✔
Large frying pan	
Small frying pan	
Large saucepan	
Medium saucepan	
Small saucepan	
Large plates	
Side plates	
Pudding/cereal bowls	
Knives, forks and spoons	
Mugs	
Teaspoons	
Large casserole dish	
Small heatproof dish	
Small heatproof bowl	
Large mixing bowl	
Measuring jug	
Sieve and/or colander	
Two wooden spoons	
Small balloon or other wire whisk	
Tablespoons	
Small sharp knife	
Bread knife	
Chopping board	

	✔
Corkscrew and bottle opener	
Potato peeler	
Grater	
Toaster	
Kettle	
Oven gloves	
Teatowels	
Hand towel	
Scissors	
Dusters	
Dish clothes	
Washing-up brush	
Pan scourers	
Lemon squeezer	
Can opener	
Garlic crusher	
Draining spoon	
Fish slice	
Draining rack	
Baking sheet	
Roasting tin (pan)	
Grill pan	
Washing-up liquid	

STOCKS AND SHARES

The kitchen is equipped with gleaming utensils and the rotas are pinned to the wall, but the cupboard is bare. Whether you're cooking together or on your own, start building up a collection of basics the whole household can share.

The following list should form the basis of your first happy household trip to the supermarket.

Buying everything on this list between you won't cost the earth and some things will last all year. As a guide buy large sizes of items you use lots – tea, coffee, cereals etc. and items that won't perish. But buy small ones of things that will be used only infrequently or in tiny quantities – chilli powder, herbs etc. Try out supermarkets' own brands too, they're usually much cheaper than well-known brands.

Photocopy the list and stick it up in the kitchen. Put an X in the box when something runs out for an instant shopping list.

The basics

Margarine

Jam (fruit conserve)

Caster (superfine) sugar (it can be used in drinks and cooking)

Coffee

Tea bags

Frozen peas (if you've got a freezer or freezer compartment in your fridge)

Salt

Pepper

Mixed dried herbs

Chilli powder

Curry powder

Garam masala and/or ground cumin

Tomato ketchup (catsup)

Mayonnaise

Vinegar (preferably cider, red or white wine or use malt)

Good quality vegetable oil (like sunflower or corn)

Olive oil (small bottle)				
Small bag of plain (all-purpose) flour				
Peanut butter (instant protein!)				
Veggie stock cubes				
Dried milk				
Soy sauce				
Worcester sauce				
Small tub of grated Parmesan cheese				
Made mustard (English, Dijon)				
Foil				
Self-cling plastic film				
Washing-up liquid				
Bathroom/kitchen cleaner				
Bin liners				
Disposable dish clothes				
Kitchen towels				
Loo rolls				

AND DON'T FORGET FRESH BREAD AND MILK!

Beyond the basics

You may find your attempt at communal living works out so well that you're able to expand the house shopping list to include items that you all cook with on a regular basis. The most common ingredients in this book are:

Canned tomatoes
Garlic/onions
Cheese
Bacon
Carrots
Potatoes
Baked beans
Red lentils
Brown rice
Pasta

Finding fresh foods

There's no point wasting your culinary efforts on manky meat or passée potatoes so:

Don't buy

- ✘ Fish that has dull scales and eyes or smells fishy (odd that).
- ✘ Dented cans of meat or fish – they may be slightly cheaper but the contents have been traumatised (fruit and veg are okay though).
- ✘ Meat with a brown tinge.
- ✘ Fruit and veg with a label saying "ripe" – it means overripe.

Do buy

- ✔ Cheap pallets of fruit and veg at the market, but check for rotten ones as soon as you get it home.
- ✔ Crisp-looking veg without dark brown spots.
- ✔ Bread that's still slightly warm (although beware of squashing it on the way home and don't expect it to last long!).

Chilling out

All food will last longer if it's kept cool until ready to use, but fridge space is limited so don't keep everything in there. Use your kitchen space sensibly and don't keep any foods too close to the cooker. If you've got a larder cupboard with ventilation use it!

In (the fridge)

milk
veg (at the bottom)
open cans (decant into covered containers)
raspberries
eggs (in the door only)
cheese
meat and fish
mayonnaise
pesto sauce
salad

Out (the fridge)

rice
pasta
all other fruit
onions
potatoes
bread (goes stale quicker in the fridge)
seasonings
garlic
tea and coffee
flour and other dry goods

Keep all raw foods (especially meat) well wrapped and low down in the fridge so it can't drip onto cooked food.

Respect is due to the fridge

Look after your fridge and it will look after you. Keep an eye on the temperature – if your food is coming out with ice crystals in it then it's too cold. But if your milk goes off in a day or so then it's probably not cold enough (or you've bought dodgy milk). Keep it clean – wipe up spills as they occur and keep all smelly foods well wrapped. If the fridge starts to smell, clear everything out, switch it off and let it DEFROST (unless it's self-defrosting). Here's how:

- ✔ Have lots of bowls and towels ready to catch the water.
- ✔ If the freezer section is really frosty sit a bowl of hot water in it to get the ice moving quicker.
- ✔ If you have frozen food you want to keep, wrap it in plastic bags, then in blankets, until the freezer is switched on again.
- ✔ Wash the inside with warm water that has a tablespoon of bicarbonate of soda dissolved in it.
- ✔ Leave to dry with the door open.

The dating game

Just about everything you buy in the supermarket these days has a date on it. The label may say:

Display until (this isn't your problem)

Best before)
Sell by) (your problem)
Use by)

Most of these dates are playing very safe and a bag of salad a day past its date won't kill you, but do be especially careful with meat, eggs and processed foods like paté and margarine. If you find you're having to throw food away because it's past its date, then you need to review how much food you're buying each week – don't over-shop.

You are what you eat

This isn't a lecture about eating healthily, but when you first start thinking about what you're going to be buying and eating, spare a thought for what you're actually putting into your body. It stands to reason that the better the fuel is, the better the engine will run. There's a lot of complicated info around on what you should and shouldn't be eating, but unless you're doing a course in nutrition, don't worry too much about it.

Just bear in mind that the majority of your diet should be based on carbohydrate (i.e. stodge like pasta, bread, potatoes and rice – and brown really is best) and fresh veg/fruit with a small amount of protein (meat, fish, eggs, cheese) and very little fat, salt or sugar. Think of it as a pyramid of pleasure.

nice stuff:–*salty/sugary/fatty foods*	Eat little
expensive stuff:–*meat, fish, eggs, cheese*	Have some daily
healthy stuff:–*veg, fruit, pulses*	Eat lots
filling stuff:–*bread, pasta, rice, potatoes*	Eat lots

RENT RD
GAS CITY
LECCY LAND
WOLF AT THE DOOR
LANDLORD FROM HELL!
SUPERMARK
ALL DONATION VERY GRATEFU RECEIVE
FINAL DEMAND
BILL
PAY OR ELSE

SPEND! SPEND! SPEND!

As a student you will have very little money. This is a fact of life, so get used to it before we go any further. What you need to work out is how to make the best of what you have got so the majority of it can be spent on having fun.

If you decide to shop and eat together it will work out cheaper, although it can be more tempting to splash out on luxuries if the cost is shared than if the money is coming directly from your pocket.

Whichever way you choose to organise your household, you'll need to sort out a way of splitting the cost – even if you're only sharing the electricity bill. The first step is to ask:

Where is all my money going?

You'll ask this question a lot. These are the essential areas of expenditure –

Rent
Electricity bill
Gas bill
Food
Phone bill
Travel

Total

Work out how much you're spending a week on each and it should give you an idea of how much you've got to spend on the nicer things in life – not to mention books and equipment.

Most of the recipes in this book work out at well under £1 a head (but don't forget to budget for breakfast and lunches away from home).

Here kitty, kitty

To cover the shared household bills – electricity, gas, phone, TV rental, food and non-food essentials like bin liners – you need to put aside a fixed sum every week.

The best way to do this is with a kitty. Each of you pays your share each week, either to a jar under someone's bed or – if you want to be sophisticated – set up a household bank account. Both methods involve you having to trust another member of your household enough to look after the money/keep the cheque book. If you don't, don't get involved with a kitty system. If the slacker in your house is claiming impecunity, don't let them get away with not paying. Give them a date – maybe the first of the month – to cough up by. If they still aren't paying up, padlock the fridge and remove their lightbulbs. If they aren't paying for food and electricity, they don't want them, right? Right.

The advantages of the kitty are that it helps you budget over the term and if there's any cash left at the end of term you can have a big booze-up. On the downside, it can lead to questions about who's spending money on what and there's usually one person who treats it as a loan system for emergency drinking sessions.

An alternative way to organise the household budget is to buy the bits and pieces you need and keep a tally in a book. Work out the totals once a month, so the people who are more efficient about buying bread, milk etc. aren't out of pocket for too long. Have a whip-round for big bills.

If you decide not to have a kitty, then it's up to you to keep control of your budget so you're able to pay the bills – even if they come in the last week of term.

Keeping the cost down

There are endless ways to cut corners and live cheaply – finding them yourself is part of the fun of living away from home – but here are my top 10 money-spinning greats.

- ✔ Check out your local market and make it the focus of shopping trips. Fruit, veg, eggs, cheese and all manner of household goods can be bought at a fraction of supermarket prices.

- ✔ When you do have to go to the supermarket, go at the end of the day when fresh produce nearing its sell-by date is marked down.

- ✔ Keep an eye on supermarket special offers – particularly own brands. They often do "three for the price of two" deals which are a bargain for essential items.

- ✔ Don't ever buy supermarket fruit and veg which is ready packed – simply by picking up a bag and filling it yourself you're saving.
- ✔ Supermarket prepared food like pizza and lasagne is often cheaper if you buy it frozen rather than from the chill cabinet.
- ✔ Collect money-off vouchers which come through the door or fall out of newspapers. Some supermarkets will accept vouchers even if you aren't buying that product, though this is getting rarer.
- ✔ Buy thin-cut bread. No one will notice the difference and you get a few more slices for your money. If it goes stale, sprinkle with a drop of water and then toast.
- ✔ Remember that electricity costs more than gas – so if you need hot water for cooking, heat it in a saucepan rather than in the electric kettle. In fact if you have a gas hob, don't bother at all with an electric kettle, one that sits on the hob will be cheaper to buy and run. And only heat the amount of water you need.
- ✔ If you're cooking something that needs the oven, a casserole for example, do baked potatoes and veg in the oven too to save fuel.
- ✔ Buy seasonally. Even though you can buy fresh goods throughout the year, strawberries cost a fortune in January and about one-tenth of the price in July and the same goes for just about every other fresh product.

(or how to cook absolutely anything)

BUT I CAN'T EVEN BOIL AN EGG!

If the last thing you cooked was that *Blue Peter* recipe for peppermint creams ten years ago, despair not. Basic cooking is a cinch. Just bear in mind that raw food + heat = delicious hot food and you can't go wrong. It's just a question of knowing how to apply which heat to what food.

The main cooking methods are boiling, steaming, baking, roasting, frying and grilling.

Boiling

You need a saucepan big enough to cook the quantity of food (see below for guidelines on quantities) plus enough room to cover the food in water. The basic principle is to bring a saucepan of water to the boil and add the food. Continue boiling until it's cooked.

Pasta: Use the biggest possible saucepan, fill two-thirds full with water and bring to the boil. Add a dash of oil and a pinch of salt. Pour in pasta and stir occasionally with a wooden spoon. Turn the heat down so the water just simmers (i.e. bubbles gently).

Pasta usually takes about 8 minutes to cook, wholemeal pasta takes a little longer. Some people suggest throwing a strand of pasta at the wall to see if it's cooked (if it sticks, it's done), but this can get messy. I suggest lifting a piece out with the wooden spoon, running it under the cold tap and eating it. You don't want pasta to be too soggy. It needs bite. Don't cover the pan or it will boil over.

Eggs: Probably one of the most difficult things to boil. Put the eggs into a saucepan of cold water and bring to the boil. Add a burnt match to the water (sounds mad, but it helps to stop the eggshell cracking). Once the water is boiling, let it simmer for exactly 4 minutes for a firm white and soft yolk, 5 minutes for a firm yolk.

Rice: White rice is tricky to cook, brown is much better behaved, as well as being higher in fibre. Boil a kettle of water and meanwhile heat a tablespoon of oil in the bottom of a saucepan. Add the rice to the oil and stir round for a minute. (This helps to stop it sticking.) Add the water and bring to the boil, stir once then turn down the heat. It should take about 15-20 minutes to cook for white, up to 30 minutes for brown. Don't stir rice too much as it goes mushy. Drain and rinse with boiling water then drain again.

Potatoes: A lot of the goodness is just under the skin, so don't peel them unless you plan to mash them. Just scrub them and take out the blemishes and bumpy bits. Chop into smallish pieces and cover with cold water. Bring to the boil and allow 10-15 minutes cooking time. (Put new baby potatoes into boiling water and cook for 8-10 minutes until soft right through when pierced.) For mash, drain thoroughly and add a splash of milk, a knob of margarine, salt and pepper and beat with a potato masher or fork until soft and fluffy.

Steaming

This is the best way to cook vegetables because it keeps in all the goodness and colour. You don't need a high-tech steamer – a metal colander over a saucepan of boiling water which is then covered with the saucepan lid does the job just as well. Many woks come with a steaming "shelf" too. Cooking time is slightly longer than with boiling, but is justified by the results.

Greens: Remove tough stalks and outer leaves. Rinse, slice finely and pack into the colander or steamer. Bring the water underneath to the boil, put a lid over the steamer and leave for 5 minutes.

Broccoli: Rinse and chop into small pieces, using the stalks as well as the florets. Steam as above.

Carrots: Top, tail and scrape or peel. Cut into slices a matchstick thick. Steam for about three minutes.

Green beans: Rinse, top and tail. Cut in two or three pieces if liked or leave whole. Steam as above.

Oven baking

It's a good idea to pre-heat the oven for 15-20 minutes before putting the food in, especially when cooking cakes and biscuits. If you're using the oven, it's worth cooking more than one dish at the same time as it saves fuel. But remember if you fill your oven up the food will all take slightly longer to cook. A warm oven is also useful for keeping food hot while you wait for everyone to come back from the pub.

Potatoes: Choose large oversized ones – and give them a good scrub. Score the longest side with a sharp knife – to stop the potato splitting and to make it easier to cut open when cooked. Put in an oven pre-heated to 190°C / 375°F / gas mark 5 for one hour. Potatoes will cook very happily at virtually any temperature so if you contemplate having the munchies after a hard night out, put them on at a low heat, so they're ready on your return.

You can speed up the cooking process by sticking a metal skewer through the centre of each potato.

Apples: Core cooking (tart) apples from top to bottom using a sharp knife and place in a shallow baking tin (pan). Fill the hole with dried fruit, nuts or muesli, sprinkle a tablespoon of sugar and a tablespoon of water over each apple and bake for 30 minutes at around 190°C / 375°F / gas mark 5.

Roasting

This is like baking except you do it in fat or oil.

Meat: Cooking a joint is very expensive but it is delicious, so choose a joint of meat that looks fresh and lean. Leave any string on to hold its shape until it's cooked. Wipe with kitchen paper, put into a roasting tin (pan). Rub over with a little oil unless it has a coating of fat. Allow 225-350 g (8-12 oz) per person if the meat's got bones in and 100-175 g (4-6 oz) per person if it hasn't. Pre-heat the oven to gas 5 / 190°C / 375°F. Roast for 25 minutes per 450 g / 1 lb plus an extra 25 minutes if you want it well done. Reduce by 5 minutes per 450 g / 1 lb for pink in the middle.

For crisp pork crackling, score rind in strips with a sharp knife. Rub with oil and sprinkle with salt. Stand meat on a rack in the tin (pan) so it is raised out of the dripping as it cooks.

Poultry: Nothing is easier to roast than a chicken, and it's cheap too. Make sure it's completely thawed if frozen. Rinse the chicken and take out any bits in the body cavity (giblets). Put the chicken into a roasting tin (pan), rub with oil. Pre-heat the oven to 190°C / 375°F / gas mark 5. Roast for 20 minutes per 450 g / 1 lb plus an extra 20 minutes.

Potatoes: Roast tatties are one of life's great pleasures. Peel more potatoes than you think you need, and boil for 5 minutes. Drain, then chuck them back into the saucepan and shake for about 30 seconds to roughen the edges so they will brown and crisp. Heat 2 tablespoons of oil in a large roasting tin (pan). Add the potatoes and roll them around until coated in oil. Put in the top of the oven while cooking meat. Baby new potatoes can be roasted too. Simply rinse them, roll around in an oiled baking tin (pan) and cook as above.

Veg: Root veg like parsnips and carrots can be roasted in exactly the same way as potatoes, but you don't need to shake them to roughen the edges.

Frying

Pour as thin a layer as possible of vegetable oil into your frying pan (skillet) and heat it gently. Whatever you're frying keep an eye on it – there's a thin line between frying and burning.

Fry chicken, vegeburgers, beefburgers, mushrooms, eggs, sliced courgettes (zucchini). Sausages and bacon can be dry-fried without fat because they have plenty of their own! Use your common sense when it comes to timing – fried food is cooked when it looks cooked.

How to fry the perfect egg: Get the oil hot, but not hissing. Crack in the egg (in a cup first if you're not very good at it) and stop it spreading too far by pushing the white back towards the yolk with a fish slice. As the white cooks, spoon the hot oil across the yolk and onto that bit of white round it that never cooks. Use the fish slice to dish it out.

Grilling

An increasingly popular option in these health-conscious times. Works like frying by cooking food one side at a time, but without the cooking oil. Again, watch the grill very carefully. Always have the grill hot before cooking.

Sausages: Turn frequently for 7-15 minutes, depending on size. Don't prick them.

Bacon: Make little cuts along the fatty edge of the bacon (this stops it curling up) and grill for about 3 minutes each side.

Courgettes (zucchini) and aubergines (eggplants): Top and tail, then slice thinly from top to bottom. Brush both sides of each slice with oil (if you don't have a pastry brush use a scrunched-up piece of kitchen towel dipped in oil) and grill for three minutes each side.

Red, green and yellow (bell) peppers: Top and tail, cut in half vertically and remove the white bits inside. Grill, skin side up, until the skin blackens. Pop the pepper pieces into a plastic bag or wrap in foil (this loosens the skin). After 10 minutes peel the skin off and serve with olive oil or French dressing (see Salads in Chapter 6). Delicious.

Flavouring

Any dish can be improved by being well seasoned. This basically means adding salt and pepper. Taste, season, then taste again. Chilli powder, mixed herbs,

Worcestershire sauce, soy sauce, mustard and curry powder are store cupboard basics which can add masses of flavour. Just add a little to start with, then more if you need to.

Quantities

Very few student kitchens are equipped with sophisticated weighing scales, but the majority of recipe books call for 100 g of this or 13 fl oz of that. Ignore all that stuff – in this book virtually all quantities are given as handfuls or easy-to-measure portions. Don't forget that tbsp = tablespoon; tsp = teaspoon.

If your first attempt at cooking results in a handful of rice between six or enough spaghetti to feed the five thousand, stop and think about how much food you'd like to see on your plate.

As a guide, rice and pasta double in size when cooking, so if you normally eat about 4 tbsp when cooked, use 2 tbsp raw and so on.

Rewriting the recipes

Once you master the basics of cooking, don't be afraid to experiment. A recipe is a guideline, not a commandment. There are no hard and fast rules in this book – if you want something spicy add chilli; if you've got lots of potatoes sitting around boil some up and chuck them into the curry/omelette/soup that's on the go.

I've tried to give alternatives in the recipes which follow, but if it says "add chopped bacon" and you haven't got any or don't eat the stuff – try chopped mushrooms or peppers instead. There are as many variations as there are people to cook them.

Getting saucy

The most easily varied recipes of all are the two basic sauces which will keep you happily fed for years. They are white sauce and tomato sauce – each one can be the basis of many different dishes. Both sauces can be poured over cooked pasta, rice, baked potatoes or even toast. They can be diluted with water to make soup.

White sauce

Put 1 tbsp margarine or vegetable oil in a saucepan. Stir in 1 tbsp of flour. Whisk in 300 ml / ½ pt / 1¼ cups of milk. Bring to the boil, whisking all the time. Season with salt and pepper.

Cheese sauce: add a handful of grated cheese after cooking.

Mushroom sauce: fry a handful of sliced mushrooms in the butter/oil before adding the flour and milk.

Leek/onion sauce: fry one thinly sliced leek/onion as above.

Tomato sauce

Peel and chop an onion. Fry in 1 tbsp oil until it's transparent then add a 400 g / 14 oz can of chopped tomatoes. Boil rapidly for 5 minutes. Season with salt, pepper and a pinch of mixed dried herbs.

Chilli sauce: add $^{1}/_{2}$ tsp chilli powder to the sauce when you season it.

Italian sauce: fry a handful of sliced mushrooms with the onion and go heavy on the herbs.

Tuna sauce: drain a 185 g / $6^{1}/_{2}$ oz can of tuna and add to the tomato

Bacon sauce: chop two rashers (slices) bacon and fry with the onion.

HELP! EXAM CRISIS AND FEEDING YOURSELF INSTANTLY

You know that feeling: starving hungry, but not a second to spare from last minute revision/all night essay frenzy or, heaven forbid, actually enjoying yourself. It's time to resort to ready-made food – open a few cans or head for the supermarket chill cabinet.

It really is important to eat properly – if you're starving in an exam you won't be able to think straight. If you really can't face food, take some glucose tablets into the exam room with you and eat them regularly. This will keep your blood sugar high, helping to keep your brain ticking over at a reasonable pace.

During my finals I lived on pasties, salad and samosas from the Indian supermarket round the corner – all instant foods. Try not to start buying prepared ready meals – they cost a fortune and aren't very good for you. Ditto takeaways. A friend of mine revised in a curry house every night for a month. Having seen the size of his gut and his overdraft afterwards I wouldn't recommend it. But there's no harm in spoiling yourself once in a while!

Don't forget the simple sandwich.
Make huge ones
with any filling you like.
Use a variety of loaves, rolls and pittas.
Add salad bits for vitamins and minerals.

Supermarket sweeps

In times of crisis the supermarket will help you – as long as you don't start helping yourself to overpriced selections of Indian and Chinese nibbles, chicken tikka or prepared tomato sauce for pasta (my tomato sauce recipe on page 38 tastes just as good and costs one-third of the price).

The best value comes from vegetables dishes and basic things like cheese and tomato pizza that you can add your own toppings to. So fill your basket with:

Smarty little packs of ready to stir-fry veg

Sachets of rice with bits in – Thai or Indian style are good and don't cost much. Add some frozen veg and soy sauce or mango chutney

Oriental noodle soup – for very little money you get a pack of noodles which takes three minutes to cook, plus a sachet of flavouring. Add a few frozen peas or any cooked leftover vegetables in the fridge

Simple chill-cabinet meals-for-one like lasagne or cauliflower cheese are a good buy

Tins of veg curry, ratatouille or stir-fry. Serve with rice noodles (they take only minutes to cook)

Baked beans with meatballs or sausages – a stodge-out for pennies

Frozen crispy pancakes

Frozen chilli or curry with rice

Frozen pizza – cheaper than the chilled variety

Hummous, taramasalata or tzatziki – Greek dips that can be served with pitta bread, tortilla chips, cucumber sticks and carrots

Store cupboard standbys

If your store cupboard is reasonably well stocked you should be able to rustle up the following recipes in minutes. All produce minimal washing up and serve one (it's every man for himself in an exam crisis).

CHEESE AND EGG TOASTIES

Serves 1

2 slices of bread
Margarine or butter
Small handful of grated cheese
1 or 2 eggs
A toasted sandwich maker

1 Pre-heat the sandwich maker.

2 Butter the bread and put one slice buttered side down in the bottom bit.

3 Sprinkle on the cheese. Then break the egg on top.

4 Split the yolk with a knife (this is the tricky bit) so it runs equally into each section.

5 Top with the other slice of bread and cook.

If you don't have a sandwich maker: make up a cheese sandwich, beat the egg and soak the sandwich in it on both sides until completely covered. Fry in a little oil until golden on both sides.

BAKED BEAN DELUXE

Serves 1

2 slices of bread
Butter or margarine
Marmite
Handful of grated cheese
200 g / 7 oz can of baked beans

1 Toast the bread, butter it and spread with Marmite.

2 Top with cheese and grill (broil) until bubbling.

3 Meanwhile heat the beans. Pour the beans over the toast.

••••••••

TUNA, MAYO, SWEETCORN

Serves 1

½ x 185 g / 6½ oz can tuna in brine, drained
Small 200 g / 7 oz can sweetcorn (corn), drained
1 tbsp mayonnaise
Pepper

1 Put the tuna and sweetcorn in a bowl.

2 Add mayonnaise and season with pepper (you won't need salt).

3 Eat as it is out of the bowl or with toast.

Add leftover cooked rice, pasta or potatoes for a filling meal.

VEG BALTI

Serves 1

1 tbsp vegetable oil

Any vegetables you have to hand – a courgette (zucchini), piece of cabbage, carrots, broccoli – chopped small

$^1/_2$ jar balti curry sauce

Portion of instant noodles

1 Heat the oil and add the vegetables. Stir around for 2-3 minutes then add sauce.

2 Let it bubble gently while you cook the noodles.

If you've got cooked, leftover vegetables to hand, chop them up, add to the sauce and heat through.

•••••••••

BEAN BAKE

Serves 1

400 g / 14 oz can bean salad
or chilli beans

Handful of grated cheese

1 packet ready-salted crisps

1 Heat the beans in a saucepan then put into a shallow, heatproof dish.

2 Mix the cheese and crisps together and sprinkle on top.

3 Pop under a pre-heated grill (broiler) for about 5 minutes until cheese bubbles and beans are heated through.

••••••••

BOILED EGG AND PEANUT BUTTER SOLDIERS

Serves 1

1 egg

2 slices of bread

Peanut butter

1 Boil the egg as described in Chapter 4.

2 Meanwhile, toast the bread and smother in peanut butter.

3 Cut toast into thin strips and dip into egg.

••••••••

SPAGHETTI SURPRISE

Serves 1

400 g / 14 oz of spaghetti in tomato sauce

1 surprise item (my mum uses chopped ham, but a little tuna, chopped mushrooms or sweetcorn (corn) would be good)

Small handful of grated cheese

1 slice bread, cut into small cubes

1 Pre-heat the grill (broiler). Heat the spaghetti and surprise item in a pan.

2 Pour into a heatproof dish and top with cheese and bread.

3 Grill (broil) for 2 minutes.

●●●●●●●●●

TUNA AND MUSHROOM SOUP

Serves 1

1 quantity mushroom sauce (see page 37)

½ x 185 g / 6½ oz can tuna in brine, drained

Pepper

To serve: lots of crusty bread

1 Make up the mushroom sauce, but only use 2 tsp flour. Add the tuna, heat through and season with lots of pepper. Serve with lots of bread.

MASH AND MUSHROOM SAUCE

Serves 1

1 portion instant mashed potato

Lump of butter or margarine

$^1/_2$ x 275 g / 10 oz can condensed mushroom soup

1 Make up the potato according to the instructions on the packet. Add the butter or margarine.

2 Heat soup gently (it will be quite thick) and pour over.

●●●●●●●●

HOT MUESLI

Serves 1

Milk

Muesli

1 Fill your favourite cereal bowl with muesli, then pour the muesli into a saucepan.

2 Fill the cereal bowl with milk, then pour that into the pan too.

3 Heat gently, stirring all the time, until the muesli has absorbed most of the milk.

4 Put it back into the cereal bowl. It's like Ready Brek with bits in.

●●●●●●●●

LEFT, RIGHT
FLIP!
LIFE, THE UNIVERSE AND EVERYTHING
UP, UP & AWAY
A shy Potato
YIKES MISSED!

AFTER LECTURES, BEFORE THE PUB

Life's too short to spend too much time in the kitchen. When you need to feed the team quickly, pasta, salads, omelettes and a few ethnic specials do the trick.

Pasta

Pasta really comes into its own when time is short – it's filling, nutritious and CHEAP. All it needs is a sauce and that can be made while it's cooking.

Use a good handful of dry pasta shapes per person – or a 250 g packet for four people. If cooking spaghetti use 1/2 a 500 g packet (or more if you're starving). Cooking time remains the same however much you cook. But make sure you have a large enough saucepan!

Large pasta, like spaghetti or tagliatelle, is best for the clingy sauces – pesto; carbonara; cheese and onion; Moroccan tomato. Short, stumpy pasta shapes are best for chunky sauces – cream, leek and bacon; slacker salmon; chickpea; spinach and mushroom.

SLACKER SALMON

Serves 4

250 g / 9 oz pasta shapes
Salt
185 g / $6\frac{1}{2}$ oz can pink salmon, drained and bones and skin removed
2 tbsp cooked peas or sweetcorn (corn) (optional)
4 tbsp mayonnaise
2 tbsp milk
Pepper

1 Cook pasta in plenty of boiling salted water according to packet directions and drain.

2 Put the salmon in a small pan with the peas or sweetcorn if using, mayonnaise and the milk.

3 Heat through very, very gently, stirring all the time. Mix into pasta. Season with pepper.

•••••••••

CHICKPEA (Garbanzos)

Serves 4

250 g / 9 oz pasta shapes
Salt
2 tbsp olive oil
1 garlic clove, crushed
2 x 430 g / $15\frac{1}{2}$ oz cans chickpeas, rinsed and drained
1 tsp chilli powder
2 red (bell) peppers, seeded and chopped

1 Cook pasta in plenty of boiling salted water until tender and drain.

2 Heat the oil and mix in all the other ingredients. Heat through for 5 minutes.

3 Add to pasta, toss well and serve.

••••••••

PESTO

Serves 4

Pesto is one of a growing number of prepared pasta sauces that are a cinch to use and it's probably the best value for money.

250 g / 9 oz large pasta
Salt
2 tbsp pesto sauce
Lump of margarine or
 2 tbsp olive oil
To serve: Grated Parmesan or Cheddar cheese.

1 Cook the pasta in plenty of boiling salted water according to packet directions. Drain and put it back in the pan.

2 Add the pesto and margarine or olive oil.

3 Stir it around and serve with grated Parmesan or Cheddar cheese.

••••••••

CARBONARA

Serves 4

If you're a garlic fan add a little garlic purée or a crushed clove with onion.

250 g / 9 oz large pasta
Salt
4 rashers (slices) bacon, chopped (or for veggies 2 handfuls sliced mushroom)
1 tbsp oil
4 eggs
2 tbsp Parmesan, or Cheddar cheese grated
2 tbsp cream or milk

1 Cook pasta in plenty of boiling salted water according to packet directions. Drain and return to pan.

2 Meanwhile fry the bacon (or mushrooms) in the oil until brown.

3 Beat the eggs, cheese, cream or milk and some pepper in a bowl and stir in the bacon.

4 Add the bacon mix to the hot pasta. Stir it around over a gentle heat until lightly scrambled but still creamy and serve with salad.

•••••••••

CHEESE AND ONION

Serves 4

250 g / 9 oz large pasta
Salt
1 onion, chopped
1 tbsp oil
300 ml / ½ pt / 1¼ cups of milk
1 tbsp flour
2 handfuls grated cheese

1 Cook pasta in plenty of boiling salted water according to packet directions and drain.

2 Meanwhile fry (sauté) the onion in the oil until transparent.

3 Add the flour and stir around. Add the milk slowly, stirring as you go. Bring to the boil. Stir all the time until thickened.

4 Add the cheese and stir until melted.

5 Stir into the pasta and serve.

••••••••

CREAM, LEEK AND BACON

Serves 4

250 g / 9 oz pasta shapes

Salt

2 large leeks, thinly sliced

4 rashers (slices) bacon, chopped

1 tbsp oil

1 small carton (150 ml / ¼ pt / ⅔ cup) double (heavy) cream

Pepper

1 Cook pasta in plenty of boiling salted water according to packet directions and drain.

2 Fry (sauté) the bacon and leeks in the oil until the leeks are soft. Add the cream and season with pepper. Leave to bubble for 2 minutes.

3 Stir into pasta and serve hot.

For a lighter sauce use natural (plain) yoghurt.

•••••••••

MORROCAN TOMATO

Serves 4

250 g / 9 oz pasta shapes
Salt
1 onion, chopped
1 garlic clove, crushed
1 small aubergine (eggplant), topped, tailed and cubed
2 tbsp oil
400 g / 14 oz can chopped tomatoes
1 tbsp raisins or sultanas (golden raisins)
1 tsp ground cumin (optional)

1 Cook pasta in plenty of boiling salted water according to packet directions and drain.

2 Fry (sauté) the onion, garlic and aubergine in the oil for five minutes, stirring.

3 Add the tomatoes, dried fruit and spice and heat through. Simmer for 5 minutes until pulpy.

4 Pile pasta onto warm plates and spoon over, or toss in, the sauce.

•••••••••

SPINACH AND MUSHROOM

Serves 4

250 g / 9 oz pasta shapes
1 tbsp oil
1 garlic clove, crushed
4 handfuls of mushrooms, sliced
4 handfuls of fresh spinach, rinsed, de-stalked and chopped
4 large tomatoes, chopped
1 small carton (150 ml / $^{1}/_{4}$ pt / $^{2}/_{3}$ cup) double (heavy) cream or thick yoghurt

1 Cook pasta in plenty of boiling salted water according to packet directions and drain.

2 Lightly fry (sauté) the garlic and mushrooms in the oil.

3 Add the spinach and tomatoes and keep stirring until the spinach has wilted. Pour in cream or yoghurt and heat through but do not boil or it will curdle.

4 Add to pasta, toss and serve.

•••••••••

Salad

Instant, nutritious and almost anything edible can go into it. All good salad needs a good base and a good dressing. Serve with plenty of crusty bread.

The salad base:
This is the veggy bit – any type of lettuce you fancy (washed and torn into pieces), shredded cabbage (red, white or green), sliced cucumber, grated or chopped carrot or other root veggies, sliced tomato, chopped (bell) peppers, sliced mushrooms, lightly boiled cauliflower or broccoli florets, grated courgette (zucchini).
Aim to cover each plate with the stuff then put the tasty bits on top.

The salad dressing:
This is the oily bit – the classic recipe is one part vinegar or lemon juice to three parts olive oil, mixed and shaken well.
This can be altered with splashes of different flavoured oils like walnut and sesame, or soy sauce for an oriental touch.
Always season dressing with salt and pepper.
A crushed garlic clove, a dash of chilli or a pinch of mixed dried herbs is good too.
Salad dressing will keep up to a week in the fridge. 3 tbsp of oil and one of vinegar will serve 4 people.

SPINACH, BACON AND AVOCADO

Serves 4

Salad base for 4 plates (see above)

4 small handfuls of spinach leaves, washed and torn into pieces

4 tbsp olive oil

4 rashers (slices) bacon, chopped, or 4 small handfuls of mushrooms, sliced

1 tbsp lemon juice

2 ripe avocados, peeled and chopped

1 Arrange the spinach leaves on the salad base.

2 Heat the oil in a small frying pan (skillet) and fry (sauté) the bacon or mushrooms until brown.

3 Add the lemon juice then pour the entire contents of the pan over the spinach (the hot dressing will wilt the spinach slightly). Chuck the avocado on top and serve straight away.

An avocado is ripe when you can move the skin around the top with your thumb

●●●●●●●●●

EGGY SALAD

Serves 4

Salad base and dressing for 4 plates

4 tomatoes, sliced

4 tbsp mayonnaise

4 eggs

Oil

4 thick slices of bread (white is best), cubed

1 Boil the eggs for around 8 minutes, then place in cold water until cool enough to shell. Quarter the eggs.

2 Put eggs and tomatoes on the salad base and spoon mayonnaise on top.

3 Heat the oil in a small frying pan (skillet). Add the bread. Keep the heat high until the bread is golden and crispy on all sides, stirring all the time.

4 Remove from pan with a draining spoon, drain on kitchen paper then scatter over salad.

For garlic croutons (bread cubes) add a crushed clove of garlic to the oil before frying bread.

••••••••

MEXICAN PASTA

Serves 4

Salad base for 4 plates (see above)

4 handfuls of pasta shapes, cooked (see page 49), rinsed with cold water and drained

425 g / 15 oz can red kidney beans, washed and drained

200 g / 7 oz can sweetcorn (corn), drained

1 ripe avocado, peeled and chopped

Salad dressing (see above) made with one tsp chilli powder

1 Mix together the pasta, beans, corn, and avocado.

2 Add the dressing, toss well and spoon onto salad base.

••••••••

HOT CHICKEN AND BACON

Serves 4

Salad base for 4 plates (see above)

4 tbsp olive oil

4 rashers (slices) bacon, chopped

2 chicken breasts, skinned and cubed

2 tbsp lemon juice

1 Arrange the salad on four plates.

2 Heat the oil in a frying pan (skillet) and fry (sauté) the bacon and chicken, stirring occasionally until both are lightly browned – about 7 minutes. Add the lemon juice and spoon onto salads. Serve straight away.

•••••••••

HOT 'N' SPICY TOFU

Serves 4

Salad base for 4 plates

2 tbsp soy sauce

1 tsp chilli powder

1 packet of firm silken tofu, cubed

2 handfuls of mushrooms, sliced

4 tbsp olive oil

Small, 200 g / 7 oz can sweetcorn (corn), drained and rinsed

1 Arrange salad bases on plates.

2 Mix the soy sauce and chilli in a bowl, add the tofu and leave to marinate for 10 minutes.

3 Fry (sauté) the mushrooms in the oil, add the tofu, mix and heat through gently, stirring. Sprinkle the sweetcorn over the salad bases and put the hot tofu mix on top.

•••••••••

GOAT'S CHEESE AND GRILLED PEPPERS

Serves 4

Salad base for 4 plates

4 red or yellow peppers

Salad dressing enough for 4 plates of salad base (see page 57)

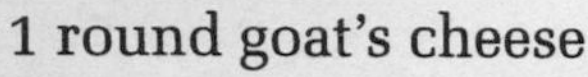

1 round goat's cheese

1 slice of toast, quartered

1 Arrange salad base on plates.

2 Grill the peppers. Peel if preferred. Slice.

3 Put slices on top of the salad and pour the dressing over.

4 Slice the cheese horizontally into four discs and place each one on a quarter of toast slice. Grill (broil) for about 2 minutes or until the cheese browns. Lay on the peppers and serve.

•••••••••

ORIENTAL NOODLE

Serves 4

4 handfuls of rice or egg noodles

Salt

4 handfuls of mangetout (snow peas)

4 handfuls of bean sprouts

Dressing: 2 tbsp soy sauce

1 level tsp chilli powder

juice of 1/2 lemon

2 tsp sesame oil

2 tbsp olive oil

1 Cook the rice or noodles in boiling water according to packet directions. Add mangetout for last 2 minutes' cooking time. Drain, rinse with cold water and drain again.

2 Add the bean sprouts and divide between four plates (or bowls). Put dressing ingredients in a screw-topped jar and shake well until blended.

3 Pour the dressing over the salad and serve.

•••••••••

Stir fries

You could live on stir-fries all year. They suit meat eaters and veggies, use cheap ingredients, take minutes to cook and never taste the same twice. There are just a few basic rules to remember:

TOP TIP

Prepare all the ingredients before you start cooking.

•

Most vegetables will work in a stir-fry – (bell) peppers, carrots, bean sprouts, courgettes (zucchini), cabbage, onions, leeks. For the meat part try skinned chicken or turkey breast (or look for prepared stir-fry poultry), pork (shoulder is cheaper than fillet – or you could try de-rinding and cutting up belly rashers into very small pieces) and – if you're feeling very flush – steak. Liver and kidneys are ideal too. Cut all meat in strips (or small pieces for kidneys). You need very little meat – 2 chicken breasts or 225 g / 8 oz meat will serve four – the veg is the most important thing.

•

All the ingredients need to be cut to the same size. Aim for chunky batons about 5 cm / 2 in long and 5 mm / ¼ in in width and thickness. You'll need 6 handfuls for four people – that's the equivalent of 2 courgettes (zucchini), 4 carrots, 2 (bell) peppers and ½ cabbage.

The flavour of stir-fry comes from the sauce. There's loads of room to experiment here – but the basic ingredients for 4 are: 4 tbsp soy sauce, 1 tbsp vinegar and 1 tsp of runny honey or sugar. Jazz it up with chilli powder, ground ginger, sherry, sesame oil or 1 tbsp prepared sauce like yellow bean (expensive, but if you use it like this it'll last for ages). Mix up all the ingredients in a bowl.

•

You must stir-fry on the hob in a wok or deep-dish frying pan (skillet). Get it really hot and then add 1 tbsp of cooking oil. Swirl the oil around.

•

If you're using meat, add to the hot oil and cook for 3 minutes, then add the veg and cook for a further 2 minutes. Add the sauce and stir thoroughly for a minute more before serving.

•

Serve with rice or noodles.

•

That's all there is to it!

•••••••••

Omelettes

Another made-in-minutes meal that suits most people. They're best made individually – but if preferred make one big one using 6-8 eggs and serve a quarter per person. Here's how:

In a bowl beat 2 eggs until they look a bit frothy. Add 2 tbsp water and season well.

•

Choose a topping if you want one – grated cheese, chopped ham, sliced mushrooms, boiled potatoes or simply a pinch of mixed dried herbs all work well.

•

Heat a small knob of margarine or 1 tbsp oil in a non-stick frying pan (skillet).

•

Pour in the egg mix. Use a wooden spatula to lift and stir the egg until it sets and browns underneath. Keep the heat low so it doesn't burn.

•

Add any topping after 2 minutes' cooking.

•

When brown underneath and almost set, pop it under the grill (broil) to finish off, if liked.

•

Cut into quarters or fold in three and serve with bread and salad.

••••••••••

CHICKEN IN WINE SAUCE

Serves 4

1 tbsp oil

4 skinned chicken breasts, cubed

2 handfuls of mushrooms, sliced

1 glass white wine (dregs will do)

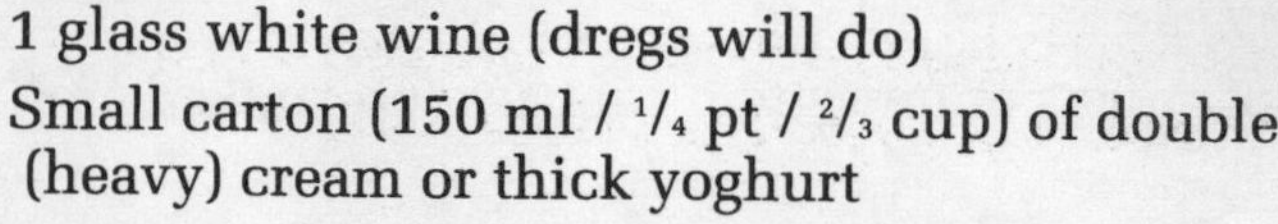

Small carton (150 ml / $^{1}/_{4}$ pt / $^{2}/_{3}$ cup) of double (heavy) cream or thick yoghurt

1 Heat the oil in a small frying pan (skillet).

2 Add the chicken and stir it around until it starts to brown (about 2 minutes).

3 Add the wine and mushrooms. Cook over a moderate heat for 5 more minutes. Add the cream, heat through and season well. Serve with rice or pasta. Luxurious, but quick.

You can use chicken thighs either whole or cubed, which are much cheaper. But remember they'll take a little longer to cook through.

●●●●●●●●●

THAI GREENS

Serves 4

2 rashers (slices) bacon, chopped small (optional)
1 tbsp oil
Juice of 1 lime
2 tsp sugar
1 tsp chilli powder
2 tbsp soy sauce
2 heads of greens or one small cabbage, de-stalked and shredded
To serve: rice noodles

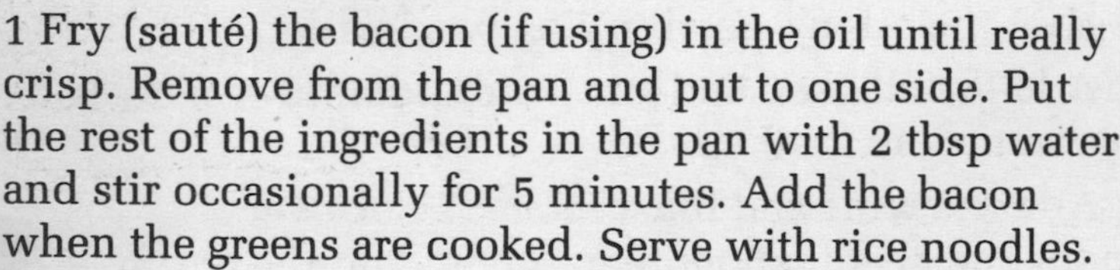

1 Fry (sauté) the bacon (if using) in the oil until really crisp. Remove from the pan and put to one side. Put the rest of the ingredients in the pan with 2 tbsp water and stir occasionally for 5 minutes. Add the bacon when the greens are cooked. Serve with rice noodles.

•••••••••

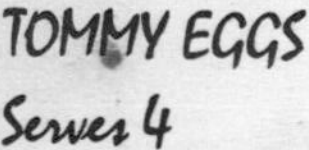

TOMMY EGGS

Serves 4

This recipe was once used in *Neighbours*. Who says Aussie soaps have no cultural worth?

1 onion, finely chopped
4 rashers (slices) bacon, chopped (optional)

1 tbsp oil
6 eggs, beaten
4 tomatoes, seeded and chopped

1 In a saucepan fry (sauté) the onion and bacon (if using) in the oil until the bacon is crisping.

2 Add the eggs and tomatoes and stir around until the eggs are cooked. This is good with chips and ketchup, but toast will do.

●●●●●●●●

MALAYSIAN PEANUT CHICKEN

Serves 4

3 chicken breasts, skinned and cut into thin strips
1 tbsp cooking oil
1 green (bell) pepper, cut into thin strips
2 tbsp peanut butter
2 tbsp soy sauce
½ level tsp chilli powder
To serve: rice or noodles

1 Fry the chicken in the oil until golden.

2 Add the other ingredients and stir until the peanut butter melts.

3 Cook for 5 minutes more, then serve with rice or noodles.

●●●●●●●●

SPINACH AND BEAN BHAJI

Serves 4

4 tbsp margarine

2 onions, peeled and sliced into fine rings

1 garlic clove, crushed

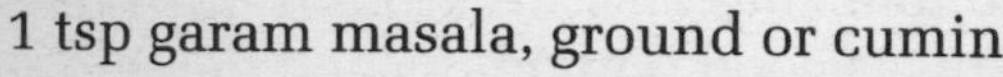

1 tsp garam masala, ground or cumin

1 tsp ground ginger or chilli powder

2 x 425 g / 15 oz cans red kidney beans, drained and rinsed

Lots and lots of spinach – NEVER underestimate how much spinach cooks down – for this you need at least 900 g / 2 lb.

To serve: natural (plain) yoghurt, naan bread or rice

1 Melt the margarine in a large pan.

2 Fry (sauté) the onion until golden, then add garlic and spices. Cook for a minute more.

3 Add the beans and spinach. Keep the spinach moving with a wooden spoon – it'll soon wilt.

4 Serve with natural (plain) yoghurt and naan bread or rice.

•••••••••

LIGHT MEALS & SNACKS

Not starving, but feel in need of nourishment? Nip into the kitchen and whip up a snack.

VEG STICKS AND AVOCADO DIP

Serves 1-2

Sticks cut from peeled carrots, cucumber, celery and anything else you fancy

For the dip:

1 ripe avocado, mashed

1 small carton (150 ml / 1/4 pt / 2/3 cup natural (plain) yoghurt

1/2 tsp chilli powder

2 tomatoes and/or a piece of cucumber, finely chopped (optional)

1 Mix all the dip ingredients and season well.

If you have to leave it around before eating, put the avocado stone in to stop it going brown.

•

BLT

Serves 1

This is the classic American sandwich – bacon, lettuce, tomato.

2-3 rashers (slices) bacon
2 slices of bread
Lots of mayonnaise
1 tomato, sliced
Handful of lettuce

1 Grill (broil) the bacon until really crisp.

2 Toast the bread and spread generously with mayonnaise.

3 Pile the tomato and lettuce onto 1 slice of bread, top with bacon then remaining toast.

Line the grill (broiler) pan with foil to save those "grilled-on grease" washing up problems.

•

Try substituting the bacon with fish fingers for an English version.

•••••••••

BCT

Another variation –
bacon, cheese, tomato.

2 rashers (slices) bacon
2 slices bread
Slices of cheese
1 tomato, sliced

1 Grill (broil) the bacon and put to one side.

2 Toast the bread and top with slices of cheese. Grill the cheese until it bubbles, top with tomatoes, bacon and rest of toast.

●●●●●●●●

PITTA PIZZA

Serves 1

1 large pitta bread
Tomato purée (paste) or
 ketchup (catsup)
Sliced mushrooms or tomato (optional)
Piece of cheese, sliced or grated

1 Grill (broil) one side of the bread and then spread the tomato purée on the ungrilled side. Top with mushrooms or tomato (if using) and the cheese. Grill again until the cheese melts.

●●●●●●●●

MAYO EGGS

Serves 1

Lump of margarine
2 eggs
1 tbsp milk
2 tsp mayonnaise
2 slices of toast

1 Melt the margarine in a saucepan on the lowest possible heat.

2 Add the eggs and beat them with a wooden spoon.

3 Pour in milk and keep stirring all the time.

4 Add mayonnaise and season well. Be patient. Don't turn the heat up or give up the stirring.

5 When the eggs begin to set serve on toast.

•••••••••

SAUCY MUSHROOMS

Serves 4

Lump of margarine
4 large handfuls of mushrooms, sliced
1 tsp mixed dried herbs
2 wine glasses of milk
1 tsp cornstarch, (cornflour) mixed with 1 tbsp water

1 Melt margarine in a saucepan and fry (sauté) mushrooms gently.

2 Add the herbs and milk and cook until the mushrooms start to absorb the milk.

3 Add the blended cornstarch (cornflour) and cook, stirring all the time, until it thickens. Simmer for 1 minute. Serve with toast.

••••••••

GARLIC BREAD

Serves 4

Totally delicious, but rather anti-social – unless you all eat it!

1 French stick

4 tbsp soft margarine

2 garlic cloves, crushed

1 tsp mixed dried herbs

1 Pre-heat the oven to 190°C / 375°F / gas mark 5.

2 Cut the loaf in half (so it will fit into the oven), then make cuts from the top almost through to the bottom, about 5 cm / 2 in apart. In a bowl, mash the margarine, garlic and herbs together and spread the mixture into the cuts in the loaf. Wrap both halves of the loaf in foil and put in the oven for 15 mins.

••••••••

Soups

There are two types of soup – creamy ones and clear ones. Creamy ones are made in the same way as the white sauce recipe in Chapter 4, using flour and milk. Clear ones have water and flavouring. You'll need around 900 ml / $1^{1}/_{2}$ pts / $3^{3}/_{4}$ cups liquid to make soup for four. If in doubt, fill a bowl with milk or water and use that as a measuring guide.

Serve soup with bread and salad for a more substantial meal.

FRENCH ONION SOUP

Serves 4

4 small onions, cut into very fine rings
2 tbsp margarine
900 ml / $1^{1}/_{2}$ pts/ $3^{3}/_{4}$ cups water
2 beef stock cubes
2 slices of bread (or 8 thin slices French stick), toasted and quartered
Handful of grated cheese

1 Melt the margarine in a large saucepan and fry (sauté) the onions until soft.

2 Add the water, bring the boil, add stock cubes and simmer gently for 5 minutes.

3 Top the toast quarters with the cheese and grill (broil) until melted. Put two into each bowl and pour the soup on top

NOODLE SOUP

Serves 4

900 ml / 1½ pts / 3¾ cups water

2 vegetable stock cubes

4 "blocks" of noodles

1 tsp chilli powder

2 tbsp soy sauce

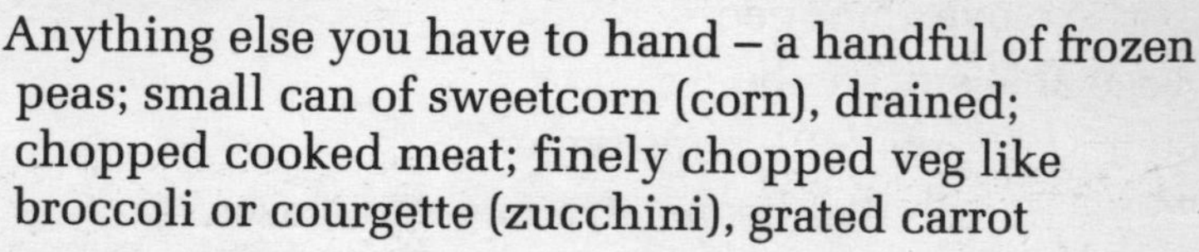

Anything else you have to hand – a handful of frozen peas; small can of sweetcorn (corn), drained; chopped cooked meat; finely chopped veg like broccoli or courgette (zucchini), grated carrot

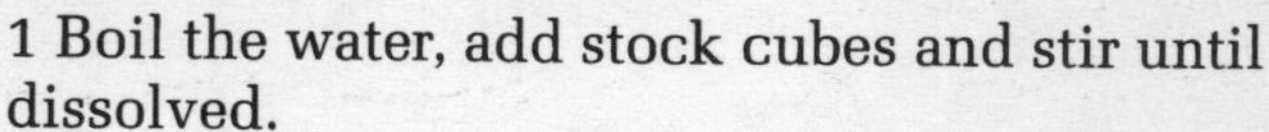

1 Boil the water, add stock cubes and stir until dissolved.

2 Add the noodles and all other ingredients.

3 Boil gently for 3 minutes or follow the instructions on the packet.

•••••••

BEAN AND BREAD SOUP

Serves 4

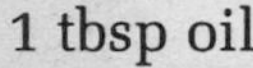

1 tbsp oil
2 leeks, thinly sliced
4 large tomatoes, sliced or
 225 g / 8 oz can chopped tomatoes
1 garlic clove, chopped
1 vegetable stock cube
900 ml / 1½ pts / 3¾ cups water
425 g / 15 oz butter beans, drained and rinsed
4 slices white bread, cubed
1 tsp vinegar

1 Heat the oil in a saucepan and fry (sauté) leeks over a low heat for 5 minutes.

2 Add the tomatoes and garlic, cook for a further 5 minutes.

3 Add the stock cube and water. Bring to the boil and simmer gently while you add the beans and bread.

4 Switch off the heat and allow soup to stand for 2 minutes before adding vinegar.

Serve straight away.

•••••••••

MUM, I MISS YOU – A BIT OF HOME COOKING

No one makes it quite like mum, right? Right. Well, now you can have a damned good try. These recipes take longer to cook, so a bit of planning is required, but they are very easy and will delight your housemates – and mum if she comes to visit. All the quantities will serve four, so multiply or divide according to numbers and hunger. All the dishes below should be served with salad or cooked vegetables.

Most of these recipes reheat well, so if you know you'll be in,
make double to save time tomorrow.
BUT do wait until the cooked food is completely cold
before putting it in the fridge.
Keep it covered and away from raw food.
Reheat in a hot oven until piping hot all through –
never just warm until palatable.

If you do burn something DON'T PANIC.
A splash of milk can take away the burnt taste of a sauce (be careful not to scrape the blackened base of the pan)
and a burnt topping can be scraped off with a pointed knife.

BAKED POTATOES

Serves 4

One of the world's best comfort foods which gives the minimum of washing up. Cook 4 potatoes following the instructions in Chapter 4. Halve, then mash a lump of margarine into each one. Season with salt and pepper then top with:

Cheese: 4 handfuls of grated cheese. Pile on top of potatoes and grill (broil) briefly.

Tuna: Mix a drained 150 g / 5 oz can tuna and 200 g / 7 oz can sweetcorn with lots of mayonnaise. OR mix the tuna into a tub of coleslaw. Pile onto potatoes.

Cathy's chilli bean: Heat 400 g / 14 oz can tomatoes, a 425 g / 15 oz can red kidney beans in chilli sauce and 2 handfuls of sliced mushrooms. Simmer gently for 10 minutes. Spoon onto potatoes and sprinkle a little grated cheese over the top.

A canny idea: Try heating a 425 g / 15 oz (approx) can of ratatouille OR baked beans with sausages OR vegetable curry OR condensed mushroom soup. Spoon over potatoes and serve.

SHEPHERD'S PIE

Serves 4

1 large onion, chopped
750 g / 1½ lb minced (ground) beef
2 carrots, grated
200 g / 7 oz can chopped tomatoes
2 large potatoes, chopped
Lump of margarine
1 tbsp milk
Salt and pepper

1 Dry-fry the onion with the meat in a saucepan, stirring until crumbly.

2 Add the carrots and tomatoes. Simmer for 20 mins.

3 Meanwhile boil the potatoes in plenty of salted water and mash with the margarine, the milk and salt and pepper to taste.

4 Pour meat mixture into a heatproof dish and top with potato. Grill (broil) for 5 minutes or until the topping is turning brown.

•

To chop an onion:
The least painful way is to cut the top off the onion then cut it in half from top to bottom. Lay each half cut side down on the chopping board. Peel off the brown skin and bin it. Hold onto the root base and make cuts from top to root. Then cut across horizontally into little squares. Discard the root.

••••••••

SAUNDERS PIE

This is a cheat's version of shepherd's pie

400 g / 14 oz can baked beans

350 g / 12 oz can corned beef

Mashed potato as before

1 Mash the corned beef and add to the beans.

2 Heat through in a saucepan, pour into a heatproof dish and top with potato.

3 Grill (broil) until the potato starts to brown.

••••••••

VEGGIE SHEPHERD'S PIE

1 tbsp oil

1 large onion, chopped

1 garlic clove, crushed

400 g / 14 oz can ratatouille

425 g / 15 oz can pulses, (cooked, dried beans), drained and rinsed

2 carrots, grated

2 large potatoes, chopped

Lump of margarine

Handful of grated cheese

1-2 tbsp milk

1 Heat the oil in a large saucepan.

2 Fry (sauté) the onion until translucent then add garlic, ratatouille, pulses and carrots. Simmer for 5 minutes.

3 Meanwhile boil the potatoes in salted water until tender then mash them with the margarine, cheese and the milk.

4 Season well then pour the vegetable mixture into a heatproof dish and top with potato.

5 Grill (broil) for 5 minutes so the potato browns slightly.

Pulses are an important part of a vegetarian diet instead of meat. Cooking them from their dried state is cheap but time-consuming – they need to be soaked overnight then boiled rapidly for 10 minutes, before simmering until tender. Do not add salt. (Only red lentils can be cooked without soaking.) Or buy them ready cooked in cans. Drain and rinse before using.

•••••••••

CHEAP FISH PIE

Serves 4

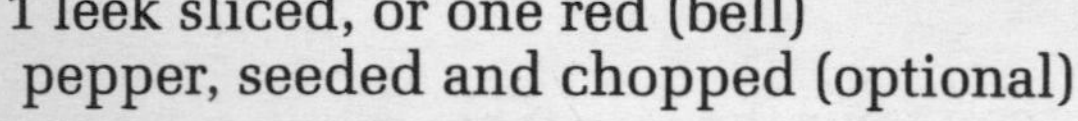

450 g / 1 lb of cheap white fish (coley, hoki, whiting)

600 ml / 1 pt / $2\frac{1}{2}$ cups milk

1 leek sliced, or one red (bell) pepper, seeded and chopped (optional)

2 large potatoes, diced

3 tbsp margarine

A splash of milk

Salt and pepper

1 tbsp flour

2.5 cm / 1 in thick slab of cheese, chopped

1 Put the fish in a saucepan. Cover with milk, add the vegetables (if using) and poach on a low heat for 10 minutes until fish flakes easily when pushed with a fork.

2 Meanwhile cook the potatoes in boiling salted water until tender.

3 Drain and mash with 1 tbsp of margarine, a splash of milk, salt and pepper.

4 Heat the remaining 2 tbsp of margarine and stir in flour. Lift cooked fish and vegetables from the milk and place in a heatproof dish. Break up with a fork. Discard the skin and any bones.

5 Pour the milk from the fish into the flour mixture. Stir constantly over a moderate heat until thickened. Add the cheese. Pour sauce onto fish and top with the mashed potato. Pop under the grill (broiler) for 5 minutes or until the potato starts to brown.

CAULI CHEESE

Serves 4

1 cauliflower, cut into florets

4 handfuls of pasta shapes

1 tbsp oil

1 tbsp flour

2 handfuls of grated cheese

600 ml / 1 pt / $2\frac{1}{2}$ cups milk

1 tbsp grated Parmesan cheese (optional)

1 Put cauliflower and pasta in a saucepan of boiling water and boil until cooked – approx 8 minutes.

2 Heat the oil, add flour and stir well.

3 Add milk slowly and a handful of the cheese.

4 Drain the pasta and cauliflower, tip into a heatproof dish.

5 Pour on sauce and top with remaining cheese, plus Parmesan (if using).

6 Grill (broil) until the cheese starts bubbling.

•••••••••

POTATO AND BACON PIE

Serves 4

4 large potatoes, scrubbed and sliced

6 rashers (slices) bacon

Oil

4 large tomatoes, sliced

5 cm / 2 in piece Cheddar cheese, thinly sliced

1 Boil the potato slices in salted water until cooked – about 5-10 minutes.

2 Grill (broil) the bacon until crisp and chop into small pieces.

3 Oil a heatproof dish and fill with alternate layers of potato, bacon, tomatoes and cheese. Finish with a layer of cheese.

4 Bake in the oven at 190°C / 375°F / gas mark 5 for 20 minutes or until hot through, bubbling and golden.

Once you've opened a packet of cheese, wrap the remainder in foil to stop it going hard.

••••••••

CHEAP CHILLI

Serves 4

1 tbsp oil

1 large onion, chopped

450 g / 1 lb minced (ground) beef

400 g / 14 oz can chopped tomatoes

400 g / 14 oz can red kidney beans, drained and rinsed

1 tsp chilli powder (or less to taste)

4 large handfuls of rice

4 handfuls of chopped lettuce

2 tomatoes, chopped

1 Heat the oil and brown the onion and mince, stirring.

2 Add the tomatoes, beans and chilli powder.

3 Simmer gently for anything between 20 minutes and 2 hours.

4 Cook the rice in boiling, salted water until tender. Drain and divide into bowls or deep plates. Pour on chilli and top with chopped lettuce and tomatoes.

When browning mince, pour off as much fat as you can so it's not too greasy.

SPAGHETTI BOLOGNESE

Serves 4

Garlic clove, crushed
1 onion, chopped
1 tbsp oil
450 g / 1 lb minced (ground) beef
400 g / 14 oz can chopped tomatoes
1 tsp mixed dried herbs
4 handfuls of spaghetti (1/2 a 500 g packet)
4 tbsp grated Cheddar or Parmesan cheese

1 Brown the garlic and onion in the oil.

2 Add the meat and fry (sauté), stirring until brown and crumbly.

3 Add tomatoes and herbs and simmer for 20 minutes.

4 Cook the spaghetti in plenty of boiling salted water according to packet directions. Drain.

5 Pile on plates, top with meat and sprinkle cheese on top.

••••••••

SPAGHETTI LENTILESE

Make as for Bolognese, but substitute the meat with four handfuls of red lentils.

(They don't need browning.)

••••••••

FRUITY BEAN STEW

Serves 4

1 onion, chopped

1 garlic clove, chopped

1 tbsp oil

1 red and one green (bell) pepper, seeded and chopped

2 carrots, peeled and sliced

2 x 425 g / 15 oz cans pulses e.g. black-eyed beans, drained and rinsed

400 g / 14 oz can chopped tomatoes

1 orange, peeled and chopped

2 handfuls of raisins or sultanas

4 tbsp orange juice

1 tsp dried mixed herbs

Small (shack-size) bag of sunflower seeds or unsalted peanuts (optional)

1 Lightly fry (sauté) the onion and garlic in the oil in a large saucepan.

2 Add all the other ingredients, except the sunflower seeds or nuts.

3 Simmer gently for 20 minutes.

4 Top with sunflower seeds or nuts (if using) and serve with potatoes or rice.

••••••••

SAUSAGE CASSEROLE

Serves 4

8 large or 12 medium sausages (meat or veggie)

1 onion, chopped

4 tomatoes, chopped

2 small apples (Coxes have the best flavour) cored and chopped

Apple juice or cider (or half and half)

1 tsp cornflour (cornstarch)

1 Dry-fry the sausages in frying pan (skillet) until lightly browned all over.

2 Place the onion, tomatoes and apples in a casserole dish (Dutch oven) and lay the sausages on top.

3 Pour in enough apple juice to half cover the sausages.

4 Mix the cornflour with 1 tbsp juice or cider and pour over the casserole. Cover (with foil if you don't have a lid).

5 Bake for 30 minutes at 190°C / 375°F / gas mark 5. Remove the cover and cook for 10 minutes more. Serve with mashed potato.

●●●●●●●●

LIVER AND BACON

Serves 4

2 onions, sliced

1 tbsp oil

4 rashers (slices) bacon

450 g / 1 lb pigs or lamb's liver
1 beef or vegetable stock cube
300 ml / $^{1}/_{2}$ pt / $1^{1}/_{4}$ cups water
1 tsp cornflour (cornstarch), mixed into 1 tbsp water.

1 Brown the onion in the oil in a large frying pan.

2 Add the bacon and liver and crumble in the stock cube. Brown gently then pour on the water, and stir in the cornflour mix.

3 Cook over a low heat for 15 minutes. Serve with rice or mashed potato.

••••••••

CHEESY LAYER

Serves 4

1 tbsp oil
4 carrots, sliced
4 large potatoes, peeled and sliced thinly
1 small cabbage, de-stalked and sliced
1 handful of mushrooms, sliced
4 handfuls of green beans – fresh or frozen
2 handfuls of grated cheese
2 eggs
300 ml / $^{1}/_{2}$ pt / $1^{1}/_{4}$ cups milk

1 Swirl the oil around in a large heatproof dish.

2 Layer in the veg and cheese, ending with cheese.

3 Beat the eggs into the milk and season well.

4 Pour over the dish and bake for 1 hour at 190°C / 375°F / gas mark 5.

FISH CHOWDER

Serves 4

2 tbsp oil

1 tbsp flour

900 ml / 1½ pts / 3¾ cups milk

4 potatoes, diced

225 g / 8 oz smoked fish e.g. haddock or cod

Selection of vegetables – sliced carrots, sliced courgettes (zucchini), shredded cabbage, peas, chopped tomatoes, watercress, spinach

4 handfuls of grated cheese

1 Heat the oil in a large saucepan.

2 Stir in flour and gradually blend in the milk.

3 Skin the fish: put it skin side down on a chopping board. Hold firmly one end and work a sharp knife between the flesh and skin, gradually pushing flesh back

4 Cut fish into pieces. Put in a pan with the vegetables.

5 Simmer for about 15 minutes until fish and vegetables are cooked.

6 Sprinkle cheese over and serve with lots of bread.

•••••••••

SHOWING OFF

Now the kitchen is your oyster (though I wouldn't recommend you go as far as cooking those), let's get a little more sophisticated. However hectic life becomes there will be a time you want to sit down with your mates (or someone you hope to mate with) and have a proper meal.

CHEESE AND AUBERGINE PIE

Serves 4

2 aubergines (eggplants)
Oil
1 onion, chopped
400 g / 14 oz can chopped tomatoes
1 tsp mixed dried herbs
4 handfuls of grated Cheddar cheese
To serve: tagliatelle

1 Top and tail the aubergines then slice into discs slightly thicker than a pound coin (5mm) and prepare as described below (if you have time).

2 Lightly oil a heatproof casserole dish (Dutch oven).

3 Fry (sauté) the onion in 1 tbsp oil until transparent.

4 Add the tomatoes and herbs and cook for five minutes.

5 Spread a thin layer of the tomato sauce on the bottom of the casserole dish. Cover with a layer of aubergine slices. Sprinkle over some of the Cheddar.

6 Continue the layers until you run out of ingredients or the dish is full. Finish with a layer of cheese. Bake in a hot oven at 200°C / 400°F / gas mark 6 for 30 minutes or until vegetables are tender when a knife is pushed down in the centre of the dish. Serve with tagliatelle.

Aubergines can be bitter so salting and draining them will improve the taste, although it's not essential: slice or cube and place in a colander over a bowl or the sink. Sprinkle with salt and leave to stand for 20-30 mins. Rinse thoroughly then cook as required.

•••••••••

CHICKEN IN A POT

Serves 4

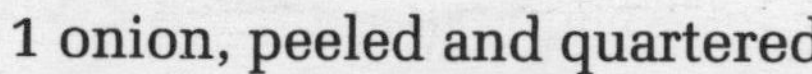

1.4 kg / 3 lb oven-ready chicken (completely thawed if frozen)

1 onion, peeled and quartered

1 lemon, cut into chunks

4 sticks celery, sliced

2 (bell) peppers (red or yellow), seeded and sliced

Small handful of stoned (pitted) olives, rinsed (optional)

3 garlic cloves, crushed

½ bottle dry white wine

1 tsp mixed dried herbs

To serve: potatoes and a green vegetable

1 Remove the giblets from the chicken cavity (if present) and rinse the chicken and dry with kitchen paper.

2 Put the onion and half the lemon chunks in the body cavity.

3 Put the celery, peppers, olives and remaining lemon in a casserole dish (Dutch oven). Place the chicken on top, season with salt and pepper and sprinkle over the garlic and herbs. Pour the wine over the top and cover with a lid or foil.

4 Cook in the oven at 190°C / 375°F / gas mark 5 for 1 hour 20 minutes. Remove cover and cook for a further 20 minutes. Serve with potatoes and a green vegetable.

●●●●●●●●●

THAI VEG CURRY

Serves 4

Salt

2 aubergines (eggplant), cubed

400 ml / 14 fl oz / ¾ cup coconut milk

2 tbsp oil

1 onion, chopped

2 garlic cloves, crushed

2 tbsp Thai red or green curry paste

4 courgettes (zucchini), cut into thick chunks

1 red (bell) pepper, seeded and sliced

Finely grated rind and juice of one lime (or lemon)

1 tsp sugar

2 tbsp soy sauce

To serve: noodles and fresh coriander leaf garnish.

1 Salt and drain the aubergines (if you have time).

2 Open the coconut milk, then leave in the fridge so the cream can rise to the top – don't stir it!

3 Heat oil in a saucepan.

4 Fry (sauté) the onion and garlic lightly, then add the curry paste.

5 Fry until it starts to separate then add prepared veg.

6 Skim off 6 tbsp of thick coconut cream and add to pan. Simmer gently for 10 minutes. Stir in lime rind and juice, sugar and soy.

STUFFED TROUT

Serves 4

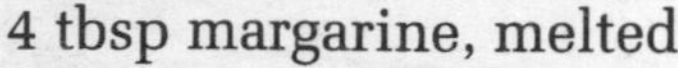

4 tbsp margarine, melted
4 tbsp lemon juice
4 mushrooms, finely chopped
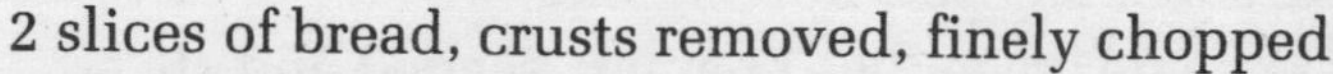
2 slices of bread, crusts removed, finely chopped
4 fresh, cleaned, rainbow trout
Salt and pepper
To serve: potatoes and a green vegetable

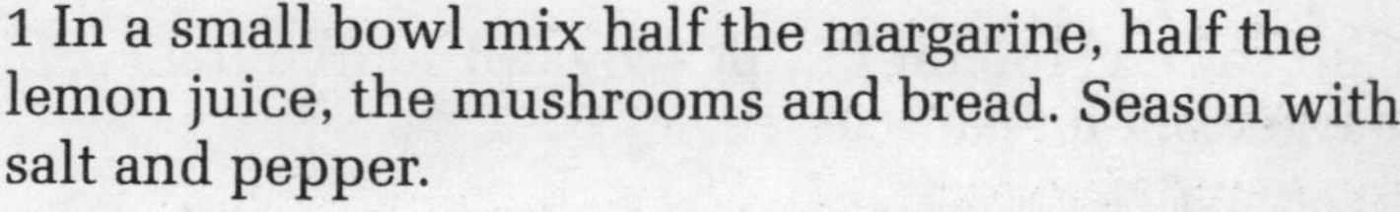

1 In a small bowl mix half the margarine, half the lemon juice, the mushrooms and bread. Season with salt and pepper.

2 Rinse the fish and wipe with kitchen paper.

3 Stuff the mushroom mixture into the cavities.

4 Place in a heatproof dish, pour over remaining margarine and lemon and cover with foil or a lid.

4 Cook for 30 minutes at 190°C / 375°F / gas mark 5. Serve with potatoes and a green vegetable.

For a cheaper dish, buy mackerel instead of rainbow trout.

•

Never re-freeze food. A lot of fish has been frozen on its way to the shop so don't store it in the freezer for a later date – use it as quickly as possible.

VEGETABLE GOULASH

Serves 4

1 tbsp oil
1 onion, chopped
1 garlic clove, crushed
2 handfuls of broccoli florets
1 red and one green (bell) pepper, seeded and sliced
4 courgettes (zucchini), thickly sliced
$^{1}/_{2}$ Savoy cabbage, de-stalked and sliced
2 x 400 g / 14 oz cans tomatoes
2 tbsp sherry
Small carton (150 ml / $^{1}/_{4}$ pt / $^{2}/_{3}$ cup) soured (dairy sour) cream for garnish
To serve: rice

1 In a large saucepan heat oil and fry (broil) the onion until transparent.

2 Add the garlic, cook briefly then add all the other vegetables. Add sherry and bring to the boil.

3 Turn down the heat and simmer gently for 15 minutes until vegetables are cooked but not soggy. Serve with rice and dollop the cream on top.

Booze adds lots of flavour to food and needn't be expensive – any old rubbish will do. It's worth investing in a bottle of cheap British sherry just to pep up dishes. Don't drink it – even in extremis – the hangover will be horrible!

STUFFED CHICKEN BREASTS

Serves 4

4 boneless chicken breasts

One red (bell) pepper, seeded and thinly sliced

$^1/_2$ small carton of cream cheese, or 1 garlic and herb cheese, like Boursin (about 85 g / $3^1/_2$ oz)

2 glasses of white wine

To serve: French Potatoes (see page 100) and broccoli

1 Place one chicken breast on a chopping board with the thickest part facing you. With a sharp knife, make a small pocket in the side (imagine it's pitta bread and you're making a donar kebab).

2 Spread a layer of the cheese along the bottom of the pocket and top with a few strips of pepper. Repeat with each chicken breast reserving about $^1/_3$ of cheese for the sauce.

3 Carefully place each piece of chicken in a casserole dish (Dutch oven), closing the "pockets" as you go.

4 Place any remaining pepper strips in the dish as well. Pour over the wine, cover and bake at 200°C / 400°F / gas mark 6 for 30 minutes until chicken is cooked through.

5 Put the chicken pieces on plates and stir the remaining cheese into the wine so it melts to form a sauce. Spoon over. Serve with French Potatoes and broccoli.

•••••••••

FRENCH POTATOES

Serves 4

1 tbsp oil

4 large potatoes,
sliced thinly

2 large onions,
sliced into fine rings

Lump of margarine

Salt and pepper

1 mugful milk

1 Swirl the oil into an ovenproof dish.

2 Put a layer of potatoes, a layer of onion rings and a few flakes of margarine into the dish and season with salt and pepper. Repeat until all ingredients are used.

3 Pour over the milk.

4 Bake for $1\frac{1}{4}$ hours at 200°C / 400°F / gas mark 6.

If serving with stuffed chicken breasts get this dish in the oven before you prepare the chicken.

••••••••

HOME-MADE PIZZA

Serves 4

2 tsp salt

1 tsp sugar

1 sachet easy-blend
dried yeast

3 mugfuls flour (preferably
strong (bread) flour but plain (all-purpose) will do)

2 tbsp olive oil
About 450 ml / $^3/_4$ pt / 2 cups warm water
Oil for greasing bag
4 tbsp tomato purée (paste)
4 handfuls sliced mushrooms
4 handfuls grated cheese
1 tsp mixed dried herbs
To serve: salad

1 Put the salt, sugar, yeast and flour in a bowl and mix with a wooden spoon.

2 Make a well in the centre, pour in the oil and mix with enough water until the mixture forms a dough which comes away from the sides of the bowl.

3 Place on a floured surface and knead well for a few minutes. Really bash it around (pretend it's someone you hate).

4 Put the dough in a oiled plastic bag. Leave 30 mins.

5 Knead the risen dough for a minute more and divide in two.

6 Flatten each half into a round and place on oiled baking sheets.

7 Spread tomato purée over each one and top with mushrooms, then cheese and herbs.

8 Bake at 230°C / 450°F / gas mark 8 for 15 minutes or until golden and bubbling. Cut up using scissors and serve with salad.

Use an ordinary drinking mug as a measure for flour.

If you don't want to make your own base, buy a ready-made one and brush with olive oil before using (they tend to be a bit dry). Try using grilled sliced peppers and courgettes (zucchini) on top.

VEGGIE PUFF PIE

Serves 4

Flour for dusting
Slab of puff pastry (approx 250 g / 9 oz), thawed if frozen
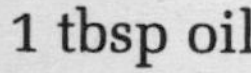
1 tbsp oil
2 leeks, sliced thinly
1 red (bell) pepper, seeded and chopped small
4 handfuls sliced mushrooms
2 handfuls of rice, cooked (see page 30) and cooled
2 tbsp soy sauce
1 tsp mixed dried herbs
1 egg, beaten
To serve: salad

1 Sprinkle some flour on a baking sheet or large chopping board.

2 Roll out the pastry until it's about 30 cm/12 in square.

3 Heat oil in a pan and lightly fry (sauté) the leeks, peppers and mushrooms. Add rice, soy sauce and herbs.

4 Rub some oil onto a baking sheet. Place the pastry on it and pile the veg mixture onto one half.

5 Spread a little of the beaten egg around the edge of the pastry (use your finger if you haven't got a pastry brush). Fold over the remaining pastry so it looks like a big Cornish pastie and pinch the edges together well and seal.

6 Brush more egg on the top and make a small slit in

the top with a knife (this stops it exploding).

7 Bake for 15-20 minutes at 220°C / 425°F / gas mark 7 until risen and golden brown. Serve with salad.

If you haven't got a rolling pin, use a clean bottle and rub some flour onto it.

●●●●●●●●●

CHEESE FONDUE

Serves 4

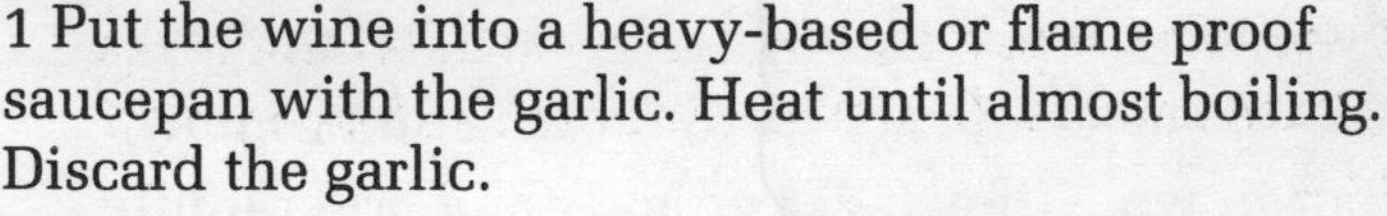

$^{1}/_{2}$ bottle white wine

1 garlic clove, peeled

450 g / 1 lb cheese, grated – Cheddar, Emmental or Gruyère

1 tbsp cornflour (cornstarch)

1 French stick, cut into small cubes

Sticks of fresh vegetables like carrots and celery

1 Put the wine into a heavy-based or flame proof saucepan with the garlic. Heat until almost boiling. Discard the garlic.

2 Mix cornflour with cheese and stir into wine. Keep stirring over a gentle heat until it's all melted and the mixture is thick and creamy.

3 Season well and serve in the pan with bread, vegetables and forks for dipping.

First person to drop their bread has to down their drink/buy a round/wash up.

●●●●●●●●●

LASAGNE

Serves 4

1 tbsp oil, plus a little for greasing
1 onion, chopped
2 garlic cloves, crushed
1 carrot, grated
350 g / 12 oz minced (ground) beef
2 glasses red wine (optional)
150 ml / 1/4 pt / 2/3 cup milk
400 g / 14 oz chopped tomatoes
1 tbsp tomato purée (paste)
1 tsp dried mixed herbs
2 packets cheese sauce mix
8-10 sheets no-pre-cook lasagne
2 handfuls of grated cheese
To serve: salad

1 Heat the oil in a large saucepan. Add the onion, garlic and carrot, cook until they start to colour.

2 Add the meat and stir until brown and crumbly.

3 Pour in wine (if using) and milk and boil rapidly until most of the liquid has evaporated.

4 Stir in the tomato purée, and herbs. Simmer over a low heat for 20-30 minutes.

5 Make up cheese sauce mix according to the packet.

6 Oil an oven proof dish, cover the bottom with a thin layer of meat sauce. Cover with a layer of lasagne. Do another layer of meat sauce then pasta then some cheese sauce. Sprinkle on grated cheese and bake for

45 minutes at 190°C / 350°F / gas mark 4 or until lasagne feels soft when a knife is pushed down through the centre. Serve with salad.

••••••••

PORK CASSEROLE

Serves 4

2

30 ml / 2 tbsp oil
450 g / 1 lb lean, cubed pork
2 apples, cored and chopped
1 red (bell) pepper, seeded and chopped
1 leek, chopped
1 tbsp flour
Apple juice
Salt and pepper
To serve: baked potatoes (see page 32) and spring greens

1 Heat the oil in a large frying pan (skillet). Brown the meat, then add the apple, pepper and leek.

2 Sprinkle over flour and stir well.

3 Turn into a heatproof dish and pour in apple juice until meat is just covered. Season with salt and pepper. Stir well.

4 Cook for at least 1½ hours at 160°C / 325°F / gas mark 3 until tender.

5 Serve with baked potatoes and spring greens.

••••••••

VEGGIE LASAGNE

Serves 4

30 ml / 2 tbsp oil plus a little for greasing
2 garlic cloves, chopped
1 aubergine (eggplant), cubed
2 leeks, sliced
8 handfuls of spinach, rinsed and torn in pieces
4 tomatoes, chopped
1 red (bell) pepper, seeded and chopped
2 small cartons (300 ml / $^1/_2$ pt / $1^1/_4$ cup) natural (plain) yoghurt
2 packets cheese sauce mix
8-10 sheets no-pre-cook lasagne
Two handfuls of grated cheese
To serve: salad

1 Heat the oil in a saucepan and lightly fry (sauté) all the veg for 5 minutes. Mix in the yoghurt.

2 Make up the cheese sauce following the instructions on the packet.

3 Oil an ovenproof dish and cover the bottom with a layer of vegetable mix.

4 Then pour over some cheese sauce, cover with lasagne sheets and repeat the layering process.

5 End with pasta, then cheese sauce and sprinkle over the grated cheese.

6 Bake for 45 minutes at 180°C / 350°F / gas mark 4 until cooked through. Serve with salad.

••••••••

SWEET TREATS

Never trust anyone who says they don't have a sweet tooth. They must be a control freak. Everyone reaches a stage in their life when they need a pudding – don't they?

LEMON ICE CREAM

Serves 4

Large carton (600 ml / 1 pt / $2^1/_2$ cups) natural (plain) yoghurt

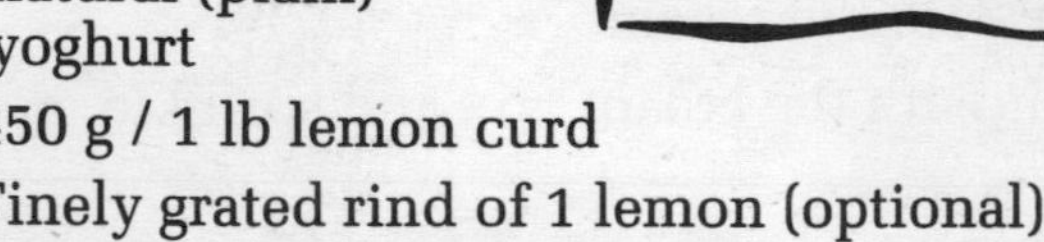

450 g / 1 lb lemon curd

Finely grated rind of 1 lemon (optional)

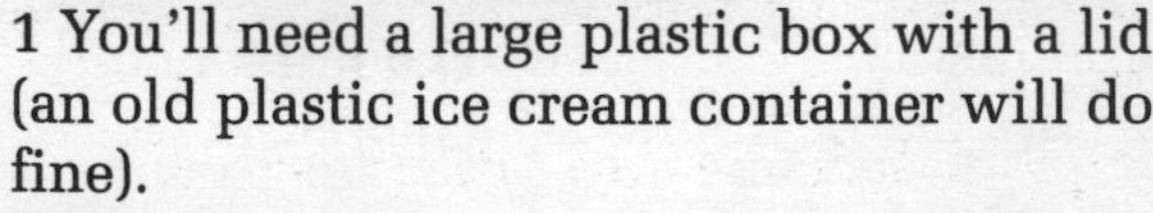

1 You'll need a large plastic box with a lid (an old plastic ice cream container will do fine).

2 Tip the ingredients into the box and mix really well.

3 Put in the freezer or freezing compartment of the fridge for at least 2 hours (it'll keep for about a month) and take out 15 minutes before you want to eat it.

•••••••••

FRUIT SALAD BRÛLÉE

Serves 4

Mixed fresh fruit – maybe
1 banana, 1 apple, 1 orange

425 g / 15 oz can peach slices in fruit juice

1 large carton (450 g / 1 lb) fromage frais OR crème fraîche OR thick natural (plain) yoghurt

1 small carton (150 ml / $^1/_4$ pt / $^2/_3$ cup) of extra thick double (heavy) cream

3 tbsp sugar (brown if you've got it)

1 Peel and slice the fruit and put in the bottom of a heatproof dish. Pour over the peaches and mix well.

2 In a separate bowl, mix the fromage frais/crème fraîche/yoghurt with the cream.

3 Cover the fruit with the cream mix and sprinkle on sugar.

4 Get the grill (broiler) really hot and pop the dish under for a couple of minutes or until the sugar starts to bubble. Eat immediately or leave to cool then chill for not much more than 2 hours.

Puddings are fattening – you can't get away from it. But you can cut the calories by substituting cream with low fat cream substitute, yoghurt or fromage frais.

●●●●●●●●

FRUIT CRUMBLE

Serves 4

4 handfuls of chopped fresh fruit – apples, plums, pears and rhubarb all work well

About 3 tbsp sugar (less for sweet apples, more for cooking (tart) apples and rhubarb)

6 tbsp flour

8 tbsp margarine

4 tbsp sugar

2 tbsp muesli (optional)

To serve: cream or custard

1 Put the fruit into a heatproof dish. Sprinkle over sugar to taste.

2 Put remaining ingredients in a separate bowl and rub in with the fingertips (imagine a small blob of Blu-Tack in your fingers and you'll soon get the hang of it). Stop when the mixture looks like breadcrumbs.

3 Spoon this on top of the fruit and bake for at least 30-40 minutes at 190°C / 375°F / gas mark 5. Crumble is very good tempered so it will sit in the oven happily for longer if need be – just don't let it burn.

4 Serve with cream or custard (the best custard comes ready made in cartons – don't worry about making it yourself).

Experiment with combinations of fruit – try raisins with apple, soft berry fruits with pear or orange with rhubarb.

●●●●●●●●●

MARS BAR SAUCE

Serves 4

3 Mars bars
3 tbsp milk (or cream)
3 tbsp sherry or brandy
Vanilla ice cream

1 Chop the Mars bars small and put in a heatproof bowl with the other ingredients.

2 Put bowl over a saucepan of gently simmering water.

3 Stir gently until the Mars bars have melted. Pour over ice cream and enjoy.

•••••••••

TRIFLE PUDDING

Serves 4

½ an un-iced banana or carrot loaf
Juice of 1 orange
Slug of sherry (optional)
3 bananas
3 small cartons (150 ml / ¼ pt / ⅔ cup) of "custard-style" fruit yoghurt
Small carton (150 ml / ¼ pt / ⅔ cup) extra thick double (heavy) cream
Kiwi fruit, sliced or a little drinking chocolate powder (optional)

1 Slice loaf thinly and line a bowl with it. Pour over juice (and sherry if using), so the bread is well soaked.

2 Peel and slice bananas, sprinkle over bread.

3 Pour over yoghurt and top with cream. Decorate with peeled and sliced kiwi fruit or a dusting of chocolate powder if liked just before serving.

•••••••••

BREAD AND BUTTER PUDDING

Serves 4

Small lump of margarine
4 slices of bread, buttered and quartered
Handful of dried fruit
3 (size 4 or 5) eggs
600 ml / 1 pt / $2^1/_2$ cups milk
4 tbsp sugar

1 Rub the margarine around a heatproof dish.

2 Arrange the bread in the bottom of the dish and sprinkle dried fruit over it.

3 Beat eggs, milk and sugar together.

4 Pour over the bread and leave to soak for 30 minutes (if you have time).

5 Bake in the oven at 180°C / 350°F / gas mark 4 for 40 minutes or until the centre has set and top is crisp and golden.

•••••••••

CHOCOLATE FONDUE

Serves 4

Large bar (about 200 g / 7 oz) plain (semi-sweet) chocolate

Small carton (150 ml / $\frac{1}{4}$ pt/ $\frac{2}{3}$ cup) double (heavy) cream

4 tbsp sherry

Fruit for dipping – orange segments, strawberries, chunks of banana, sliced pear, grapes

1 Break the chocolate into squares and put in a heatproof bowl with the cream and sherry.

2 Stand the bowl over a saucepan of gently simmering water and stir until chocolate melts (don't let it get too hot or it will go grainy).

3 Give everyone a plate of fruit and a fork to make dipping easier. If the chocolate starts to solidify, pop it back onto the saucepan for a minute and stir well.

Cut fruit goes brown very quickly, so leave chopping until the last minute or sprinkle the fruit with lemon juice. (The lemon juice trick works for avocados too.)

•••••••••

BAKED STUFFED PEACHES

Serves 4

4 ripe peaches OR large (600 g / 1¼ lb) can of peach halves in juice

Small carton (175 g / 6 oz) cream cheese

4 tbsp chopped mixed nuts

5 tbsp sugar

1 Carefully peel the peaches, halve and remove stones (pits) OR drain juice from canned ones.

2 In a small bowl, mix cheese, nuts and 1 tbsp of the sugar. Stuff the cheese mix into the hole in the peach where the stone was. Sprinkle remaining sugar over the peaches. Place the peach halves, stuffed side up, in a heatproof dish and bake for 10 minutes at 160°C / 325°F / gas mark 3.

For quickness flash peaches under a hot grill (broiler) for 2-3 minutes instead.

●●●●●●●●

BANANA LOAF

5 tbsp oil plus a little for greasing
10 tbsp self-raising wholemeal (ground) flour
2 handfuls of sultanas (golden raisins) or raisins
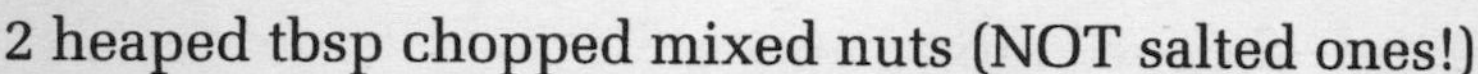
2 heaped tbsp chopped mixed nuts (NOT salted ones!)
3 tbsp sugar
1 tsp baking powder
Pinch of salt
3 ripe bananas
2 eggs, beaten
Juice of 1 orange
To serve: margarine for spreading (optional)

1 Grease a 450 g / 1 lb loaf tin with a little oil.

2 Mix the flour, fruit nuts, sugar, baking powder and salt together in a large bowl.

3 In a separate bowl, mash the bananas with a fork and beat in eggs, oil and 5 tbsp of the juice (it won't look that great at this stage!). Pour this into the dry ingredients and mix well.

4 Spoon into tin and bake for 45 minutes at 180°C / 350°F / gas mark 4. Cover with foil and cook for another 30 minutes or until cooked through.

5 Cool slightly, loosen edge then turn out onto wire rack to cool completely. Serve cut in slices and spread with margarine if liked.

A cake is cooked when a sharp knife in the middle comes out clean.

**If you haven't got a loaf tin,
a small cake tin or heatproof basin
(about 18-20 cm / 7-8 in diameter) will do.**

●●●●●●●●●

BANANA BREAD PUDDING

Serves 4

4 tbsp margarine
3 tbsp sugar
Small carton (150 ml / $^1/_4$ pt / $^2/_3$ cup) single (light) cream
4 slices banana bread (see previous recipe)
Vanilla ice cream

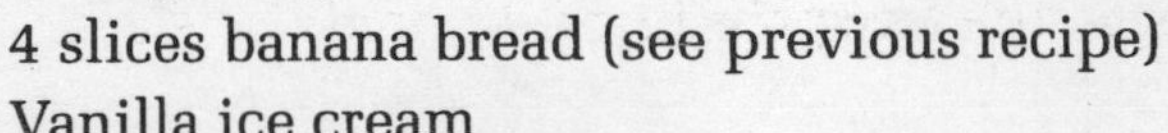

1 Melt margarine and sugar in a saucepan over a very low heat, stirring all the time.

2 When it's golden coloured (don't let it go brown) stir in the cream. Keep warm.

3 Toast the banana bread and put each slice on a plate. Top with ice cream and pour over sauce.

This sauce is great poured over slices of orange or coffee ice cream.

●●●●●●●●●

ALL-IN-ONE CHOCCY CAKE

Cake:

Oil for greasing

1 small bar (75 g / 3 oz) plain (semi-sweet) chocolate

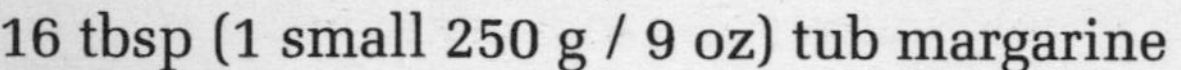

16 tbsp (1 small 250 g / 9 oz) tub margarine

8 tbsp sugar

3 tbsp milk

8 tbsp self-raising (self-rising) flour

$1^{1}/_{2}$ tbsp baking powder

4 tbsp cocoa (unsweetened chocolate) powder

4 eggs, beaten

Icing:

8 tbsp sugar

1 large bar (200 g / 7 oz) plain (semi-sweet) chocolate

6 tbsp milk

1 Make the cake first: Grease a 20 cm / 8 in cake tin with oil and then shake some flour around it.

2 Melt the chocolate and margarine very slowly in a large saucepan. Switch off the heat and mix in the other ingredients, adding the eggs last.

3 Pour into cake tin and bake for 1 hour at 180°C / 350°F / gas mark 4.

4 Put all the icing ingredients in a saucepan and melt together. Bring to the boil. Switch off heat and leave to cool.

5 Once the cake is cooked, remove from oven and

leave to stand for 10 minutes.

6 Carefully turn out onto a wire rack (the grill pan rack will do). When it's cool, cut in half and sandwich back together with a little of the icing. Spread remaining icing over top and sides of cake.

•

If you're investing in a cake tin get a deep one with a removable base.

•••••••••

YUK CAKE

Oil for greasing
8 tbsp margarine
200 g / 7 oz plain chocolate
16 (about 250 g / 9 oz) digestive biscuits (Graham crackers), crushed
1 small bag (100 g / 4 oz) mixed chopped nuts
2 tbsp sugar
1 tbsp sherry or rum (optional)
1 small carton (150 ml / 1/4 pt / 2/3 cup) of double (heavy) cream

1 Lightly oil a 20 cm / 8 in cake tin.

2 Melt margarine in a large saucepan, add chocolate and melt it over a very low heat.

3 Remove from heat, stir in other ingredients and spoon into cake tin. When cold, chill for at least 2 hours or until firm. Turn out and cut in wedges.

••••••••••

QUICK APPLE CAKE

Serves 4

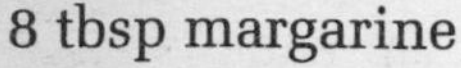

8 tbsp margarine
7 tbsp sugar
2 eggs, beaten
10 tbsp plain (all-purpose) flour
3 tsp baking powder
2 tbsp orange juice
4 eating apples, peeled, cored and chopped
3 tbsp chopped walnuts

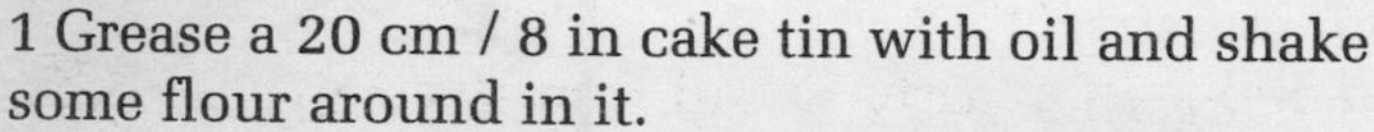

1 Grease a 20 cm / 8 in cake tin with oil and shake some flour around in it.

2 Melt the margarine in a large saucepan, beat in 5 tbsp of the sugar and beat with a wooden spoon or a balloon whisk until the mixture is pale and creamy.

3 Mix in eggs, flour, baking powder and orange juice.

4 Stir the apples into cake mixture.

5 Pour into prepared cake tin. Spread walnuts over top of cake and sprinkle rest of sugar on top.

6 Bake for about 1 hour at 160°C / 325°F / gas mark 3 until centre springs back when lightly pressed and top is golden. Remove from oven and leave to stand. for 10 minutes.

Keep cakes wrapped in foil or in an airtight tin.

•••••••

READY TO PARTY!

Student parties fall into two camps – the ones you're still talking about ten years later and the ones everyone bundles into after the pub and mooches round, optimistically shaking lager cans in the vain hope that they're not all completely empty.

If you want your party to fall into the first category then you need to work out a game plan. Should it be fancy dress or have a theme? What time do you want to have it? Who provides the booze? Getting the alcoholic content of a party right is vital – you want everyone to have a good time without throwing up all over your bathroom.

The best student parties I've been to have been hosted by one household (usually a fairly large one) who've got their act together and provided all the drink and music, then covered the cost by selling tickets to their friends. This means that you know what people are drinking and have control over how many turn up. You do have to be confident that you've bought enough drink and have enough friends to make it economically viable.

Lots of off licences do a drink-or-return deal to help prevent those "out-of-booze" nightmares. But DO keep your drink supplies out of sight – or you could end up with a huge bill and a lot of very drunk people. They will also supply glasses – sometimes free, sometimes for a small hire charge.

If this all seems a bit too organised, then plan a punch and suggest to guests what sort of drink they should bring. You'll need a clean bucket or large washing up bowl, about five bottles of cold white wine, three litres of orange juice and a bottle of cheap brandy. This should keep 10-15 people happy, so multiply according to guest list. Add some chopped fresh fruit to make it look like you've tried and provide soft drinks for drivers and non-drinkers. Don't forget to get enough cups or glasses (paper ones are cheapest).

Do try to keep drinks cold – it makes a big difference. Clear out the fridge and pack it with booze. Even better, see if a tame medical student can get you a great sack of ice (don't ask where from) and fill the bath with it. At worst stand bottles in buckets of cold water outside in the garden if you have one.

•

Stay ahead of the game by drinking lots of water on the night – it really will help prevent a hangover the next day. And don't forget to eat as well as drink.

••••••••

Some more party themes

◆ Fancy dress can be a laugh: try pop stars; parent of the opposite sex; anything that begins with the letter H (or any other letter of the alphabet); Blackadder characters; soap opera characters; train stations; the Seventies; New Romantics

◆ Try a salsa party: beg, borrow or steal lambada tapes, buy in Mexican beer and set up a tequila bouncer on the door. The bouncer has to give everyone a traditional tequila shot – lick of salt on the back of the hand, shot of tequila and a slice of lemon to bite on. (This can be expensive so it's worth considering charging people for it)

◆ Vodka jelly is another conversation piece: break two packets of lime jelly into cubes and dissolve in 600 ml / 1 pt / 2½ cups vodka. Pour into ice cube trays and chill (it will take a while to set, so start early)

◆ If it's Christmas or New Year, try Gluwein: simmer 600 ml / 1 pt / 2½ cups of orange juice with two cinnamon sticks, a handful of cloves and 4 tbsp sugar for 10 minutes and then strain. In a big saucepan heat one bottle of cheap red wine, 600 ml / 1 pt / 2½ cups water, a large slug of brandy and a ladle of the orange syrup. Alternatively, buy Gluwein sachets (they look like teabags) and follow instructions on the packet

◆ Upside-Downers are guaranteed to make the party go with a swing: you'll need three different spirits – try tequila, vodka and white rum – a bottle of lime cordial and shot measures (egg cups will do).

Get the "victim" to lie across a table with their feet facing away from it and the back of their head resting on it. The Upside-Downer Master of Ceremonies pours out one shot of each spirit and one of lime. These are all poured into the victim's mouth. The victim gives them a quick swill then stands up straight WHILE SWALLOWING. Head rush? I should say so. Don't do this late on in a party when guests are already half way out of it. It can be dangerous.

A word of warning

Student parties are notorious for good reason. They're easy to crash and easy to trash. Keep an eye on who knows about your party beforehand and who's coming in on the night. If necessary, get a burly mate to stand on the door and check invitations. You don't want to be the ones losing your deposit on the house or talking to the police at 2 am if things get out of hand.

DO warn your neighbours if it's going to be a biggie because you don't want them calling the police. It's even worth inviting them. They probably won't come but if they've been invited, they're less likely to complain.

Timing of food

If you're not asking guests to turn up until 10 pm or so, it's fair to expect them to have eaten before they arrive. But that means you get the dreaded post-pub crowd, so it can be a good idea to get people to pitch up a bit earlier and then provide them with some food to soak up the alcohol yourself. Of course, this makes the party more expensive, but it also makes it more of an event and is a good excuse to limit numbers – perhaps to your corridor in hall or a few of your favourite neighbouring households.

Party food divides into two sections – easy-to-eat-with-the-fingers nibbles and huge servings of easily prepared nosh.

Nibbles

Aim for about 8 nibbles per person

Make bulk-bought cheap crisps more exciting by serving them with a dip (see below).

Pumpkin and sunflower seeds can be cheaper than nuts.

Check out Indian supermarkets for interesting snacks.

●●●●●●●●

MINI PIZZAS

Mini pitta breads
Tomato purée
Mixed dried herbs
Sliced mushrooms
Grated cheese

1 Toast pitta breads on one side, spread purée on the other. Top with herbs, mushrooms then cheese.

2 Grill (broil) for about 4 minutes or until the cheese is bubbling. These taste fine cold.

TORTILLA CHIPS, CHEESE AND SALSA

Serves 8

Big bag of tortilla chips
Jar of salsa sauce
4 handfuls grated cheese

1 Put chips onto a heatproof plate or shallow bowl.

2 Spread sauce over the top and sprinkle on cheese. Grill for about three minutes. Serve quickly.

●●●●●●●●

MINI MEATBALLS

Makes about 20

450 g / 1 lb minced (ground) beef
1 egg, beaten
1 garlic clove, peeled and crushed
1 tbsp tomato purée
1 tsp mixed dried herbs
Oil
To serve: dips (see below) and wooden cocktail sticks

1 Mix the first five ingredients together in a bowl. Roll into little balls.

2 Heat a little oil in a frying pan (skillet) and fry for about 5 minutes, turning until browned all over. Serve with a dip.

●●●●●●●●

CURRY SAUCE DIP

1 small carton (150 ml / $^{1}/_{4}$ pt/ $^{2}/_{3}$ cup) natural yoghurt

1 small carton (150 ml / $^{1}/_{4}$ pt/ $^{2}/_{3}$ cup) double (heavy) cream

2 tbsp mayonnaise

1 or 2 tsp curry powder (depending on your taste)

1 Mix all the ingredients together and serve chilled.

••••••••

CUCUMBER DIP

2 small cartons (300 ml / $^{1}/_{2}$ pt/ $1^{1}/_{4}$ cup) natural yoghurt

$^{1}/_{2}$ cucumber, grated

1 garlic clove, crushed

1 Mix everything together and serve chilled.

••••••••

TOMATO DIP

1 onion, finely chopped

1 tbsp oil

400 g / 14 oz chopped tomatoes with garlic and herbs

1 tsp mixed dried herbs

1 Fry (sauté) the onion in the oil until transparent then add tomatoes and herbs. Boil for 5 minutes then allow to cool.

Large scale party nosh

If you don't want to cook, simply provide loads of French bread, slabs of cheese and a few pickles.

•

Make sure you have enough plates and cutlery for everyone – borrow like mad or splash out on paper plates to make the clearing up operation less painful.

•

You can feed a lot of people quite cheaply by bulking out the dishes with lots of stodge – pasta, potatoes etc. – but if the cost is prohibitive, consider asking people to contribute a couple of quid.

TWO SALMON PASTA SALAD

Serves 10

10 handfuls of pasta shapes – bows look nice
Salt
1 large can (about 400 g / 14 oz) salmon
Small packet of smoked salmon trimmings (from a fishmonger – they are much cheaper than a slice)
Small carton (150 ml / 1/4 pt / 2/3 cup) natural (plain) yoghurt
5 tbsp mayonnaise
1/2 small carton (75 g / 5 tbsp) double (heavy) cream
1 garlic clove, crushed
Small bunch of fresh dill (dillweed), chopped
To serve: green salad and lots of bread

1 Cook the pasta in plenty of boiling salted water according to packet directions (use 2 pans if necessary). Drain and rinse with cold water. Drain the can of salmon and chop the smoked salmon, removing any bones and skin from both. Mix all the ingredients together really well. Serve with green salad and fresh bread.

•••••••••

CORONATION CHICKEN

Serves 10

1.75 g / 4 lb oven-ready chicken

6 tbsp mayonnaise

1/2 small carton (75 ml / 5 tbsp) double (heavy) cream

3 tbsp mango chutney

2 tsp curry powder

2 handfuls sultanas (golden raisins) or raisins

To serve: green salad and Rice Salad (see page 128)

1 Roast the chicken for 1 hour 40 minutes (see page 33). Leave to cool. (This can be done the day before.)

2 Remove the skin from the chicken and remove as much meat as you can. Chop it up and mix with all the other ingredients.

3 Serve with green salad and rice salad.

•••••••••

RICE SALAD

Serves 10

10 handfuls rice
Salt
2 handfuls frozen peas
1 red or green (bell) pepper, finely chopped
1 small can (200 g / 7 oz) sweetcorn (corn), drained
4 tbsp olive oil
2 tbsp vinegar
Salt and pepper

1 Boil the rice in plenty of salted water for 20 minutes or until just tender. Add peas in the last 5 minutes of cooking.

2 Drain and rinse with cold water.

3 Put in a serving bowl and mix in all the other ingredients. Season with salt and pepper.

•••••••••

CLASSY CHILLI

Serves 10

Double the quantities for the Cheap Chilli on page 87. Using two pans if necessary, cook 10 handfuls rice (see page 30 or Rice Salad on this page), drain, rinse with hot water and drain again. Leave rice and chilli in separate saucepans on a low heat on the top of the stove. Let people serve themselves. Put out bowls of garnishes, e.g.

finely chopped lettuce and tomato salad
large carton soured (dairy sour) cream, or natural (plain) yoghurt
bowl of grated Cheddar cheese
tortilla chips
Avocado Dip (see page 71)

●●●●●●●●

VEG CHILLI

Serves 10

2 onions, chopped
3 tbsp oil
2 garlic cloves, chopped
2 aubergines (eggplant), cubed
2 courgettes (zucchini), thickly sliced
Large can (350 g / 12 oz) sweetcorn (corn), drained
2 x 425 g / 15 g cans red kidney beans in chilli sauce
400 g / 14 oz can chopped tomatoes
Chilli powder to taste

1 Fry (sauté) the onions in the oil until transparent.

2 Add the garlic, aubergines and courgettes and fry for 2-3 minutes.

3 Add the other ingredients and simmer for 20 minutes. Serve as above, using vegetarian Cheddar.

●●●●●●●●

CHICKEN AND CAULI CURRY

Serves 10

2 onions, chopped

3 tbsp oil

2 garlic cloves, chopped

4 tbsp curry powder

20 boneless chicken thighs

1 large carton (300 ml / $^1/_2$ pt / $1^1/_4$ cups) double (heavy) cream

2 handfuls of red lentils

2 x 400 g / 14 oz cans chopped tomatoes

1 large cauliflower, broken into small florets

To serve: rice (see Chilli on page 30), mango chutney and Cucumber Dip (see page 125)

1 Fry (sauté) the onions in the oil until transparent.

2 Add the garlic, curry powder and chicken, and fry, stirring, for 5 minutes.

3 Add all remaining ingredients except the cauliflower, cover, and cook gently for 20 minutes.

4 Add the cauliflower. Cook, uncovered, for another 10 minutes. Serve with rice, mango chutney, and Cucumber Dip.

•

Taste your curry near the end of cooking and, if it's not hot enough, add chilli powder rather than curry powder – curry powder needs time to cook properly to release its flavour.

••••••••

VEG CURRY

Serves 10

2 onions, chopped
3 tbsp oil
2 garlic cloves, chopped
6 large potatoes, diced
10 handfuls of spinach, washed and torn into pieces
4 tbsp curry powder
2 x 400 g / 14 oz cans chopped tomatoes
2 tbsp lemon juice
To serve: natural (plain) yoghurt, rice (see Chilli on page 30) and poppadoms

1 Fry (sauté) the onion in the oil until transparent and then add remaining ingredients.

2 Cook, uncovered, for 20 minutes.

3 Serve with yoghurt, rice and poppadoms.

•

**If your curry is too hot,
stir some yoghurt or cream in to cool it down.**

One final party tip

Don't forget to stock up on loo paper when doing your party shopping!

••••••••

The morning after . . .

So it was a party never to be forgotten, which is strange as you can't remember most of it. The house looks like a bomb site and your head feels like one. Grab a bin liner each, get the Slacker out of bed and give him/her the vacuum cleaner and clear up NOW. Within half an hour the mess will have gone (I promise) and you can contemplate curing your hangover. The best way to do this is with a big FRY UP. It's one of the most difficult things to cook, but follow this minute-by-minute guide and you can't go wrong.

FRY UP –

for four very hungry people

8 sausages/veggie bangers
8 rashers (slices) bacon (or hash browns for veggies)
2 x 420 g / 15 oz cans baked beans
Oil
4 handfuls sliced mushrooms
Salt and pepper
Pinch of mixed dried herbs
8 slices of bread
8 eggs
Tea and coffee

FRY-UP MINUS 15 MINUTES. Assemble ingredients, fill kettle, switch grill (broiler) on to medium and oven to 160°C / 325°F / gas mark 3 (if they're separate).

MINUS 14. Place 4 sausages in the centre of the grill (broiler) pan and 4 rashers (slices) of bacon/hash browns round the edge (don't worry if the bacon overlaps – it will shrink). Start cooking.

MINUS 12. Open beans and put in a saucepan ready to go on the cooker. Check on bacon and sausages – turn if necessary.

MINUS 11. Heat about 2 tbsp oil in a large pan (skillet). Fry mushrooms, season with salt and pepper and a pinch of mixed dried herbs, turn into a heatproof bowl and place in bottom of oven to keep warm. Check bacon and sausages, turn sausages again if necessary.

MINUS 10. Put bacon/hash browns and sausages in the oven to keep warm.

MINUS 9. Put on kettle and first round of toast in toaster.

MINUS 8. Put first round of toast in oven along with all the plates you'll be using.

MINUS 6. Put on more toast and rest of bacon/hash browns and sausages. Put 2-3 tbsp oil into frying pan and crack in four eggs. Push the whites together with a fish slice to stop them spreading everywhere.

MINUS 4. Put second round of toast in the oven and start another lot. Check on grill. Get someone else in to make the tea and coffee, get the cutlery and find the ketchup.

MINUS 3. Put first lot of eggs in the oven and start the rest. Ditto toast. Put the heat on under the beans.

MINUS 2. Get warm plates and food out of the oven (use an oven glove) and start dividing up. By the time you've done this, the other eggs, toast and beans will be ready to dish up.

ZERO HOUR. Sit down and get stuck in.

If you really feel so bad after your party-to-end-all-parties that you can't face an onslaught of fat and washing up then drink lots of water, take a painkiller, a vitamin C tablet and try one of these:

FRUIT SHAKE (Serves 1)

Mash a banana in a bowl. Add juice of two oranges and mix well. Pour into a glass and add ice cubes.

PORRIDGE (Serves 1)

Half-fill a mug with porridge oats. Put the oats in a saucepan. Fill the mug with milk or water, pour into pan. Sprinkle in some raisins, if you have some. Heat gently, stirring all the time for 3-4 minutes. Alternatively make Hot Muesli (see page 47).

DRIED FRUIT (Serves 1)

Pour a glass of orange juice into a saucepan. Add a large handful of mixed dried fruit (pear, apple, prunes etc.). Bring to boil and simmer for 15 minutes.

ENTERTAINING

If all this talk of parties sounds a little too raucous for you, then how about entertaining your chums to an elegant dinner party? This involves feeding between six and ten friends with your best recipes and them sitting down, rather than standing up, to get drunk.

Before you even start to think about what to cook consider these questions:

- Do I invite my housemates? If not, how are you going to ask them politely to get lost while you entertain more favoured friends? If yes, how many others have you got room for?

- Do I have enough cutlery, crockery and chairs for everyone? If you're serving soup and a pudding you'll need a lot of bowls and spoons. Or can you face washing up in the middle?

- Am I going to be able to cook everything on my own, or do I need to enlist a willing helper? (Try to get someone else to wash up!)

Menu planning

When you're happy with the logistics, then plan a menu. As you decide on your menu decide on a time plan too. Work out when you intend to start eating and work backwards from there. If your menu is too complicated, find another one. The last thing you want is to be sweating in the kitchen while your guests are having a fine old time without you.

◆ Keep the menu varied – each course should have different flavours and texture. Don't go for dairy product overkill: creamy mushroom soup, followed by pasta with cream, leek and bacon sauce then fruit brûlée.

◆ Don't be afraid to serve old favourites like curry and chilli – just jazz them up a bit with side dishes (see the party section). All sorts of recipes can be upgraded with a bit of thought – extra cream, spices, fresh herbs and slighter better quality ingredients can make all the difference.

◆ Here are some suggested menus to delight your guests with, gathered from recipes in this book. (Increase quantities of ingredients according to numbers.) Each has a rough time guide to help you.

Menu 1 (vegetarian)

AVOCADO DIP WITH CRUNCHY RAW VEG AND TORTILLA CHIPS (see page 71)

Bump up the chilli powder to make it spicier

SPINACH AND MUSHROOM PASTA (see page 56)

Add a small can of stoned (pitted) olives, drained and chopped. Serve with salad.

BANANA BREAD PUDDING (see page 115)

TIME PLAN

Earlier that day: cut carrots, cucumbers, peppers etc. into matchsticks for dip. Make banana bread (or buy some) and sauce.

1 hour to go: make pasta sauce. Measure pasta into a saucepan and fill kettle. Prepare all the ingredients for the dip except avocado and put in serving bowl. Make salad and dressing, but keep separate.

Just before serving: add avocado to dip ingredients. Cook pasta, reheat sauce. Assemble salad. Assemble pudding.

•

When cooking pasta for a second course like this, cover it with boiling water or bring to the boil and then switch the heat off as you serve up the starter – it should be nearly cooked by the time you start to assemble the main course.

••••••••

Menu 2

GREEK STARTER

Serve shop-bought hummous and taramasalata with Cucumber Dip (see page 125), chunks of cucumber and olives and warm pitta bread cut into fingers.

CHICKEN IN A POT (see page 95)

Serve with baked potatoes (see page 32) and a green veg like broccoli.

CHOCCY CAKE OR YUK CAKE (see page 116 or 117)

Serve with sauce made by sieving a can of raspberries.

TIME PLAN

Earlier that day: prepare the chicken so it's completely ready to go in the oven. Make cake and sauce.

One hour to go: put chicken and potatoes in preheated oven. Prepare green vegetables and put in saucepan.

Just before serving: assemble starter. Steam or boil green vegetables. Assemble pudding.

Menu 3 (vegetarian)

HOT 'N' SPICY TOFU SALAD (see page 61)

Leave out the sweetcorn (corn).

CHEESE AND AUBERGINE PIE (see page 93)

Substitute the Cheddar with a small pack of Mozzarella cheese, chopped, and a small slab of Emmental, grated. Serve with pasta shapes tossed in olive oil or margarine and fresh herbs.

QUICK APPLE CAKE (see page 118)
Serve with shop-bought apple sauce and crème fraîche or fromage frais.

TIME PLAN

Earlier that day: make the pie up to the point it goes into the oven. Make the cake.

One hour to go: marinate the tofu. Assemble salad ingredients.Put pasta in saucepan and fill kettle.

Just before serving: Cook Tofu Salad. Cook pasta. Assemble pudding.

Menu 4

FRENCH ONION SOUP (see page 76)
Substitute stock cubes and water with 2 x 275 g / 10 oz cans consommé (clear beef soup) and 3 tbsp cooking sherry. Use slices of French stick instead of ordinary bread (see alternative in recipe).

PASTA WITH CREAM, LEEK AND BACON SAUCE (see page 54)
Serve with salad.

TRIFLE PUDDING (see page 110)
Top with slices of kiwi fruit or strawberries.

TIME PLAN

Earlier that day: make pudding and store in fridge.

One hour to go: make pasta sauce. Put pasta in saucepan so it's ready to go. Make soup up to the point where you toast the bread. Assemble salad ingredients.

Just before serving: finish soup. Cook pasta and reheat sauce. Pour dressing onto salad.

Menu 5 (suitable for vegans)

BEAN AND BREAD SOUP (see page 78)

THAI VEG CURRY (see page 96)

Try to include fresh coriander, if available.

BAKED STUFFED PEACHES (see page 112)

Use a soya-based cream cheese.

TIME PLAN

Earlier that day: make soup up to point where you add the bread.

One hour to go: make curry, but don't add coriander. Prepare pudding.

Just before serving: finish soup. Reheat curry and add coriander. Don't put boiling water on noodles until just before serving. Preheat grill, then cook pudding.

Menu 6 (vegetarian)

LEEK AND CHEESE SOUP (see page 77)

Use blue-veined cheese suitable for vegetarians.

VEGGIE PUFF PIE (see page 102)

Serve with salad or with green vegetables and boiled potatoes.

FRUIT SALAD BRÛLÉE (see page 108)

TIME PLAN

Earlier that day: make pie and pudding.

One hour to go: make soup. Prepare potatoes and salad/vegetables. Preheat oven.

Just before serving: put potatoes on to boil. Reheat soup and put pie in oven.

Menu 7

SPINACH, BACON AND AVOCADO SALAD (see page 58)

Don't use too many ingredients in salad base - just lettuce (for effect use radicchio) would be OK.

STUFFED TROUT (see page 97)

Serve with boiled potatoes and broccoli.

BREAD AND BUTTER PUDDING (see page 111)

Substitute 150 ml / $^1/_4$ pt / $^2/_3$ cup milk for double (heavy) cream and add 2 tbsp of sherry or brandy. Slice a banana, toss in lemon juice and sandwich between the bread.

TIME PLAN

Earlier that day: prepare trout. Assemble pudding, but don't cook.

One hour to go: preheat oven. Prepare potatoes and veg. Fry bacon.

Just before serving: assemble salad, put fish and pudding in oven at the same time. Boil potatoes, cook broccoli.

Menu 8

GOAT'S CHEESE AND GRILLED PEPPER SALAD (see page 62)

Use slices from a French stick as the base for the cheese.

PORK CASSEROLE (see page 105)

Use cider instead of apple juice. Serve with jacket potatoes and spring greens or mangetout (snow peas).

FRUIT CRUMBLE (see page 109)

Serve with cream.

TIME PLAN

Earlier that day: grill peppers and leave to marinade in dressing. Assemble casserole and put in fridge. Make crumble topping.

One hour to go: put casserole and potatoes in preheated oven. Assemble pudding.

Just before serving: finish salad and put pudding into oven. Cook vegetables.

Menu 9

NOODLE SOUP (see page 77)

Use a small bag of defrosted prawns or stick to one vegetable and add some fresh coriander.

STUFFED CHICKEN BREASTS (see page 99)

Serve with French Potatoes (see page 100) and a green vegetable.

CHOCOLATE FONDUE (see page 112)

TIME PLAN

Earlier that day: prepare chicken breasts and put in fridge. Peel potatoes and leave completely covered in cold water so they don't go brown.

One hour to go: preheat oven. Start cooking potatoes. Make fondue. Defrost prawns.

Just before serving: put chicken in oven. Make soup. Prepare fruit for fondue.

Menu 10 (vegetarian)

TORTILLA CHIPS, CHEESE AND SALSA (see page 124)

VEGETABLE GOULASH (see page 98)

Serve with rice.

MARS BAR SAUCE AND ICE CREAM (see page 110)

TIME PLAN

Earlier that day: make goulash.

One hour to go: grate cheese. Make Mars Bar Sauce.

Just before serving: Cook rice. Assemble starter. Reheat goulash and add cream. Reheat sauce and assemble pudding.

Stir-fries make good dinner party main courses – just stick to three main ingredients – mushrooms, red pepper and meat for example.

•

Hot salads can be used as main courses – serve with lots of good bread.

Dinner party do's and don'ts

✔ Prepare as much food as you can in advance.

✔ Ask guests to bring booze – but buy some yourself in case there isn't enough or it isn't cold.

✔ Chill white wine – chuck it in the freezer for half an hour but DON'T forget about it because it will explode if you leave it overnight.

✔ Check that your corkscrew works.

✔ Provide mineral water or a jug of iced tap water.

✔ Leave yourself plenty of time to get the food and yourself ready – it's bound to take longer than you think.

✔ Put candles on the table and play music.

✘ Run out of milk for coffee.

✘ Apologise if things go wrong.

✘ Skimp on quantities.

✘ Cut the bread or dress the salad until the last minute.

✘ Panic!

Sunday lunches

Dinner parties don't have to happen in the evenings. Why not invite people round for Sunday lunch like mum makes? They'll love you forever.

Every good Sunday lunch needs:

A roast or casserole
Stuffing
Gravy
A sauce or relish
Roast potatoes
At least two different vegetables
A stodgy pudding

Roast: You'll need a deep roasting tin (pan) to sit the meat in. Follow the cooking instructions on page 33. Add some chopped onion or mixed dried herbs to the pan to add flavour. If you're unsure what sort of meat will roast well, look at guidelines on supermarket packets or ask your butcher, but loin, shoulder or leg are always good bets. When the meat is cooked let it rest for about 10 minutes. This makes it easier to carve and gives you time to make the gravy. If you're cooking vegetarian make deluxe stuffing below.

Chicken is cooked if clear juices run out when you stab the thickest part of the leg with a sharp knife. If they look a bit pink, it needs longer in the oven.

Casseroles: These are a good alternative to a slab of meat. Try the pork casserole (see page 105) or Fruity Bean Stew (see page 89).

Stuffing: Can be made from a packet or with breadcrumbs, melted margarine and flavouring like chopped onion, herbs, lemon juice and chopped apple. Stuffing can be baked separately in a small heatproof dish. If you're cooking for vegetarians as well as meat-eaters, make lots of deluxe stuffing out of wholemeal breadcrumbs, onion, melted butter, a glass of wine, chopped dried apricots and nuts. Serve it as an alternative to the meat.

Gravy: Once the meat is cooked, put it on a large plate and leave to rest. Spoon all but a couple of tbsp of fat out of the roasting tin (leave the juices) and put it on the hob. Sprinkle in 2 tbsp of flour and cook for about four minutes or until it's really brown – keep stirring. Add 450 ml / ¾ pt / 2 cups of water (preferably from cooking the vegetables) and cook until thick. Make vegetarian gravy by frying a chopped onion in 1 tbsp of oil. Add 1 tbsp of flour then stir in the water, a veggie stock cube and one tbsp of tomato purée (paste).

Sauces: Each type of meat has a traditional accompaniment and they can all be bought virtually ready-made: bread sauce for chicken; apple sauce for pork; mint sauce or redcurrant jelly (clear conserve) for lamb; cranberry sauce for turkey. If you're vegetarian, serve a selection.

Potatoes and vegetables: Follow instruction on page 33 to 34 and don't skimp on quantities – everyone will eat at least five roasties. Oven baked veg will cook alongside the roast – try sliced aubergine (eggplant), courgettes (zucchini) and (bell) peppers with a little crushed garlic and olive oil, cooked in a roasting tin; or shredded red cabbage with raisins, a chopped apple, some sugar and a little water, and a dash of vinegar cooked in a casserole dish (Dutch oven) with a lid.

Pudding: Classic puddings to follow a roast are: bread and butter pudding, fruit crumble and trifle (see pages 109 to 111). Serve with shop-bought custard and cream or ice cream.

TIMINGS

The hardest thing about cooking a roast is getting everything ready at once. Work backwards from the time you want to dish up. Anything that's been cooked in the oven will sit there on a low heat quite happily, so don't panic if you get it a bit wrong. Leave green veg and gravy until the last minute – prepare the ingredients and boil a kettle, then cook them while someone else carves and dishes up the rest of the food.

HOME SWEET HOME
aromatic whif.
ART STUDENT
BON APETITE
I LOVE YOU
hunger pangs...

LEFTOVERS

13 LEFTOVERS

There are two types of leftovers – the small amount of food left after a meal and the large amount of term left after the money's run out. Both call for drastic measures.

Leftover food

The majority of food that gets left is stodgy – mashed potato, cold rice and pasta.

◆ The easiest thing to do with rice or pasta is to turn it into a salad with some dressing and anything else you have to hand – chopped cucumber, tomatoes, sweetcorn, tuna, canned pulses etc.

◆ Mashed potato can be covered with grated cheese and grilled, or warmed gently in the oven and topped with a fried egg.

◆ Reheat rice or pasta by shoving it into a sieve and steaming over a saucepan of boiling water for 4-5 minutes, stirring occasionally.

◆ Use leftover cooked veg or salad (including dressing) to make a soup with boiling water, a stock cube, soy sauce and noodles.

◆ Spice up boiled eggs or cooked meat with a curry sauce made by frying a chopped onion, a chopped apple and 1 tbsp of curry powder in a little oil. Add 1 tbsp flour and stir. Add 300 ml / 1/2 pt / 1 1/4 cups water, a 200 g / 7 oz can chopped tomatoes and 1 tsp lemon juice. Simmer for 10 minutes then add 1 tbsp of natural (plain) yoghurt if you have some.

Leftover term

When the money suddenly seems to run out look to your stock cupboard. You've probably got at least 10 meals staring you in the face right there. But if the cupboard really is bare, call home, see your Student Union Welfare Officer or your bank – no one should go hungry.

If there is SOMETHING in the cupboard try the following – they won't win Michelin stars, but as my mother says, they'll keep the wolf from the door.

POTATO NESTS

Serves 4

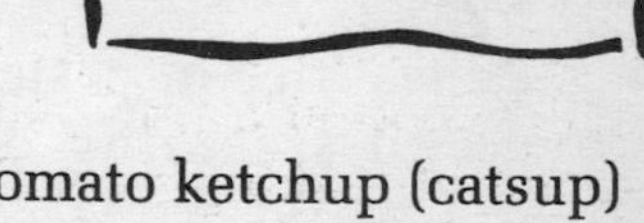

4 large potatoes, cut up
Dash of milk
Margarine
Salt and pepper
1 tbsp pesto sauce OR 1 tbsp tomato ketchup (catsup) OR 1 tsp made mustard
4 eggs

1 Boil the potatoes in boiling salted water until tender.

2 When they're cooked, mash them with the milk, margarine, salt and pepper and whichever flavouring you have to hand.

3 Oil a heatproof dish and put the mash in it. Make four little wells in the potato and break an egg into each one. Bake for 10 minutes or until set to your liking.

•••••••••

PANCAKES

Serves 4

4 tbsp flour

1 egg

300 ml / $^1/_2$ pt / 1$^1/_4$ cup milk

Oil

Grated cheese OR sugar and lemon juice

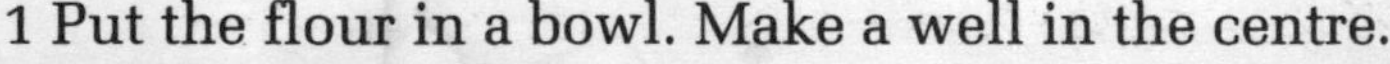

1 Put the flour in a bowl. Make a well in the centre.

2 Add the egg and half the milk.

3 Gradually draw the flour into the liquid, beating as you go until you have a thick batter. Add the rest of the milk. The batter can be left in the fridge for up to 24 hours before cooking.

4 Heat a very little oil in a non-stick frying pan (skillet) and pour off the excess. Add the batter 1 tablespoon at a time, swirling the pan as you go. The secret of making pancakes is to put in as little batter as humanly possibly (usually 2 tbsp). Loosen the sides with a fish slice and toss with a dramatic flourish. Cook underside briefly. Then repeat until all the batter is used. Serve rolled up with cheese or with lemon and sugar.

CARROT AND MARMITE SOUP

Serves 4

2 tbsp oil
3 onions, chopped
4 carrots, grated
4 handfuls of red lentils
Stock cube
900 ml / 1½ pts / 3¾ cups water
2 tsp Marmite or other yeast extract

1 Heat the oil in a saucepan and fry (sauté) the onion until transparent. Add the carrot, lentils, stock cube and water. Simmer for 20 minutes. Stir in Marmite and serve.

••••••••

PEA PASTA

Serves 4

4 handfuls of pasta
Salt
4 handfuls of frozen peas
185 g / 6½ oz can tuna, drained
3 tbsp mayonnaise or double (heavy) cream
Pepper

1 Cook the pasta in plenty of boiling salted water according to packet directions. Add peas for the last 5 minutes of cooking. Drain them quickly then mix in tuna and mayonnaise or cream. Season with pepper.

••••••••

PEANUT NOODLES

Serves 4

4 blocks quick-cook egg noodles

4 tbsp peanut butter

4 tbsp soy sauce

1 tbsp vinegar

1 tsp sugar

1 Cook the noodles in boiling water according to packet directions.

2 Put the remaining ingredients in a small pan and heat gently, so the peanut butter melts.

3 Drain the noodles and mix in sauce. Serve straight away.

••••••••

CHEAPO RISOTTO

Serves 4

Six handfuls of rice

Lump of margarine

1 tbsp grated Parmesan

1 tbsp tomato purée (paste) (optional)

Anything else you have around – frozen veg, grated carrot, canned pulses, tuna etc.

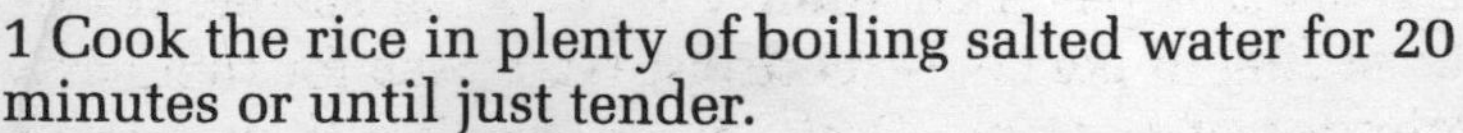

1 Cook the rice in plenty of boiling salted water for 20 minutes or until just tender.

2 Drain and stir in margarine, cheese and tomato purée (if using). Add any extra ingredients, heat through and serve.

VEGGIE CRUMBLE

Serves 4

4 handfuls of any chopped veg – carrot, potato, courgette (zucchini), aubergine (eggplant), cabbage etc.

400 g / 14 oz can chopped tomatoes

1 tsp mixed dried herbs

8 tbsp flour

4 tbsp margarine

Salt and pepper

1 onion, chopped

1 Simmer the vegetables with the tomatoes and herbs for 15 minutes in a covered pan.

2 Put the flour in a bowl with the margarine. Season well with salt and pepper.

3 Rub the fat into the flour with your fingertips as if rolling a small ball of Blu-Tac. When mixture looks like breadcrumbs, stop.

4 Put the tomato mixture into a heatproof dish and top with crumble mix.

5 Bake for 30 minutes at 190ÞC / 375ÞF / gas mark 5 until top is golden brown.

•••••••••

CHILLI CABBAGE PASTA

Serves 4

4 handfuls of pasta shapes

1 small cabbage, de-stalked and shredded

$^1/_2$ tsp chilli powder (or more if you like)

2 tbsp grated Parmesan cheese

3 tbsp olive oil

1 Cook pasta in plenty of boiling salted water according to packet instructions. Add cabbage for last 4 minutes. Drain.

2 Add remaining ingredients and stir.

••••••••

LENTIL SOUP WITH RICE

Serves 4

4 handfuls of rice

400 g / 14 oz can lentil soup

2 tbsp curry powder

3 onions, sliced into rings

2 tbsp oil

1 Cook the rice in plenty of boiling salted water for 20 minutes or until just tender. Drain.

2 Fry (sauté) onions in the oil slowly until golden. Heat the soup with the curry powder. Serve rice with soup poured over. Top with the fried onions.

••••••••

STALE BREAD SALAD

Serves 4

8 slices stale (but not mouldy) bread

½ cucumber or 1 courgette (zucchini), chopped

4 tomatoes, chopped

1 (bell) pepper, seeded and chopped

1 tsp mixed dried herbs

4 tbsp olive oil

2 tbsp vinegar

Salt and pepper

1 Remove the crusts from the bread then soak in enough cold water to cover it. After a few minutes squeeze out excess.

2 Put bread in a bowl and mash with a fork.

3 Add remaining ingredients and mix well.

•••••••••

ONION PIZZA

If you made the pizza recipe in this book when you had more money then you'll probably have the necessary flour and yeast left in the cupboard. Make up a pizza base and cover it with fried onions. French people live on it!

INDEX

THE SEVILLE COMMUNION

Arturo Pérez-Reverte was born in Cartagena in 1951. Since the publication of his first novel, *The Fencing Master*, Pérez-Reverte has become one of Spain's best-selling authors: his novels have been translated into twenty-eight languages and published in fifty countries. *The Flanders Panel* was awarded the Grand Prix Annuel de Littérature Policière and *The Dumas Club* was made into a film entitled *The Ninth Gate*, directed by Roman Polanski and starring Johnny Depp. In 2002, he was elected to the Spanish Royal Academy.

Sonia Soto is half Spanish and was educated at the French Lycée in London and at the University of Cambridge. She is a translator from Spanish, French and Russian and is the translator of *The Ages of Lulu* by Almudena Grandes.

ALSO BY ARTURO PÉREZ-REVERTE

The Fencing Master

The Flanders Panel

The Dumas Club

ARTURO PÉREZ-REVERTE

The Seville Communion

TRANSLATED FROM THE SPANISH BY

Sonia Soto

VINTAGE BOOKS

London

Published by Vintage 2003

15

First published with the title *La piel del tambor* by Alfaguara S.A., Madrid in 1995

First pubished in Great Britain in 1998 by The Harvill Press

Vintage
Random House, 20 Vauxhall Bridge Road,
London SW1V 2SA

www.vintage-books.co.uk

Addresses for companies within The Random House Group Limited can be found at: www.randomhouse.co.uk/offices.htm

The Random House Group Limited Reg. No. 954009

A CIP catalogue record for this book is available from the British Library

ISBN 9780099453963

Penguin Random House is committed to a sustainable future for our business, our readers and our planet. This book is made from Forest Stewardship Council® certified paper.

Printed and bound in Great Britain by Clays Ltd, Elcograf S.p.A.

To Amaya, for her friendship,
To Juan, for keeping at me,
And to Rodolfo, for doing his bit

Clerics, bankers, computer hackers, duchesses, and scoundrels – the characters in this novel are all imaginary. And any resemblance to real events is entirely coincidental. Only the setting is true. Nobody could invent a city like Seville.

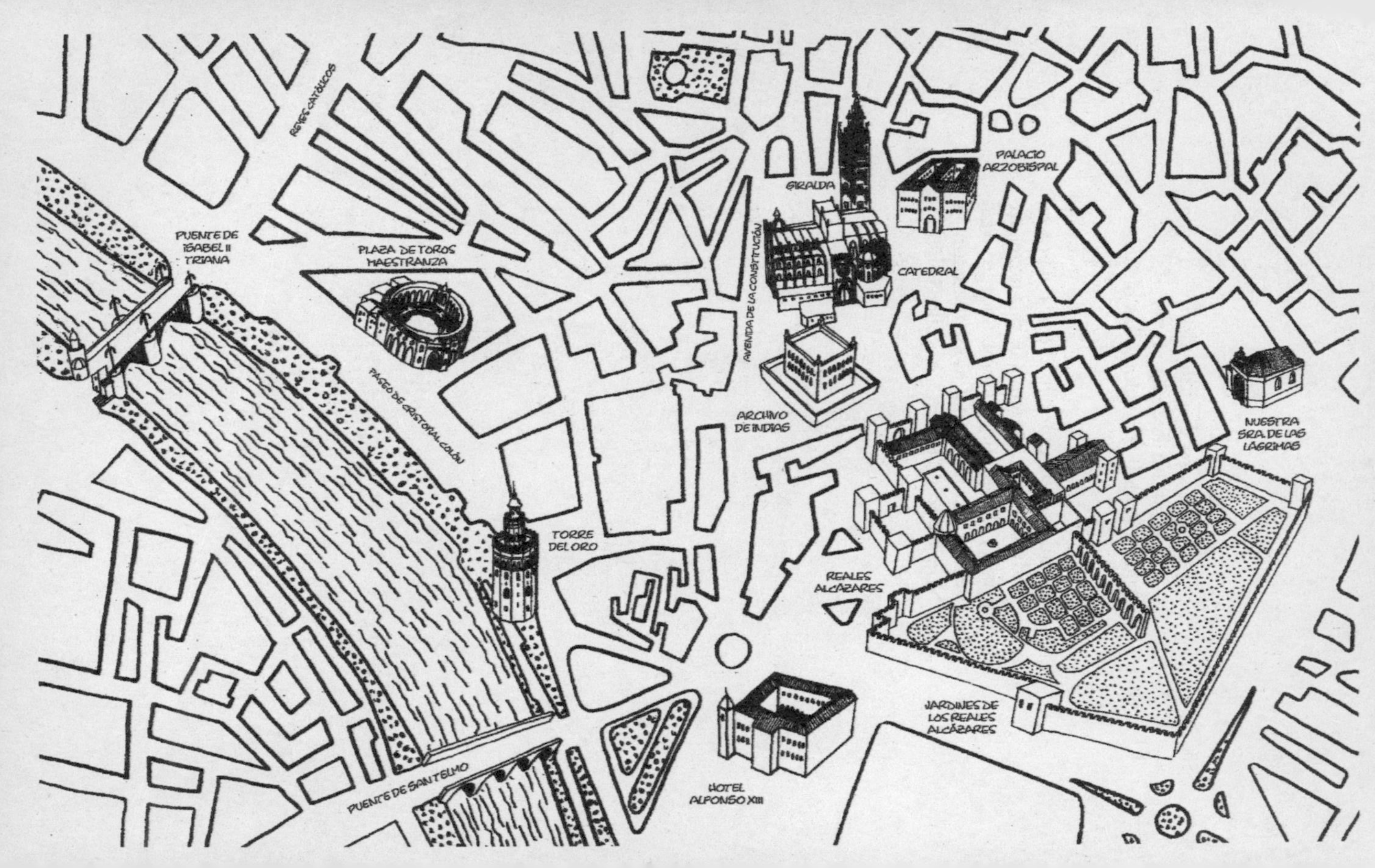

REYES CATÓLICOS
PUENTE DE ISABEL II TRIANA
PLAZA DE TOROS MAESTRANZA
PASEO DE CRISTÓBAL COLÓN
GIRALDA
AVENIDA DE LA CONSTITUCIÓN
PALACIO ARZOBISPAL
CATEDRAL
ARCHIVO DE INDIAS
NUESTRA SRA. DE LAS LÁGRIMAS
TORRE DEL ORO
REALES ALCÁZARES
JARDINES DE LOS REALES ALCÁZARES
HOTEL ALFONSO XIII
PUENTE DE SAN TELMO

Contents

The hacker broke into the central Vatican system eleven minutes before midnight. Thirty-five seconds later, one of the computers triggered the alarm. Rapid changes on the screen tracked the progress of the automatic security protocols. The letters HK appeared in a corner, and the duty officer, a Jesuit inputting data from the latest census of the Papal State, picked up the telephone to inform his superior.

"We've got a hacker," he said.

Father Ignacio Arregui, also a Jesuit, came out into the hallway buttoning his cassock and walked the fifty metres to the computer room. He was thin and bony, with shoes that squeaked as he passed the frescoes in the dimly lit corridor. He glanced out of the windows at the deserted Via della Tipografia and the dark façade of the Belvedere Palace, muttering to himself. Being woken bothered him more than hackers in the system. They got in quite often but their forays were usually harmless. Generally they kept to the outer security perimeters, leaving only slight traces of their presence – a message or small virus. Hackers liked attention. They were mostly teenage boys surfing the Net for ever harder systems to crack. Microchip junkies, tech addicts, getting their kicks trying to break into Chase Manhattan Bank, the Pentagon, or the Vatican.

The priest on duty was Father Cooey, a plump young Irish Jesuit with glasses. Bent over his keyboard, he frowned as he followed the hacker. He looked up, relieved, when Father Arregui came in.

"You don't know how glad I am to see you, Father."

His superior stood beside him, hands on the table, watching the blue and red icons blinking on the screen. The automatic search system was keeping in constant contact with the intruder.

"Is it serious?"

"It might be."

In the past two years there had been only one serious case, when a hacker had managed to slip in a worm program that multiplied inside the system until it crashed. Decontaminating and repairing the network had cost half a million dollars. The hacker was tracked down after a long and complicated search. He turned out to be a sixteen-year-old boy from a small village in Holland. Other serious attempts to corrupt the system with killer viruses – by a Mormon from Salt Lake City, a fundamentalist Islamic organisation based in Istanbul, and a mad priest who opposed celibacy – had all been stopped before they could do too much damage. The priest, a Frenchman, working from the computer of his lunatic asylum by night, had pestered them for six weeks and managed to infect forty-two files with a virus that filled the screens with Latin insults.

Father Arregui pointed at the cursor, now flashing red:

"Is this our hacker?"

"Yes."

"What have you called him?"

They always gave them a name – it made identifying and following them easier. Some were like old friends. Father Cooey pointed to a line on the screen:

"'Vespers'," he said, "because of the time he appeared. It was the first name that came into my head."

On the screen, files appeared and disappeared. Father Cooey watched them intently. He moved the cursor to one of them and clicked twice. Now that his superior was there to take responsibility, he was more relaxed, expectant even. Any hacker was a challenge to his expertise.

"He's been inside for ten minutes," he said, and Father Arregui thought he heard a tone of admiration. "At first he just looked at the different entry points. Then

he suddenly slipped in. He already knew the way. He must have visited us before."

"What do you think he's up to?"

Cooey shrugged. "I don't know. But he's pretty good, and he's quick. He's using a three-pronged approach to get past our defences. He starts by trying simple permutations of names of known users, then tries names from our own Dictionary and finally a list of four hundred and thirty-two passwords." As he said this, the Jesuit twisted his mouth slightly, as if suppressing a smile. "Now he's probing the entrances to INMAVAT."

Father Arregui drummed his fingers anxiously on one of the computer manuals littering the table. INMAVAT was a confidential list of the high-ranking members of the Roman Curia. Access was possible only with a secret personal code.

"Signal tracker?" he suggested.

Cooey jerked his chin towards the monitor at the neighbouring table, as if to say, "I've already thought of that". Connected to the police and to the Vatican's telephone network, the system recorded all information on an intruder's signal. It even contained a trap, a series of paths that slowed intruders long enough for them to be located and identified.

"This won't get us very far," said Cooey after a few moments. "Vespers has hidden his entry point by jumping between different telephone networks. Every time he makes a loop through one of them, we have to trace him right back to the exchange. He'd have to be here a long time before we could do anything about him. And he'd still be able to do some damage, if that's what he wants."

"What else could he want?"

"I don't know," the younger man answered, looking both intrigued and amused. He went on, his face serious again. "Sometimes they just want to have a look around, or leave a message – 'Captain Zap was here', that kind of thing." He paused, watching the screen. "But this one's going to a lot of trouble just for a saunter around the system."

Father Arregui nodded twice, still absorbed in what was happening on the screen, but then he seemed to come to. He glanced at the telephone inside the cone of lamplight. He reached for it, but stopped midway.

"Do you think he'll get into INMAVAT?"

"He just has."

"Dear God." Now the red cursor was flickering rapidly, moving down the long list of files on the screen.

"He's good," said Cooey, no longer hiding his admiration. "God forgive me, but this hacker is very good." He paused and smiled. "Diabolically good."

He'd given up on the keyboard and was now simply watching, his elbows on the table. The restricted-access list was there on the screen, in full view. Eighty-four cardinals and high-ranking officials, each given with a corresponding code. The cursor moved up and down the list, twice, then stopped with a flicker beside VoIA.

"Swine," muttered Father Arregui.

The data transfer log was registering a tiny decrease in free memory. The intruder had cracked the security lock and was transferring a file into the system.

"Who's VoIA?" asked Father Cooey.

Father Arregui didn't answer immediately. He unfastened the collar of his cassock and passed his hand over his head. He looked at the screen again in disbelief. Then he picked up the telephone receiver slowly and, after another moment's hesitation, he dialled the emergency number of the Vatican palace secretariat. It rang seven times before a voice answered in Italian. Father Arregui cleared his throat and announced that an intruder had broken into the Holy Father's personal computer.

I
The Man from Rome

He carries a sword for a reason. He is God's agent.
Bernard de Clairvaux, *Eulogy of the Templar Militia*

At the beginning of May, Lorenzo Quart received the order that would take him to Seville. An area of low pressure was moving towards the eastern Mediterranean and that morning it was raining on St. Peter's Square, so Quart had to skirt the square, taking shelter under Bernini's colonnade. As he walked up to the Portone di Bronzo, he saw the sentry standing with his halberd in the gloomy marble-and-granite corridor and preparing to ask for his identification. The man, tall and strong with a crew cut, was wearing the red, yellow, and blue-striped Renaissance uniform and black beret of the Swiss Guard. He stared at Quart's well-cut suit, matching black silk shirt with a Roman collar, and his fine, handmade leather shoes. Definitely not, the guard seemed to be thinking, one of the grey bagarozzi – the officials of the complex Vatican bureaucracy who passed through every day. But neither was the visitor a high-ranking member of the Curia, a prelate or monsignor. They wore a cross, a purple trim or a ring at the very least, and they definitely didn't arrive on foot in the rain. They entered the Vatican palace by another gate, St. Anne's, in comfortable chauffeur-driven cars. Anyway, despite grey hair cut short like a soldier's, the man looked too young to be a prelate. He stood politely before the guard and searched amongst the various credit cards in his wallet for his ID card. Very tall, slim, sure of himself, he looked calmly at the guard. His nails were well kept, and he wore an elegant watch and simple silver cufflinks. He couldn't have been over forty.

"Guten Morgen. Wie ist der Dienst gewesen?"

The guard stiffened and held his halberd straight, not so much at the greeting – in perfect German – as at the sight of the letters IEA in the upper right-hand corner of the man's identity card, next to the tiara and the keys of St. Peter. The Institute of External Affairs was entered in the thick red volume of the Pontifical Yearbook as a department of the secretariat of state. But even the newest recruits to the Swiss Guard knew that for two centuries the Institute had been the executive arm of the Holy Office and now co-ordinated all the secret activities of the Information Services of the Vatican. Members of the Curia, masters of the art of euphemism, referred to it as God's Left Hand. Others called it the Dirty Work Department, but only in a whisper.

"*Kommen Sie herein.*"

"*Danke.*"

Quart walked past the sentry through the ancient Portone di Bronzo and turned right. He came to the wide staircase of the Scala Regia and, after stopping at the checkpoint, mounted the echoing marble steps two at a time. At the top, beyond glass doors guarded by another sentry, was the Courtyard of St. Damaso. He crossed it in the rain, watched by yet more sentries in blue capes. There was a sentry at every door of the Vatican palace. After another short flight of steps Quart stopped outside a door with a discreet metal plate: *ISTITUTO PER LE OPERE ESTERIORE*. He took a tissue from his pocket and dried the rain from his face, then bent down and wiped his shoes. He screwed the handkerchief into a ball and threw it into a brass ashtray by the door. At last, after checking his shirt-cuffs and smoothing his jacket, he rang the bell. Lorenzo Quart was perfectly aware of his failings as a priest: he knew he lacked charity and compassion, for instance. And humility, despite his self-discipline. He may have been without these qualities, but he was thorough and adhered strictly to the rules. This made him valuable to his superiors. The men waiting behind the door knew that Father Quart was as precise and reliable as a Swiss Army knife.

The room was in semidarkness. There was a power cut in the building and the only light – from a window facing the Belvedere Gardens –

was dim and grey. A secretary left, closing the door behind him, as Quart entered and stood in the middle of the room. Quart knew the room well. Its walls were lined with bookshelves and wooden filing cabinets partly covering frescoes of the Adriatic, Tyrrhenian, and Ionian seas by Antonio Danti. Ignoring the figure standing at the window, he nodded briefly to a man sitting at a large desk covered with files.

"Monsignor," he said.

Without a word, Archbishop Paolo Spada, director of the Institute of External Affairs, smiled at him conspiratorially. He was from Lombardy, a strong, solid, almost square man, with powerful shoulders beneath a black suit that bore no emblem of his ecclesiastical rank. With his large head and thick neck, he resembled a truck driver or boxer, or – perhaps more appropriately in Rome – a veteran gladiator who had exchanged his sword and helmet for a priest's habit. This impression was reinforced by his black, bristly hair and huge hands, with no sign of an archbishop's ring. He held a brass paperknife shaped like a dagger and waved it in the direction of the man at the window.

"I assume you know Cardinal Iwaszkiewicz."

Only then did Quart look to his right and greet the motionless figure. Of course he knew him. His Eminence Jerzy Iwaszkiewicz, Bishop of Kraków, promoted to cardinal by his compatriot Pope Wojtyla, and Prefect of the Sacred Congregation for the Doctrine of the Faith, known until 1965 as the Holy Office, or Inquisition. Even as a thin dark shadow at the window, Iwaszkiewicz and what he represented were unmistakable.

"*Laudeatur Jesus Christus*, Eminence."

The director of the Holy Office remained silent. It was Monsignor Spada's husky voice that intervened. "You may sit if you wish, Father Quart. This is an unofficial meeting. His Eminence prefers to remain standing."

He'd used *ufficioso* for "unofficial", and Quart caught the nuance. In Vatican parlance, there was an important distinction to be made between *ufficioso* and *ufficiale. Ufficioso* conveyed the special sense of what is thought rather than said, or even, what is said but always disowned. Quart glanced at the chair the archbishop had indicated, and gently shook his head. He clasped his hands behind his back and stood in the centre of the room, calm and relaxed, like a soldier awaiting orders.

Monsignor Spada regarded him approvingly. The whites of the archibishop's small cunning eyes were streaked with brown like those of an old dog. This, together with his solid appearance and bristly hair, had earned him a nickname – the Mastiff. But only the most high-ranking, secure members of the Curia dared use it.

"Pleased to see you again, Father Quart. It's been some time."

Two months, thought Quart. Then, as now, there had been three men in the room: himself, Monsignor Spada, and a well-known banker, Renzo Lupara, chairman of the Italian Continental Bank, one of the banks involved with Vatican finances. Lupara had an untarnished reputation. He was handsome, elegant, and a happy family man blessed with a beautiful wife and four children. He had made his fortune using the cover of Vatican banking activities to get money out of the country illegally for businessmen and politicians who were members of the Aurora 7 lodge, of which he himself was a member and holder of the 33rd degree. This was exactly the sort of worldly matter that required Lorenzo Quart's special skills. He spent six months trailing Lupara through offices in Zurich, Gibraltar, and St. Barthélemy in the West Indies, and produced a lengthy report on his findings. Lying open on the desk of the director of the IEA it left the banker two choices: he could go to prison, or he could make a discreet exit, thus saving the good name of the Continental Bank and the Vatican, not to mention Mrs Lupara and her four offspring. Staring blankly at the fresco of the Tyrrhenian Sea in the archbishop's office, the banker had clearly grasped the thrust of Spada's speech, which was most tactfully expressed and illustrated with the parable of the bad slave and the talents. Then, despite the salutary moral that, technically, an unrepentant mason always died in mortal sin, Lupara went straight to his beautiful villa in Capri and leaped, apparently without saying confession, from a terrace over the cliff. According to a commemorative plaque, Curzio Malaparte had once drunk vermouth at that very spot.

"We have a matter suitable for you."

Quart stood listening to his superior, conscious that the dark figure of Iwaszkiewicz was watching him from the window. For ten years, Monsignor Spada had always had a matter suitable for Father Lorenzo Quart. These all came with a place-name and a date – Central America, Latin America, the former Yugoslavia – and were listed in the black leather notebook Quart used as a travel diary. It was a kind of logbook where he had entered details, day by day, of the long journey taken since he had acquired Vatican nationality and joined the operations section of the Institute of External Affairs.

"Take a look at this."

The director of the IEA held out a sheet of computer paper. Quart went to take it from him, but at that moment the outline of Cardinal Iwaszkiewicz shifted uneasily at the window. Still holding the paper, Monsignor Spada gave a small smile.

"His Eminence believes this to be a delicate matter," he said looking at Quart, though his words were obviously intended for the cardinal. "And he considers it unwise to involve anyone else."

Quart drew his hand away without taking the document and looked calmly at his superior.

"Naturally," added Spada, his smile almost gone, "His Eminence doesn't know you as I do."

Quart nodded. He asked no questions and showed no impatience; he waited. Spada turned towards Cardinal Iwaszkiewicz.

"I told you he was a good soldier," he said.

There was silence. The cardinal stood against the cloud-filled sky and the rain falling on the Belvedere Gardens. Then he moved away from the window, and the grey light, cast diagonally, revealed a bony jaw, a cassock with a purple collar, and the gold cross on his chest. He extended the hand on which he wore his pastoral ring, took the document from Monsignor Spada, and handed it himself to Lorenzo Quart.

"Read this."

Quart obeyed the order, which was spoken in Italian with a guttural Polish accent. On the sheet of paper were these printed lines:

Holy Father,
My audacity is justified by the gravity of the matter. At times the Holy See seems very far away, beyond the reach of the voices of the humble.

In Spain, in Seville, there is a place where merchants are threatening the house of God and where a small seventeenth-century church, neglected both by the power of the Church and the lay authorities, kills to defend itself. I beg you, Your Holiness, as a pastor and priest, to cast your eyes upon the most humble sheep in your flock and demand an explanation from those who have abandoned them to their fate.

I beg for your blessing, in the name of Our Lord Jesus Christ.

"This appeared on the Pope's personal computer," explained Monsignor Spada when Quart had finished reading. "Anonymously."

"Anonymously," echoed Quart. He was in the habit of repeating certain words aloud, like a helmsman or NCO repeating his superior's orders. As if he were giving himself, or others, the chance to think about what had been said. In his world, certain words, certain orders – sometimes no more than an inflection, a nuance, a smile – could turn out to be irreversible.

"The intruder," the archbishop was saying, "cunningly hid his exact location. But our enquiries have confirmed that the message was sent from Seville, from a computer with a modem."

Quart slowly reread the letter. "It mentions a church that . . ." He broke off, waiting for someone to finish the sentence for him. The part that followed sounded too ridiculous to speak aloud.

"Yes," said Spada, "a church that kills to defend itself."

"Appalling," said Iwaszkiewicz. He didn't specify whether he meant the notion or the church.

The archbishop went on. "We've checked, and it does exist. The church." He glanced quickly at the cardinal and then ran his finger along the edge of the paperknife. "We've also found out about a couple of irregular and unpleasant occurrences."

Quart put the document on the desk. The archbishop looked at it as if the thing was dangerous to touch. Cardinal Iwaszkiewicz picked up the paper, folded it, and slipped it into his pocket. He turned to Quart.

"We want you to go to Seville and find out who sent it."

He was very close. Quart could almost smell his breath. The proximity was unpleasant, but he locked eyes with the cardinal for a few seconds. Then, making an effort not to take a step back, he glanced over the cardinal's shoulder at Spada who smiled briefly, grateful to Quart for indicating his loyalty in such a way.

"When His Eminence says 'we'," the archbishop explained, "he is referring not only to himself and me but also, of course, to the will of the Holy Father."

"Which is God's will," added Iwaszkiewicz, almost provocatively. He was still standing very close to Quart, his hard black eyes staring.

"Which is, indeed, God's will," said Monsignor Spada without allowing the slightest hint of irony into his voice. Despite his power, the director of the IEA knew he could only go so far, and his look contained a warning to his subordinate – they were both swimming in dangerous waters.

"I understand," said Quart and, again meeting the cardinal's eye, nodded briefly. Iwaszkiewicz seemed to relax slightly. Behind him Spada inclined his head approvingly.

"I told you that Father Quart . . ."

The Pole raised his hand – the one that bore his cardinal's ring – to interrupt the archbishop. "Yes, I know." He gave Quart a final glance and then moved back to the window. "A good soldier." His tone was weary, ironic. He looked out at the rain as if the matter no longer concerned him.

Spada put the paperknife on his desk, opened a drawer, and took out a thick blue folder.

"Finding out who sent the message is only part of the job," he said. "What do you gather from reading it?"

"It could have been written by a priest," answered Quart without hesitation. Then he paused before adding: "And he might very well be mad."

"It's possible." Spada opened the folder and leafed through a file full of press cuttings. "But he's a computer expert, and what he says is true. That church does have problems. And causes them too. Two people have died there in the last three months. There's a whiff of scandal about the whole business."

"It's more than that," said the cardinal without turning. Again he was a dark shape against the grey light of the window.

"His Eminence," explained Spada, "believes that the Holy Office should intervene." He paused deliberately. "As in the old days."

"The old days," repeated Quart. He'd never much liked the methods of the Congregation for the Doctrine of the Faith. For an instant he saw the face of Nelson Corona, a priest from the Brazilian *favelas*, a proponent of liberation theology. Quart had supplied the wood for his coffin.

"The thing is," Spada was saying, "the Holy Father wants the investigation to be appropriate to the situation. He believes it would be excessive to involve the Holy Office. Like swatting a fly with a cannon." He paused and turned to Iwaszkiewicz. "Or a flame-thrower."

"We don't burn people at the stake any more," the cardinal said, still looking out of the window. He seemed to regret it.

"In any case," the archbishop went on, "it's been decided, for the time being" – he stressed these last words – "that the Institute of External Affairs is to carry out the investigation. You, in other words. And only if more serious evidence emerges is the matter to be referred to the official arm of the Inquisition."

"I would remind you, brother in Christ, that the Inquisition hasn't existed for thirty years," the cardinal said.

"You're right. Forgive me, Your Eminence. I meant to say the official arm of the Congregation for the Doctrine of the Faith."

Monsignor Spada fell silent a moment. His look at Quart seemed to say, Beware of this Pole. When he spoke again, he was reserved and formal. "You, Father Quart, are to spend a few days in Seville. You are to do everything possible to find out who sent the message. Maintain contact with the local church authority. And above all, conduct the investigation in a prudent, discreet manner." He placed another file on top of the first one. "This contains all the information we have. Do you have any questions?"

"Only one, Monsignor."

"Yes?"

"The world is full of churches beset by problems and the threat of scandal. What's special about this one?"

The archbishop glanced at Iwaszkiewicz, but the inquisitor said nothing. Spada scrutinised the folders on the desk as if searching for the right words. "I suppose," he said at last, "it's because the Holy Father appreciates that the hacker went to a lot of trouble."

"I wouldn't say that he appreciates it," said Iwaszkiewicz distantly.

Spada shrugged. "Then let's say His Holiness has decided to give the matter his personal attention."

"Despite the hacker's insolence," added the Pole.

"Yes," said the archbishop. "For some reason the message on his private computer has aroused his curiosity. He wants to be kept informed."

"To be kept informed," repeated Quart.

"Regularly."

"Once I'm in Seville, am I to consult the local church authority as well?"

"Your only authority in this matter is Monsignor Spada," said the cardinal. At that moment, the electricity came on. A large chandelier lit up the room, making the cardinal's diamond cross and ring glint as he pointed at the director of the IEA. "You report to him and only to him." The light softened the angles of his face slightly, blurring the obstinate line of his thin, hard lips. Lips that had kissed only vestments, stone, metal.

Quart nodded. "Yes, Eminence. But the diocese of Seville has an ordinary: the archbishop. What are my instructions with regard to him?"

Iwaszkiewicz linked his hands beneath his gold cross and looked at his thumbnails. "We are all brothers in Christ. Good relations, co-operation even, would be desirable. Once there, however, you will have a dispensation from your vow of obedience. The nunciature of Madrid and the local archbishopric have received instructions."

Quart turned to Spada. "Perhaps His Eminence is unaware," he said, "that I don't enjoy the sympathies of the archbishop of Seville . . ."

Two years ago, a disagreement over security measures during the Pope's visit to the Andalusian capital had caused a confrontation between Quart and His Grace Aquilino Corvo, archbishop of Seville.

"We know of your problems with Monsignor Corvo," said Iwaszkiewicz. "But the archbishop is a man of the Church. He will be capable of putting the higher good before his personal dislikes."

"We're all part of the Church of Peter," said Spada, and Quart realised that although Iwaszkiewicz was a dangerous player on the team, the IEA was in a strong position in this case. Help me to keep it that way, said his superior's expression.

"The archbishop of Seville has been informed, out of courtesy," said the Pole. "But you have full rein to obtain the information you need, and you may use whatever means you think necessary."

"Legitimate means, of course," said Spada.

Quart forced himself not to smile.

Iwaszkiewicz was watching them both. "That's right," he said after a moment. "Legitimate means, of course." He touched his eyebrow with a finger, as if to say, Take care with your little schoolboy games. One slip, and I'll get you both.

"You must remember, Father Quart," the cardinal went on, "that the purpose of your mission is only to gather information. You are to remain strictly neutral. Later, depending on what you discover, we'll determine how to proceed. For the time being, whatever you find, you must avoid any publicity or scandal. With God's help, of course." He paused to look at the fresco of the Tyrrhenian Sea and moved his head from side to side as if reading some secret message there. "Remember that nowadays the truth doesn't always set us free. I refer to the truth that is made public."

Imperiously, abruptly, he held out the hand that wore the ring. He stared at Quart with a taut mouth and dark, menacing eyes. But Quart was the kind of soldier who chose his own master, so he waited a second longer than necessary before dropping on one knee to kiss the ruby ring. The cardinal raised his hand and slowly made the sign of the Cross over him, which seemed more of a threat than a blessing. Then he left the room.

Quart breathed out and stood up, brushing the trouser leg he'd knelt on. He looked enquiringly at Spada.

"What do you think?" asked the director of the IEA. He'd picked up the paperknife again and was smiling anxiously at the door through which Iwaszkiewicz had left.

"Officially or unofficially, Monsignor?"

"Unofficially."

"I wouldn't have wanted to fall into his hands two or three hundred years ago," said Quart.

Spada's smile widened. "Why not?" he asked.

"He seems a very hard man."

"Hard?" The archbishop glanced again at the door, and Quart saw the smile disappear slowly from his lips. "If it wasn't being uncharitable towards a brother in Christ, I'd say His Eminence was an absolute bastard."

Together they walked down the stone steps that led to the Via del Belvedere, where Monsignor Spada's official car was waiting. The archbishop had an appointment with Cavalleggeri and Sons, near where Quart lived. For a couple of centuries the Cavalleggeri had been tailors to the entire upper echelons of the Curia, including the Pope. The workshop was on the Via Sistina, near the Piazza di Spagna, and the archbishop offered Quart a lift. They drove out through St. Anne's Gate, and through the misted car windows they saw the Swiss Guards standing to attention as they passed. Quart smiled, amused – Spada wasn't popular with the Swiss in the Vatican. An IEA investigation into alleged cases of homosexuality in the Guard had resulted in half a dozen dismissals. And just to pass the time, the archbishop also occasionally dreamed up perverse schemes to test internal security. Such as slipping one of his agents into the Vatican palace, dressed as a member of the public and carrying a phial of mock sulphuric acid intended for the fresco of the Crucifixion of St. Peter in the Pauline Chapel. The intruder had himself photographed standing on a bench in front of the painting, grinning from ear to ear. Spada delivered the photo, together with a rather teasing note, to the colonel of the Swiss Guard. That was six weeks ago, and heads were still rolling.

"He's been called Vespers," said Spada.

The car turned right and then left after passing under the arches of the Porta Angelica. Quart stared at the chauffeur, who was separated from them by a glass partition.

"Is that all the information you have about him?"

"He could be a priest. And he has access to a computer with a modem."

"Age?"

"Unknown."

"Your Reverence isn't giving me much to go on."

"I'm telling you what I know."

The Fiat made its way through the traffic on the Via della Conciliazione. The rain had stopped, and the sky was clearing slowly towards the east, over the Pincio Gardens. Quart adjusted the crease in his trousers and looked at his watch even though he didn't particularly care what time it was.

"What's going on in Seville?"

Spada took a few moments to answer. He was staring absently at the street. "There's a baroque church, Our Lady of the Tears. It's old, small, dilapidated. It was being restored, but the money ran out. It seems it's situated in an area of great historical importance, Santa Cruz."

"I know Santa Cruz. It's the old Jewish quarter, rebuilt at the turn of the century. Very near the cathedral and the archbishop's palace." Quart frowned at the thought of Monsignor Corvo. "A lovely district."

"It must be, because the threat of the church falling into ruin and the halting of the work have stirred up rather passionate feelings. The city council wants to expropriate the site, and an aristocratic Andalusian family with links to one of the banks has also dug out age-old rights of some sort."

They passed the Castle of Sant'Angelo, and the Fiat moved along the Lungotevere towards the Ponte Umberto I. Quart glanced at the dun-coloured walls which he felt symbolised the worldly side of the Church he served. He pictured Clement VII gathering up his cassock, running to take refuge there while Charles V's soldiers plundered Rome. *Memento mori.* Remember you must die.

"What about the archbishop of Seville? I'm surprised he's not involved."

The director of the IEA was looking at the grey waters of the Tiber through the rain-spattered window. "He's an interested party, so they don't trust him here. Our good Monsignor Corvo is trying to do some speculating of his own. His concern is, of course, only for the material benefit of Our Holy Mother the Church. Meanwhile, Our Lady of the Tears is falling to bits and nobody's repairing her. It seems she's worth more demolished than standing."

"Does the church have a priest?"

At this the archbishop sighed. "Yes, astonishingly. There's a fairly elderly priest in charge there. Apparently he's a difficult character and, according to our information, all his appeals have been ignored by our good friend Corvo. Any suspicions about Vespers must point to him or his assistant, a young priest who's about to be transferred to another diocese." Spada smiled reluctantly. "It wouldn't be unreasonable to suspect that one of the two priests or both were responsible for this rather original method of reaching the Holy Father."

"It must be them."

"Maybe. But it has to be proved."

"And if I get proof?"

The director of the IEA frowned and lowered his voice. "Then they will bitterly regret their inopportune interest in computers."

"What about the two who died?"

"That's the awkward part. Without it, this would have been just one more conflict over a plot of land involving speculators and a great deal of money. The church would simply have been pulled down when it became too dilapidated and the money from the sale of the land used for the greater glory of God. But these deaths complicate matters." Spada's eyes, streaked with brown, gazed distractedly out of the window. The Fiat was now caught in traffic leading up to the Corso Vittorio Emmanuele. "Within a very short time two people involved with Our Lady of the Tears have died. One of them was a municipal architect carrying out a survey of the building for the purpose of declaring it a ruin and ordering it to be vacated. The other was a priest, Archbishop Corvo's secretary. He was there, apparently, putting pressure on the parish priest on behalf of His Grace the Archbishop."

"I don't believe it."

The Mastiff turned to look at Quart. "Well, you'd better start believing it. As from today you're dealing with it."

They were stuck in a huge and noisy traffic jam. The archbishop craned his neck and glanced up at the sky. "Let's get out and walk. There's plenty of time. I'll buy you a drink in that café you like so much."

"The Greco? That would suit me, Monsignor. But your tailor

awaits. Cavalleggeri himself. Not even the Holy Father would dare keep him waiting."

The prelate, already getting out of the car, laughed huskily. "That's one of my rare privileges, Father Quart. After all, not even the Holy Father knows some of the things I know about Cavalleggeri."

Lorenzo Quart was very fond of old cafés. Almost twelve years earlier, when he'd just arrived in Rome to study at the Gregorian University, he'd been immediately captivated by the Caffè Greco with its imperturbable waiters and two-hundred-year history as a port of call for travellers such as Byron and Stendhal. Now he lived just around the corner, in a top-floor apartment rented by the IEA at 119 Via del Babuino. From the small terrace he had a good view of the church of Trinità dei Monti and the azaleas in bloom on the Spanish Steps. The Greco was his favourite place to read. He'd go and sit there at quiet times of the day, beneath the bust of Victor Emmanuel II, at a table said to have been Giacomo Casanova's and Louis of Bavaria's.

"How did Monsignor Corvo take his secretary's death?"

Spada was peering at his vermouth. There weren't many people in the café: a couple of regulars reading the paper at tables at the back, a smartly dressed woman with Armani and Valentino shopping bags talking into a mobile, and some English tourists taking photos of each other at the bar. The woman with the phone seemed to make the archbishop uncomfortable. He glanced disapprovingly at her before answering Quart.

"He took it badly. Very badly, in fact. He swore to raze the church to the ground."

Quart shook his head. "That sounds extreme. A building doesn't have a will. And certainly not to cause harm."

"I hope not." The Mastiff looked serious. "Better for everyone that way."

"You don't think Monsignor Corvo's simply looking for an excuse to demolish the church and have done with it?"

"It's definitely an excuse. But there's something else. The archbishop has a personal grudge against that church, or against its priest. Or both."

He fell silent and stared at the picture on the wall: a Romantic landscape depicting Rome when it was still the city of the pope as monarch, with Vespasian's arch in the foreground and the dome of St. Peter's in the background, surrounded by roofs and ancient walls.

"Were there any suspicious circumstances surrounding the deaths?" asked Quart.

The archbishop shrugged. "It depends on what you consider suspicious. The architect fell from the roof, and a stone from the vault fell on the priest."

"Definitely spectacular," said Quart, raising his glass to his lips.

"And bloody. The secretary was quite a mess." Spada pointed at the ceiling. "Imagine a watermelon crushed by a ten-kilo chunk of cornice. Splat."

Quart winced. He could picture it clearly. "What about the Spanish police?" he asked.

"They say both were accidents. That's what makes the line about 'a church that kills to defend itself' so disturbing." Spada frowned. "And now, thanks to some cheeky computer hacker, the Holy Father is worried about it too. So it's the job of the IEA to ease his anxiety."

"Why us?"

The archbishop laughed under his breath. His profile reminded Quart of an old engraving of the centurion who crucified Christ. His big, strong hands now rested in front of him on the table. Beneath the rough exterior of a Lombard peasant, the Mastiff held the key to all the secrets of a state that had three thousand employees in the Vatican itself, three thousand archbishops around the world, and responsibility for the spiritual guidance of a billion souls. It was rumoured that during the last conclave he'd dug up the medical records of all the candidates to the papacy and examined their cholesterol levels in order to get an idea how long the new pontiff would last. The director of the IEA had forecast Wojtyla's investiture and the swing to the right even while the smoke issuing from the Sistine Chapel was still black.

"Why us?" he said at last. "Because in theory we have the Pope's confidence. Any pope's. But there's more than one faction vying for power in the Vatican, and lately the Holy Office has been gaining in influence at our expense. We used to work together as brothers in

Christ." He waved his hand dismissively. "You know about that better than anyone."

Quart did indeed. Until the scandal that caused the entire financial apparatus of the Vatican to be dismantled and until the swing of the Polish team towards orthodoxy, relations between the IEA and the Holy Office had been cordial. But the hounding and defeat of the liberal element had unleashed a pitiless settling of old scores within the Curia.

"These are difficult times," the archbishop said with a sigh, absorbed in staring at the picture on the wall. Then he sipped his drink and sat back in his chair, clicking his tongue. "Only the Pope is allowed to die there," he added, pointing to Michelangelo's dome in the background. "Forty hectares containing the most powerful state on earth, but with the structure of an absolutist medieval monarchy. A throne now bolstered only by a religion that has become little more than a show – televised papal visits and that *totus tuus* business. But underneath it all there is the reactionary fanaticism of Iwaszkiewicz and company."

He looked away from the picture almost contemptuously. "Now it's a fight to the death," he went on sombrely. "The Church can function only if its authority goes unchallenged and its structure remains compact. The trick is keeping it that way. In that task, the Congregation for the Doctrine of the Faith is such a valuable weapon that it's been growing in influence since the eighties, when Wojtyla took to going up Mount Sinai and chatting to God every day." His mastiff eyes looked around vaguely, in a pause charged with irony. "The Holy Father is infallible even in his errors, and reviving the Inquisition is a good way of keeping the dissidents quiet. Who remembers Kung, Castillo, Schillebeeck, or Boff now? Throughout history the Church of Peter has resolved its struggles by silencing the disobedient or eliminating them. And we still use the same weapons: defamation, excommunication and the stake . . . What are you thinking, Father Quart? You're very quiet."

"I always am, Monsignor."

"True. Always loyal and careful, isn't that so? Or should I say professional?" The prelate's tone was light-hearted, if grudging. "Always that damned discipline that you wear like chain mail . . . You would have got on well with Bernard de Clairvaux and his gang of Knights Templar. If you'd been captured by Saladin, I'm sure you'd rather have had your throat cut than renounce your faith. But not from devotion, from pride."

Quart laughed. "I was thinking of His Eminence Cardinal Iwaszkiewicz," he said. "They don't condemn people to the stake anymore." He swallowed the last of his drink. "Or excommunicate them."

Spada grunted ferociously. "There are other ways of casting someone into darkness. Even we've done it. You have yourself."

The archbishop fell silent, watching Quart's eyes. He wondered if he'd gone too far. But he'd spoken the truth. In the early days, when they hadn't been in opposing camps, Quart supplied Iwaszkiewicz's henchmen with ammunition. Again Quart saw Nelson Corona – his myopic frightened eyes, his glasses misted, sweat running down his face. He'd been defrocked a week later, and a week after that he was dead. That was four years ago, but the memory was as sharp as ever.

"Yes, I have," he said.

Spada studied Quart, curious. "Corona, still?" he asked gently.

Quart smiled. "May I speak frankly, Monsignor?"

"Yes."

"Not just him. Also Ortega, the Spaniard. And the other one, Souza."

There had been three priests, proponents of so-called liberation theology. They had opposed the reactionary tide from Rome. And in all three cases the IEA had done the dirty work for Iwaszkiewicz and his Congregation. Corona, Ortega, and Souza were prominent progressive priests working in marginal dioceses, poor districts of Rio de Janeiro and São Paulo. They believed in saving man here on earth, not waiting for the Kingdom of Heaven. Once they'd been identified as targets, the IEA set to work, finding the weak points to put pressure on. Ortega and Souza soon gave in. As for Corona – a popular hero in the *favelas* of Rio and the scourge of local police and politicians – it had been necessary to remind him of certain dubious details of his work with young drug addicts. Quart had spent several weeks investigating the matter, not leaving a stone unturned. But the Brazilian priest refused to mend his ways. Hated by the extreme right, Corona was murdered by death squads seven days after he was suspended *a divinis* and expelled from his diocese. His photo was on the front pages of all the papers. They found the body on a rubbish dump near his former parish. His hands were tied and he'd been shot in the back of the head. COMUNISTA E VEADO: Communist and fag, read the sign around his neck.

"Father Quart. Corona forgot his vow of obedience and the priorities of his ministry. He was asked to reflect on his mistakes. That's all. But things got out of hand. It had nothing to do with us. It was Iwaszkiewicz and his Congregation. You were just obeying orders. What happened wasn't your fault."

"With all due respect, Your Grace, it was. Corona's dead."

"Well, we both know others who died. The financier Lupara, for instance."

"But Corona was one of us, Monsignor."

"One of us, one of us . . . There is no 'us'. We're all on our own. We answer to God and the Pope." The archbishop paused deliberately. "In that order." Popes died, but God was immortal.

Quart looked away, as if he wanted to change the subject. Then he lowered his head. "Your Grace is right," he said, inscrutable.

Exasperated, the archbishop clenched his huge fist as if to bang the table. But he didn't raise it. "Sometimes," he said, "I detest your damned discipline."

"What am I to say to that, Monsignor?"

"Tell me what you think."

"In situations like these I try not to think."

"Don't be ridiculous. I'm ordering you to tell me."

Quart said nothing for a moment, then shrugged. "I still believe that Corona was one of us. And an honest man."

"A man with weaknesses."

"Maybe. What happened to him happened precisely because of that, a weakness, a mistake. But we all make mistakes."

Spada laughed. "Not you, Father Quart. I've been waiting for you to make a mistake for ten years. The day it happens, I'll have the pleasure of giving you a hair shirt, fifty lashes, and a hundred Hail Marys as punishment." Suddenly his tone became acid. "How do you manage always to be so virtuous?" He passed his hand over his bristly hair. He shook his head, not waiting for an answer. "But about that unfortunate business in Rio, you know the Almighty works in mysterious ways. It was just bad luck."

"Luck or not, Monsignor, it's a fact. It happened. And some day I may have to answer for what I did."

"When that day comes, God will judge you as he judges all of us. Until then – only in official matters, of course – you know you have my general absolution, *sub conditione*."

He raised one of his large hands in a brief gesture of blessing. Quart smiled.

"I'll need more than that. But can Your Grace assure me that we would do the same today?"

"By 'we' do you mean the Church?"

"I mean the Institute for External Affairs. Would we be quite so quick now to bring those three heads on a tray to Cardinal Iwaszkiewicz?"

"I don't know. A strategy consists of tactics." The prelate broke off, looking worried, and glanced sharply at Quart. "I hope none of this will affect your work in Seville."

"It won't. At least I don't think so. But you did ask me to speak frankly."

"Listen. You and I are both career churchmen. But Iwaszkiewicz has either bought or intimidated everyone in the Vatican." He looked around, as if the Pole might appear at any moment. "Only the IEA hasn't yet fallen into his hands. The Secretary of State, Azopardi, went to college with me. He's the only one who still puts in a good word for us to the Holy Father."

"You have many friends, Your Grace. You've done favours for a lot of people."

Spada laughed sceptically. "In the Curia, favours are forgotten and slights remembered. We live in a court of tattling eunuchs, where promotion comes only with the support of others. Everyone rushes to stab a fallen man, but otherwise nobody dares do anything. Remember when Pope Luciani died: to determine the hour of death it was necessary to take his temperature but nobody had the guts to stick a thermometer in his rectum."

"But the Cardinal Secretary of State . . ."

The Mastiff shook his bristly head. "Azopardi is my friend, but only in the sense that the word has here. He has to look out for his own interests. Iwaszkiewicz is very powerful." He fell silent for a few moments, as if weighing Iwaszkiewicz's power against his own. "Even the hacker is a minor matter," he said at last. "At any other time it wouldn't have occurred to them to give us this job. Strictly speaking, it's a matter for the archbishop of Seville and the parishioners of his diocese. But with the situation as it is, the slightest thing gets blown out of all proportion. The Holy Father shows an interest, and it's enough to set off another round of internal reprisals. So I've chosen the best man for the job. What I need above all is information. We need to present a report this thick"– he held his thumb and index finger five centimetres apart – "which leaves us looking good. Let them see that we're doing something. It'll satisfy His Holiness and keep the Pole quiet."

A group of Japanese tourists peered inside the café admiringly. A few of them smiled and bowed politely when they saw the priests. Monsignor Spada smiled back absently.

"I think highly of you, Father Quart," he went on. "That's why I'm letting you know what's at stake here, before you leave for Seville . . . I don't know whether you're always 'the good soldier', but you've never given me reason to think otherwise. I've kept an eye on you since you were a student at the Gregorian University, and I've grown fond of you. Which may cost you dear, because if I fall from grace some day, you'll be dragged down with me. Or you might go first. You know how it is, the pawns are sacrificed."

Quart nodded, impassive. "What if we win?"

"We'll never really win. As your fellow countryman Saint Ignatius Loyola would have said, we've chosen what God has to spare and others don't want: torment and struggle. Our victories only postpone the next attack. Iwaszkiewicz will be a cardinal for the rest of his life, a prince by protocol, a bishop whose investiture is irrevocable, a citizen of the smallest and – thanks to men like you and me – most secure state in the world. And, for our sins, one day he may even be pope. But we'll never be *papabili,* and possibly never even cardinals. As they say in the Curia, we've got an impressive CV but not much of a pedigree. We do have some power, however, and we know how to fight. That makes us formidable opponents, and for all his fanaticism and arrogance, Iwaszkiewicz knows it. We can't be crushed like the Jesuits and the liberals in the Curia, to the benefit of the Opus Dei, the fundamentalist Mafia, or God on Sinai. *Totus tuus* is all very well, but they'd better not mess with me. Mastiffs don't go down without a fight."

The archbishop looked at his watch and called the waiter. He put his hand on Quart's arm to stop him paying the bill and put some banknotes on the table. Eighteen thousand lire exactly, Quart noticed. The Mastiff never left a tip. His childhood had been poor.

"It's our duty to fight, Father Quart," he said as he stood up. "Because we're right, not Iwaszkiewicz. He and his friends would like to go back to imprisoning and torturing people, but the Church can be strong and retain authority without that. I remember when Luciani was appointed pope – he lasted thirty-three days. That was twenty years ago, before your time, but I was already involved in this kind of work." The archbishop frowned. "When he made that speech just after his investiture, about 'the Almighty being more of a mother than a father', Iwaszkiewicz and his hard-liners were climbing the walls. And I thought to myself, 'This isn't going to work.' Luciani was too soft. I suppose the Holy Spirit got rid of him before he could cause too much trouble. The press called him the smiling pope, but everyone in the Vatican knew his was a strange smile." He grinned mischievously, baring his teeth. "A nervous smile."

The sun had come out and was drying the paving stones of the Piazza di Spagna. Flower sellers were removing tarpaulins from their stalls, and tourists were coming to sit on the still-damp steps leading to Trinità dei Monti. Quart walked up the steps with the archbishop. He was dazzled by the light – an intense Roman light, like a good omen. Halfway up, a tourist – a young woman with a rucksack on her back, in jeans and a striped T-shirt – was sitting on one of the steps. She took a photo of Quart as the two priests came level with her. A flash and a smile. Spada half-turned, irritated but also amused. "Do you know, Father Quart? You're too good-looking to be a priest. It would be crazy to appoint you to a convent."

"I'm sorry, Monsignor."

"Don't be sorry, it's not your fault. But how do you manage? To keep temptation at bay, I mean. You know, woman as the Devil's creation and all that."

Quart laughed. "Prayer and cold showers, Your Grace."

"You always follow the rules, don't you? Aren't you bored with being so good?"

"That's a trick question, Monsignor."

Spada looked at him out of the corner of his eye and nodded approvingly. "All right. You win. Your virtue passes the test. But I haven't lost hope. One day I'll catch you out."

"Of course, Monsignor. For my countless sins."

"Shut up. That's an order."

"Very good, Your Reverence."

When they reached the obelisk of Pius VI, the archbishop looked back at the girl in the striped T-shirt. "Regarding your eternal salvation," he said, "remember the old proverb: 'If a priest can keep his hands off money and his legs out of a woman's bed until he's fifty, he has every chance of saving his soul.'"

"That's what I'm striving for, Monsignor. I have twelve years to go."

They passed the impressive façade of the Hassler Villa Medici Hotel and then turned down the Via Sistina. The only sign on the tailor's door was a discreet plate. None but élite members of the Curia passed through that door. With the exception of the popes. They alone enjoyed the privilege of having Cavalleggeri and Sons – granted a minor title of nobility by Pope Leo XIII – come to their residence to take measurements.

The archbishop turned and scrutinised the priest's perfectly cut suit, silver cufflinks, and black silk shirt. "Listen, Quart," he said, and the name without a title sounded harsh. "Pride is a sin to which we're not immune, but there's more to it than that. Over and above our personal weaknesses, you and I – and even Iwaszkiewicz and his sinister brotherhood, and the Holy Father with his maddening fundamentalism – we're all responsible for the faith of millions of people. Faith in a Church that is infallible and eternal. And that faith – which is sincere, whatever we cynical members of the Curia might think – is our only justification. It absolves us. Without it, you, I, Iwaszkiewicz, we'd all be hypocritical bastards. Do you understand what I'm trying to say?"

Quart returned the Mastiff's look evenly. "Perfectly, Monsignor," he said. Almost instinctively he had adopted the rigid stance of a Swiss Guard before an official: his arms at his sides, thumbs lined up with his trouser seams.

Spada watched him a moment longer, then seemed to relax slightly. There was even a hint of a smile on his face.

"I hope you do," he said, his smile widening. "Because when I stand at the gates of Heaven and the grumpy fisherman comes out to greet me, I'll say: Peter, be lenient with this old soldier of Christ who's worked so hard bailing out water from your ship. After all, even Moses had to resort to Joshua's sword. And you yourself stabbed Malchus to defend our Teacher."

It was Quart's turn to laugh. "In that case I'd like to go first, Monsignor. I don't think they'll accept the same excuse twice."

II
Three Villains

When I arrive in a city, I always ask who are the twelve most beautiful women, the twelve richest men, and the man who could have me hanged.
Stendhal, *Lucien Leuwen*

Celestino Peregil, personal assistant to Pencho Gavira the banker, flicked bad-temperedly through *Q&S* magazine. He was on his way to the Casa Cuesta Bar in the heart of Seville's Triana district. There were several reasons for Peregil's bad mood: his recalcitrant ulcer, the delicate mission that now took him across the Guadalquivir, and the cover of the magazine he was holding. Peregil was a squat, nervous man. To hide his premature baldness he combed his hair over his head from a parting on a level with his left ear. He was fond of white socks, loud silk ties, double-breasted jackets with gold buttons, and hookers in hostess bars. But above all, fond of the magical pattern of numbers on the gaming tables of any casino that still let him in. This, together with the appointment he was grudgingly keeping, was why the ulcer bothered him more than usual. And the cover of *Q&S* did nothing to improve his mood. Even a man as unfeeling as Celestino Peregil couldn't but be worried by a photograph of his boss's wife with another man. Especially if he'd tipped off the magazine himself.

"The little tart," he said aloud, and a couple of passers-by turned to look at him.

Then he remembered the purpose of the appointment. He took a mauve silk handkerchief from his breast pocket and wiped his forehead. Before his eyes the numbers 7 and 16 danced nightmarishly on a green baize background. If I get out of this mess, he said to himself, I swear it'll be the last time. I swear on the Virgin Mary.

He threw the magazine into a dustbin. Then, turning the corner under a sign for Cruzcampo beer, he stopped at the door of the bar. He hated that kind of place, with its marble tables, tiled walls and shelves full of dusty bottles of Terry Centenario brandy. It stood for the Spain of castanets and guitars, stuffy, squalid and vulgar, so difficult to escape. He'd been a small-time private investigator specialising in sordid adultery and social security fraud until good luck brought him Pencho Gavira and the great bank. Now he hung out in fashionable bars drinking whisky on the rocks to ambient music; he frequented plush offices humming with faxes, air-conditioning and trilingual secretaries, where the *Financial Times* lay about and guys in expensive cologne casually mentioned Zurich, New York, or the Tokyo Stock Exchange. Just like in the ads.

The sight of Don Ibrahim, El Potro del Mantelete and La Niña Puñales soon brought him down to earth. They were already waiting for him, sure as fate. He saw them as soon as he entered, to the right of the dark wooden bar decorated with gilded flowers. Above them hung a sign that must have been there since the turn of the century: *SEVILLE-SANLUCAR-COAST STEAM LINE: TRAINS DAILY BETWEEN SEVILLE AND THE GUADALQUIVIR ESTUARY*. They were sitting at a marble table, and Peregil noticed that La Ina fino was already flowing. At eleven in the morning.

"How you doing?" he said, and sat down.

It wasn't a question. He didn't give a damn how they were doing, and they knew it. He could see it in the three pairs of eyes that watched him adjust his shirt-cuffs – a gesture copied from his elegant boss – and then carefully place his elbows on the table.

"I've got a job for you," he announced.

Peregil saw El Potro del Mantelete and La Niña Puñales glance at Don Ibrahim, who nodded gravely and twirled the ends of his moustache – a thick, bristly, reddish-grey, handlebar moustache. Despite this rather fierce appendage, Don Ibrahim appeared good-natured and placid. He was tall, very fat, and he did everything solemnly. The Lawyers' Association of Seville had long ago discovered that his legal credentials were spurious, but the time he'd spent practising the law under false pretences had given him a grave and dignified presence. He carried a silver-handled walking stick and wore a wide-brimmed panama hat and a watch and chain curving between two pockets of his waistcoat. He claimed he'd won the watch from Ernest Hemingway in a poker game at the Chiquita Cruz brothel in Havana, in the days before Castro.

"You have our full attention," he said, his paunch causing him to sit at a distance from the table.

Triana and all of Seville knew that Don Ibrahim the Cuban was a con man and a crook, but also a perfect gentleman. For instance, only after a courteous glance at El Potro del Mantelete and La Niña Puñales had he spoken for the three of them, indicating that he would be honoured to represent them.

"There's a church and a priest," Peregil began.

"Not a good start," said Don Ibrahim. In one hand – sporting a gold signet ring – he held a smoking cigar, while with the other he brushed ash from his trousers. From his misspent youth in Cuba he'd retained a taste for immaculate white suits, panama hats and Montecristo cigars. He looked like one of the Spaniards who made their fortune in Latin America at the turn of the century then sailed back to Seville with a roll of gold coins, a dose of malaria and a mulatto servant. All Don Ibrahim had brought back was the malaria.

Peregil looked at Don Ibrahim, confused. Was it a bad start because he'd dropped ash on his trousers or because the job involved a church and a priest?

"An *old* priest," he said, to probe Don Ibrahim and also to make the job seem less daunting. But then he remembered: "Well, two priests actually – an old one and a young one."

"*Othu!*" exclaimed La Niña Puñales, using the Gypsy slang from the banks of the Guadalquivir. "Two priests."

Her silver bracelets jangled on her flaccid arms as she drained her sherry glass. Beside her, El Potro del Mantelete shook his head, apparently mesmerised by the thick mark of lipstick on the edge of La Niña's glass.

"Two priests," Don Ibrahim repeated anxiously as cigar smoke spiralled through his moustache.

"Well, actually there are three of them," Peregil added truthfully.

Don Ibrahim shuddered, dropping ash on his trousers again. "I thought you said two."

"No, three. The old one, the young one and another one on his way."

Peregil saw them exchange cautious glances.

"Three priests," said Don Ibrahim, peering at the nail on the little finger of his left hand. It was as long as a spatula.

"That's right."

"A young one, an old one and another one coming."

"Yes, from Rome."

"From Rome."

La Niña Puñales jangled her bracelets again. "Too many priests," she said lugubriously. She touched the wooden table leg for luck.

"So we've run into the Church," said Don Ibrahim with gravity, as if his remark had been the product of lengthy pondering. Peregil suppressed the urge to get up and leave. This isn't going to work, he thought, looking at the three of them: the former bogus lawyer with ash on his trousers, La Niña with a beauty spot and kiss-curl on her withered forehead, and the former bantamweight with a squashed nose. Then he remembered the numbers 7 and 16 on the card table, and the photographs in the magazine. Suddenly it seemed unbearably hot. But maybe it wasn't the temperature in the bar but fear that was drenching his shirt with sweat and making his mouth feel rough and dry. Find a professional, Pencho Gavira told him. You've got six million pesetas to sort this out. It's up to you how you manage the money.

Peregil had indeed managed the money in his own way: six hours in a casino and he'd lost three out of the six million. Five hundred thousand an hour. He'd even spent what he got for the magazine tip-off about his boss's wife, or ex-wife. And on top of that, Ruben Molina, the loan shark, was about to set the dogs on him for another six million.

"It's an easy job," Peregil heard himself say. He knew he had no choice. "Clean. No complications. A million each."

"Why us?" asked Don Ibrahim.

Peregil looked straight into his sad, bleary eyes and for an instant glimpsed the anxiety in their depths. Peregil swallowed and then ran a finger round the inside of his collar. He glanced again at the fat bogus lawyer's cigar, El Potro's deformed nose, La Niña's beauty spot. Three losers who should be locked up. Shipwrecks. Dregs. But with the money that was left, they were all he could afford.

Blushing, he answered, "Because you're the best."

On his first morning in Seville it took Lorenzo Quart almost an hour to find the church. Several times he inadvertently wandered out of Santa Cruz and then had to find his way back. He realised his tourist map was useless in the maze of silent, narrow streets. Once or twice a passing car forced him to take refuge in cool, dark archways, their wrought-iron gates leading to tiled courtyards full of roses and geraniums. He came at last to a small square with white and ochre walls and railings hung with flowerpots. Tiled benches showed scenes from *Don Quixote* and there was an intense scent of orange blossom from the half-dozen trees. The church was small, its brick façade barely twenty metres across, and it formed a corner with another building. It looked in poor condition: the belfry was shored up by wooden struts, thick beams propped up the outer wall, and scaffolding partially obscured a tile depicting Christ, flanked by rusty iron lamps. There was also a cement mixer beside a mound of gravel and some sacks of cement.

So there she was. Quart stood and stared at the building for a couple of minutes. Seen through the orange trees and beneath a bright blue Andalusian sky on that perfect morning, it didn't seem remotely sinister. Two twisted Solomonic columns stood on either side of the baroque portico. Above it was a niche containing a statue of the Virgin. Our Lady of the Tears, he almost said aloud. Then he walked towards the church and, as he came closer, saw that the Virgin had been beheaded.

Nearby, bells began to ring and a flock of pigeons rose from the roofs around the square. He watched them fly off, then looked back to the church façade. Something had changed. Now, despite the Andalusian sunlight and the orange trees with their fragrant blossom, the church seemed different. Suddenly, the old beams shoring up the walls, the ochre paint of the belfry peeling in strips like skin, the bell hanging motionless from the crossbeam overgrown with weeds, all gave the place a sombre, dull, disturbing atmosphere. A church that kills to defend itself, Vespers' mysterious message had said. Quart glanced again at the headless Virgin while inwardly laughing at himself for feeling uneasy. There didn't seem much left to defend.

To Quart, faith was relative. Monsignor Spada had not been wrong to speak of him, if half-joking, as a good soldier. Quart's creed didn't consist of revealed truths; it rested, rather, on the assumption that one had faith and acted accordingly. In this light, the Catholic Church from the start was to Quart what the army was to other young men: a place where rules provided most of the answers as long as one didn't question the basic concept. In Quart's case, this self-discipline replaced faith. And the paradox, which the veteran archbishop had sensed, was that it was precisely the lack of faith, with all the pride and rigour needed to sustain it, that made Quart so good at his job.

Everything has its source, of course. The son of a fisherman who drowned at sea, Lorenzo Quart was taken under the wing of a rough village priest who helped him enter the seminary. A brilliant and conscientious student, to such an extent that his superiors took an interest in his progress, Quart was possessed of that southern clarity of mind that is like a quiet affliction sometimes brought on by the easterly winds and blazing Mediterranean sunsets. One day, as a child, he stood for hours on the breakwater of the port, lashed by wind and rain, while out to sea some helpless fishing boats fought the huge waves. In the distance they looked tiny and pitifully fragile in the mountainous foaming seas, their motors struggling to bring them back to port. One boat had been lost. And when one fishing boat was lost, that meant sons, husbands, brothers, fathers were lost along with it. Women in black with children clinging to their skirts stood by the lighthouse, moving their lips in silent prayer, trying to make out which boat was missing. And when the little boats finally entered the port, the men on board looked to where Lorenzo stood on the breakwater, clasping his mother's hand, and they took off their caps. The rain, the wind, and the waves roared on. No more boats returned. That day, Quart realised that it was no use praying to the sea. And he vowed that no one would ever stand in the rain waiting for him to return to port.

* * *

The church door, made of oak and decorated with thick nails, was open. As Quart went inside, a cold breath of air came to meet him, as if he'd just lifted a gravestone. He took off his sunglasses and dipped his fingers in holy water. He felt its coolness as he made the sign of the Cross on his forehead. The gilded altar gleamed gently at the other end of the nave. Half a dozen wooden pews sat facing it. The rest had been piled in a corner to make room for the scaffolding. The place smelled of wax, stale air and the mildew of centuries. The entire church was in gloom, except for the top left-hand corner, lit by a spotlight. Quart looked up at the light and saw a woman on the scaffolding, photographing the leaded windows.

"Good morning," she said.

Her hair was grey, but unlike Quart's not prematurely – she must have been well over forty, he thought as she looked down from the scaffolding. Holding on to the metal poles, she climbed nimbly to the ground. She had her hair in a small plait and she wore a polo shirt, jeans covered in plaster, and trainers. From behind she could have been a young girl.

"My name is Quart," he said.

The woman wiped her right hand on her jeans and gave him a firm, brief handshake. Her hand felt rough.

"Gris Marsala. I work here."

She had an American accent. Her eyes, edged with lines, were bright and friendly, and her smile was easy and open. She looked him over curiously.

"You're a good-looking priest," she said at last, forthright. Her gaze rested on his dog collar. "We were expecting someone rather different."

"We?"

"Yes. We've all been waiting for the envoy from Rome. An anonymous little man in a cassock, with a briefcase full of missals and crucifixes."

"Who is all?"

"I don't know. All of us." She started counting on her plaster-covered fingers. "Father Priamo Ferro, the parish priest. His assistant, Father Oscar. The archbishop, the mayor, and quite a few others."

Quart tensed his mouth. He hadn't realised his mission would be public knowledge. He thought the IEA had informed only the nunciature of Madrid and the archbishop of Seville. The nuncio wouldn't have told anyone, but Quart could well imagine the archbishop, Monsignor Corvo, spreading rumours. Damn His Grace.

"I wasn't expecting such a reception," he said coldly.

The woman shrugged, ignoring his tone. "It's not over you, but the church." She gestured at the scaffolding, the paint on the blackened ceiling coming away between patches of damp. "This church has aroused a lot of strong feeling lately. And nobody in Seville can keep a secret." She leaned towards him slightly and lowered her voice, parodying a confidence. "They say even the Pope is giving the matter his attention."

Dear God. Quart was silent a moment, his gaze on his shoes. Then he looked into the woman's eyes. This was as good a time as any to start untangling some of the threads, he thought. So he moved closer until he was almost touching her shoulder and looked round with theatrical suspicion.

"Who says so?" he whispered.

Her laughter was relaxed, like everything else about her. "The archbishop of Seville, I think," she said. "By the way, he doesn't seem to like you much."

I must be sure to repay His Grace's kindness at the first opportunity, Quart thought. The woman watched him mischievously. He was reluctant to be as open as she was, so he just raised his eyebrows with the practised innocence of a Jesuit. He had in fact learned the gesture from a Jesuit, at the seminary.

"You're very well informed. But you shouldn't believe everything you hear."

Gris Marsala laughed. "I don't," she said. "But the rumours amuse me. Anyway, as I said, I work here. I'm the architect in charge of restoring the church." She looked round again and sighed. "Doesn't say much for my skills, does it? But it's been one long sorry tale of estimates not being approved and money not coming through."

"You're American, aren't you?"

"Yes. I've been working here for two years. I was appointed by the Eurnekian Foundation. It put up a third of the money for the initial restoration project. At first there were three of us working here, two

Spaniards and me, but the others left . . . The work more or less ground to a halt some time ago." She looked at him to see what effect her next words would have. "And there were the two deaths, of course."

Quart showed no reaction. "You mean the accidents?"

"You could call them that, yes. Accidents." She was still watching him closely and seemed disappointed when he said nothing more. "Have you met the parish priest?"

"Not yet. I arrived only last night. I haven't even seen the archbishop. I wanted to see the church first."

"Well, here it is." She waved her hand, indicating the nave with the high altar at the end, barely visible in the gloom. "Seventeenth-century baroque, with an altarpiece by Duque Cornejo . . . A small treasure that's falling to pieces."

"And the headless Virgin at the door?"

"Some citizens of the town chose to celebrate the proclamation of the Second Republic in 1931 in their own special way." She said it kindly, as if deep down she forgave the vandals. Quart wondered how long she'd been in Seville. Definitely quite some time. Her Spanish was perfect and she seemed very much at ease.

"How long have you lived here?"

"Nearly four years. But I visited the city lots of times before I settled. I came on a scholarship and never really left."

"Why not?"

She shrugged. "I don't know. It happens to a lot of Americans, particularly young ones. They come here, and then they just can't leave. They stay and scrape a living somehow, playing the guitar or sketching in the squares." She looked thoughtfully at the patch of sunlight on the floor by the door. "There's something about the light here, the colour of the streets, that saps your will. It's almost like an illness."

Quart took a few steps up the nave and stopped. On the left the pulpit with its spiral staircase was half-obscured by scaffolding. The confessional was on the right, in a small chapel that led to the vestry. He ran his hand over one of the wooden pews, blackened with age.

"What do you think of the church?" she asked.

Quart looked up. A barrel vault inset with lunettes rose above the single nave and the short-armed transept. The elliptical dome, surmounted by a blind lantern, was decorated with frescoes that had been almost completely obliterated by smoke from the candles and by fire. Around the edges of a large soot stain he could just make out a few angels, and some bearded prophets covered with patches of damp that made them look like lepers.

"I don't know," he answered. "It's small. Very pretty. Old."

"Three centuries old," she said. Their steps echoed as they walked past the pews towards the high altar. "Where I come from, a three-hundred-year-old building would be a historical jewel that no one could touch. But around here there are lots of places like this falling into ruin. And nobody lifts a finger."

"Maybe there are just too many."

"That sounds strange coming from a priest. Although you don't look much like one." Again she regarded him with amused interest, this time observing the impeccable cut of his lightweight black suit. "If it weren't for your collar and black shirt . . ."

"I've worn a dog collar for twenty years," he interrupted coldly. Then, glancing over her shoulder, "You were telling me about the church and places like it."

She tilted her head, disconcerted, obviously trying to make him out. Quart could tell that despite her self-assurance she was intimidated by the collar. All women were, he thought, young and old. Even the most determined ones lost their confidence when a word or gesture suddenly reminded them he was a priest.

"The church, yes," said Gris Marsala at last. But her thoughts seemed elsewhere. "I don't agree that there are too many places like this. After all, they're part of our collective memory, aren't they?" She wrinkled her nose and tapped a foot on the worn flagstones, as if they were her witnesses. "I'm convinced that every ancient building, picture, or book that's lost or destroyed, leaves us bereft. Impoverished."

Her tone was unexpectedly vehement, bitter. When she saw Quart's surprise, she smiled. "I'm American, it really has nothing to do with me," she said apologetically. "Or maybe it has. It's the heritage of all humanity. We have no right to let it fall into ruins."

"Is that why you've stayed in Seville so long?"

"Maybe. At any rate, that's why I'm here now, in this church." She glanced up at the window where she'd been working when Quart arrived. "Did you know, this was one of the last churches built in Spain under the Hapsburgs? The work was officially completed on the first of November, 1700, while Charles II, the last of his dynasty, lay dying. Next day, the first mass celebrated here was a requiem for the king."

They stood before the high altar. The light fell diagonally from the windows and made the gilding high on the altarpiece gleam gently. Reliefs kept the rest in shadow. Through the scaffolding Quart could make out the central section with the Virgin beneath a wide baldachin, above the tabernacle. He bowed his head briefly before it. In the side sections, separated from the portico by carved columns, were niches containing figures of cherubs and saints.

"It's magnificent," he said with feeling.

"It's slightly more than that."

Gris Marsala moved behind the altar to the foot of the altarpiece. She switched on a light to illuminate it. The gold leaf and gilded wood came to life, and a stream of light poured through exquisitely carved columns, medallions and garlands. Quart admired the way all the different elements blended so harmoniously.

"Magnificent," he repeated, impressed, crossing himself. Then he saw that Gris Marsala was watching him intently, as if she thought it incongruous.

"Haven't you seen a priest cross himself before?" He smiled coldly to hide his embarrassment. "I can't be the first to have done that before this altarpiece."

"I suppose not. But they were a different kind of priest."

"There's only one type of priest," he said quickly. "Are you Catholic?"

"Partly. My great-grandfather was Italian." She looked at him mischievously. "I have a fairly precise understanding of sin, if that's what you mean. But at my age . . ." She touched her grey hair.

Quart thought he ought to change the subject. "We were discussing the altarpiece," he said. "I said it was magnificent . . ." He looked her in the eye, serious, courteous, distant. "How about starting again?"

Gris Marsala tilted her head as before. An intelligent woman, he thought, but she made him uneasy. His instincts were well honed by his work for the IEA and he sensed a discordant note. Something about her didn't quite add up. He peered at her, hoping for a clue, but there was no way of getting any closer without being more open himself, something he was reluctant to do.

"Please," he added.

She seemed about to smile but didn't. "All right," she said at last. They both turned to the altarpiece. "The sculptor Pedro Duque Cornejo completed it in 1711. He was paid two thousand silver *escudos*. And as you say, it's magnificent. All the energy and imagination of the Sevillian baroque are there."

The Virgin was a beautiful polychrome sculpture in wood, almost a metre tall. She wore a blue mantle and held her hands open, palms out. The pedestal was shaped like a crescent moon, and her right foot rested on a serpent.

"She's very lovely," said Quart.

"Sculpted by Juan Martínez Montañés almost a century before the altarpiece . . . It belonged to the dukes of El Nuevo Extremo. One of the dukes helped to construct the church, and his son donated the sculpture. The tears gave the church its name."

Quart looked more closely. From below he could see tears glistening on the face, crown and mantle.

"They are rather exaggerated."

"Originally they were smaller and made of glass. But now they're pearls. Twenty perfect pearls, brought from America at the end of the last century. The rest of the story lies in the crypt."

"There's a crypt?"

"Yes. There's a concealed entrance over there, to the right of the high altar. It's a kind of private chapel. Several generations of the dukes of El Nuevo Extremo are buried inside. In 1687, one of the them, Gaspar Bruner de Lebrija, ceded land from his estate for the church, on condition that a Mass would be said for his soul once a week." She pointed to a niche to the right of the Virgin, containing a figure of a knight kneeling in prayer. "There he is: carved by Duque Cornejo, as was the figure on the left, of the duke's wife . . . He commissioned his favourite architect, Pedro Romero, also the duke of Medina-Sidonia's favourite architect, to design the building. That's the origin of the family's link with this church. Gaspar Bruner's son Guzman had figures of his parents added, which completed the altarpiece, and the image of the Virgin brought here in 1711. The family still has links with the church today, although they're diminished. And this has a great deal to do with the conflict."

"What conflict?"

Gris Marsala gazed at the altarpiece as if she hadn't heard the question. Then she rubbed the back of her neck and sighed. "Well, call it what you like." She was trying to sound light-hearted. "The stalemate, you might say. With Macarena Bruner, her mother the old duchess, and all the rest of them."

"I haven't yet met the Bruners, mother and daughter."

When Gris Marsala turned to look at Quart, there was a malevolent gleam in her eyes. "Haven't you? Well, you certainly will."

Quart heard her laugh as she switched off the light. The altarpiece was once again in shadow.

"What's really going on here?" he asked.

"In Seville?"

"In this church."

She took a few moments to answer. "It's up to you to decide," she said at last. "That's why you were sent."

"But you work here. You must have some ideas on the subject."

"Of course I have, but I'm keeping them to myself. All I know is that more people would like to have this church pulled down than to keep it standing."

"Why?"

"That I don't know." Her friendliness disappeared. Now it was her turn to become closed off and distant. "Maybe because a square metre of land in this part of Seville is worth a fortune . . ." She shook her head as if to rid it of unpleasant thoughts. "You'll find plenty of people to tell you all about it."

"You said you had some ideas."

"I did?" Her smile looked forced. "Maybe. Anyway, it's none of my business. My job is to save as much as I can of the building as long as there's money for the work. Which there isn't."

"So why are you staying on alone?"

"I'm putting in some overtime. Anyway, since I began working on the church, I haven't found anything else to do, so I have a lot of spare time."

"A lot of spare time," repeated Quart.

"That's right." She sounded bitter again. "And I have nowhere else to go."

Intrigued, he was about to ask more when the sound of footsteps made him turn. A small, motionless figure dressed in black stood in the doorway. It cast its compact shadow on the flagstones.

Gris Marsala, who had also turned, smiled strangely at Quart. "It's time for you to meet the parish priest, don't you think? Father Priamo Ferro."

As soon as Celestino Peregil left the Casa Cuesta Bar, Don Ibrahim began discreetly counting the banknotes that Pencho Gavira's assistant had left them to cover initial expenses.

"A hundred thousand," he said when he'd finished.

El Potro del Mantelete and La Niña Puñales nodded in silence. Don Ibrahim made three bundles of thirty-three thousand, put one bundle in the inside pocket of his jacket, and passed the others to his companions. He placed the remaining thousand-peseta note on the table.

"What do you think?" he asked.

Frowning, El Potro del Mantelete smoothed the banknote and peered at the figure of Hernán Cortés on the front. "Looks real to me," he ventured.

"I mean the job, not the note."

El Potro stared gloomily at the banknote and La Niña Puñales shrugged.

"It's money," she said, as if that summed it all up. "But the job looks dodgy, with all those priests."

Don Ibrahim waved his hand dismissively, dropping ash on his trousers again. "We will proceed with the utmost tact," he said, leaning with effort over his paunch to brush off the ash.

La Niña Puñales said *othu* and El Potro nodded, still staring at the banknote. El Potro must have been about forty-five, and every one of his years showed in his face. In his younger days, between stints in the

Spanish Legion, he'd been a luckless apprentice bullfighter. It had left him with the dust of failure in his eyes and throat, and a scar from a bull's horn under his right ear. And all he got from a brief, obscure career as a contender for the bantamweight championship of Andalusia was a broken nose, lumpy scarred eyebrows and a certain slowness in combining thought, speech and action. When he was conning tourists in the streets, he was very good at playing the innocent. His vacant stare was utterly convincing.

"Very important to be tactful," he said slowly.

He went on frowning, as he did whenever he was thinking. This was what he'd been doing – frowning and pondering a question deeply – when he came home one day to find his brother, who was in a wheelchair, with his trousers down to his knees and his wife – El Potro's wife – sitting on top of him panting eloquently. Unhurriedly and without raising his voice, nodding as his brother assured him that there was a misunderstanding and he could explain everything, El Potro del Mantelete pushed the wheelchair almost tenderly to the landing and tipped it and its occupant down the stairs. His brother bumped down the thirty-two steps and suffered a fractured skull that turned out to be fatal. El Potro's wife got off more lightly: he beat her methodically, gave her two black eyes and then knocked her out with a left hook. Half an hour later, she came to, packed her bags and left for good.

The business with his brother didn't work out so well. It was only thanks to the skill of El Potro's lawyer that the judge was persuaded to change the charge from murder (with a possible thirty-year sentence) to involuntary manslaughter, resulting in an acquittal *in dubio pro reo*. The lawyer was Don Ibrahim. The Lawyers' Association of Seville didn't yet have doubts as to the authenticity of the diploma issued in Havana. But El Potro didn't care whether Don Ibrahim was a bona fide lawyer or not. The former bullfighter and boxer would never forget how Don Ibrahim had made an impassioned defence and won him his freedom. A home torn apart, Your Honour. A cheating brother, the heat of the moment, my client's intellect, the absence of *animus necandi*, the lack of brakes on the wheelchair. Since then, El Potro del Mantelete had been blindly, heroically, unfailingly loyal to his benefactor. And his devotion became even greater, if that was possible, after Don Ibrahim's ignominious expulsion from the legal profession. Faithful as a hound, silent and unswerving, El Potro would do anything for his master.

"Still too many priests for my liking," said La Niña, her silver bracelets jangling as she twirled her empty glass.

Don Ibrahim and El Potro exchanged glances. Then the bogus lawyer ordered three more fino sherries and some tapas of spicy pork sausage. As soon as the waiter put the sherries on the table, La Niña emptied her glass in a single gulp. Don Ibrahim and El Potro averted their eyes.

> Sour wine, so full of happiness,
> though I drink to drown my sorrows,
> I will never forget . . .

She sang low and from the heart, licking her red-painted lips moist with sherry. El Potro whispered *olé* without looking at her, gently tapping the rhythm on the table. As she sang the folk song her eyes – dark, tragic, rimmed with too much eyeliner – showed enormous in a face once beautiful. When she had too much sherry, she would recall how, as in the song, a dark man had once stabbed another to death over her. And she would search her handbag for a newspaper cutting she'd lost long ago. If it had ever really happened, it must have been when La Niña appeared on posters for shows in all her Gypsy glory, wild and beautiful, the young hope of Spanish song. The successor, they said, of Doña Concha Piquer.

Now, three decades after her brief moment of fame, she worked in seedy clubs and bars on the tourist circuit – dinner and a show included, Seville by night – the tired stamp of her dancing shoes making the rickety stages splinter.

"Where do we start?" she asked, looking at Don Ibrahim.

El Potro glanced up too at the man he most respected in the world after the late bullfighter Juan Belmonte. Aware of his responsibility, the bogus lawyer took a long drag on his cigar and twice read the list of tapas on a blackboard behind the bar. Croquettes. Tripe. Fried anchovies. Eggs in bechamel. Tongue in sauce. Stuffed tongue.

"As Caius Julius Caesar said, and he put it well," Don Ibrahim said when he judged enough time had elapsed for his words to have greatest impact, "'*Galia est omnia divisa in partibus infidelibus.*' In other words, before taking any action, ocular reconnaissance is recommended." He looked round like a general before his staff officers. "Visualisation of the territory, if you see what I mean." He blinked doubtfully. "Do you see what I mean?"

"*Othu.*"

"Yes."

"Good." Don Ibrahim stroked his moustache, satisfied with troop morale. "What I mean is, we have to go and take a look at that church and all the rest of it." He glanced at La Niña, knowing she was devout. "With due attention to the fact that it is a sacred building, of course."

"I know the church," she said in her gravelly voice. "It's old and always has the builders in. I go to Mass there sometimes."

Like a good flamenco singer, she was highly religious. For his part, although he professed to be agnostic, Don Ibrahim respected freedom of worship. He leaned forward enquiringly. Rigorous research was mother to all victories, he'd read somewhere – Churchill, perhaps, or Frederick the Great.

"What's he like, the parish priest?"

"Old-school." La Niña frowned in concentration. "Ancient, bad-tempered . . . He once threw out some tourists, young girls, who came in during Mass. He got down from the altar, in his chasuble and everything, and gave them a real scolding for wearing shorts. This isn't the beach, he said to them, off you go. And he chucked them out."

Don Ibrahim nodded, pleased. "A holy man, I see. A man of God."

"To his fingernails."

After a thoughtful pause, Don Ibrahim blew a smoke ring and watched it float away. He appeared preoccupied. "So what we have here," he said, "is a clergyman of character."

"I don't know about character," said La Niña. "He certainly has a temper."

"I see." Don Ibrahim blew another smoke ring, but this time it didn't come out right. "So this honourable priest may cause problems. I mean, he may hinder us."

"He could ruin the whole thing."

"And the young priest, his assistant?"

"I've seen him helping during Mass. Nice and quiet he looks. Not so tough."

Don Ibrahim glanced across the street, at the knee-high leather boots from Valverde del Camino hanging outside the La Valenciana Shoe Shop. Then, with a melancholy shudder, he turned back to El Potro and La Niña. At any other time he would have told Peregil where to put his little job. Or, more likely, he would have asked for more money. But as things were, he had no choice. He stared sadly at La Niña with her fake beauty spot, her chipped nail varnish, her bony fingers clasping the empty glass. He looked to his left and met the faithful gaze of El Potro. Then he regarded his own hand resting on the table. The ring he wore was a fake. Every so often he managed to sell one – he had several like it – for five thousand pesetas to some sucker in a bar in Triana. El Potro and La Niña were his people, his responsibility. El Potro, for his loyalty in adversity. La Niña, because Don Ibrahim had never heard anyone sing "Cape of Red and Gold" the way she sang it, in a *tablao*, on his arrival in Seville. He didn't meet her until much later. She was playing a really seedy club and was already wrecked by alcohol and by the years, the embodiment of the songs she sang in a cracked, sublime voice that made the hairs stand on the back of your neck. "The She-Wolf", "Ballad of Bravery", "False Coin", "Tattoo". The night they met, Don Ibrahim swore to himself that he would save her from oblivion, to do justice to her art. For despite the calumny heaped upon him by the Lawyers' Association and the articles in the local papers when he was thrown in jail over an absurd diploma that nobody else gave a damn about, and despite the scams he'd had to set up to earn his living ever since, Don Ibrahim was not a scoundrel. He held his head high as he adjusted his watch chain. He was simply an honourable man who'd had no luck.

"This is merely a matter of strategy," he said thoughtfully, to convince himself more than anything else. He felt his companions' hopes pinned on him. Peregil had promised three million, but Don Ibrahim had heard that he worked for a banker who was really loaded, so there might be more money where that came from. And he and his companions needed funds to make a long-cherished dream come true.

Don Ibrahim had read extensively – how else could he have practised law for so long in Seville without being exposed? – if superficially, and he hoarded quotations as if they were gold dust. The best quotation about dreams came from that Thomas D. H. Lawrence, the one from Arabia who wrote *Madam Butterfly*: men who dream with their eyes open, will always succeed, or something like that. He doubted whether El Potro and La Niña had their eyes open, but it didn't matter, he'd keep his open for them.

He looked affectionately at El Potro, who was slowly chewing a slice of sausage. "What do you think, champ?"

El Potro went on chewing in silence for half a minute. "I think we can do it," he said at last, when the other two had almost forgotten the question. "If God gives us luck."

Don Ibrahim sighed. "That's the problem. With all these priests involved, I don't know whose side God will be on."

El Potro smiled for the first time that morning. His smile always seemed be a great effort for his face, battered by bulls and other boxers. "Everything for the Cause," he said.

La Niña Puñales let out a low, tender *olé*:

A man without fear of death
swore his love to me . . .

She sang quietly, laying her hand on the hand of El Potro. Since his divorce he had lived alone. Don Ibrahim suspected that he silently loved La Niña but had never declared himself, out of respect. She, for her part, remained faithful to the memory of the man with green eyes still waiting for her at the bottom of every bottle. As for Don Ibrahim, nobody had definite evidence of his love affairs. On evenings of Manzanilla and guitar, he liked to talk vaguely of the romantic adventures of his youth in Cuba, when he was a friend of Beny Moré, the Brute of Rhythm, and of "Carafoca" Perez Prado, and of Jorge Negrete, the Mexican actor – until they had words, that is. He liked to talk of the time when Maria Felix, the divine Maria, the lady Maria, gave him an ebony walking stick with a silver handle, on the night she was unfaithful to Agustin Lara with him and a litre bottle of tequila. And slim and elegant Lara, devastated, wrote an immortal song to ease the pain of being deceived. Don Ibrahim's smile became young again at the supposed memory of Acapulco, the nights, the beaches, Maria my love, pretty Maria. Between glasses of Manzanilla, La Niña softly hummed the song in which he was the guilty seducer. And El Potro sat there with his hard, silent profile.

After destiny had brought them together in Seville, a quaint friendship had sustained the three companions through the endless hangover of their lives. One peaceful, drunken dawn, they found a noble purpose, as they sat watching the wide, tranquil Guadalquivir: the Cause. Some day they would have the money to set up a sensational *tablao*. They would call it The Temple of Song, and there, at last, justice would be done to La Niña Puñales's art, and traditional Spanish song would be kept alive.

> Darling, he would say,
> burning with passion . . .

La Niña sang quietly. Don Ibrahim called the waiter so that he could sort out the bill, and with a grandiose air asked for Pretty Maria's walking stick and his pale straw panama. He rose with difficulty while El Potro del Mantelete, who stood up as if the bell had just been rung, withdrew La Niña's chair, and they both escorted her to the door. They left the banknote with the picture of Hernán Cortés on the table, as a tip. It was, after all, a special day. And, as El Potro put it, humbly justifying the expense, Don Ibrahim was a gentleman.

The dark figure entered the church. The light behind him blinded Quart. By the time his eyes had readjusted to the darkness inside the church, Father Priamo Ferro had reached his side. And Quart saw that things were worse than he'd feared.

"I'm Father Quart," he said, holding out his hand. "I've just arrived in Seville."

His hand remained in midair while two piercing black eyes stared at him suspiciously.

"What are you doing in my church?"

Not a good start, Quart thought as he slowly lowered his hand and observed the man standing before him. Ferro's appearance was as rough as his voice. He was small and thin, and his white hair was poorly cut and untidy. He wore a threadbare cassock covered with stains and a pair of clumpy old shoes that looked as if they hadn't been polished in a long time.

"I thought it would be a good idea if I took a look round," Quart answered calmly.

The most disturbing thing about the old priest was his face. It was covered in marks, lines and small scars, which gave him a harsh, tormented look, like an aerial photograph of a desert. And then there were his eyes – black, defiant, deep-set, peering out at the world with little sympathy. He scrutinised Quart, taking in his cufflinks, the cut of his suit, and finally his face. He didn't look pleased by what he saw.

"You have no right to be here."

Quart thought of appealing to Gris Marsala, who had been listening to their exchange without a word. He realised immediately that she would be no help.

"Father Quart was asking for you," she said reluctantly.

Father Ferro's gaze remained fixed on the visitor. "What for?"

The envoy from Rome raised his left hand slightly in a placatory gesture. He noticed that Father Ferro was looking disapprovingly at his expensive Hamilton watch. "I'm here to compile a report on the church," he said. He was now almost certain that this first meeting was a disaster, but he decided to try a little longer. It was his job, after all. "We need to have a chat, Father."

"I have nothing to say to you."

Quart breathed in and out slowly. His worst fears had been realised, and old, unwelcome memories were returning. In his worn cassock Father Ferro embodied everything Quart hated: the poverty and stubborn wariness of the rough village priest, who was capable only of threatening with the torments of hell, or hearing confession from pious old women from whom he differed only in that he had spent a few years in a seminary and had a smattering of Latin. If Father Ferro was Vespers, he was doing a brilliant job of hiding it. This would not be an easy mission.

"I'm sorry, but I think we have much to discuss," Quart insisted, taking an envelope showing the tiara and keys of St. Peter from his jacket pocket. "I'm the special envoy from the Institute of External Affairs. You'll find my credentials in this letter from the Secretary of State."

Father Ferro took the letter and tore it up without even looking at it. The pieces fluttered to the floor.

"I don't give a damn about your credentials."

Small and defiant, he glared up at Quart. Sixty-four years old, said the report lying on Quart's desk back at the hotel. Twenty years as a country priest, ten years as a parish priest in Seville. He and the Mastiff would have made a good pair at the Colosseum in Rome. Quart could picture Father Ferro with a trident in one hand and a net over his shoulder, circling his opponent while the spectators cried out for blood. In his work, Quart had learned to tell instantly whom to be wary of. Father Ferro was the character at the end of the bar who drinks quietly while everyone else is shouting, then suddenly shatters a bottle to slit your throat. Or the soldier wading across the lake of Tenochtitlan holding a cross above his head. Or the Crusader massacring infidels and heretics.

"And I don't know what all that business about external affairs is," the priest added, not taking his eyes off Quart. "My superior is the archbishop of Seville."

Who, very obviously, had carefully prepared the reception for this tiresome envoy from Rome. Quart remained calm. He again put his hand inside his jacket and half-pulled out another envelope, identical to the one lying in pieces at his feet.

"That's precisely the person I see next," he said.

Father Ferro nodded contemptuously. "Then go and see him," he said. "I obey the archbishop, and if he orders me to speak to you, I will. Until then, forget about me."

"I was sent specially from Rome. Somebody requested that we intervene. I assume you know about it."

"I haven't requested anything. Rome's far away, and this is my church."

"Your church."

"Yes."

Quart counted silently to five. He could feel Gris Marsala watching them expectantly.

"This is not *your* church, Father Ferro. It's *our* church," he said.

For a moment, the old priest stared in silence at the shreds of envelope on the floor. Then he turned his scarred face without looking at any precise point, and Quart saw a strange expression, between a smile and a frown.

"You're wrong there too," Father Ferro said at last, as if that settled it. Then he walked off down the nave towards the vestry.

Quart forced himself to make one last attempt at conciliation. "I'm here to help you, Father," he said to Father Ferro's receding back. He'd made the effort, now he could let things take their course. He'd done his bit for humility and priestly solidarity. Father Ferro didn't have the monopoly on anger.

Father Ferro had paused to genuflect before the high altar, and Quart heard him laugh briefly and unpleasantly. "Help me? How could somebody like you help me?" He turned to face Quart, and his voice echoed around the nave. "I know your type . . . What this church needs is a different kind of help, and you haven't brought any of it in those elegant pockets of yours. So leave now. I have a baptism in twenty minutes."

Gris Marsala walked with Quart to the door. He had to summon all his self-control to conceal his dislike of the old priest. He only half-listened to her attempts to make excuses for Father Ferro. He was under a lot of pressure, she said. Politicians, bankers, the archbishop, they were all circling like vultures. If it hadn't been for Father Ferro, the church would have been demolished long ago.

"Thanks to him, they may end up pulling it down anyway. With him inside," said Quart, venting his ill-feeling.

"Please don't say that."

She was right. Once more in control, Quart reproached himself. He inhaled the scent of orange blossom as they came outside. A builder was busying himself next to the cement mixer. Quart glanced absently in his direction as they walked through the orange trees in the square.

"I don't understand his attitude," he said. "I'm on his side. The Church is on his side."

Gris Marsala looked sceptical. "And which Church might that be? The Church of Rome? Or the archbishop of Seville? Or you yourself?"

She shook her head. "No. He's right. Nobody's on his side, and he knows it."

"He seems to be trying to make things more difficult for himself."

"They're difficult enough already. He's in open opposition to the archbishop. And the mayor is threatening libel action – he thinks Father Priamo insulted him a couple of weeks ago during the homily in the Sunday service."

Quart stopped, interested. Monsignor Spada's report hadn't mentioned anything about this.

"What did he call him?"

She smiled wryly. "He said he was an unscrupulous and corrupt politician and a vile speculator." She looked at Quart to see his reaction. "If I remember correctly."

"Is that the kind of thing he usually says in his sermons?"

"Only when he gets really mad." Gris Marsala became thoughtful. "I suppose lately it's happened rather often. He talks about the merchants in the temple, that sort of thing."

"The merchants," repeated Quart.

"Yes. Among others."

"Not bad," said Quart. "It would seem our Father Ferro is an expert at making friends."

"He does have friends," she protested. She kicked a bottle top and watched it spin away. "And he has parishioners. Good people who come here to pray and who need him. You shouldn't judge him by what you've just seen."

This sudden warmth made her seem younger. Quart shook his head, embarrassed. "I'm not here to pass judgement." He turned to look at the belfry, not wanting to meet her eye. "It must be others who are doing that."

"Of course." She stopped in front of him, her hands in her pockets. He didn't like the way she was watching him. "You're the type who writes his report and then washes his hands of the whole business, aren't you? You just take people to the praetorium and all that. It's up to others to say *ibi ad crucem.*"

"I would never have imagined you so well versed in the Gospels."

"I think there are rather too many things you can't imagine."

Embarrassed, the priest shifted from one foot to another. Then he passed a hand over his grey hair. The builder next to the cement mixer had stopped and was leaning on his shovel, watching them. He was young and wore old army-surplus clothes covered with plaster.

"All I'm trying to do," said Quart, "is make sure there's a thorough investigation."

Still facing him, Gris Marsala shook her head. "No, you're not," she said, her blue eyes piercing into his. "Father Priamo was right: you've come to make sure there's a swift execution."

"Is that what he said?"

"Yes. When the archbishop announced you were coming."

Quart looked away, over the woman's shoulder. He could see a window with a grille hung with pots of geraniums and a canary in a cage. "I just want to help," he said in a flat voice that suddenly sounded alien to him. At that moment the church bell began to ring and the canary sang, glad of the accompaniment.

This was not going to be an easy mission.

III
Eleven Bars in Triana

> *You have to cut and cut and cut again. You have to fell the trees without mercy, until their rows have been cleared and the forest can be considered healthy.*
>
> Jean Anouilh, *The Lark*

There are dogs that define their masters and cars that announce their owners. Pencho Gavira's Mercedes was enormous, dark and shiny, with its menacing three-pointed star on the front like the sight of a machine gun. Celestino Peregil jumped out before the car had quite come to a halt and held the door open for his boss. The traffic on La Campana was heavy and the henchman's salmon-pink shirt collar was grimy. His red, yellow and green flower-print tie blazed like some monstrous set of traffic lights. The exhaust fumes made his lank, thinning hair flutter, ruining the shape he carefully constructed each morning with much patience and hair gel to hide his bald patch.

"You've lost more hair," said Gavira cruelly. He knew that nothing tormented his assistant more than mention of his baldness. But the financier believed that periodic use of the spur kept the animals in his stables alert. Besides, Gavira was a hard man and given to such exercises of Christian virtue.

It looked as if it was going to be a beautiful day despite the pollution. Standing very straight on the kerb, Gavira adjusted his shirt-cuffs so that his twenty-four-carat gold cufflinks glinted in the May sunshine. He looked like a male model. He touched the knot of his tie and then ran his hand over his thick, black hair, slightly wavy behind the ears and slicked back. Pencho Gavira was dark, handsome, ambitious, elegant. He had money and was about to have a lot more. He was proud of the fact that most of his success was due entirely to his own efforts. Confident and pleased, he looked round before heading for the corner of the calle Sierpes with Peregil trailing behind him.

In the La Campana Café, Don Octavio Machuca sat at his usual table, looking through the papers that his secretary, Canovas, passed to him. For several years now the chairman of the Cartujano Bank had spent his mornings at a table on this café terrace in the very heart of the city rather than in his office, full of paintings and fine furniture, on the Arenal. He spent the morning reading the *ABC* newspaper, watching the world go by and attending to business matters until it was time for lunch at his favourite restaurant, Casa Robles. Nowadays he almost never got to the bank before four o'clock, so if there were any urgent matters to be dealt with, his employees and clients had no choice but to go and see him at La Campana. This included Gavira; as vice-chairman and general manager, he had to make the rather inconvenient journey almost every day.

No doubt this was why his confident expression grew dark as he approached the table where the man to whom he owed his present and his future sat in front of a coffee and half a buttered muffin. Gavira's face grew darker still when he inadvertently glanced to his left and saw the cover of *Q&S* prominently displayed at a newspaper kiosk. He walked on as if he hadn't seen it, sensing Peregil's eyes on the back of his head. The black cloud was taking over, and his belly, its muscles firmed by a daily workout, was tense with fury. The magazine had been lying on his desk for two days now, and Gavira was as familiar with the photographs as if he'd taken them himself. The cover picture was slightly grainy from the use of a telephoto lens, but he could clearly recognise his wife, Macarena Bruner de Lebrija, heiress to the title of El Nuevo Extremo and descendant of one of the three most noble families of the Spanish aristocracy – Alba and Medina-Sidonia were the other two – as she was leaving the Alfonso XIII Hotel at four in the morning with a bullfighter, Curro Maestral.

"You're late," said the old man.

Gavira knew, without even glancing at his expensive watch, that he wasn't. It was just that Don Octavio liked to keep up the pressure. Indeed, Gavira himself used the tactic having learned it from Don Octavio. Peregil, with his ridiculous hairdo, was his victim.

"I don't like people arriving late," Machuca insisted loudly, as if he were telling this to the waiter standing by the table waiting to take his order. They always reserved the same table for him, by the door.

Gavira nodded, calmly taking in Machuca's words. He ordered a beer, unbuttoned his blazer and sat down in the chair the chairman of the Cartujano Bank indicated next to him. After bowing his head abjectly a couple of times, Peregil went and sat at a table further off, where Canovas was putting documents away in a black leather briefcase. Canovas was a thin, mouse-like man, a father of nine and morally beyond reproach. He had worked for the banker since the days when Machuca smuggled cigarettes and perfume from Gibraltar. Nobody had ever seen Canovas smile, maybe because his sense of humour had been crushed beneath the weight of family responsibility. Gavira didn't like Canovas and secretly planned to dismiss him as soon as the old man decided to vacate his office on the Arenal.

Like his boss and patron, Gavira looked in silence at the passing pedestrians and cars. When his beer arrived, he leaned forward and took a sip, taking care not to let any drip on his perfectly pressed trousers. He dried his lips with a handkerchief and sat back.

"We have the mayor," he said at last.

Not a muscle moved in Octavio Machuca's face. He stared straight ahead, at the green-and-white sign of the PEÑA BÉTICA (1935) on the second-floor balcony across the street, beside the neo-mudéjar building of the Poniente Bank. Gavira considered the old financier's bony, claw-like hands covered with liver spots. Machuca was thin and tall, with a large nose and eyes circled with dark rings as if from permanent insomnia. He scanned his surroundings like a bird of prey. The years had imparted not tolerance or mercy to those eyes but weariness. A lookout and smuggler in his youth, later a moneylender in Jerez and, by the time he was forty, a banker in Seville, the founder of the Cartujano Bank was about to retire. Now his only known ambition was to have breakfast every morning at the café on the corner of the calle Sierpes, opposite the Peña Bética and the head office of the rival bank. Which the Cartujano had recently annexed, having engineered its gradual downfall.

"About time," said Machuca, still staring across the street.

Following the direction of his gaze, Gavira wasn't sure whether he meant the Poniente Bank takeover or the fact that they now had the mayor's support.

"I had dinner with him last night," Gavira said, glancing at the old man's profile out of the corner of his eye. "And this morning I had a long friendly chat with him on the telephone."

"You and your mayor," muttered Machuca, looking as if he was trying to place a vaguely familiar face. Anyone else might have thought it a sign of senility. But Gavira knew his chairman too well.

"Yes," he said, appearing keen, alert to nuances – exactly the kind of attitude that had got him where he was. "He's agreed to reclassify the land and sell it to us immediately." He might well have allowed a note of triumph into his voice, but he didn't. This was an unwritten rule at the Cartujano Bank.

"There'll be an outcry," said the old man.

"He doesn't care. His term of office ends in a month and he knows he won't be re-elected."

"What about the press?"

"The press can be bought, Don Octavio. Or it can be fed more tasty morsels."

Machuca nodded. In fact Canovas had just put away in the brief-case an explosive dossier obtained by Gavira about irregularities in welfare payments by the Junta de Andalucia. The plan was to make it public at the same time as the deal went through, to act as a smoke screen.

"With no opposition from the city council," Gavira added, "and with the Heritage Department in our pocket, all we have to sort out is the ecclesiastical side of the matter." He paused, expecting some remark, but the old man said nothing. "As for the archbishop . . ."

He left the sentence hanging, giving Machuca the chance to respond. He needed some response – a hint or warning.

"The archbishop wants his share," Machuca said at last. "Render unto God the things that are God's, you know what I mean."

"Of course," Gavira answered cautiously.

The old banker now turned to him. "Well, give him what he wants and get it over with."

He knew as well as Gavira that it wasn't as simple as that. The old bastard.

"I agree, Don Octavio," said Gavira.

"So there's nothing more to discuss."

Machuca stirred his coffee and went back to regarding the PEÑA BÉTICA sign. At the other table, unaware of the conversation, Peregil and the secretary were eyeing each other with hostility. Gavira chose his words and his tone carefully.

"With respect, Don Octavio, I think we do have more to discuss. This is the biggest development coup since Expo '92: three thousand square metres bang in the middle of Santa Cruz. And linked to it, the purchase of Puerto Targa by the Saudis. In other words, one hundred and eighty to two hundred million dollars. But you'll allow me to make the best deal we can." He sipped his beer, letting the word "deal" resonate. "I don't want to pay ten for something we could get for five. And the archbishop's started to ask for a fortune."

"We have to reward Monsignor Corvo somehow for washing his hands of the whole business." Machuca screwed up his eyes. "Or, as you'd put it, for facilitating the operation. It's not every day you can get an archbishop to agree to secularise a piece of land like this, evict the parish priest, and pull down the church . . . Is it?" He'd raised one of his bony hands to list the points and now let it fall to the table wearily. "It's a delicate manoeuvre."

"I'm aware of that. I've made plenty of personal sacrifices, if you'll permit me to say so."

"That's why you've got where you are today. Now pay the archbishop the compensation he's hinted he wants and have done with that side of things. After all, the money you're working with belongs to me."

"And the other shareholders, Don Octavio. That's my responsibility. If I've learned anything from you, it's to honour my commitments, but without paying too much."

The banker shrugged.

"Do what you like. It's *your* deal."

And so it was, for better or for worse. It was a warning, but it took more than that to unnerve Pencho Gavira.

"Everything's under control," he said.

Old Machuca was as sharp as a razor. Gavira saw the predatory eyes go from the white-and-green PEÑA BÉTICA sign to the façade of the Poniente Bank. The Santa Cruz and Puerto Targa operations were more than just profitable deals. Pulling them off meant for Gavira the difference between succeeding Machuca as chairman and standing defenceless before a board of directors who came from the "old money" of Seville and took a dim view of ambitious young lawyers on the make. Gavira felt five beats more at his wrist, under his gold Rolex.

"What about the priest?" asked the old man, with a flicker of interest. "I hear the archbishop still isn't sure he'll co-operate."

"Something like that." Gavira smiled reassuringly. "But we've taken steps to address the problem." He looked to the other table, at Peregil, and paused uncertainly. He felt he had to add something. "He's just a stubborn old man."

It was a mistake, and he knew it at once. With visible enjoyment, Machuca struck.

"That's unworthy of you," he said, looking straight into Gavira's eyes – a snake relishing its victim's terror. Gavira counted another ten beats at least. "I'm an old man too, Pencho. And you know better than anyone that I still have sharp teeth. It would be dangerous to forget that, wouldn't it?" He narrowed his eyes. "Just when you're so close to your goal."

"I never forget it." It's difficult to swallow imperceptibly, but Gavira managed it twice. "As for that priest, there's no comparison between you and him."

The banker shook his head reprovingly. "You're not in good form today, Pencho. You, resorting to flattery."

"You don't know me, Don Octavio."

"Don't be ridiculous. I know you very well, and that's why you've got where you are. And why you're about to go even further."

"I'm always frank with you. Even when you don't like it."

"I always appreciate your frankness, which is as calculated as everything else. Like your ambition and your patience . . ." The banker stared into his cup, as if he might find there clues to Gavira's personality. "Maybe you're right. Maybe all that priest and I have in common is our age. I don't know, because I haven't met him. Now I'm going to give you some good advice, Pencho . . . You appreciate my advice, don't you?"

"You know I do, Don Octavio."

"Good, because this is some of my best. Always beware of an old man who clings to an idea. It's so rare to reach old age with any ideas one is passionate about. Only a lucky few won't have them snatched away." He stopped, as if he'd remembered something. "Anyway, haven't things become more complicated? A priest from Rome or something?"

Pencho Gavira's sigh sounded sincere. Maybe it was. "You keep up on developments, Don Octavio."

Machuca exchanged glances with his secretary, who sat motionless at the other table, saying and seeing nothing until further orders. Peregil, on the other hand, sitting opposite the secretary, fidgeted anxiously and glanced nervously at Gavira. The proximity of Don Octavio, his conversation with Gavira, and the imperturbable presence of Canovas all intimidated him.

"I don't know why that should surprise you. This is my town, Pencho," said Machuca.

Gavira took out a packet of cigarettes and lit one. The chairman didn't smoke, and Gavira was the only person allowed to do so in his presence. "Don't worry," Gavira said as he took his first puff. "Eveything's under control." He exhaled, calmer now. "No loose ends."

"I'm not worried." The banker shook his head, absently watching the passers-by. "As I said, it's your deal, Pencho. I'll be retiring in October. However this turns out, it won't make any difference to my life. But it might to yours."

With that the old man seemed to consider the matter closed. He drank the rest of his coffee, then turned back towards Gavira.

"By the way, have you heard from Macarena?" he asked.

It was a low blow. He'd obviously been saving it till the end. Gavira glanced at the newspaper kiosk and anger again knotted his stomach. It was also a rather unfortunate coincidence: just when he'd ordered Peregil to keep a discreet eye on his wife's adventures, the journalists from *Q&S* had caught her gallivanting with a bullfighter and got it all on film. Damn his luck and damn Seville.

* * *

In the three hundred metres from Casa Cuesta to the Triana Bridge there were exactly eleven bars. That meant an average of one bar every twenty-seven metres and twenty-seven centimetres, Don Ibrahim worked out in his head. He was more used to books and numbers than the other two, but any one of them could recite the entire list of bars forwards, backwards or in alphabetical order: La Trianera, Casa Manolo, La Marinera, Dulcinea, La Taberna del Altozano, Las Dos Hermanas, La Cinta, La Ibense, Los Parientes, El Bar Angeles, and the stand of Las Flores at the end, almost on the bank, by the tile showing the Virgen de la Esperanza and the bronze statue of the bullfighter Juan Belmonte. They had stopped at each and every one of the bars to discuss their strategy, and now crossed the bridge in a state of grace, not looking to their left, at the hideous modern buildings on the island of La Cartuja, and enjoying the view to their right, Seville as she had always been, beautiful Moorish queen, with her palm trees all along the other bank, the Torre del Oro, the Arenal and La Giralda. And only a stone's throw away, looking out over the Guadalquivir, was the Maestranza bullring: the cathedral of the universe where people went to pray to the brave men of La Niña's songs.

They walked across the bridge, shoulder to shoulder as in the old American films, with La Niña in the middle and the two of them, Don Ibrahim and El Potro del Mantelete, on either side like two loyal gentlemen. And in the blue, ochre, and white morning reflected in the river, lulled by the gentle vapours of La Ina fino sherry that had generously tempered their spirits, an Andalusian guitar strummed which only they could hear. Imaginary music, or maybe it was real, that gave their short and somewhat hurried walk – leaving familiar Triana behind to cross to the other side of the Guadalquivir – the purposefulness of an afternoon paseo. Don Ibrahim, El Potro, and La Niña were about to begin their campaign, to earn their living in enemy territory, leaving the safety of their usual haunts. The bogus lawyer had, in the Los Parientes Bar, they seemed to remember, raised his panama hat – the hat he once removed to slap Jorge Negrete, who had questioned whether there were any real men left in Spain – and solemnly quoted a writer named Virgil. Or was it Horace? One of the classics, anyway:

Then, like predatory wolves in darkest night,
we set out
for the centre
of blazing Hispalis.

Or something like that. The sun sparkled on the calm waters of the river. A young girl with long black hair rowed under the bridge in a little boat. As they passed the Virgen de la Esperanza, La Niña crossed herself beneath Don Ibrahim's agnostic but benevolent gaze. He even took his cigar out of his mouth, in respect. El Potro furtively made the sign of the Cross with his head bowed, just as when the bugle sounded in wretched bullrings full of dust, fear, and flies, or when the bell forced him to prise himself from his corner and return to the ring, staring at his own blood on the canvas. But he hadn't made the sign of the Cross at the Virgin. He'd directed it towards the bronze profile, hat and cape of Juan Belmonte.

"You should have taken better care of your wife."

On the terrace of La Campana, old Machuca shook his head as he watched the passers-by. He took out a handkerchief, white batiste with his initials embroidered in blue, and wiped his nose. Gavira stared at the liver spots on his claw-like hands and thought of an old, malevolent eagle, motionless, watching.

"Women are complicated, Don Octavio. And your goddaughter even more so."

The banker carefully folded his handkerchief. He seemed to ponder Gavira's words. "Macarena," he said, nodding slowly, as if the name summed it all up. And Gavira nodded too.

Octavio Machuca had been a friend of the dukes of El Nuevo Extremo for forty years. The Cartujano Bank had put up money for several disastrous business ventures on which Rafael Guardiola y Fernández-Garvey, duke consort and Macarena's late father, had squandered the remains of the family fortune. When the duke died – of a heart attack in the middle of a Gypsy party, in his underwear at four in the morning – it became apparent that the family was ruined. Machuca paid off the creditors himself and raised funds by selling the properties that hadn't been sequestrated; he invested the proceeds in his bank at the highest rate of interest. In this way he was able to retain the family home, the Casa del Postigo, for the widow and daughter, and provide an annual income that enabled the duchess, Cruz Bruner, to live out her years in dignity if not in luxury. In Seville, everyone who was anyone knew one another, and many claimed that this alleged annual income didn't exist and that it was Octavio Machuca who provided the money directly from his own pocket. It was also rumoured that in so doing the banker was honouring a relationship that went beyond friendship, begun while the late duke was still alive. With regard to Macarena, people even said that certain goddaughters were regarded with the same affection as if they were daughters. But nobody had any proof or dared confront the old man about it. Canovas, who dealt with all the banker's paperwork, secrets, and private accounts, was as talkative on that subject (as on so many others) as a plate of tongue stew.

"That bullfighter . . ." said Machuca after a while. "Maestral, isn't that his name?"

Gavira felt a sour taste in his mouth. He threw away his cigarette and took a long drink of his beer. But it didn't make things any better. He put his glass back down on the table and stared at a drop that had fallen on his trousers. A very sonorous and typically Spanish blasphemy hung temptingly on his lips.

The old man went on watching the people as if searching for a familiar face. He had held Macarena Bruner over the font at her baptism, and he had walked her – looking beautiful in white satin – to the altar where Pencho Gavira stood waiting. Rumour had it in Seville that the marriage was the old banker's doing, as it guaranteed a financially secure future for his goddaughter in return for the social recognition of his protégé. At the time Gavira was an ambitious young lawyer at the bank rising meteorically through the ranks.

"Something ought to be done about it," added Machuca thoughtfully.

Despite his humiliation Gavira burst out laughing. "You surely don't expect me to go and shoot the bullfighter."

"Of course not." The banker half-turned, an over-curious look in his cunning eyes. "Would you be capable of shooting your wife's lover?"

"She's my ex-wife, Don Octavio."

"Yes. That's what she says."

Gavira rubbed at the little beer stain and adjusted the crease in his trousers. Of course he'd be capable of it, and they both knew it. But he wasn't going to.

"It wouldn't change anything," he said.

It was true. Before the bullfighter there had been a banker from a rival firm, and before him a well-known winemaker from Jerez. Gavira would need a lot of bullets if he was going to shoot her lovers, and Seville wasn't Palermo. Anyway, he himself had recently found solace in the arms of a Sevillian model whose speciality was fine lingerie. Old Machuca slowly nodded twice – there were better methods.

"I know a couple of branch managers." Gavira smiled, calm and dangerous. "And you know a few bullfighting promoters . . . That young man, Maestral, might have a hard time of it next season."

The chairman of the Cartujano Bank screwed up his eyes. "A shame," he said. "He's not a bad bullfighter."

"He's pretty," said Gavira bitterly. "He can always turn to soap operas."

He glanced over at the newspapers, and the black cloud that had been lurking in the background again darkened his morning. Curro Maestral wasn't the problem. There was something more important than the blurry photo of him and Macarena, taken in poor light with a telephoto lens, on the cover of *Q&S*. What was at stake was not Gavira's honour as a husband but his very survival at the Cartujano and his succeeding Machuca as chairman of the board. He had almost clinched the deal involving Our Lady of the Tears. There was only one problem. A document dating back to 1687 set out a series of conditions that, if not met, would cause the land ceded to the church to be returned to the Bruner family. But a law passed in the nineteenth century, when the confiscation of ecclesiastical property was ordered by a government minister, Mendizabal, made ownership of the land revert, in the event of its secularisation, to the municipality of Seville. It was a matter of some legal complexity, and if the duchess and her daughter decided to resort to the law, things would grind to a halt for some time. But the deal was in its final stages; there was too much money invested and too many measures taken. Failure would mean that Octavio Machuca would undermine his successor's authority before the board of directors – where Gavira had enemies – just when the young vice-chairman of the Cartujano was about to seize absolute power. His head would be on the block. But as *Q&S*, half of Andalusia, and all of Seville knew, Pencho Gavira's head wasn't something Macarena Bruner had much time for lately.

Quart came out of the Doña Maria Hotel, but instead of walking the thirty metres or so to the archbishop's palace, he wandered over to the Plaza Virgen de los Reyes and looked around. He was standing at the crossroads of three religions: the old Jewish quarter behind him, the white walls of the convent of La Encarnación on one side, the archbishop's palace on the other, and at the far end, adjoining the wall of the old Arab mosque, the minaret that had become a bell-tower for the Catholic cathedral, La Giralda. There were horse-drawn carriages, postcard vendors, begging Gypsy women carrying babies, and tourists looking up in awe as they queued to get in to see the tower. A young girl with an American accent left her group to ask Quart for directions to some place close to the square; an excuse to get a closer look at him. Quart gave a brief, polite answer to get rid of her. The girl went back to her friends and they glanced at him, giggling and whispering. He heard the words "He's gorgeous". It would have amused Monsignor Spada. Quart smiled at the thought of the director of the IEA and the advice he'd given him on the Spanish Steps during their last conversation in Rome. Then, still smiling, he looked up at La Giralda, at the weather vane that gave the tower its name. Spain, the south, the ancient culture of Mediterranean Europe, could be sensed only in places such as that. In Seville different histories were superimposed and interdependent. A rosary stringing together time, blood, and prayers in different languages, beneath a blue sky and wise sun that levelled everything over the centuries. Stone survivors that could still be heard. You just had to forget for a moment the camcorders, postcards, coaches full of tourists and cheeky young girls, and put your ear to the stones and listen.

He still had half an hour before his appointment at the archbishop's palace, so he walked up the Calle Mateos Gago and had a coffee in the Bar La Giralda. He felt like sitting at the bar and enjoying the black-and-white tiled floor, the prints of old Seville and the coloured tiles on the walls. From his pocket he took the *Eulogy of the Templar Militia*, by Bernard de Clairvaux, and read a few pages at random. It was an extremely old octavo edition which he read every day between matins, lauds, vespers and compline; a routine he followed rigorously, with a strictness that had more to do with pride than piety. Often, during the many hours spent in hotels, cafés, and airports, in between appointments or work trips, the medieval sermon that for two hundred years had served as spiritual guide for the soldier-monks fighting in the Holy Land helped him bear the loneliness his work entailed. Sometimes he let himself be carried away by the mood that reading it induced, imagining himself as the last survivor from the defeat at Hattin, the Tower of Acre, the dungeons of Chinon, or the fires of Paris: a weary, solitary Knight Templar whose brothers in arms had all died.

He read a few lines (although he could have recited them from memory): "They are tonsured, covered with dust, black from the sun that scorches them and the chain mail that protects them . . ." He looked out at the bright street, the people walking beneath the orange trees. A slim young woman, probably foreign, stopped a moment to check her reflection in the half-open café window. She looked beautiful as she raised her bare arms gracefully to tie back her hair. Suddenly her eyes met Quart's through the window. For an instant she held his gaze, surprised and curious, before becoming self-conscious. Just then a young man with a camera round his neck and a map in his hand came up and drew her away, slipping an arm round her waist.

It wasn't exactly envy, or sadness. There was no word to define the desolate feeling familiar to any cleric who beholds the closeness of couples: men and women lawfully playing out the ancient ritual of intimacy, with gestures such as stroking a neck down to the shoulders, a hand following the gentle curve of a hip, a woman placing her fingers over a man's mouth. For Quart, who would have had no difficulty in becoming intimate with many of the beautiful women who crossed his path, the certainty of his self-discipline was even stronger and more painful. He was like an amputee who still feels tingling or discomfort in a limb that is no longer there.

He looked at his watch, put his book away, and stood up. On his way out he almost bumped into a very fat man dressed in white. The man apologised politely, removing his panama hat, and then watched Quart as he went out into the square. When Quart reached the brick-red baroque building behind a row of orange trees, a caretaker stepped forward to check his identification, but immediately let him through when he saw the dog collar. Quart passed under the main balcony bearing the coat of arms of the archbishops of Seville carved in stone, supported by two double columns, and he entered the courtyard in the shadow of La Giralda. He mounted the magnificent staircase beneath Juan de Espinal's vault with cherubs looking down at the pedestrians with a bored air, killing time in their centuries-old immobility. Upstairs were corridors of offices, busy priests coming and going with the self-assurance of those who know the terrain. They almost all wore suits with round collars, shirt fronts and black or grey shirts, and some wore ties or polo shirts under their jackets. They looked like civil servants rather than priests. Quart didn't see a single cassock.

Monsignor Corvo's new secretary came to meet him. He was a soft little cleric, bald, very clean-looking and with a gentle manner, in a grey suit and dog collar. He had replaced Father Urbizu, killed by the chunk of cornice from Our Lady of the Tears falling on his head. Without saying a word the secretary led Quart through a reception room. The ceiling was divided into sixty coffers containing biblical scenes and symbols intended to inspire virtue in the Sevillian prelates as they governed the diocese. The room also contained some twenty frescoes and canvases, among them four by Zurbarán, one Murillo and one Mattia Preti depicting St. John the Baptist with his throat slit. As Quart walked along beside the secretary, he wondered why there was always a head on a tray in archbishops' and cardinals' anterooms. This thought was still in his mind when he saw Don Priamo Ferro. The priest of Our Lady of the Tears was standing at one end of the room, stubborn and dark in his old cassock. He was talking to a very young, fair-haired priest with glasses. Quart recognised the young priest as the builder outside the church who had stared at him when he met Father Ferro and Gris Marsala. The two priests stopped talking and looked at him, Father Ferro expressionless, the young man sullen, defiant. Quart nodded briefly at them, but neither responded. They had obviously been waiting some time and had not been offered a chair.

His Grace Don Aquilino Corvo, archbishop of Seville, liked to adopt a pose rather like the *Gentleman with his Hand on his Chest* that hangs in the Prado. Against his dark suit he would rest his white hand bearing the emblem of his rank: a ring with a large yellow stone. Thinning hair, a long angular face, and the gold cross on his chest all reminded one of the painting, an impression the archbishop was happy to go along with. Aquilino Corvo was a pedigree prelate, the result of a careful process of ecclesiastical selection. Skilful, manipulative, accustomed to sailing on stormy seas, he had not been appointed archbishop by chance. He enjoyed considerable support within the nunciature of Madrid, had the backing of Opus Dei, and had excellent relations with both the government and the opposition in the Junta de Andalucia. None of this prevented him from engaging in marginal, even personal activities. He was, for instance, a bullfighting aficionado and always had a front-row seat when Curro Maestral or Espartaco were appearing. He was also a supporter of both local football clubs, Betis and Sevilla, out of pastoral neutrality as well as prudence, his eleventh commandment being "Don't put all your eggs in one basket". Last but not least, he detested Lorenzo Quart.

As Quart had expected after his reception from the secretary, the first part of the meeting was cold but polite. Quart handed over his credentials – a letter from the cardinal secretary of state and another from Monsignor Spada. He gave the archbishop some general information on his mission, facts with which the archbishop was already well acquainted. The archbishop offered him his unconditional support and asked to be kept informed of his progress. Quart knew that in fact the archbishop would do everything possible to sabotage his mission. Corvo, under no illusion that Quart would tell him anything, would have exchanged a year in purgatory for a front-row seat if the special envoy from Rome slipped on a banana skin. But they were professionals and knew the rules, at least as far as appearances went. They eyed each other across the desk like fencers waiting to strike.

The shadow of their last meeting in that office hung over them. It was a couple of years ago, His Grace had just been appointed archbishop. Quart had handed him a thick report listing the lapses in security during the Holy Father's visit to Seville during the previous ecclesiastical year. A married priest, suspended *a divinis*, had tried to stab the Pontiff while ostensibly handing him a memorandum on celibacy. An explosive device was found in the convent where His Holiness was staying, in a basket of clean clothes delicately embroidered for the occasion by the nuns. And thanks to continuous leaks to the press from the archbishop's palace, the schedule and itinerary for the Pope's visit was entered with horrifying precision in the diaries of all the Islamic terrorists in the Mediterranean. It was the IEA, and specifically Quart, who stepped in quickly, changing all His Grace's original security arrangements, as the Curia scolded the archbishop. In despair, the nuncio mentioned the matter to His Holiness, in terms that nearly cost Monsignor Corvo his recently awarded rank and in addition almost gave him an apoplectic fit. Once he'd got over this setback, the archbishop proved to be an excellent prelate. But in a most unpriestly way he allowed this early crisis, the humiliation, and the part Quart had played in it to gnaw away at him and disturb his equanimity. That very morning he confided the loss of equanimity to his long-suffering confessor, an elderly cleric at the cathedral who heard him on the first Friday of every month.

"That church is under sentence," the archbishop told Quart. His voice, clear and priestly, was made for giving sermons. "It's only a matter of time."

He spoke with all the authority of his ecclesiastical rank, possibly overemphasising it in Quart's presence. Although he might not be important in Rome, a prelate in his own see was not to be trifled with. Corvo was aware of this, and he liked to stress the fact of his considerable local power and independence. He would boast that all he knew of Rome was the Pontifical Yearbook, and that he never touched the Vatican's telephone directory.

"Our Lady of the Tears," the archbishop went on, "is in ruins. In order to obtain an official declaration to that effect we have had to overcome a series of administrative and technical difficulties . . . It would seem that the administrative ones are about to be resolved, because the Heritage Department, for lack of funds, has given up its effort to preserve the building, and the mayor's office is about to approve the decision. But the file hasn't yet been closed because of the accident that cost the municipal architect his life. A case of bad luck."

Monsignor Corvo paused and contemplated the dozen English pipes lined up in a little wooden stand on his desk. Behind him, through the net curtains, you could just see La Giralda and the flying buttresses of the cathedral. There was a patch of sun on his green leather desk, and the prelate placed his hand there casually. The light made the yellow stone of his ring glint.

Quart smiled slightly. "Your Grace mentioned technical difficulties," he said.

He was sitting on an uncomfortable chair opposite the archbishop's desk, at one end of the room. The walls were lined with the works of the Church fathers and papal encyclicals, all bearing the archbishop's coat of arms on the spine. At the other end of the room there was a prie-dieu beneath an ivory crucifix. There were also a low table, a small sofa and two armchairs where the archbishop gave a somewhat warmer reception to people he held in high esteem. The special envoy of the IEA was obviously not one of them.

"The secularisation of the building, which is required prior to demolition, has become rather complicated." The archbishop's mistrust of Quart was apparent. He chose his words with utmost care, weighing the implications of each one. "An ancient privilege dating from 1687, granted that same year with papal approval by one of my illustrious predecessors in this see, states categorically that the church is to preserve its privilege as long as a Mass is said there every Thursday for the soul of its benefactor, Gaspar Bruner de Lebrija."

"Why Thursday?"

"It was the day he died. The Bruner family was powerful, so I imagine that Don Gaspar must have had my predecessor by the throat."

"And Father Ferro, I assume, celebrates Mass every Thursday . . ."

"He says Mass every day of the week," said the archbishop. "At eight in the morning, except on Sundays and public holidays, when he holds two Masses."

"But surely Your Grace has the authority to make him stop," said Quart innocently.

The archbishop glared at him. His hand twitched impatiently, destroying the effect of the light on his ring. "Don't make me laugh," he said, not sounding the least inclined to laugh. "You know this isn't a question of authority. How can an archbishop forbid a priest to celebrate Mass? It's a question of discipline. Father Ferro is elderly and, especially in certain aspects of his ministry, ultra-conservative, and he has very strong opinions. One of them is that he doesn't give a damn how many times I issue him a pastoral letter or call him to order."

"Has Your Grace considered suspending him?"

"Have I considered, have I considered . . ." Corvo gave Quart a look of irritation. "It's not that simple. I've asked Rome to suspend Father Ferro *ab officio*, but these things take time. And I fear that since that unfortunate break-in to the Vatican computer system, they're waiting for you to return with your scalp hunter's report."

Quart ignored the sarcasm. You don't want to get involved, he thought. This is a hot potato, and you're throwing it to us. You want someone else to play executioner so you don't get your hands dirty.

"And until then?"

"Everything's up in the air. The Cartujano Bank is about to clinch a deal involving the plot of land that would greatly benefit my diocese." Corvo seemed to reconsider his choice of possessive pronoun and then corrected himself softly. "This diocese. Although we may only have a moral right to the land, after three centuries of worship there, the Cartujano is going to pay us a generous sum in compensation. Which is good, because nowadays the collection boxes in most parish churches aren't exactly overflowing." The archbishop allowed himself a smile, to which Quart made sure he didn't respond. "In addition, the bank will pay for a church to be built in one of the poorest districts of Seville, and set up a foundation to support our charitable work in the Gypsy community. What do you think?"

"Very convincing," said Quart calmly.

"So there you are. All brought to a halt by the obstinacy of a priest on the verge of retirement."

"I've heard he's well liked by his parishioners."

Monsignor Corvo raised the hand wearing the ring and placed it on his chest again next to his gold cross. "I wouldn't say that. The local people know him by sight to say hello to and maybe a couple of dozen pious old women hear him celebrate Mass. But it doesn't mean anything. People cry, 'Blessed is he who comes in the name of the Lord,' but then they get bored and crucify you." The archbishop peered indecisively at the row of pipes on his desk. At last he chose a curved one with a silver ring. "I have tried to find something dissuasive. I even considered rebuking him in the presence of his parishioners, but changed my mind after giving thought to the consequences. I'm afraid of going too far, and that the cure would be worse than the disease. We too have a duty to these people. Father Ferro is obstinate but sincere." He tapped the bowl of the pipe lightly against the palm of his hand. "Maybe, as you have more practice in delivering people from Caiaphas to Pontius Pilate . . ."

The words were insulting, but the tone was polite, so Quart could not object. His Grace opened a drawer, took out a tin of English tobacco, and began filling his pipe, leaving it to Quart to keep up the conversation. Quart bowed his head slightly, and only from his eyes was it possible to see that he was smiling. But the archbishop wasn't looking.

"Of course, Monsignor. The Institute for External Affairs will do everything possible to sort out this mess." He noted with satisfaction that His Grace tensed. "Maybe 'mess' is not the right word . . ."

Monsignor Corvo almost lost his composure, but he recovered himself admirably. He said nothing for several seconds while he filled his pipe. When at last he spoke, his tone was sharp: "You're too big for your boots, aren't you? You and your mafiosi in Rome. Playing God's police."

Quart held the archbishop's gaze calmly. "Your Grace's words are harsh."

"Don't give me that 'Your Grace' business. I know why you're here in Seville, and I know what your boss, Archbishop Spada, has to lose over this."

"We all have a lot to lose in this matter, Monsignor."

This was true, and the archbishop knew it. Cardinal Iwaszkiewicz was dangerous, but so were Paolo Spada and even Quart himself. As for Father Ferro, he was a walking time bomb that had to be deactivated. In the Church, harmony was often a question of keeping up appearances, but in the case of Our Lady of the Tears, appearances were being seriously threatened.

"Listen, Quart," said Corvo, trying to sound conciliatory. "I don't want to make my life complicated, and this business is getting out of hand. I admit that the thought of a scandal fills me with terror. I don't want to be seen by the public as a prelate blackmailing a poor parish priest to make a profit from selling the land. Do you understand?"

Quart nodded, accepting the olive branch.

"Anyway," the archbishop went on, "the whole thing might backfire on the Cartujano, because of the wife or ex-wife, I'm not sure which, of the man managing the operation, Pencho Gavira. He has a lot of influence and he's on the up. But he and Macarena have serious personal problems. And she's come out openly on Father Ferro's side."

"Is she devout?"

The archbishop laughed dryly. That wasn't exactly the word, he said. She'd recently been scandalising high society in Seville, which wasn't easy to shock. "Maybe it would be useful for you to talk to her," he said to Quart. "And to her mother, the old duchess. If they withdraw their support, we might be able to put Father Ferro in his place while we're waiting for his suspension and the demolition notice."

Quart had taken some cards from his pocket to make notes; he always used the back of visiting cards, either other people's or his own. The archbishop stared disapprovingly at Quart's Mont Blanc fountain pen. Maybe he felt it was unsuitable for a clergyman.

"How long has the process for issuing the demolition notice been stopped?" asked Quart.

Corvo now looked anxious. "Since the deaths," he said cautiously.

"In rather mysterious circumstances, from what I've heard."

About to light his pipe, the archbishop frowned. There was nothing mysterious about them, he told Quart. Just two cases of bad luck. The municipal architect, a certain Mr Peñuelas, was commissioned by the city council to draw up the demolition notice. An unpleasant man, he had a couple of notable run-ins with Father Ferro, who wasn't exactly an example of pleasantness himself. During the course of Peñuelas's inspection, a wooden handrail on the scaffolding gave way, and he fell from the roof, impaling himself on a metal pole protruding from some half-assembled structure below.

"Was anybody with him?" asked Quart.

Corvo shook his head. He understood Quart's implication. "No, nothing suspicious in that sense. Another council employee was there at the time. Father Oscar, the assistant priest, was also present. It was he who pronounced the last rites."

"And Your Grace's secretary?"

The archbishop, eyes half-closed, blew out a puff of smoke. The aroma of the English tobacco reached Quart. "That was more painful. Father Urbizu had worked with me for years." He paused, as if he felt he ought to add something in memory of the deceased. "An excellent man."

Quart nodded sympathetically. "An excellent man," he repeated thoughtfully. "They say he was putting pressure on Father Ferro on Your Grace's behalf."

Monsignor Corvo didn't like that at all. He took the pipe out of his mouth and scowled at Quart. "That's a nasty way of putting it. And an exaggeration." Quart noticed that the archbishop was tapping impatiently on the table. "I can't go round churches arguing with the priests. So Urbizu had meetings in my name with Father Ferro. But Father Ferro refused to budge, and some of their discussions became rather heated. Father Oscar even threatened my secretary."

"Father Oscar again?"

"Yes. Oscar Lobato. He had an impressive CV, and I assigned him to Our Lady of the Tears so that he would eventually replace the old priest. As in that Bing Crosby film . . ."

"*Going My Way*," prompted Quart.

"Well, he certainly did that. Within a week, my Trojan horse had gone over to the enemy. I've taken steps, of course." The archbishop made a gesture as if to sweep Father Lobato out of the way. "My secretary continued to pay visits to the church and the two priests. I even decided to remove the image of Our Lady of the Tears. It's an ancient carving and very valuable. But on the very day poor Urbizu was going to tell them, a chunk of cornice fell from the ceiling and smashed his skull."

"Was there an investigation?"

The archbishop blinked at Quart in silence, his pipe in his mouth, as if he hadn't heard the question. "Yes," he said at last. "Because this time there were no witnesses, and I took it . . . Well . . . personally." He laid his hand on his chest. Quart thought of Spada's words: He's sworn not to leave a single stone standing. "But the investigation concluded that there was no evidence of murder."

"Did the report rule out the possibility of foul play?"

"No, but technically that would have been almost impossible. The stone fell from the ceiling. Nobody could have thrown it from there."

"Except Providence."

"Don't play the fool, Quart."

"That wasn't my intention, Monsignor. I'm only trying to test the truth of Vespers' claim that the church itself killed Father Urbizu. And the other man."

"That's outrageous and absurd. And exactly what I'm afraid of: that people will start muttering about the supernatural, with us involved, as if this were a Stephen King novel. We've already got a journalist hanging about. An unpleasant character who's been digging into the story. He works for a gossip magazine called *Q&S*. They've just published photos of Macarena Bruner in a compromising situation with a bullfighter. Be careful if you come across the journalist. His name is Honorato Bonafé."

Quart shrugged. "Vespers pointed a finger at the church. He said it kills to defend itself."

"Yes. Very dramatic. Now tell me, to defend itself from whom? From us? The bank? The Evil One? I have my own ideas about Vespers."

"Would you care to share them, Monsignor?"

When Aquilino Corvo lowered his guard, his dislike of Quart was clearly visible. It showed in his eyes for a few seconds and was then hidden behind the pipe smoke. "Do your own work," he said. "That's what you're here for."

Quart smiled, polite, disciplined. "Well, would Your Grace care to tell me about Father Ferro, then?"

For the next five minutes, puffing on his pipe and showing little sign of pastoral charity, Corvo told the parish priest's life story. From his twenties to the age of fifty-four, a rough village priest in a remote part of the Alto Aragón, a godforsaken place where all his parishioners gradually died, until he was left without a congregation. Followed by ten years at Our Lady of the Tears. Uncouth, fanatical, uneducated and stubborn as a mule. Without the slightest sense of what was possible, the sort who believed *omnia sunt possibilia credenti*, who couldn't distinguish between their own point of view and the reality surrounding them. Quart ought to go and hear one of his Sunday sermons, the prelate said. Quite a show. Father Ferro dealt in the torments of hell with the ease of a Counter-Reformation preacher; he kept his parishioners on the edge of their seats with the old tale of eternal damnation that nobody dared use any more. A sigh of relief swept through the pews when he finished his sermon.

"And yet, in complete contradiction," said the archbishop, "in other respects his views are highly modern. Inappropriately so, I would say."

"Such as?"

"His stance on contraception, for one thing. He's unashamedly in favour. Or his views on homosexuality, divorce and adultery. A couple of weeks ago he baptised a child whose parents weren't married. A priest from another parish, who had refused to do the baptism, came to demand an explanation. Father Ferro told him that he baptised whomever he wished."

His Grace's pipe had gone out. He struck a match and glanced at Quart over the flame. "To sum up," he said, "Mass at Our Lady of the Tears is like travelling in a time machine that jumps backwards and forwards."

"I can imagine," Quart said, suppressing a smile.

"No. I assure you, you can't. You have to see him in action. He performs part of the Mass in Latin, because he says it inspires more respect." Corvo managed to relight his pipe and sat back in his chair, relaxed. "Father Ferro belongs to an almost extinct species: the old-style country priest without training or vocation, ordained simply to escape a life of poverty, who turned even wilder in a godforsaken rural parish. He also has tremendous pride, which makes him quite intractable . . . In the past we would have excommunicated him immediately, or sent him to America, to see if God the Father could get him to return to the fold thanks to a fever in the Gulf of Darien, and then convert the natives by beating them on the back with a crucifix. But nowadays we have to be very careful. All the journalists and the political manoeuvring complicate things."

"Why hasn't he been suspended *ex informata conscientia*? That would allow Your Grace to exclude him from the ministry for confidential reasons, without publicity."

"He would have to have committed some civil or ecclesiastical offence, which isn't the case. Anyway, that might only strengthen his resolve. I would rather things followed the usual course in the case of *ab officio*."

"In other words, Monsignor, you would prefer it if Rome dealt with this."

"You've said it, not I."

"What about Father Oscar?"

With the pipe still in his mouth the archbishop made a very sour face. I wouldn't like to be in that young priest's shoes, thought Quart.

"Oh, that one's different," said the archbishop. "Good education, seminary in Salamanca. He's thrown a promising future out of the window. Anyway, we *have* taken care of him. He has until the middle of next week to leave the parish. We're transferring him to a rural diocese in Almeria, a kind of desert near the Cabo de Gata, where he can devote himself to prayer and reflect on the dangers of letting oneself get carried away by youthful enthusiasm."

"Could he be Vespers?"

"Yes. He fits the profile, if that's what you mean. But rooting around in dustbins isn't an archbishop's job." Corvo paused deliberately. "I'll leave that to the IEA and to you."

"What are his duties?" asked Quart, ignoring the remark.

"The usual ones for an assistant priest: he assists during services, performs Mass, takes the afternoon rosary. . . . He also does some building work for Sister Marsala in his spare time."

Quart stiffened in his chair. "Forgive me, Your Grace, did you say *Sister* Marsala?"

"Yes. Gris Marsala. She's a nun. American, been in Seville for years. An expert – so they say – in restoring religious buildings. Haven't you met her yet?"

Quart, distracted by the sound of pieces of the puzzle clicking into place, paid little attention to the prelate's words. So that was it, he thought. The jarring note. "I met her yesterday. I didn't realise she was a nun."

"Well, she is." Corvo's tone was grim. "She, Father Oscar and Macarena Bruner are Father Ferro's allies. She's here in Seville in a private capacity. She has a dispensation from her order, so she's not under my jurisdiction. I don't have the authority to order her to leave Our Lady of the Tears. Anyway, I can't go persecuting priests and nuns."

He exhaled smoke like a squid hiding behind a cloud of ink. He looked again at Quart's Mont Blanc. "Let me summon the parish priest now," he said. "I called him here for a meeting this morning, but I wanted to talk to you privately first. I think it's time to see what's what, don't you? Let the opposing sides confront each other."

The archbishop glanced at the bell on his desk, next to a well-thumbed copy of *The Imitation of Christ* by Thomas à Kempis.

"One last point, Quart. I don't like you, but you're a career priest, and you know as well as I that even in this profession there are plenty of mediocrities. Father Ferro is one of them." He took his pipe out of his mouth and gestured at the bound volumes lining his study walls. "All the thinking of the Church – from Saint Augustine to Saint Thomas, and the encyclicals of all the pontiffs – is here within these four walls, and I'm its temporal administrator. I have to deal with stocks and shares while maintaining a vow of poverty, make pacts with enemies and sometimes condemn friends . . . Every morning I sit at this desk and, with God's help, I manage priests of all kinds: intelligent, stupid, fanatical, honest, wicked; political priests, priests opposed to celibacy, saints and sinners. Given time, we would have sorted out this problem with Father Ferro. But now you and Rome have stepped in, so it's up to you. *Roma locuta, causa finita*. From now on I'm just an observer. May the Almighty forgive me, but I'm washing my hands of the whole business and leaving the field for the executioners." He rang the bell and motioned towards the door. "Let's not keep Father Ferro waiting any longer."

Quart slowly screwed the cap back on his pen and put it in his pocket, together with the cards covered with his cramped, meticulous handwriting. He sat well forward in his chair, rigid, at attention.

"I have my orders, Monsignor," he said. "And I follow them to the letter."

His Grace grimaced. "I wouldn't want your job, Quart," he said at last. "I assure you, by my soul's salvation, I wouldn't want it one little bit."

IV
Seville Oranges and Blossom

"Now you've seen a hero," he said. "And that's worth something."
Eckermann, *Conversations with Goethe*

"I believe you've met," said His Grace.

He sat in his armchair like a boxing referee who keeps well back so as not to get his shoes spattered with blood. Quart and Father Ferro looked at each other in silence. The parish priest of Our Lady of the Tears refused to sit when Corvo offered him a chair. Small and obstinate, he stood in the middle of the study, with his face that looked as if it had been hewn with a chisel, and his untidy white hair. As usual, he wore an old, threadbare cassock and a huge pair of scuffed shoes.

"Father Quart would like to ask you some questions," added the archbishop.

The priest's face, covered with wrinkles and scars, remained impassive. He stared blankly out of the window, where the blurred ochre outline of La Giralda was visible through the net curtains.

"I have nothing to say to Father Quart."

Corvo nodded slowly, as if he'd expected such an answer. "Very well," he said. "But I am your bishop, Don Priamo. And you owe *me* a vow of obedience." He took his pipe from his mouth and gestured with it to the two priests, one after the other. "So, if you prefer, you may give me your answers to Father Quart's questions."

For a moment there was uncertainty in Father Ferro's dark, dull eyes. "That's ridiculous," he said abruptly, half-turning to Quart, whom he held responsible.

The archbishop smiled disagreeably.

"I know it is," he said. "But this jesuitical device will keep us all happy. Father Quart can do his job, I'll be glad to witness your conversation, and you will ensure that your incredible pride isn't compromised." He blew out a puff of smoke menacingly and leaned to one side. His eyes shone in anticipated amusement. "You may now begin, Father Quart. He's all yours."

So Quart began. He was harsh, brutal at times, getting back at Father Ferro for the cold reception he had been given at the church the previous day, and for Father Ferro's open animosity now towards Quart in His Grace's office. Quart no longer concealed the disdain he felt for Father Ferro the poor, stubborn country priest. The feeling was more complex, more profound than mere personal dislike, or than what was dictated by his mission here in Seville. To Corvo's surprise, and ultimately to Quart's own, Quart conducted himself like a public prosecutor entirely devoid of pity. Only he knew the source of the stinging cruelty with which he harried the old man. And when at last he stopped to catch his breath, aware of how unjust it all was, he was disturbed by the sudden thought that His Eminence the Inquisitor Jerzy Iwaszkiewicz would have given the entire performance his unqualified approval.

The two men stared at him; the archbishop frowning uneasily, his pipe in his mouth; Father Ferro motionless, his eyes, red and watery after an interrogation more appropriate to a criminal than to a sixty-four-year-old priest, fixed on Quart. Quart shifted in his chair and, to hide his embarrassment, made some notes. He'd been kicking the man when he was down.

"To sum up," he said, trying to sound slightly less harsh and looking down at his notes to avoid the priest's eyes, "you deny that you wrote the message that was sent to the Holy See. You also deny that you have any idea who sent it or any clues as to the author or his intentions."

"Yes," said Father Ferro.

"Before God?" asked Quart, feeling ashamed of himself – this was going too far.

The old priest turned to Corvo, in an appeal for help that the archbishop could not ignore. Corvo cleared his throat and raised his hand bearing the ring.

"Let's leave the Almighty out of this, shall we?" the prelate said through the smoke from his pipe. "I don't think we need put anyone on oath in this conversation."

Quart accepted this in silence and turned once more to Father Ferro. "What can you tell me about Oscar Lobato?" he asked.

The old priest shrugged. "Nothing. Just that he's a fine young man and an honourable priest." His unshaven chin trembled slightly. "I'll be sorry to see him go."

"Does your assistant know computers?"

Father Ferro narrowed his eyes. His expression was wary now, like that of a peasant watching storm clouds approach.

"You should ask him." He jerked his chin at the door. "He's out there, waiting for me."

Quart smiled almost imperceptibly. He appeared confident, but there was something about all this that made him feel he was crossing a void. Something out of place, a wrong note. *Nearly* all that Father Ferro said was true, but there was a lie in it somewhere. Maybe only one, and maybe not a serious one, but a lie.

"What can you tell me about Gris Marsala?"

The old priest's lips tensed. "Sister Marsala has a dispensation from her order." He glanced at the archbishop as if for corroboration. "She's free to come and go as she pleases. Her work is entirely voluntary. Without her, the building would have fallen down by now."

"A piece of it did fall down," said Corvo, unable to stop himself. He was obviously thinking of his secretary's death.

Quart went on questioning Father Ferro. "What kind of relationship does she have with you and your assistant?"

"Normal."

"I don't know what you consider normal." Quart's contempt was calculated to the millimetre. "You old village priests have always had a questionable notion of normality regarding your housekeepers and nieces . . ."

Out of the corner of his eye Quart saw Corvo nearly jump in his chair. Quart had been provocative but with a purpose.

Father Ferro's knuckles were white. "I hope you're not implying . . ." He broke off and glared at Quart. "Someone might kill you for that."

The threat did not seem incongruous, given Father Ferro's style of preaching, rough exterior and hard, dry body now shaking with fury. He seemed capable of violence himself, but his exact meaning was open to interpretation.

Quart looked back at him calmly. "Your church, for instance?" he asked.

"For the love of God!" the archbishop interrupted. "Have you both lost your minds?"

There was a long silence. The patch of sunlight on Monsignor Corvo's desk had shifted to the left, away from his hand. The copy of *The Imitation of Christ* now fell exactly within it and Father Ferro stared at the book. Quart observed the old man intently. He was reminded of that other priest he'd wanted never to resemble; the man he had almost managed to forget. Since Quart left the seminary, a letter or a postcard had come occasionally; but then, silence. And Quart remembered him only when the wind from the south revived smells and sounds buried in his memory. The sea pounding against the rocks and the humid, salty air, and the rain. The smell of the brazier and the *mesa camilla* in winter, *Rosa Rosae, Quoúsque tandem abutere Catilina, Nox atra cava circumvolat umbra*. Water dripping on the misted window, bells at dawn, an unshaven, greasy face leaning over the altar and muttering prayers to a deaf God. Man and boy, officiant and server, turned towards a barren land edged by a cruel sea. And thus it was, after the Last Supper. For this is my blood. May you go in peace. And the muffled breathing, like a tired animal's, later in the damp vestry as the young Lorenzo helped him remove his vestments. The seminary, Lorenzo. You will go to a seminary. One day you'll be a priest, like me. You'll have a future, like me. With all his might and memory Quart hated the roughness, the poverty of spirit, the limited existence – Mass at dawn, naps in his smelly rocking chair, rosary at seven, hot chocolate with the pious old women, a cat in the doorway, a housekeeper or niece who one way or another eased the solitude and the passing years. And then the finale: senile dementia, a sordid, barren life ending in a nursing home, soup dribbling down his chin. For the greater glory of God.

"A church that kills to defend itself . . ." Quart made an effort to return to the present, to Seville; to what was rather than what might have been. "I want to know what Father Ferro thinks this means."

"I don't know what you're talking about."

"It was a sentence from the message somebody slipped into the Holy See. It refers to your church . . . Do you think there could be an element of Providence in all this?"

"I don't have to answer that."

Quart turned to Corvo, but the archbishop refused to get involved.

"It's true," he said with a dipomatic smile, delighted by Quart's difficulties. "He wouldn't answer me either."

It was a waste of time. The IEA agent realised that he wasn't getting anywhere, but he had to follow the form. So, portentously, he asked Father Ferro if he was aware of what was at stake. The old man answered sarcastically. Impassive, Quart continued to work his way through the questionnaire: the necessity for a report, possible cause for serious disciplinary measures, etc. That Father Ferro was one year away from retirement was no guarantee that his superiors would be lenient. At the Holy See . . .

"I don't know anything about those deaths," the old priest interrupted. He obviously couldn't care less about the Holy See. "They were accidents."

Quart leaped in. "Convenient accidents, from your point of view?"

There was a slight tone of camaraderie, a hint of "Come on, man, open up, and let's sort this out". But the old priest didn't drop his guard. "You mentioned Providence earlier," he said. "Well, why don't you ask God the question and I'll pray that you receive an answer."

Quart took a couple of slow, deep breaths before trying again. What annoyed him most was the thought that His Grace must be enjoying this, wreathed in pipe smoke in his front-row seat.

"Can you state categorically, as a priest, that there was no human intervention in the two deaths at your church?"

"Go to hell."

"I beg your pardon?"

Corvo had again jumped in his chair. Father Ferro looked at him and said, "With all due respect to Your Grace, I refuse to answer any more questions."

Quart wondered if he was joking. In their twenty-minute meeting, Father Ferro had not answered a single question. Corvo just frowned and blew out more smoke; he was only the server here. Quart stood up, and the top of Father Ferro's head reached his chest. The wiry grey hair reminded Quart of another priest. Quart had been back once only since his ordination: a brief visit to his widowed mother, another to the dark shape crouching in the church like a mollusc in its shell. Quart performed Mass there, in the church where he'd been an altar boy for so long. And in the cold, damp nave, haunted by the ghost of the lonely little boy looking out to sea in the rain, he had felt like a stranger. He'd left and never returned, and the church, and the old priest, and the little white village, and the cruel sea had gradually faded from memory; a bad dream from which he'd managed to awaken.

The embodiment of everything he hated now stood before him. He could see it in the dull, stubborn eyes boring into him. "I have one more question. Only one," he said, putting away his cards and fountain pen. "Why do you refuse to leave Our Lady of the Tears?"

Father Ferro looked him up and down. Tough as old leather. That was the best description, though Quart could think of a couple more.

"It's none of your business," the priest said. "It concerns me and my bishop."

Quart expected the answer. He gestured to indicate that the absurd meeting was at an end. To his surprise, Corvo came to his aid.

"Answer Father Quart please, Don Priamo."

"Father Quart would never understand."

"I'm sure he'll do his best. Please try."

The old priest shook his head stubbornly, muttering that Quart had never heard the confession of a poor woman on her knees seeking consolation, the cry of a newborn child, the breath of a dying man whose sweating hand he held. So even if Father Ferro talked for hours, nobody would understand a single damned word. And Quart, despite the diplomatic passport in his pocket, the official support of the Curia, the tiara and keys of St. Peter on his papers, realised that he didn't have the slightest authority over the hostile, wretched-looking old man, the exact antithesis of what any churchman would link with the glory of God. With a sudden stab of anxiety he saw the outline of a ghost from the past: Nelson Corona. He remembered the same distancing from officialdom, the same determined expression.

The only difference was that Quart had glimpsed fear as well as determination in the Brazilian's eyes, while Father Ferro's dull gaze was as firm as a rock. Before resuming his obstinate silence, the old priest concluded by saying that his church was a refuge. It sounded quaint, and the Vatican envoy arched an eyebrow derisively. In search of equilibrium, he tried to reawaken his old contempt for the village priest. Once again he was a dignitary confronting an underling, and the ghost of Nelson Corona faded.

"That's an odd way to describe it."

Quart smiled, sure of himself, once more strong, firm and remorseless. Once more he saw only the priest's threadbare, stained cassock and unshaven chin. It was strange how calming contempt was, he thought. Like an aspirin, a drink, or a cigarette. He decided to ask another question.

"A refuge. From what?"

He knew even before he'd finished the sentence that he was going to regret asking. Small and hard, Father Ferro looked up and fixed Quart with a stare.

"From all the bullshit," he said.

Horse-drawn carriages, painted black and yellow, were lined up waiting for customers in the shade of the orange trees. Leaning against the window of a souvenir shop, El Potro del Mantelete watched the entrance to the archbishop's palace. His hands were in the pockets of his tight, checked jacket which he wore over a close-fitting white polo-neck jumper that showed off his hard, lean pectorals. He moved a toothpick rhythmically from one side of his mouth to the other. He narrowed his eyes beneath his scarred eyebrows, his gaze fixed on the gap between the twin columns of the baroque portico. Don't let him out of your sight, Don Ibrahim ordered before he went into the shop to browse. They would look too conspicuous if all three of them hung around outside on the pavement. But they'd had to wait a long time – Don Ibrahim and La Niña Puñales had looked through all the post-cards, T-shirts, fans, castanets and plastic models of La Giralda and the Torre del Oro under the suspicious gaze of the shopkeeper. El Potro was trustworthy, so they had decided to repair to the nearest bar, on the corner opposite. La Niña was already on her fifth Manzanilla. El Potro, lacking new orders, wasn't taking his eyes off the entrance. The tall priest had been inside a whole hour, and in all that time El Potro had looked away only twice – when a couple of policemen walked past him on their way up the street and back down again. Both times he stared hard at the tips of his shoes. A certain character had been imparted by four gorings in the bullring, two stints in the Spanish Legion and a brain that ran on fixed rails, stunned by blows and the ringing of bells in round after round. Had Don Ibrahim and La Niña forgotten about him, he would have stood there motionless day and night, come rain or shine, his eyes fixed on the entrance to the archbishop's palace until they came to relieve him or he dropped dead. Twenty years earlier, during an awful quarrel in a third-rate bullring, his manager said something like, "If the bull doesn't kill you, you creep, the crowd'll kill you at the exit," and El Potro, sweat on his face and fear in his eyes, went back out into the ring with his red matador's cape at his waist and stood motionless until the bull, known as Butcher, charged and gave him his fourth and final goring, ending his bullfighting career. Later, during similar episodes in the boxing ring, the Legion and prison, his body and brain acquired more scars. El Potro was an idiot, but he had the makings of a hero.

Suddenly the tall priest emerged from the palace. He paused for a moment at the entrance and looked back, as if someone had called him from inside the building. A young man with fair hair and glasses followed him out, and they stood talking at the door. El Potro glanced at the bar where Don Ibrahim and La Niña were waiting, but they were engrossed in their Manzanillas. So he spat the toothpick from his mouth and went to let them know. He walked round the square past the archbishop's palace, and as he came nearer, he got a better look at the priest. But for the dog collar and crew cut the man could have been a movie star. The young priest was scruffy, pale, and spotty, like a teenager. And he looked more like a priest than the tall one.

"Leave him alone," El Potro heard the fair-haired priest say.

The tall one frowned. "Father Ferro's crazy," he said. "He's living in a fantasy world. If it was you who sent the message, you didn't do him, or his church, any favours."

"I didn't send anything."

"We have to have a talk about that, you and I. A quiet talk."

"I have nothing to tell you," said the fair-haired priest, his voice trembling but defiant.

"People keep saying that." The tall priest smiled unpleasantly. "You're wrong. There's a lot you can tell me. For instance . . ."

The conversation faded out of earshot as El Potro moved past. He quickened his pace and entered the bar. Prawn shells and sawdust littered the floor, and sausages and hams hung over the counter. At the bar Don Ibrahim and La Niña drank in silence. On the radio, Camarón was singing:

Wine kills the pain
and the memories . . .

Don Ibrahim, separated from the bar by his paunch, was smoking a cigar and dropping ash on his white jacket. Beside him, La Niña had progressed from Manzanilla to Machaquito anis. She raised the lipstick-rimmed glass to her lips. She wore silver earrings and a blue dress with white polka dots. Her eyes were heavily made up and a kiss-curl stuck to her withered forehead: a down-at-heel flamenco singer like the pictures on the covers of the old singles that Don Ibrahim hoarded like gold dust in his room at the boarding house. He had records by Nat King Cole, Los Panchos, Beny Moré, Antonio Machín, and an antediluvian Telefunken gramophone. The former bogus lawyer and La Niña turned to look at El Potro, who jerked his head towards the street.

"There," he said.

The three partners went to the door and looked. The tall priest was walking away from the other one, past the mosque.

"Some priest," said La Niña huskily.

"Not bad-looking," admitted Don Ibrahim impartially, inspecting him with narrowed eyes.

The drop of Machaquito made the flamenco singer's eyes shine mischievously. "*Othu.* I wouldn't mind getting the last rites from him."

Don Ibrahim exchanged a grave look with El Potro. When they were on a job, as now, such frivolity was out of place. "What about the old one?" he asked, to concentrate their minds.

"He's still inside," said El Potro.

The former bogus lawyer drew thoughtfully on his cigar. "Let's split up the armed retinue," he said at last. "You, Potro, follow the old priest when he appears. Once he's home, come back here and report to me. La Niña and yours truly will watch the tall priest." He paused and solemnly consulted Don Ernesto Hemingway's watch. "Before taking action, we need information: the mother of victories, and so on. Don't you agree?"

His companions must have, because they nodded. His eyebrows meeting in the middle, El Potro was grave, as if teasing out the meaning of a word pronounced five minutes earlier. With a faraway look, La Niña watched the tall priest walk away. She still held her glass and looked as if she was going to finish off the Machaquito. On the radio, Camarón still sang of wine and longing, and behind the bar the waiter, in white shirt and black tie, clapped quietly in time to the music. Don Ibrahim surveyed his troops and decided to raise morale with a few suitably stirring words. Something about Seville being the greatest place on earth. And this job's in the bag.

"He who dares, wins," he said after a little thought, drawing on his cigar.

"*Othu.*"

La Niña finished her anis. Still frowning, El Potro shook his head and asked, "What does 'retinue' mean?"

Lorenzo Quart's extreme conscientiousness was the source of his composure. So, when he returned to his room, the first thing he did was to open his leather briefcase and take out his laptop. He spent an hour working on his report for Monsignor Spada. As soon as it was finished, he sent it by modem to the director of the IEA. In its eight pages Quart was careful not to draw any conclusions regarding the church, the people involved with it, or the identity of Vespers. He limited himself to a fairly faithful account of his conversations with Monsignor Corvo, Gris Marsala and Priamo Ferro.

Once he'd shut down the computer and gathered up the cables, he relaxed a little. He was in shirtsleeves, collar unbuttoned. He walked round the two canopied beds to the window that looked on to the

Plaza Virgen de los Reyes. It was too early to eat, so he flicked through some guidebooks he'd bought in a small bookshop opposite the town hall. He'd also bought a copy of *Q&S* on the recommendation of Monsignor Corvo. "So you can acquaint yourself with the situation," the prelate had suggested caustically. Quart looked at the cover and then the photographs inside. "A Marriage In Crisis" ran the headline. Alongside the pictures of the woman and her companion, there was one of a very serious, well-dressed man with perfectly parted hair. "Their separation is confirmed. While financier Pencho Gavira consolidates his position as the strong man of Andalusian banking, Macarena Bruner is out and about in Seville until the early hours." Quart tore out the pages and put them in his briefcase. He suddenly noticed that the copy of the Gideon bible was on his bedside table. He didn't remember leaving it there. He thought he'd put it in a drawer with all the other stuff he wanted out of the way: pamphlets, advertisements, notepaper and envelopes. He opened the bible at random and found an old postcard. The caption read: "Church of Our Lady of the Tears. Seville. 1895." A bleached halo surrounded the central image, but the church, although faded, was unmistakable: the portico with its Solomonic columns, the bell-tower and the figure of the Virgin in its niche, head intact. Everything looked in better condition than it did now. In the square in front there was a stall with a man in a wide belt and typical Andalusian hat selling vegetables to two women dressed in black with their backs to the photographer. On the other side, a donkey carrying two barrels of water was walking away down the narrow street that led off the square, the man on its back scarcely more than an outline, a ghost about to disappear from the picture into the surrounding white halo.

Quart turned the card over. There were a few lines written in a gently sloping copperplate hand. The ink had faded to a pale brown making the words barely legible.

I come here to pray for you every day and wait for you to return to the sacred place where you swore your love and gave me such happiness.

I will always love you.

Carlota

* * *

The stamp, showing Alfonso XIII as a child, had no postmark, and there was a stain over the date handwritten at the top. Quart could make out a 9 and maybe a 7 at the end, so it could have been 1897. The address, on the other hand, was perfectly legible: "Captain Manuel Xaloc. On board the ship *Manigua*. Port of Havana. Cuba".

He picked up the telephone and dialled Reception. The receptionist said that his shift had started at eight that morning and no one had been up to Quart's room or asked for him in all that time, but maybe Quart should ask the cleaners. Quart was put through to them, but they weren't much help. They didn't remember having moved the bible, and they couldn't say whether it had been in the drawer or on the bedside table when they cleaned the room. Nobody had been in except them.

He sat by the window and examined the postcard in his hand. A ship docked in the port of Havana in 1897. A captain called Manuel Xaloc and someone called Carlota who had loved him and prayed for him at Our Lady of the Tears. Did the message on the back of the postcard have any special meaning, or was it the picture of the church that was significant? Suddenly he remembered the Gideon bible. Had the postcard been placed inside at random or was it marking a specific page? He cursed himself for not having noticed. He went over to the bedside table and saw that by chance he'd left the book open face down. It was open at pages 168 and 169 – John 2. There was nothing underlined but he quickly found the relevant lines. It was too obvious.

15. And when he had made a scourge of small cords, he drove them all out of the temple, and the sheep, and the oxen; and poured out the changers' money, and overthrew the tables;
16. And said unto them that sold doves, Take these things hence; make not my Father's house an house of merchandise.

Quart glanced from the bible to the postcard. He thought of Monsignor Spada and His Eminence Cardinal Iwaszkiewicz – they wouldn't be very happy about this turn of events. He wasn't that happy about it himself. Somebody was playing disturbing games, breaking into papal computer systems and people's hotel rooms. Quart thought of all the people he had met, and wondered if the

Iglesia de Nuestra Señora de las Lagrimas - Sevilla. 1895

Carta Postal – Carte Postale – Postkarte

Aquí rezo por ti cada día, y espero tu regreso, en el lugar sagrado de tu juramento y mi felicidad.

Te amaré siempre.

Carlota

Capitan don Manuel Xalos

A bordo del buque "Maniguá"

Puerto de la Habana

Cuba

Nº 560

person he was looking for was one of them. Dear God. He could feel his exasperation mounting, and he threw the book and postcard on to the bed. This was all he needed: a ghost playing hide-and-seek.

Quart came out of the lift on the ground floor. He walked past the display case full of fans and along the corridor round the lobby. He looked slightly out of place in his dark suit. The Doña Maria was a four-star hotel, a beautiful building in the Calle Don Remondo, a stone's throw from Santa Cruz. The interior decorator had got slightly carried away with the Andalusian folk motifs, bullfighters and pictures of dancers with mantillas and hair combs. At the door a tired-looking young woman tour guide, holding up a small Dutch flag, herded a brightly dressed group equipped with cameras. As he handed in his key at the reception desk, Quart read her name on the little plastic badge she wore: V. Oudkerk. He smiled sympathetically. The young woman smiled back resignedly and walked off at the head of the group.

"There's a lady waiting for you, Father Quart. She's just arrived."

Quart looked at the receptionist in surprise, then turned round. A woman, tanned, with black hair reaching to below her shoulders, sat on one of the sofas in the lobby. She wore sunglasses, jeans, moccasins, a pale-blue shirt and a brown jacket. She was very beautiful. She stood up as Quart came towards her and he noticed her ivory necklace – pale against her tanned skin – and her gold bracelet and the leather handbag beside her. She held out a slender, elegant and perfectly manicured hand.

"Hello. I'm Macarena Bruner."

He'd recognised her a few seconds before, from the photographs in the magazine. He couldn't help staring at her mouth. It was large and well defined, lips slightly parted with very white teeth showing. Her upper lip was heart-shaped. She wore pale-pink, almost colourless lipstick.

"Well," she said, surprised, keeping her sunglasses on, "you really are very good-looking."

"So are you," answered Quart calmly.

She was only slightly shorter than he, and he was nearly one metre eighty-five. Beneath her jacket he could make out a generous, attractive figure. Uneasy, he looked away and checked his watch. She was staring at him thoughtfully.

"I'd like to talk to you," she said at last.

"Of course. You've done me a favour. I was thinking of coming to see you." Quart looked round. "How did you know where I was staying?"

"My friend Gris Marsala told me."

"I didn't know you were friends."

She smiled and he saw her white teeth again. They echoed the ivory necklace against her caramel skin. She was sure of herself, because of her social standing and because of her beauty. But Quart could tell that she, like Gris Marsala, found his severe black suit and dog collar intimidating. They had that effect on women, whether beautiful or not.

"Could we talk now?"

"Of course."

They sat facing each other, she with legs crossed on the sofa where she'd waited; he in the armchair next to it.

"I know why you're here in Seville."

"I hope you're not expecting me to be surprised," Quart said with a smile, resigned. "My visit seems to be public knowledge."

"Gris said I should come to see you."

He looked at her with renewed interest. He wondered what her eyes were like behind her dark glasses. "That's strange. Your friend wasn't very helpful yesterday."

Macarena Bruner's hair slid over her shoulders, half-covering her face, and she pushed it back. It was very thick and black, Quart noticed. An Andalusian beauty like those painted by Romero de Torres. Or maybe Carmen of the Tobacco Factory, as described by Mérimée. Any man, whether painter, Frenchman or bullfighter, could have lost his head over that woman. A priest could too.

"I hope you didn't get the wrong impression of the church," she said. After a pause she added, "Or of Father Ferro."

To dispel his uneasiness Quart resorted to humour: "Don't tell me you too are a member of Father Ferro's fan club."

His hand was hanging over the arm of the chair, and he knew, despite the dark glasses, that she was looking at it. He moved it discreetly and interlaced its fingers with the fingers of his other hand.

Macarena Bruner said nothing for a few moments. She pushed her hair from her face again. She seemed to be debating how to continue the conversation.

"Look," she said at last, "Gris is my friend. And she thinks your presence here might be useful, even if your view isn't sympathetic."

Quart realised she was being conciliatory. He raised his hand and saw her follow its movement with her eyes. "You know," he said, "there's something about all this that I find somewhat irritating . . . But what should I call you? Señora Bruner?"

"Please, call me Macarena."

She took off her glasses, and Quart was taken aback by the beauty of her large, dark eyes with glints of honey. Praise God, he would have said aloud had he thought that God bothered Himself with that kind of prayer. He forced himself to hold her gaze as if the salvation of his soul depended on it. And maybe it did – if there was a soul, that is, and a God.

"Macarena," he said, leaning forward and resting his elbows on his knees. As he did so, he smelled her perfume: gentle, like jasmine. "There's something irritating about this whole business. Everyone assumes I'm in Seville to give Don Priamo Ferro a hard time. I'm not. I'm here to write a report on the situation. I don't have any preconceptions. But Father Ferro won't co-operate." He sat back. "In fact, nobody will."

Now it was her turn to smile. "It's understandable. Nobody trusts you."

"Why?"

"Because the archbishop has been speaking ill of you. He calls you a scalp hunter."

Quart grimaced. "Yes. We're old acquaintances."

"Father Ferro could be made to see things differently," Macarena said, biting her lower lip. "Maybe I can help."

"It would be better for everyone, especially him. But why would you do this? What would you gain?"

She shook her head as if that was irrelevant, and her hair once more slid over her shoulder. She pushed it back, looking intently at Quart.

"Is it true that the Pope received a message?"

Macarena Bruner was obviously aware of the effect her eyes had on people. Quart swallowed. It was partly her eyes, partly her question.

"That's confidential," he answered, trying to soften his words with a smile. "I can neither confirm nor deny it."

"It's a secret that's being shouted from the rooftops."

"In that case, I don't need to join in."

Her dark eyes shone thoughtfully. She leaned on the arm of the sofa, which made her blouse move suggestively. "My family has the final say regarding Our Lady of the Tears," she explained. "That means my mother and I. If the building is condemned and the archbishop allows it to be demolished, the final decision about the land is left to us."

"Not entirely," said Quart. "According to my information, the council has some say."

"We'd take legal action."

"Technically you're still married. And your husband . . ."

"We've been living apart for six months," she interrupted, shaking her head. "My husband has no right to take any action independently."

"He hasn't tried to change your mind?"

"Yes." Macarena's smile was contemptuous now, distant, almost cruel. "But it makes no difference. The church will outlive all of this."

"Strange choice of words," said Quart, surprised. "You make it sound as if the church is alive."

She was staring at his hands again. "Maybe it is. Lots of things are alive and you wouldn't think it." She was lost in thought for a moment, then suddenly came to. "But what I meant was that the church is needed. Father Ferro is too."

"Why? There are plenty of other priests and churches in Seville."

She burst out laughing. A loud, frank laugh. It was so contagious that Quart almost laughed too. "Don Priamo's special. And so is his church." She was still smiling, her eyes fixed on Quart. "But I can't explain it in words. You have to go and see it."

"I've already been. And your favourite priest kicked me out."

Macarena Bruner burst out laughing again. Quart had never heard a woman laugh in such a forthright, appealing way. He realised he wanted to hear her laugh more. He was astonished at himself. In his well-trained brain, alarm bells were ringing. It was beginning to seem as if he had wandered into the garden that his old mentors at the seminary had warned him to keep a healthy distance from: serpents, forbidden fruit, incarnations of Delilah and the like.

"Yes," she said. "Gris told me. But do try again. Go to Mass and see what goes on there. Maybe you'll understand."

"I will. Do you go to eight o'clock Mass?"

The question was well-meaning but Macarena's expression suddenly became suspicious, serious. "That's none of your business," she said, opening and closing her sunglasses.

Quart raised both hands apologetically, and there was an awkward silence. He looked round for a waiter and asked her if she wanted anything. She shook her head. She seemed more relaxed so he asked her another question. "What do you think about the two deaths?"

Her laugh this time was unpleasant. "The wrath of God," she said.

Quart looked at her seriously. "A strange point of view."

"Why?" She seemed genuinely surprised. "They, or whoever sent them, were asking for it."

"Not a very Christian sentiment."

She picked up her bag impatiently and put it down. She wound and unwound the shoulder strap round her fingers. "You don't understand, Father . . ." She looked at him hesitantly. "What should I call you? Reverend? Father Quart?"

"You can call me Lorenzo. I'm not going to be your confessor."

"Why not? You're a priest."

"A rather unusual one," said Quart. "And I'm not really here in that capacity."

As he spoke, he looked away for a couple of seconds, unable to meet her eyes. When he looked back, she was watching him with interest, almost mischievously.

"It would be fun to say confession to you. Would you like me to?"

Quart took a breath. He frowned, as if considering. The cover of *Q&S* flashed before his eyes. "I'm afraid I wouldn't be an impartial confessor, in your case," he said, "you're too . . ."

"Too what?"

She wasn't playing fair, he thought. She was going too far even for a man with the nerves of Lorenzo Quart. He breathed in and out to calm himself, to keep his composure.

"Attractive," he answered coolly. "I suppose that's the word. But you know more about that than I do."

Macarena Bruner said nothing, weighing his answer. She seemed pleased. "Gris was right," she said finally. "You're not like a priest."

Quart nodded. "I expect Father Ferro and I seem like different species . . ."

"You're right. And he's my confessor."

"A good choice, I'm sure." He paused, then continued, to make his words sound less sarcastic, "He's a very rigorous man."

"You know nothing about him."

"Quite true. And so far I haven't found anyone to enlighten me."

"I will."

"When?"

"I don't know. Tomorrow evening. Join me for dinner at La Albahaca."

"La Albahaca," he repeated.

"Yes. In the Plaza de Santa Cruz. They usually require a tie, but I'm sure they'll make an exception in your case. You dress rather well for a priest."

He didn't answer for a few seconds. Why not? After all, that was what he was in Seville for. And he could drink to the health of Cardinal Iwaszkiewicz.

"I can wear a tie if you like, though I've never had a problem in a restaurant."

Macarena Bruner stood up, and so did Quart. She was staring at his hands again. "It's up to you," she said, smiling as she put her sunglasses back on. "I've never had dinner with a priest before."

Don Ibrahim fanned himself with his hat. He was sitting on a bench in the Plaza Virgen de los Reyes, and the air smelled of Seville oranges and blossom. Beside him, La Niña Puñales was crocheting while they watched the entrance of the Doña Maria Hotel: four chain, miss two, one double and one treble. She moved her lips silently, as if in prayer, repeating the sequence, the ball of yarn in her lap, while the crochet grew and her silver bracelets jangled. She was making yet another bedspread for her trousseau. For almost thirty years now it had lain yellowing between mothballs, in a wardrobe at her apartment in the district of Triana. But she still added to it, as if she held time in her fingers, waiting for the dark man with green eyes to come for her.

A carriage crossed the square, with four English football fans in the back wearing sombreros. Real Betis was playing Manchester United. Don Ibrahim gazed after it and fingered his moustache, sighing. Poor Seville, he murmured, fanning himself more vigorously with his panama. La Niña muttered in agreement without looking up, intent on her crochet: four chain, miss two. Don Ibrahim threw away his cigar butt and watched it smoulder on the ground. He stubbed it out carefully with the tip of his walking stick. He hated those brutal types who ground out cigarettes as if they were murdering them. Thanks to Peregil's advance he'd treated himself to a whole, brand-new box of Montecristo cigars, something he hadn't done since Adam was a lance corporal. Two of the magnificent cigars were peeping out of the breast pocket of his crumpled white linen suit. He patted them tenderly. The sky was blue, the air smelled of orange blossom, and he was in Seville. He had a good little deal going, cigars in his pocket and thirty thousand pesetas in his wallet. All he needed to make his happiness complete were three tickets to the bullfight; three good seats in the shade to see Faraón de Camas, or that promising young bullfighter Curro Maestral. According to El Potro, Maestral's technique wasn't bad but there was no comparison with the late Juan Belmonte, God rest his soul. The same Curro Maestral who was in the papers chasing after bankers' wives.

And, speaking of women, the tall priest had just emerged from the hotel talking to a pretty classy one. Don Ibrahim nudged La Niña, who stopped crocheting. The lady was still young, good-looking, and wore dark glasses and casual but stylish clothes with the relaxed elegance typical of upper-crust Andalusian women. She and the priest shook hands. Don Ibrahim and La Niña exchanged meaningful glances. This introduced all sorts of unexpected possibilities.

"A slight complication, Niña."

"You're right there."

With some difficulty, given his bulk, the former bogus lawyer got to his feet, placed his panama on his head, and grasped Maria Felix's walking stick resolutely. He told La Niña to go on crocheting while not losing sight of the tall priest. He himself set off after the woman with the sunglasses. She headed into Santa Cruz, turning down the Calle Guzmán el Bueno and disappearing into a palace known as the Casa del Postigo. A renowned building in Seville, it had been the residence of the dukes of El Nuevo Extremo since the sixteenth century. Frowning and alert, Don Ibrahim walked past the obligatory orange trees in the little square in front of the building, which was painted ochre and white, to carry out a tactical reconnaissance of the place. The windows were protected by iron grilles. Beneath the main balcony an escutcheon presided over the entrance: a helmet with a lion for a crest, a bordure of anchors and heads of Moors and American Indian chiefs, a bend with a pomegranate and the motto *ODERINT DUM PROBENT*. Don Ibrahim translated it – "Smell before you touch," or something like that – and approved the message. He entered the dark portal casually and looked through the wrought-iron gate to the inner courtyard, a beautiful Andalusian patio of Mozarabic columns and large pots with plants and flowers around a pretty marble and tiled fountain. A maid in a black uniform came up to the gate looking rather suspicious, so he smiled his most innocent smile, raised his hat and made his way back out to the street, as if he were simply a tourist who'd lost his way. He stood for a moment facing the building. Still smiling beneath his bushy, nicotine-stained moustache, he pulled one of the cigars from his pocket and carefully removed the band bearing the words MONTECRISTO, HAVANA around a tiny fleur-de-lis. He cut one end with the penknife hanging on his watch chain. The little knife had been a present, he claimed, from his friends Rita and Orson, a memento of an unforgettable afternoon in Old Havana when he took them to see the Partagas Cigar Factory on the corner of the Calle Dragones and Calle Barcelona. Later, Rita and he danced at the Tropicana until the early hours. Orson and Rita were there filming *The Lady from Shanghai* or something. They all hugged and kissed, and Orson got drunk as a lord and gave him the little penknife that Citizen Welles used to cut the tips off his cigars. Lost in the memory, or the fantasy, Don Ibrahim put the cigar between his lips and savoured the leaf of pure tobacco wrapped round the outside. The tall priest certainly had interesting lady friends, he thought. Then he held his lighter to the end of the Montecristo, looking forward to the half hour of pleasure he had before him. Don Ibrahim couldn't imagine life without a Cuban cigar. With his first puff, Seville, Havana – how similar they were – and his Caribbean youth, in which even he couldn't distinguish fact from fiction, all merged in a dream as extraordinary as it was perfect.

The light inside the brothel was red, and Julio Iglesias was playing on the stereo. Dolores la Negra put more ice in Celestino Peregil's glass of whisky.

"You look great, Loli," said Peregil.

Dolores wiggled her hips behind the bar and ran an ice cube over her bare navel. Her enormous breasts, inside a very short T-shirt, swung in time to the music. She looked like a Gypsy; she was a large woman well into her thirties who'd had more men than were in the army.

"I'm going to give you the fuck of your life," announced Peregil, smoothing the hair over his bald patch. "It'll take your breath away."

Accustomed to such protocol and to Peregil's sexual prowess, Dolores took two dance steps, looking straight into his eyes. She stuck out the tip of her tongue, dropped the ice cube she'd rubbed over her navel into her glass, and went to pour another glass of Catalan champagne for one of the other customers. The girls had already brought out two bottles for the man and he was now well on his way to a third. Iglesias sang on. Peregil swallowed some whisky and eyed Arab Fatima, who was dancing by herself on the dance floor, wearing a skirt that barely covered her bottom, knee-high boots and a low-cut top that showed her merrily jiggling tits. Fatima was his second choice for the evening, and he seriously started to weigh the pros and cons of each girl.

"Hello, Peregil."

He hadn't heard them arrive. They came and leaned on the bar, one on either side of him, and looked straight ahead at the rows of bottles on the mirror-lined shelves. Peregil could see their reflections in front of him: to his right, the Gypsy Mairena, dressed in black, thin and dangerous, with the manner of a flamenco dancer, wearing a huge gold ring beside the stump of his little finger. He'd chopped it off himself during a riot at Ocaña Prison. To Peregil's left, El Pollo Muelas, fair-haired, neat and slight. The cutthroat razor he carried in his left-hand trouser pocket made him look as if he had a permanent hard-on, and he always said "Excuse me" before slashing someone.

"Aren't you going to buy us a drink?" asked the Gypsy slowly, amicably. He was enjoying himself. Peregil suddenly felt very hot. With a despairing look, he called Dolores over. A gin and tonic for Mairena, the same for El Pollo Muelas. Neither touched his drink. Both stared at Peregil in the mirror.

"We've come to give you a message," said the Gypsy.

"From a friend," added El Pollo.

Peregil swallowed, hoping that in the red light of the bar they wouldn't notice. The "friend" was Ruben Molina, a moneylender from El Baratillo. For months Peregil had been writing IOUs, and he felt quite faint when he thought how much he owed Molina. Ruben Molina was well known in certain circles in Seville. He sent his debtors only two reminders: the first by word, the second by deed. Mairena and El Pollo Muelas were his errand boys.

"Tell him I'll pay him. There's money coming in."

"That's what Frasquito Torres said."

El Pollo smiled, menacingly sympathetic. In the mirror, the Gypsy's long, ascetic face was about as cheerful as if he'd just returned from his mother's funeral. Peregil saw his own reflection between the two of theirs. He wanted to swallow again but couldn't, the mention of Torres had made his throat dry. Frasquito came from a good family and was well known in Seville as an idler. For a time, like Peregil, he'd called on the services of Molina. But when the time came, he wasn't able to pay up. Somebody waited for him at the entrance to his house and broke every tooth in his head. They left him there, with his teeth inside a cone of newspaper tucked into his top jacket pocket.

"I just need another week."

Mairena put an arm round Peregil's shoulders, in a gesture that was so unexpectedly friendly that Peregil almost lost his head with terror. Mairena stroked Peregil's chin with the stump of his little finger. "What a coincidence," said the Gypsy. His black shirt smelled of stale sweat and cigarette smoke. "Because that's exactly what you have, my friend. Exactly seven days and not a minute more."

Peregil gripped the bar, trying to stop his hands from trembling. On the shelves the bottle labels merged. Life is dangerous, he thought. It always ends up killing you.

"Tell Molina that's no problem," he stammered. "I'm a man of my word. I'm about to clinch a good deal." He grabbed his glass and downed the drink. An ice cube crunched in a sinister fashion against his teeth, reminding him how Frasquito Torres had had to borrow from another moneylender to pay for a set of false teeth that cost him nearly half a million pesetas. The Gypsy still had his arm round Peregil's shoulders.

"That sounds so pretty," mocked El Pollo Muelas. "To clinch."

Julio Iglesias sang on. Swinging her hips in time to the music behind the bar, Dolores La Negra came up to make conversation. She dipped a finger in Peregil's whisky and sucked it noisily, rubbed her stomach against the bar, and then shook the contents of her shirt with consummate professionalism before stopping to stare at the three men, disappointed. Peregil was as pale as if he'd just seen a ghost, and the other two didn't look at all friendly. They hadn't even touched their drinks. So Dolores turned and walked away, still moving her hips in time to the music. After a lifetime on one side of a bar or the other, she knew when to get out of the way.

V
Captain Xaloc's Twenty Pearls

I've also loved women who were dead.
Heinrich Heine, *Florentine Nights*

Deputy Superintendent Simeon Navajo, head of investigations at police headquarters in Seville, finished eating his tortilla and glanced amicably at Quart.

"Listen, Padre," he said. "I don't know if it's the church itself, mere chance or the Archangel Gabriel." He paused and took a swig from the bottle of beer on his desk "But there's something sinister about that place."

Navajo was a small, thin, amiable man, constantly gesticulating. He wore round steel-rimmed glasses, and his bushy moustache seemed to sprout from his nose. He looked like the caricature of a seventies intellectual. This impression was emphasised by his jeans, baggy red shirt, and receding hair, worn long and in a ponytail. For the past twenty minutes he and Quart had been going through reports on the two deaths at Our Lady of the Tears. The police investigation had come to the same conclusion as the forensic reports: accidental death. Navajo was sorry he didn't have a handcuffed culprit to parade before the envoy from Rome. Just bad luck, Father, he was saying, a loose handrail, a chunk of plaster coming away from the ceiling. Poor devils, their number was up. Wham, straight to heaven. At least, the deputy superintendent assumed they'd gone to heaven, since they'd been in church.

"We know exactly how Peñuelas, the municipal architect, died." Navajo walked two fingers along his desk to illustrate his account. "He spent half an hour wandering about under the roof of the church looking for evidence to support a condemnation order and then leaned against one of the wooden handrails up in the belfry. The wood was rotten and gave way. Peñuelas fell and was impaled on one of the metal poles sticking out of the half-assembled scaffolding below, like a kebab." The deputy superintendent now held one finger up, as if it were the pole, and slammed the palm of his other hand down on it. Quart assumed the hand was meant to represent the skewered architect. "There were witnesses present when it happened, and on subsequent inspection the handrail didn't appear to have been tampered with."

The deputy superintendent took another swig of beer and wiped his moustache with the finger on which Peñuelas had been impaled. Then he smiled enthusiastically. He and Quart had met a couple of years before, during the Pope's visit. Simeon Navajo had been acting as liaison for the Seville police, and the two had got along famously. The envoy from Rome let the policeman take the credit for all the spectacular successes, such as catching the priest who planned to stab the Holy Father or finding the Semtex hidden in the basket of laundry at the Convent of the Holy Sacrament. Navajo was personally congratulated by the minister of the interior and His Holiness himself. His photo was on the front page of the newspapers and he was awarded a special commendation. Now, nobody at headquarters dared call him Miss Magnum for wearing his hair in a ponytail. The magnum, a .357-calibre, lay among a pile of papers on his desk. He only wore it when he went to his ex-wife's house to pick up his kids. That way, he said, she respected him. And the kids thought it was cool.

Quart looked around the office. Through a glass partition he could see a North African with a black eye. The man sat facing a thickset police officer in shirtsleeves. The officer was saying something to him and didn't look too friendly. It was like a silent movie. On this side of the partition, a framed photograph of the king and a calendar, its passing days energetically ticked off, hung on the wall. There was a grey filing cabinet with an Expo '92 sticker and a sticker of a marijuana leaf, a fan, a pin-board covered with photographs of criminals, a dart-board with holes in the wall all around it, and a poster of some American policemen beating the daylights out of a black man under the words TOUGH LOVE.

"What about Father Urbizu?" asked Quart.

The deputy superintendent scratched his ear. "It seems his death was accidental too, Padre. For him there weren't any witnesses, but my people went over every inch of the church afterwards. Maybe he leaned against part of the scaffolding or knocked it accidentally." He imitated the motion of swaying scaffolding with his hands so realistically that he stopped, as if it gave him vertigo. "The top of it could have knocked off a section of the cornice. The cornice might already have been loose, and by some miracle – if you'll excuse the word – only the scaffolding was keeping it in place. So when the scaffolding got knocked, ten kilos of plaster came down on his head. He must have heard the sound, looked up, and then splat."

He illustrated his story with the appropriate hand movements. At the end, he lay one hand palm upwards to show Father Urbizu passing to a better life. He looked for a moment at his dying hand, then took a swig of beer. "Another case of bad luck," he said thoughtfully.

Quart took out a couple of name cards, to take notes. "Why did the chunk of cornice come down?" he asked.

"Depends." Navajo glanced suspiciously at the cards. He brushed some tortilla crumbs from his shirt. "According to Newton, the attraction of the earth causes any unsupported object to acquire vertical velocity and fall on the heads of archbishops' secretaries who got out of bed on the wrong side that morning." He looked to see Quart's reaction. "I hope you've written that down. And people say the police don't base their work on scientific principles."

Quart got the message. He laughed and put his cards and pen away. "So, why do you think it happened?" he asked.

Navajo shrugged. None of this information was particularly important or confidential, but he obviously wanted to keep things on an official footing. Since the investigation confirmed that the two deaths were accidental, Our Lady of the Tears was still exclusively a matter for the Church. There were rumours that the council and the banks were bringing pressure to bear, and the deputy superintendent's bosses wanted to keep well out of it. Quart may have been a Spaniard, a priest and an old friend, but he was still an agent for a foreign state.

"According to our experts," answered Navajo, "the chunk of cornice was already loose. This was proved by an inspection after the accident. We found a pocket of damp behind it. The roof had been leaking for years."

"You've definitely ruled out human intervention?"

The deputy superintendent began to sneer but caught himself. After all, he was in Quart's debt.

"Listen, Padre, we're the police. We wouldn't even rule out a hundred per cent that Judas wasn't actually bumped off by one of his eleven colleagues. So let's say we're ninety-five per cent sure. It's hardly likely that someone said to the poor bastard, 'Hey, stand there a moment,' climbed up the scaffolding, pulled off a chunk of cornice, and dropped it on him while he just stood there looking up." Navajo's fingers illustrated the climb up the scaffolding and the cornice crashing down. Then a finger lay inert, waiting for the forensic people. "That only happens in cartoons."

When he left the deputy superintendent, Quart felt sure that Vespers had been exaggerating. Maybe the statement about the church killing to defend itself – freely interpreted, metaphorically, symbolically – was true. It was quite another thing to establish how a dilapidated three-hundred-year-old building could, either on its own or with the help of Providence, do away with anyone who threatened it. Establishing that was no longer a matter for Quart, or even the IEA. The supernatural was the province of another kind of expert, closer to Cardinal Iwaszkiewicz's sinister brotherhood than to the rough centurion embodied by Monsignor Spada. In the monsignor's world, and in the good soldier Quart's, two and two always added up to four.

He was turning all this over in his mind when he thought he heard footsteps behind him as he entered the narrow streets of Santa Cruz. He stopped a couple of times but could see nothing suspicious. He walked on, keeping to the narrow strip of shade provided by the eaves of the houses. The sun beat down on Seville, and the white and ochre façades shimmered in the heat like the walls of an oven. Quart's jacket felt as heavy as lead. If there really was a hell, he thought, sinning Sevillanos would feel quite at home – having already lived in an inferno for several months each year, here on earth. When he came to the little square with the church, he stopped before the railing hung with geraniums. He watched enviously as a canary dipped its beak into a bowl of water in its shaded cage. There wasn't a breath of air and nothing stirred, neither the curtains at the windows nor the leaves of the geraniums and orange trees. Sails on the Sargasso Sea.

It was a relief to cross the threshold of Our Lady of the Tears. Inside he found an oasis of cool shade that smelled of wax and damp. He stopped to catch his breath, still dazzled by the sun outside. By the door there was a small carved figure of Jesus of Nazareth. A tormented baroque Christ who'd been put through the third degree in the judgement hall: How many of you are there? Where do you keep your followers' gold and silver coins? What's all this about you being the son of God? Guess who ratted on you. His wrists were bound with rope, and large drops of blood dripped from his crown of thorns. He was looking up, hoping for someone to get him out of there on a habeas corpus. Unlike his peers, Quart had never felt a link with this man whose image he now had before him. Not even at the seminary, during the years of what he thought of as his breaking in, where his theology teachers meticulously took apart and reassembled the mechanisms of faith in the minds of young men destined for the priesthood. "My God, my God, why hast thou forsaken me?" was the question to be avoided at all cost. But for Quart, who had already posed the question by the time he entered the seminary and was convinced there was no answer, this theological programming was superfluous. Being a prudent young man, he said nothing.

He glanced at the carved figure again. The Nazarene certainly had had guts. Nobody need feel ashamed to carry His Cross like a flag. Quart often regretted not having another kind of faith. Men black with dust beneath their chain mail had once shouted the name of God as they charged into battle, to win eternal life and a place in heaven with their slashing swords. Living and dying had been so much simpler then.

Mechanically, he made the sign of the Cross. Around the figure of Christ, which was in a glass display case, hung fifty or so ex-votos: brass or wax models of hands, legs, eyes, children's bodies, locks of hair, letters, ribbons, notes, and plaques giving thanks for a healing. Even a military medal from Africa tied to an old bridal bouquet. As always when he came across such devotion, Quart wondered how much anxiety, how many sleepless nights by a sickbed, how many prayers or stories of hope, pain, life and death were summed up by each of those objects that Don Priamo Ferro, unlike other priests more in tune with the times, allowed people to place around the figure of Christ in his small church. This was old-style religion, with a priest in a cassock intoning Mass in Latin, the vital link between man and the great mysteries. A church of faith and solace, when cathedrals, gothic windows, baroque altarpieces, images and paintings depicting the glory of God served the same purpose as television screens nowadays: to reassure man confronted with the horror of his own solitude, death and the void.

"Hello," said Gris Marsala.

She had climbed down from the scaffolding and now stood before him expectantly, hands in the pockets of her jeans. As before, her clothes were covered with plaster.

"You didn't tell me you were a nun," Quart said reproachfully.

She suppressed a smile, smoothing her grey hair tied in a plait. "True, I didn't," she said, surveying him with a friendly expression, as if she wanted something confirmed. "I assumed a priest would sense it without anyone's help."

"I'm a rather slow-witted priest."

There was a brief silence. Gris Marsala smiled and said, "That's not what I've heard."

"From whom?"

"You know . . . Archbishops, angry priests." Her American accent was more pronounced with certain words. "Attractive women who ask you out to dinner."

"You can't possibly know about that," Quart said, laughing.

"Why not? Haven't you heard of the telephone? You just dial and speak. Macarena Bruner's my friend."

"Strange friendship. A nun and a banker's wife who's the talk of Seville . . ."

"That's not at all funny."

He nodded placatingly, realising he'd gone too far. His remark, no matter what tactical purpose it might have served, was unfair. And as ye would that men should do to you, do ye also to them likewise.

"You're right. I'm sorry," he said looking away, embarrassed by his faux pas. He wondered why he'd been so rude. He could see Macarena Bruner, the ivory necklace against her brown skin and those eyes of hers.

"You don't know her as well as I do," said Sister Marsala sadly.

"That's true."

Quart took a few steps up the nave and again looked at the scaffolding along the walls, the pews pushed into a corner, the blackened ceiling. At the far end, in front of the altarpiece in gloom, burned the candle of the Holy Sacrament. "What have you got to do with all of this?" he asked.

"I told you. I work here as an architect and restorer. Fully qualified. I have degrees from UCLA and Seville."

Quart's footsteps echoed in the nave. The nun walked beside him noiselessly in her trainers. The remains of pictures were visible between the damp and soot stains on the vault: the wings of an angel, the beard of a prophet.

"They're lost for ever," she said. "It's too late to restore them."

Quart looked up at a cherub that had a crack across its forehead as if it had been struck with an axe. "Is the church really falling down?" he asked.

Gris Marsala looked weary. She'd heard that question too many times. "The council, the bank and the archbishop all claim it is, to justify demolishing it." She waved her hand, taking in the nave. "The building is in a bad state. It's been neglected for the last hundred and fifty years. But the basic structure is still sound. There aren't any irreparable cracks in the walls or the vault."

"But part of the ceiling came down on Father Urbizu's head," said Quart.

"Yes. There. Do you see?" The woman pointed at a gap almost a metre long in the cornice all round the nave ten metres up. "That chunk of gilded plaster missing above the pulpit. An unfortunate accident."

"The second unfortunate accident."

"If the municipal architect fell from the ceiling, it was his own fault. Nobody said he could go up there."

For a nun, Gris Marsala didn't sound that sympathetic towards the dead. She seemed to be implying that they'd deserved it. He wondered if she too, like Macarena Bruner, sought absolution from Father Ferro. It was rare to find a flock so faithful to its pastor.

"Imagine," said Quart, eyeing the scaffolding, "that you had nothing to do with this church and I asked you to give me a technical assessment of it."

She answered immediately, without hesitation. "It's old and neglected, but not in ruins. The damage is mostly to the internal walls, because of the leaking roof. But we've repaired that now. I carried nearly ten tons of lime, cement, and sand fifteen metres up with my own hands." She held them up. They were strong, calloused, with short, broken nails encrusted with plaster and paint. "And Father Oscar helped. Father Ferro's too old to go clambering about on the roof."

"And the rest of the building?"

The nun shrugged. "It won't fall down if we get the essential repairs finished. Once we've got rid of all the leaks, it would be a good idea to reinforce the wooden beams, which have rotted in places. Ideally they should be replaced, but we don't have the funds." She sighed. "That's for the actual structure of the building. As far as the ornamentation goes, we just have to restore, gradually, the most damaged parts. I've found a way of doing the windows. A friend of mine works in a stained-glass workshop, and he's promised to make me some pieces to replace the damaged ones, for free. It'll be a slow process, because the leadwork also needs to be restored. But there's no hurry."

"Isn't there?"

"Not if we win this battle."

Quart looked at her with interest. "It sounds as if you take it very personally."

"I do," she said simply. "I stayed in Seville because of this. I came here to try to solve a certain problem, and this is where I found the solution."

"A personal problem?"

"Yes. You could call it a crisis, I suppose. They happen from time to time. Have you had yours?"

Quart nodded politely, his thoughts elsewhere. I must ask Rome for her file. As soon as possible.

"We're talking about you, Sister Marsala."

She screwed up her eyes. "Are you always so detached, or is it a pose? By the way, call me Gris. 'Sister Marsala' sounds ridiculous. I mean, look at me. Anyway, as I was saying, I came here to put my heart and mind in order, and I found the answer in this church."

"What answer?"

"The one we're all searching for. A cause, I suppose. Something to believe in and to fight for." She said nothing for a moment, then added, more quietly, "Faith."

"Father Ferro's."

She looked at him without saying anything. Her plait was coming undone. She re-plaited it without taking her eyes off Quart.

"We all have a kind of faith," she said at last. "And it's something we all very much need, with this century ending so disreputably, don't you think? All those revolutions made and lost. The barricades deserted. The heroes who fought as one are now simply loners clinging to whatever they can find." Her blue eyes rested on him curiously. "Have you never felt like one of the those pawns forgotten in a corner of the board, with the sounds of battle fading behind them? They try to stand straight but wonder if they still have a king to serve."

As they walked round the church, Gris Marsala showed Quart the only picture of any worth: a painting of the Virgin, attributed without too much conviction to Murillo, hanging over the entrance to the vestry from the nave, next to the confessional. Then they went to the crypt. It was closed off by a wrought-iron gate at the top of marble steps descending into darkness. The woman explained that small churches such as this didn't usually have a crypt. Our Lady of the Tears, however, was specially privileged. Fourteen dukes of El Nuevo Extremo lay there, among their number some who died before the church was built. After 1865 the crypt fell into disuse, and members of the family were buried in the family vault in San Fernando. The only exception was Carlota Bruner.

"*Who?*"

Quart was resting a hand on the arch at the entrance to the crypt, decorated with a skull and crossbones. The stone was like ice.

"Carlota Bruner," Gris Marsala said, surprised by his surprise. "Macarena's, great-aunt. She died at the turn of the century and was buried here in the crypt."

"Could we see her tomb?"

The anxiety in Quart's voice, though concealed, was evident. The woman stared at him, unsure.

"Of course," she said and went to fetch a bunch of keys from the vestry. She unlocked the gate and flicked a very antiquated light switch. A dusty bulb cast a dim light over the steps. Quart had to bow his head as he went down. At the bottom he came to a small square area with walls covered with flat stones laid out in three rows. There were large patches of damp on the brick walls, and the air smelled musty. One of the walls bore an escutcheon, carved in marble, with the motto *ODERINT DUM PROBENT*. Let them hate me, so long as they respect me, he translated to himself. Above it was a black cross.

"Fourteen dukes," said Gris Marsala beside him. Her voice was hushed, as if the place made her feel awkward. Quart read the inscriptions on the stones. The oldest bore the dates 1472–1551: Rodrigo Bruner de Lebrija, conquistador and Christian soldier, first Duke of El Nuevo Extremo. The most recent was by the door, between two empty niches. In a vault occupied by explorers, statesmen and warriors, it was the only one with a woman's name:

CARLOTA VICTORIA AMELIA
BRUNER DE LEBRIJA Y MONCADA
1872–1910
GOD REST HER SOUL

Quart ran his fingers over the words carved in marble. He was absolutely certain that the postcard in his pocket had been written by the same woman, ten or twelve years before she died. Disparate characters and events were now starting to fall into some sort of order. And in the centre, like a crossroads, was the church.

"Who was Captain Xaloc?"

Disconcerted, Gris Marsala watched Quart's fingers touch the name "Carlota".

"Manuel Xaloc was a sailor from Seville who emigrated to the Americas at the end of the last century. He was a pirate around the West Indies before disappearing at sea, during the war between Spain and the United States in 1898."

Quart saw the lines again, in his mind's eye: I come here to pray for you every day and wait for you to return.

"What was his relationship with Carlota Bruner?"

"She lost her mind over him. That is, over his absence."

"What do you mean?"

"Exactly what I said." The nun was intrigued by Quart's interest. "Or did you think that only happened in novels? The story could have come straight out of a cheap romance series. Only this one didn't have a happy ending. A girl from an aristocratic family stands up to her parents, and a young sailor goes to seek his fortune overseas. The family makes sure no letters are delivered. The young woman pines at her window, her heart with every ship that passes on the Guadalquivir." It was Gris Marsala's turn to touch the stone, but she withdrew her hand immediately. "She couldn't bear it and lost her mind."

Quart saw the remaining line in his mind: To the sacred place where you swore your love and gave me such happiness. He suddenly felt a strong urge to be outside, where the sun would banish the words, promises and ghosts he'd stirred up in the crypt.

"Did they ever meet again?"

"Yes. In 1898, shortly before war broke out in Cuba. But she didn't recognise him. She didn't recognise anybody any more."

"What did he do?"

The woman's blue eyes seemed to be gazing out over a calm sea. "He went back to Havana just in time to take part in the war. But first he left the dowry he'd brought for her. The twenty pearls on the Virgin of the Tears are the ones that Manuel Xaloc collected for a necklace that Carlota Bruner was to have worn on her wedding day." She glanced one last time at the stone. "She wanted to be married in this church."

They left the crypt, and Gris Marsala locked the gate. Then she switched on the light to the high altar for Quart to get a better look at the Virgin of the Tears. On her chest the Virgin had a heart pierced with seven daggers, and her face, crown of stars and blue mantle were encrusted with Captain Xaloc's pearls.

"There's something I don't understand," said Quart, thinking of the lack of a postmark on the card. "A moment ago you mentioned letters that weren't delivered. And yet Manuel Xaloc and Carlota Bruner must have maintained a correspondence . . . What happened?"

The nun smiled sadly. She didn't seem to enjoy recounting this story. "Macarena told me that you and she are having dinner tonight. Ask her. Nobody knows more about the tragedy of Carlota Bruner than she does."

She switched off the light, and the altarpiece was once again in shadow.

Gris Marsala climbed back up the scaffolding while Quart left through the vestry. Instead of going straight out, he took a look around. A very dark, damaged painting, an unsigned Annunciation, hung on one of the walls. There was also a battered carving of Saint Joseph with the Infant Jesus, a crucifix, two dented brass candelabra, an enormous mahogany chest of drawers and a cupboard. He stood in the middle of the room, looking, then went and opened drawers at random. They contained missals, liturgical objects, vestments. In the cupboard he found a pair of chalices, a monstrance, an ancient brass ciborium, and half a dozen chasubles. Quart closed the drawers without touching anything. The parish was obviously not prosperous.

The vestry had two doors. One of them gave access to the church via the small chapel with the confessional through which Quart had entered. The other door led out into the square through a narrow hall that was also the entrance to the priest's living quarters. A staircase led to a landing lit by a skylight. Quart glanced at his watch. He knew that Father Ferro and Father Oscar were at the archbishop's palace attending an administrative meeting which had been conveniently suggested by Quart himself. If all went well, he had about half an hour.

He walked slowly up the creaking wooden stairs. The door at the top was locked; but finding a way round such obstacles was part of the job. The most difficult lock Quart had ever come across in his career was at the Dublin home of a certain Irish bishop. It had an alphanumeric combination, and he had to crack the code at the door itself, by the light of his Maglite, using a scanner connected to his laptop. The bishop, a rosy-cheeked red-haired little man named Mulcahy, was later summoned urgently to Rome. There, the prelate's cheeks turned pale when he was presented with a copy of the correspondence between himself and members of the IRA by a stern Monsignor Spada – letters that the bishop had been unwise enough to keep, filed in chronological order, behind the volumes of the *Summa Teologica* lined up on his library shelves. This curbed Monsignor Mulcahy's nationalist fervour and convinced the special units of the SAS that it was no longer necessary to eliminate the man physically. According to information obtained by IEA informers, this rather drastic step had been planned – at a cost of ten thousand pounds charged to the secret funds of the Foreign Office – for the upcoming visit of the bishop to his colleague in Londonderry. An operation for which the British intended Loyalist paramilitaries to be blamed.

The lock on Don Priamo Ferro's door, an old-fashioned, conventional type, was no problem. Examining it briefly, Quart took a slim metal strip from his pocket and inserted it into the hole. He moved the strip gently, without forcing it, until he felt several small clicks. Then he turned the knob and opened the door.

He walked along the corridor, looking around. The accommodation was modest, consisting of two bedrooms, a kitchen, bathroom and small sitting room. Quart started with the sitting room but found nothing of interest other than a photograph in one of the sideboard drawers. It was a poor-quality Polaroid snapshot of an Andalusian patio. The floor of the patio was decorated with a mosaic, and there were pots of flowers and a tiled fountain. It showed Don Priamo Ferro, as ever in his long black cassock, sitting at a table set for breakfast, or possibly tea. There were two women beside him: an old lady, dressed in light, summery, slightly dated clothes, and the other one was Macarena Bruner. They were all three smiling at the camera. It was the first time Quart had seen Father Ferro smile, and the old priest looked quite different from the man Quart had met at the church and in the archbishop's office. The smile made him seem younger, softening the hard expression of his black eyes and stubborn chin, unshaven as always. It made him look gentle and sad. More innocent, more human.

Quart put the photograph in his pocket and shut the drawer. He went over to a portable typewriter on a small desk and took off the cover. By professional reflex, he inserted a sheet of paper in the roller and tapped several keys. That way he'd have a sample, in case he ever needed to identify anything typed on the machine. He folded the sheet and put it in his pocket with the photograph. There were about twenty books lined up on the sideboard. He glanced over them, opening some and checking to see if anything was hidden behind them. They were all on religious themes, well-thumbed volumes – the liturgy, a 1992 edition of the Catechism, two volumes of Latin quotations, the *Dictionary of the Ecclesiastical History of Spain*, Urdanoz's *History of Philosophy*, and Menéndez y Pelayo's three-volume *History of Spanish Heterodoxy*. Not the kind of book Quart would have expected. He was surprised, too, to find several books on astronomy. He leafed through them curiously but found nothing significant. The rest of the books were of no interest, except, possibly, the only novel there: a very old, battered paperback copy of *The Devil's Advocate*; Quart detested Morris West's bestsellers with their tormented priests. A paragraph was underlined in ballpoint pen.

. . . you and I and others like us have been removed too long from pastoral duty. We have lost touch with the people who keep us in touch with God. We have reduced the Faith to an intellectual conception, an arid assent of the will, because we have not seen it working in the lives of the common folk. We have lost pity and fear and love . . . . We work by canon, not by charity.

He put the novel back and checked the telephone. It had an old-fashioned, fixed connection. Nowhere to plug in a modem. He went out of the room, leaving the door exactly as he'd found it, at an angle of forty-five degrees, and walked along the passage to a bedroom he guessed was Father Ferro's. It smelled stale, like a priest's solitude. It was a simple room with a window looking on to the square. There was a metal bed with a crucifix on the wall above it, and a wardrobe with a mirror. He saw a book of prayers on the bedside table and, on the floor, an old pair of slippers and a chamber pot. He smiled. Inside the wardrobe he found a black suit, a cassock hardly in better condition than the one Father Ferro wore every day, a few shirts and some underwear. One of the only other personal possessions was a yellowish photograph in a wooden frame. It showed a man and a woman – they looked like peasants in their Sunday best – standing beside a priest.

Despite the black hair and grave young face, Quart easily recognised the priest of Our Lady of the Tears. The photograph was very old and stained. Quart guessed it must have been taken forty years ago. The look of solemn pride on the faces of the man and woman – on whose shoulders the young cleric was resting his hands – suggested that the snapshot had been taken to celebrate his recent ordination.

The other bedroom was without doubt Oscar Lobato's. On the wall was a lithograph of Jerusalem seen from the Mount of Olives, and an *Easy Rider* poster with Peter Fonda and Dennis Hopper on motorbikes. Quart also saw a tennis racket and a pair of trainers in a corner. There was nothing of interest in either the bedside table or the wardrobe, so he searched the desk at the window. He found various bits of paper, books on theology, on the history of the Church, Royo Marín's *Moral Doctrine*, Altaner's *Patristics*, the five volumes of *Mysterium Salutis*, the lengthy essay *Clerics* by Eugen Drewermann, an electronic chess set, a guidebook to the Vatican, a small packet of antihistamine pills and an old copy of one of the adventures of Tintin, *The Sceptre of Ottokar*. And in a drawer – a reward for Quart's patience – twenty pages on St. John of the Cross printed in New Courier font, and five plastic boxes each containing a dozen 3.5" diskettes.

He might be Vespers or he might not. This was pretty slender proof; anway there was too much to go through then and there, Quart realised, annoyed, as he looked quickly through the boxes. He'd have to find a way to come back and copy the contents of the diskettes on to the hard disk of his laptop, to search them for clues later at his leisure. Copying the diskettes could take an hour, so he'd need to devise another excuse for getting the priests out of the way.

Quart could feel the heat of the sun through the curtains, and he was sweating beneath his lightweight black alpaca jacket. He mopped his forehead with a tissue, then rolled the tissue into a ball and put it in his pocket. He put the diskettes back and closed the drawer, wondering where Father Oscar kept his computer. The hacker would have needed a very powerful computer connected to an easily accessible telephone line, as well as additional equipment. Such facilities were not to be found in these quarters. Whether he was Oscar Lobato or someone else, Vespers obviously didn't work from here.

Quart looked round indecisively. It was time to leave. And at that moment, just as he glanced at his watch, he heard footsteps on the stairs. He realised that his problems had only just begun.

Peregil hung up and stared thoughtfully at the telephone. Don Ibrahim had just called from a bar near the church to give him the latest report on the movements of each of the characters in the story. The former bogus lawyer and his henchmen were taking their commission very seriously. Too seriously, in Peregil's view. He was fed up with receiving calls every half hour telling him that such-and-such a priest had just bought a newspaper, or that such-and-such a priest was sitting on the terrace of the Laredo Bar enjoying the evening air. So far, the only valuable information was that Macarena Bruner had met the envoy from Rome at the Doña Maria Hotel. Peregil reacted to this news with disbelief at first, then with a kind of expectant satisfaction. You could bet this would be interesting.

And speaking of betting. In the last twenty-four hours the gaming tables had brought him a few more problems. After paying Don Ibrahim and his companions the hundred-thousand-peseta advance on the three million promised for the entire job, Pencho Gavira's assistant gave in to temptation: he used the remaining two million nine hundred thousand to try to repair his dire financial situation. The idea had come to him in a flash, with the dangerous intuition that some days are special and that this was one of them. Also, a certain Moorish fatalism stirred in the man's Andalusian blood. Luck will not knock at the same door twice unless you do something to attract its attention. That was the only piece of advice his father gave him when he was little, the day before his father went out for cigarettes and ran off with the butcher's wife. So, as Peregil stood eating tapas at the bar, he suddenly realised, although he knew he was walking along the edge of a precipice, that if he didn't act on his instinct, he'd spend the rest of his life regretting what might have been. Because he, the sidekick of the strong man at the Cartujano Bank, could be many things: a scoundrel, a man ashamed of his baldness, or a gambler who would sell his old mother, his boss or his boss's ex-wife for the price of a bingo card; but just imagining the sound of a rolling roulette ball made him brave as a lion. So that evening Peregil put on a clean shirt and a tie with mauve and red flowers, and headed for the casino like a Greek on his way to Troy. He nearly pulled it off, and that said much for his intuition as an habitué of the gaming tables. But, as Seneca said, what isn't to be isn't to be. Or maybe he never said anything of the sort. The two million nine hundred thousand went the way of the other three million. So Celestino Peregil was without a cent, and the shadows of Mairena the Gypsy and El Pollo Muelas hovered over him like a black cloud.

He got up and paced the cubbyhole, full of photocopiers and paper, that he occupied two floors below his boss, with views on the Arenal and the Guadalquivir. From here he could see the Torre del Oro, San Telmo Bridge and couples walking along the river. Even in his shirtsleeves and with the air-conditioning on, he couldn't breathe. So he went to get the bottle and some ice, and downed a glass of whisky in one. He wondered how long things could go on this way.

A tempting idea was taking shape in his mind. Nothing specific yet, but something that might provide him with a little liquidity and breathing space. He'd be playing with fire again, but the truth was he didn't have much choice. The main thing was to make sure that Pencho Gavira never found out that his assistant was playing a double game. As long as Peregil was discreet about leaking the story to the press, this business could bring him quite a bit more money. The tall priest was much more photogenic than Curro Maestral.

Slowly turning the idea over, he went to the desk in search of his address book. His finger paused over a telephone number he'd dialled before. Suddenly he slammed the address book shut, as if struggling against temptation. You're a low-down rat, he said to himself with an objectivity unusual in the type he was. But the former detective wasn't really that concerned about the state of his morals; he was worried that some remedies, if you overdid it, could kill you. But debts could also kill you, especially if they were owed to the most dangerous money-lender in Seville. So, after weighing things again, he opened the address book once more and found the number of *Q&S* magazine. What have I got to lose? he thought. Somebody once said that betrayal was just a matter of timing; and for Peregil time was running out. Anyway, calling it betrayal wasn't right. He was just trying to survive.

"What are you doing here?"

Father Oscar hadn't been detained at the archbishop's palace long enough. There he was in the corridor, blocking Quart's way out, and not looking too friendly. Quart smiled coldly, barely managing to conceal his annoyance and embarrassment.

"I was taking a look round," he said.

"So it would seem."

Oscar Lobato kept nodding, as if answering his own questions. He wore a black polo shirt, grey trousers and trainers. His skin was pale, although he was now flushed from having run up the stairs. He was considerably shorter than Quart and didn't look very strong – his appearance (from Father Oscar's CV, Quart knew he was twenty-six) indicated that he spent more time sitting over a book than doing physical exercise. But he looked furious, and Quart knew you should never underestimate a man in that state. His eyes were wild behind his glasses, his fair hair flopped untidily over his forehead and his fists were clenched.

There was nothing Quart could say to get out of this mess, so he raised a hand, requesting calm, and turned sideways, as if to go out into the narrow corridor. But Father Oscar moved to the left, blocking him. The envoy from Rome realised that things were going to go further than he had bargained for.

"Don't be stupid," he said, undoing the button on his jacket.

Even before Quart finished the sentence, Father Oscar struck, blindly, furiously, dispensing with priestly meekness. But Quart stepped back quickly, and the punch missed.

"This is ridiculous," Quart protested.

It was true. None of this was worth a fight. Quart raised both hands to placate. But his opponent, still in a rage, tried again to hit him. This time the blow glanced off his jaw. It was a feeble haymaker, but Quart was now angry. The assistant priest seemed to believe that people went at each other in real life as they did in films. Not that Quart was an expert at this sort of thing; but during the course of his work he had acquired a few skills unusual for a priest. Nothing spectacular, just half a dozen tricks to get him out of tight spots. Quart kicked the flushed, panting young man in the groin.

Father Oscar stopped dead, a look of astonishment on his face. Quart knew that it would take about five seconds for the kick to have its full impact, so he also punched him behind the ear, not too hard, to make sure he didn't strike out again. The assistant priest fell to his knees, his head and right shoulder against the wall, and stared fixedly at his glasses lying undamaged on the tiled floor.

"I'm sorry," said Quart, rubbing his sore knuckles.

He really was sorry – and embarrassed that he hadn't been able to prevent this ridiculous scene: two priests fighting like a couple of louts. His opponent's youth only added to his discomfort.

Father Oscar didn't move. Red in the face and gasping for breath, he was still staring myopically at his glasses on the floor. Quart picked them up and handed them to him, then put an arm under his shoulders and stood him on his feet. After Quart helped him to the sitting room, the assistant priest, still doubled up in pain, collapsed into a plastic sofa on top of a pile of *New Life* magazines. Quart brought him a glass of water from the kitchen and Father Oscar gulped it down. He put his glasses back on. One of the lenses was smudged. Sweat plastered his fair hair to his forehead.

"I'm sorry," Quart said again.

The assistant priest nodded weakly, staring at a vague point in space. He brushed his hair off his forehead. He looked truly pathetic. His glasses had slipped down his nose and he was very pale. He must have been under a lot of pressure to have lost control like that.

"I was just doing my job," Quart said, as gently as he could, leaning over the table. "There's nothing personal about it."

Father Oscar nodded again, avoiding his eyes. "I lost my head," he said, subdued.

"We both did," Quart said with a smile, trying to soothe the young man's wounded pride. "But I'd like to make one thing very clear: I didn't come here to persecute anyone. I'm just trying to understand."

Still avoiding Quart's eye and with his hand on his forehead, Father Oscar asked what the hell Quart thought he'd understand by going through other people's belongings.

Trying to sound as friendly as he could, Quart told Father Oscar about the hacker and the message to Rome. As he talked, he paced.

Then he stopped in front of the young priest. "Some believe," he said, in a tone that implied that *he* didn't believe it, "that you're Vespers."

"That's absurd."

"But your age, qualifications, interests, they all fit the profile . . ." He leaned on the table again. "How much do you know about computers?"

"The same as everyone."

"What about these boxes of diskettes?"

The assistant priest blinked. "That's private. You have no right."

"Of course not" – Quart held up his palms to placate – "but could you tell me where your computer is?"

"That's not important."

"I think it is."

Father Oscar looked more resolute now, and less like a humiliated young man. "Listen," he said, "there's a war going on here, and I've chosen which side I'm on." He sat up straight and looked Quart in the eye. "Don Priamo is a good and honourable man. The others aren't. That's all I have to say."

"Who are the others?"

"Everyone. From the people at the bank to the archbishop." He smiled for the first time. A smile of anger. "And I include those who sent you from Rome."

Quart couldn't have cared less; he wasn't bothered by insults to his team. Assuming that Rome was his team. "All right," he said neutrally. "I'll put all this down to your youth. At your age, life is much more dramatic. Ideas and lost causes carry you away."

The assistant priest glared at him contemptuously. "Ideas are what made me join the priesthood," he said, as if wondering what Quart's motivation had been. "And Our Lady of the Tears isn't a lost cause yet."

"But if anyone's going to win in this, it won't be you. You're being transferred to Almeria . . ."

The young man sat up even straighter, defiantly. "Maybe that's the price I have to pay for my dignity and a clear conscience."

"Nice words," said Quart. "So you're prepared to throw a brilliant career out the window. Is it really worth it?"

"For what shall it profit a man, if he shall gain the whole world, and lose his own soul?" The assistant priest faced Quart firmly as if there could be no argument with this.

Quart managed not to laugh in Father Oscar's face. "I don't see what your soul has to do with this church," he said.

"You don't see a lot of things. That some churches are more needed than others, for instance. Maybe because of what they hold within them, or symbolise. Some churches are refuges."

Quart remembered Father Ferro's using exactly the same expression during their meeting in Corvo's office. "Refuges," he echoed.

"Yes."

"From what?"

Still facing Quart, Father Oscar stood up and walked with difficulty to the window. He drew back the curtains, letting in the air and the light. "From Our Holy Mother the Church," he said at last. "So Catholic, Apostolic and Roman that it's ended up betraying its original purpose. In the Reformation it lost half of Europe, and in the eighteenth century it excommunicated Reason. A hundred years later, it lost the workers, because they realised it was on the side of the masters and oppressors. And now, as this century draws to a close, it's losing the young and the women. Do you know how this will end? With mice running around empty pews."

Father Oscar fell silent for a few moments. Quart could hear him breathing.

"Above all," the assistant priest went on, "some churches allow us to defend ourselves from what you came to impose here: submission and silence." He contemplated the orange trees in the square. "At the seminary I realised that the entire system is based on appearances, and on a game of ambition without principles. In the priesthood you only get close to people if they can advance your career. Very early on, you choose a teacher, a friend, a bishop who will further you," Father Oscar laughed quietly. He didn't look so young now. "I thought there were only four types of bow that a priest makes before the altar, until I met priests who were experts at hundreds of bows. I was such a priest myself. People look for a sign from us, and when we fail to give it, they fall into the hands of palmists, astrologers and other charlatans peddling the spirit. But when I met Don Priamo, I saw what faith is. Faith doesn't even need the existence of God. It's a blind leap into a pair of welcoming arms. It's solace in the face of senseless fear and suffering. The child's trust in the hand that leads out of darkness."

"And have you told many people this?"

"Of course. Whoever will listen."

"Well, I think you're going to get into trouble."

"As you know better than anyone, I already am. I could start over, somewhere else. I'm only twenty-six. But I'm not leaving the priesthood. I will stay and fight, wherever they send me . . ." He stared at Quart defiantly. "Do you know something? I think I quite enjoy being a nuisance to the Church."

Pencho Gavira sat back in his black leather armchair, staring at his computer screen. The e-mail message read:

> `They parted his garments, casting lots upon them, but they could not destroy the temple of God. The stone which the builders rejected, the same is become the head of the corner. It remembers those that were torn from our hand.`

For his own amusement, the intruder had also slipped in a harmless virus: an irritating little white ball that bounced around the screen and multiplied. When two balls bumped into each other, they exploded in a mushroom cloud, and then the whole thing started over again. Gavira wasn't too worried; the virus could be deleted. The bank's computer department was already working on it, and checking to make sure there weren't other, more destructive viruses lurking. What worried him was how easily the hacker – a bank employee or just a prankster? – had slipped in the little bouncing balls, and the strange quotation from the Gospels that must have been an allusion to the operation involving Our Lady of the Tears.

Trying to think of something more cheerful, the vice-chairman of the Cartujano looked up from his computer at the painting hanging on the main wall of his office. It was by Klaus Paten and extremely valuable. It had been acquired a little over a month ago, together with the rest of the stocks and assets of the Poniente Bank. Old Machuca wasn't keen on modern art, so Gavira appropriated it when they divided up the spoils. In the past, generals wrapped themselves in flags captured from the enemy, and the Klaus Paten was exactly that: the standard of the defeated army, a 2.2m x 1.8m expanse of cobalt blue with one red stroke and one yellow stroke crossing it diagonally, entitled *Obsession No. 5*. For thirty years it had presided over board meetings at the bank recently absorbed by the Cartujano. A trophy for the victor.

The victor. Gavira almost said the word aloud. But he was frowning as he turned back to his computer screen, now covered with little balls bouncing in all directions. At that moment two of them collided and set off the mushroom cloud. Boom. A single ball started the sequence again. Exasperated, Gavira swivelled his chair one hundred and eighty degrees to face the enormous window looking out on the banks of the Guadalquivir. In his world he had to keep moving, like that bloody little ball. If he stood still he was vulnerable, like a wounded shark. Old Machuca, calm and cunning as ever, said to him once: It's like riding a bicycle: if you stop pedalling, you fall. It was Pencho Gavira's fate to keep pedalling, finding new paths, constantly attacking his enemies, real or imagined. Every setback spurred him on, every victory entailed a new struggle. That was how the vice-chairman of the Cartujano Bank spun his web of ambition. He would know his ultimate objective when he reached it. If he ever reached it, that is.

He exited his e-mail, typed his password, and entered a private file to which only he had access. There, safe from prying eyes, was a confidential report that could cause him serious trouble. Commissioned by board members opposed to Gavira's succeeding Octavio Machuca as chairman of the Cartujano, it was drawn up by a private financial information agency and was a lethal weapon. The conspirators were planning to produce it at a meeting the following week. They didn't know that Gavira, by paying a considerable sum, had managed to obtain a copy:

S&B Confidential
Summary of CB internal investigation re PT deal and others
In the middle of last year an abnormal increase was noted in the reserves of the Bank, and consequently in the interbank debt of previous months. Vice-chairman Fulgencio Gavira (who is, in addition, invested with all powers except those that may not be delegated) maintains that said increases occurred principally as a result of funding to Puerto Targa

and its shareholders, but that these were specific, provisional transactions which would be normalised with the imminent sale of the Puerto Targa company to a foreign group (Sun Qafer Alley, with Saudi capital). The sale would produce a substantial capital gain for the shareholders and a large commission for the Cartujano. The sale has been authorised by the Junta de Andalucia and the Council of Ministers.

Puerto Targa is a company with an original share capital of five million pesetas. Its aim is the creation, in a protected zone near the Coto de Doñana National Park, of a golf course and a development of luxury villas with a marina. The administrative restrictions on construction in a protected zone have recently and unexpectedly been lifted by the Junta de Andalucia. The Junta previously vehemently opposed the project. Seventy-eight per cent of the shares in the company were purchased by the Bank at the request of the vice-chairman (Gavira), following an increase that raised the capital to nine billion pesetas. The other twenty-two per cent has remained in private hands, and we have good reason to believe that the company H. P. Sunrise, based in St. Barthélemy in the West Indies, which retained a substantial block of shares, may have links with Fulgencio Gavira.

Time has passed, and the sale of Puerto Targa still has not been concluded. Meanwhile the risk mounts. For his part, the vice-chairman has continued to maintain that the increase noted was caused partly by the liquidation of assets, paper discount, and pure funding, but that the sale of shares will take place imminently, thus ensuring the expected significant reduction in exposure. Our investigation has, however, revealed that the increase in exposure is due to items that were deliberately concealed at the time and that came to light only upon probing. These amounted to twenty billion pesetas, of which only seven corresponded to the Puerto Targa operation. The vice-chairman continues to maintain that the purchase of the Puerto Targa shares by Sun Qafer Alley will rectify the situation.

The investigation has revealed that Puerto Targa is a company that, following a complex operation revolving around Gibraltar-based companies, has been financed, from its foundation to the present day, almost entirely by the Cartujano Bank. This situation has been kept hidden from the majority of Board members. It could be said that the company was set up, firstly, to record a fictitious profit on the previous balance sheet of the Cartujano Bank, in that the seven billion pesetas spent on the purchase of the company were entered as profits, when the Bank actually paid itself that sum when it sold itself Puerto Targa through the Gibraltar companies acting as fronts for the operation. The second purpose of the company was, with the capital gains produced by its subsequent sale to Sun Qafer Alley, to restore the Bank's balance sheet. In other words, to restore the shortfall of over ten billion pesetas produced at the Cartujano Bank by the present vice-chairman's dealings and the burden resulting from previous transactions.

The sale, which, according to the present vice-chairman, will triple the value of the company, has not yet taken place. A new date for the sale has been set for the middle or end of this month of May. It is possible that, as the vice-chairman maintains, the Puerto Targa operation may return the bank's internal situation to normal. But, for the time being, it is definite that the systematic concealment of the true situation is proof of a cover-up in the income statement of the Cartujano Bank. This means that for the past year, the Board has been kept in the dark concerning the risks of the situation and the lack of positive results, as well as with respect to management errors and irregularities, although in truth the vice-chairman cannot be held entirely responsible.

Some of the methods used to conceal the true situation were as follows: frenetic searching for new and expensive sources of funds; false accounting and infringement of banking regulations; and risk-taking that – should the expected sale of Puerto Targa to Sun Qafer Alley (forecast to fetch some hundred and eighty million dollars) not take place – will deal a serious blow to the Cartujano Bank and cause a public scandal, considerably diminishing the Bank's high standing with its shareholders, most of whom are conservative by nature and have small shareholdings.

As for the irregularities for which the present vice-chairman is directly responsible, the investigation has uncovered a general lack of financial prudence. Considerable sums have been paid to professionals and private individuals without due documentary proof. These include cases of payments to public figures and institutions that can only be described as bribery. The investigation has also discovered that the vice-chairman has intervened in transactions with clients and, although this is not proven, has received certain sums as commission.

For the reasons set out above, and quite apart from the management irregularities uncovered, it is evident that the failure of the Puerto Targa operation would place the Cartujano Bank in serious difficulties. Another cause for concern is the possible negative effect that knowledge of the operations carried out by the vice-chairman involving the church of Our Lady of the Tears and the entire Puerto Targa project might have on public opinion and on the traditionally middle-class, conservative and Catholic customer-base of the bank.

In general terms, it was all true. In the past two fiscal years, Gavira had needed to perform great feats of juggling in order to present his management of the bank in a favourable light. He had taken over a bank damaged by uninspired, conservative policies. Puerto Targa and other, similar operations were simply ways of playing for time while he strengthened his position at the helm of the Cartujano. It was like building the staircase on which one climbed; but until the final coup, which would ensure his position, this was the only possible tactic. He needed a breathing space and credit, and the deal involving Our Lady of the Tears – bait for the Saudis buying Puerto Targa – was crucial: it would turn north Santa Cruz into a prime location for upmarket tourism. The project was a small, exclusive luxury hotel only five hundred metres from Seville's ancient mosque, a personal whim of Kemal Ibn Saud, brother of the King of Saudi Arabia and principal shareholder of Sun Qafer Alley. The file with all the plans was protected by a password on his computer, along with the report on his management of the bank and a few other sensitive documents. Copies on diskette and CD were stored in the safe just below the Klaus Paten. He couldn't let four board members ruin things. There was too much at stake.

He glanced at the screen again, frowning. The intruder and his little bouncing ball worried him. It was unlikely, but possible, that the hacker had cracked the password and got into the file. The thought made Gavira feel hot; it wasn't pleasant imagining a hacker wandering about so close to that kind of information. As old Machuca would say, better safe than sorry. Gavira deleted the file.

Afterwards he stared at the grey-green Guadalquivir and the Calle Betis running along the opposite bank. Sunlight glinted on the river, and the glare framed the compact outline of the Torre del Oro. It could all be his one day. He lit a cigarette and opened his desk drawer. For the hundredth time he pulled out the magazine with the photographs of his wife outside the Alfonso XIII Hotel with a bull-fighter. Again he felt a morbid fascination as he turned the pages and looked at the photographs that were already burned in his memory. He glanced from the magazine to the silver-framed photograph on his desk of Macarena in a white off-the-shoulder blouse. He had taken the photograph at a time when he thought she was his – his all the time, not just during sex. Then things went wrong, this business with the church, Macarena wanting a child, Macarena becoming bored in bed.

He shifted uneasily in his leather armchair. Six months. He remembered his wife sitting naked on the edge of the bath. He was taking a shower, unaware that they would never make love again. She looked at him as she had never done before, as if he were a stranger. She left suddenly, and when Gavira came into the bedroom in his dressing gown, she was dressed and packing her suitcase. Not one word of reproach. She just looked at him darkly and went to the door before he had time to say or do anything. Six months ago today. And she had refused to see him since.

He put the crumpled magazine away and stubbed out his cigarette viciously. If only he could stub out the old priest, and that nun who looked like a lesbian, and all those priests in their confessionals, and the catacombs, and the dark, useless past, everything that was complicating his life. If only he could stub out miserable, moth-eaten Seville; this city that was only too pleased to remind him that he was nothing but a parvenu the minute the duchess of El Nuevo Extremo's daughter turned her back on him. Gritting his teeth, he knocked the photograph of his wife face down with the back of his hand. By God, or the devil, or whoever was responsible, he was going to make them all pay dearly for the humiliation. First they'd taken his wife, now they were trying to take the church, and his future.

"I'll wipe you out." He spat the words. "All of you."

He switched off the computer and watched the rectangle of light on the monitor shrink and disappear. A few priests out of circulation, taught a lesson – a broken hip or something – wouldn't cause Pencho Gavira any remorse. He picked up the telephone, determined.

"Peregil," he said into the receiver, "are your people reliable?"

Solid as rocks, the henchman answered. Gavira glanced at the picture frame lying on his desk. His face had the fierceness now that had earned him the nickname Shark in Andalusian banking circles. It was time to take action. Those damned priests were going to learn a lesson.

"Set fire to the church," he ordered. "Do whatever you think necessary to settle this once and for all."

VI
Lorenzo Quart's Tie

All the women in the world are in you.
Joseph Conrad, *The Golden Arrow*

Lorenzo Quart had only one tie. It was navy blue silk, and he'd bought it at a shirt maker's on the Via Condotti a hundred and fifty paces from where he lived. He always bought the same kind: a very traditional cut, slightly narrower than was fashionable. When it became worn or dirty, he bought another, identical, to replace it. He rarely wore the tie – no more than a couple of times a year. Mostly he wore black shirts with a Roman collar that he ironed himself with the precision of a veteran soldier preparing for inspection by superiors obsessed with regulations. Quart's life revolved around regulations; he had adhered to them rigorously ever since he could remember – long before he was ordained a priest, face down on cold flagstones with his arms out. At the seminary, from the very start, he accepted Church discipline as an efficient way of organising his life. In return he was given security, a future, and a cause to devote his talents to. Unlike his fellow students, he had never sold his soul to a patron or powerful friend, neither then or since. He believed – and this was perhaps his only point of naivety – that following the rules would gain him the respect of others. Many of his superiors were indeed impressed by the young priest's intelligence and discipline and helped him in his career. He spent six years at the seminary, two at the university studying philosophy, theology, and the history of the Church, and was then awarded a scholarship to Rome for a Ph.D. in canon law. There, the professors at the Gregorian University put his name forward to the Pontifical Academy for Ecclesiastics and Noblemen, where Quart studied diplomacy and relations between Church and State. After that, the Vatican Secretariat assigned him to a couple of European nunciatures, until Monsignor Spada formally recruited him into the Institute for External Affairs. Quart was just twenty-nine. It was then that he went to Enzo Rinaldi and paid 115,000 lire for his first tie.

That was ten years ago, and he still had trouble tying the knot. He knew how to do it in theory, but, standing in front of the bathroom mirror and looking at the white shirt collar and the blue silk tie in his hands, he felt vulnerable. He felt particularly vulnerable to be without his Roman collar and black shirt for a dinner with Macarena Bruner. Like a Knight Templar setting aside his armour to go and parley with the Mamelukes beneath the walls of Tyre. The thought made him smile uneasily as he glanced at his watch. There was just enough time to dress and walk to the restaurant. He'd found it on the map, in the Plaza de Santa Cruz, a stone's throw from the ancient Arab wall. The connotations of which the modern Knight Templar found rather disturbing.

Lorenzo Quart was as punctual as the robot-like Swiss Guard at the Vatican. He always worked out his schedule by dividing the hours precisely and making efficient use of every second. He had enough time to deal with the tie, so he made himself do the knot calmly, adjusting it carefully. He liked to move slowly, because his self-control was a source of pride. In his dealings with the world he was constantly striving to avoid a hurried gesture, an inappropriate word, an impatient move that might break the serenity of the regulations. Even when he broke rules that were not his own – something that Spada, with his gift for euphemism, called "walking along the outer edge of the law" – the appearance of morality was safe with him. In his case the old curial saying, *Tutti i preti sono falsi*, wasn't accurate. He was quite indifferent as to whether or not all priests were frauds; *he* would be an honourable Knight Templar.

Maybe that was why, after regarding himself for a moment in the mirror, he removed the tie and white shirt and put on a black shirt with a round collar. As he buttoned the shirt, his fingers brushed the scar beneath his left clavicle, a memento of the American soldier who struck him with the butt of his rifle during the invasion of Panama. It was the only scar Quart had acquired in the line of duty; the red badge of courage, Spada called it wryly. His Grace and the pusillanimous head-hunters in the Curia were impressed. Quart himself would have preferred for the lunatic with the Kevlar helmet, M-16, and badge that said J. KOWALSKY on his bulletproof vest – "Another Pole," Spada said later caustically – to have taken Quart's Vatican diplomatic passport more seriously when it was brandished under his nose at the nunciature, the day that Quart negotiated General Noriega's surrender.

Apart from the broken-shoulder incident, the operation in Panama had proceeded flawlessly, and the IEA considered it a classic of diplomacy in a crisis. Following a hazardous flight from Costa Rica, Quart landed in Panama a few hours after the American invasion and Noriega's admission to the Vatican diplomatic legation. Officially, his task was to assist the nuncio, but really he would be monitoring the negotiations and keeping the IEA directly informed. He had come to relieve Monsignor Hector Bonino, an Argentine-Italian who had no diplomatic experience. The secretary of state didn't trust Bonino to handle a matter like this. It was indeed an unusual situation. The Americans, behind wire fences and tank traps, had installed powerful loudspeakers blasting out rock music twenty-four hours a day to psychologically weaken the nuncio and his refugees. Inside the building, spread throughout the offices and corridors, an assortment of people sat waiting: a Nicaraguan, head of Noriega's counter-intelligence; five Basque separatists; a Cuban economic adviser who kept threatening to commit suicide if he wasn't returned safe and sound to Havana; an agent for CESID, the Spanish central intelligence agency, who went in and out of the building as he pleased to play chess with the nuncio and keep Madrid informed; three Colombian drug traffickers; and General Noriega, Pineapple Face himself, on whose head the Americans had put a price. In return for asylum, Monsignor Bonino required that his guests attend Mass daily; and it was moving to see them wishing each other peace – Noriega all prayers and chest beating – under the watchful eye of the nuncio, with Bruce Springsteen's *Born in the USA* blaring outside. On the crucial night of the siege, when Delta commandos with their noses painted black tried to storm the nunciature, Quart maintained telephone contact with the archbishops of New York and Chicago until President Bush agreed to call off the raid. At last Pineapple Face gave himself up without laying down too many conditions, the Nicaraguan and the Basque separatists were discreetly transported out of Panama, and the drug traffickers ran – to reappear later in Medellin. Only the Cuban, who came out last, had problems. The Marines found him in the trunk of an old Chevrolet Impala that Quart had rented. The CESID agent had agreed to drive the man out of the nunciature, just for the hell of it, risking his career. The agreement negotiated for the Cuban's release was kept secret, so Marine Kowalsky knew nothing about it, nor was he particularly concerned about the subtleties of diplomacy. So Quart, despite his collar and Vatican passport, ended up with a broken shoulder when he attempted to mediate. As for the Cuban, a nervous type by the name of Girón, he spent a month in a Miami jail. And not only did he break his promise to commit suicide, but on his release he obtained political asylum in the United States after giving an interview to *Reader's Digest* entitled "I Too Was Fooled by Castro".

As Quart came out of the lift the man waiting in the lobby stood up. Quart had never seen him before. He was about forty and rather thick around the waist. His lank, thinning hair was lacquered down, and he had a double chin that seemed an extension of his cheeks.

"The name's Bonafé," the man said. "Honorato Bonafé."

Quart thought he'd never met anyone with a more inappropriate name. This person looked anything but honourable. His cunning little eyes seemed to be calculating how much he'd get for Quart's suit and shoes if he stole them.

"Could we talk for a moment?" Bonafé's smile made him more repellent still. It was a grimace, both obsequious and malicious, like a priest of the old school trying to curry favour with a bishop. In fact, Quart thought a cassock would have suited the man much better than the crumpled beige suit and the leather bag in his hand. His hands were small and podgy, promising a limp handshake.

Quart stopped. He was prepared to listen but didn't drop his guard. He glanced over the man's head at the clock on the wall. Fifteen minutes till his appointment with Macarena Bruner. Bonafé followed Quart's gaze, said again that he would take only a moment of his time, and raised his hand as if to place it on the priest's arm. Quart stared hard at the hand, stopping Bonafé dead. The hand remained in midair while Bonafé told him what he wanted in a conspiratorial tone. Quart didn't want to listen, but the name *Q&S* magazine set alarm bells ringing.

"To sum up, Father, I'm at your disposal."

Quart frowned, disconcerted. He could have sworn the man had winked at him. "Thank you. But I don't see what this has to do with me."

"You don't." Bonafé nodded as if sharing a joke. "But it's all quite clear, isn't it? What you're doing in Seville."

Dear God. Just what he needed: someone like this turning up when Rome wanted the matter resolved as discreetly as possible. Quart wondered how so many people could have found out about it. "I don't know what you mean," he said.

The man looked at him with barely concealed insolence and said, "Really?"

Quart consulted his watch. He'd had enough. "Excuse me, I have an appointment." He walked away, towards the entrance. But Bonafé followed him.

"Do you mind if I walk with you? We could talk as we go."

"I have nothing to say."

He left his key at Reception and went out into the street, trailed by the journalist. The dark shape of La Giralda was visible against the remaining light of the sky. At that moment the streetlights came on in the Plaza Virgen de los Reyes.

"I don't think you understand," insisted Bonafé, pulling a copy of *Q&S* from his pocket. "I work for this magazine." He held it out but put it away again when Quart ignored him. "All I want is a short, friendly chat. You tell me a couple of things, and I'll be decent. I assure you, co-operation will benefit us both." On his pink lips, the word "co-operation" acquired obscene connotations.

Quart had to make an effort to contain his revulsion. "Please go away."

"Come on. Just the time to have one drink," he said, at once rude and friendly.

They were now under a street lamp at a corner of the archbishop's palace. Quart stopped and turned. "Listen, Buenafé."

"Bonafé."

"Bonafé or whatever your name is. What I'm doing in Seville is none of your business. And in any case, I would never dream of telling the world about it."

The journalist protested, quoting the usual journalistic clichés: freedom of information, the quest for truth, the public's right to know. "And anyway," he added after thinking a moment, "better for you lot to be in than out."

It sounded like a threat. Quart was beginning to lose patience. "Us lot?"

"You know what I mean." Again the obsequious smile. "The clergy and all that."

"Ah. The clergy."

"I see we understand each other," Bonafé said, his double chin wobbling hopefully.

Quart looked at him calmly, his hands clasped behind his back. "And what exactly do you want to know?" he asked.

"Well. Let's see." Bonafé scratched his armpit beneath his jacket. "What's the view in Rome on that church, for instance. What's the position of the parish priest in terms of canon law . . . And whatever you can tell me about your mission here." His smile was slimy. "That shouldn't be too difficult."

"And if I refuse?"

The journalist clucked his tongue, as if to say that wouldn't do, especially as they'd been getting on so well. "I'll write the article anyway, of course. And he that is not with me, is against me." He stood on tiptoe as he spoke. "Isn't that what it says in the Gospels?"

Quart stared at him for a moment without a word. He glanced to the right and left before moving closer to the journalist, as if to speak in confidence. But there was something in his demeanour that made Bonafé step back. "I really couldn't care less what your name is," said Quart quietly. "I can't decide whether you're rude, stupid, criminal, or all three. In any case, even though I'm a priest, I have a bad temper. So if I were you, I'd get out of my sight. Now."

The street lamp cast vertical shadows on the journalist's face. No longer smiling, he gave Quart an aggrieved look. "Not very priestly," he complained, his double chin trembling. "Your attitude."

"You think?" Now it was Quart's turn to smile unpleasantly. "In that case, you'd be surprised how unpriestly I can be."

He turned his back on him and walked away, wondering what he'd have to pay for his small victory. Clearly, he had to conclude his investigation before the situation became too complicated, if it wasn't already. A journalist rooting around in church matters was the final straw. Absorbed in these thoughts, Quart crossed the Plaza Virgen de los Reyes without noticing a couple – a man and a woman – sitting on a bench. They stood up and followed him at a distance. The man was fat and wore a white suit and a panama hat; the woman was in a polka-dot dress and had a strange kiss-curl on her forehead. They walked behind Quart, arm in arm like a husband and wife enjoying the cool evening air. But when they came to the Bar La Giralda, they exchanged looks with a man in a polo-neck sweater and checked jacket in the doorway. At that moment, bells began to ring throughout Seville, startling the pigeons dozing under the eaves.

When the tall priest went into La Albahaca, Don Ibrahim gave El Potro del Mantelete a coin and told him to telephone Peregil from the nearest call box and fill him in. A little less than an hour later, Pencho Gavira's henchman turned up to see how things were going. He carried a Marks & Spencer's plastic bag and looked tired. He found his troops strategically deployed about the Plaza de Santa Cruz outside the restaurant, a converted seventeenth-century mansion. El Potro leaned against a wall, motionless, near the exit leading to the Arab wall; La Niña Puñales sat crocheting at the foot of the iron cross in the middle of the square; and Don Ibrahim's bulky shadow moved from one side of the square to another, swinging his walking stick, the ember of a Montecristo cigar visible beneath the broad brim of his pale straw hat.

"He's inside," he told Peregil. "With the lady."

He made his report, pulling his watch from his waistcoat and consulting it by the light of the street lamp. Twenty minutes earlier, he had sent La Niña into the restaurant for reconnaissance, pretending to sell flowers. Later he himself exchanged a few words with the waiters when he went in to buy the cigar he was now smoking. The couple were sitting at a good table beneath a reasonable copy of *The Topers* by Velázquez. The lady had ordered scallop salad with basil and truffles, while the Reverend Father had chosen sautéed goose liver with honey vinaigrette. They were drinking uncarbonated mineral water and red wine, a Pesquera from the banks of the Duero. Don Ibrahim apologised that he hadn't been able to ascertain the vintage. But, as he told Peregil, twirling his moustache, excessive curiosity might have aroused the suspicions of the staff.

"And what are they talking about?" asked Peregil.

The former bogus lawyer shrugged. "That," he said, "is beyond the scope of my investigation."

Peregil considered the situation. Things were still under control. Don Ibrahim and his colleagues were doing well, and the cards they had given him looked good. In his world, as in almost every other, information meant money. It was a question of knowing how to get the best deal, the highest bid. Of course, he would have preferred to take all this back to his boss, Pencho Gavira, who was the principal interested party here, being both banker and husband. But the missing six million and Peregil's debt to loan shark Ruben Molina made it hard to think straight. Peregil had been sleeping badly for the last few days, and his ulcer was troubling him again. When he stood in front of the bathroom mirror this morning, constructing the complicated edifice that concealed his baldness, Peregil saw only despair in the sour face staring back at him. He was going bald, his digestion was wrecked, he owed his boss six million and almost twice that to a moneylender, and he very much suspected that his last glorious spasm with Dolores La Negra had left him with the alarming little itch in his urogenital tract. Just what he needed.

And there was worse. Peregil glanced at the rotund form of Don Ibrahim, who awaited instructions, at La Niña Puñales crocheting in the lamplight, and at El Potro del Mantelete on the corner. To all the things complicating Peregil's life could be added another: the information obtained by the three partners was already circulating on the market, because Peregil needed cash urgently. Bonafé had slipped him another cheque, this time as payment for confidential information about the priest from Rome, Peregil's boss's wife (or ex-wife or whatever she was), and the business of Our Lady of the Tears. The next step was obvious: Macarena Bruner and the elegant priest would make the front page of every magazine in Seville. Their dinner at La Albahaca, rang the cash register in Peregil's brain. Bonafé paid well, but he was a dangerous and unpredictable character. Selling him one priest, or several, had its attraction. But blowing the whistle on Peregil's boss's wife for a second time was more than a little mischief – it was institutional betrayal.

He had to foresee every eventuality. Gathering information was a type of life insurance for him. With that in mind, he turned to Don Ibrahim, who stood solemnly in the shadows with his smoking cigar, walking stick over one arm, and thumbs hooked in his waistcoat, awaiting instructions. Peregil was pleased with him and his colleagues and felt a little more optimistic. He almost put his hand in his pocket to pay for the Montecristo from the restaurant, but he stopped himself in time. He shouldn't encourage their bad habits.

"Good work," he said.

Don Ibrahim didn't answer. He merely drew on his cigar and glanced at La Niña and El Potro, giving Peregil to understand that the credit was to be shared with them.

"Carry on like this," added Pencho Gavira's henchman. "I want to know everything, right down to when the priest takes a piss."

"What about the lady?"

This was touchier. Peregil chewed his lower lip anxiously. "Absolute discretion," he said at last. "I'm only interested in her business with this priest or with the older one. But I want every detail."

"What about the other business?"

"What other business?"

"You know. The other business."

Don Ibrahim looked around, embarrassed. He read the newspaper *ABC* every day, but he also glanced at *Q&S* from time to time. La Niña bought it along with ***Hola***, ***Semana***, and *Diez Minutos*. In the former bogus lawyer's opinion, *Q&S* was more sensationalist and tacky than the rest. The photos of Señora Bruner and the bullfighter were in very poor taste. She was from a distinguished family, and a married woman to boot.

"The priests," said Peregil. "Concentrate on the priests." Suddenly he remembered what he had in the bag: a Canon camera with a long zoom. He'd just bought it, second-hand, and he hoped that the outlay – another gash in the soft underbelly of his straitened finances – would prove worthwhile. "Are you any good with a camera?"

Don Ibrahim looked offended. "Of course." He put his hand on his heart. "In my youth I was a photographer in Havana." He thought a moment, then added, "That's how I paid for my studies."

In the dim light of the square, Peregil could see the gold chain, with Hemingway's watch gleaming against Don Ibrahim's paunch. "Your studies?" he asked.

"That's right."

"Your law studies, I suppose."

The fraud had been exposed a few years ago in the papers, and they both knew it, as did all of Seville. But Don Ibrahim swallowed and gravely held Peregil's gaze. "Of course." He paused with dignity. "What else?"

Peregil said nothing and handed him the bag. After all, he thought, what would become of us if we didn't have ourselves? In life's shipwreck we cling to what we can.

"I want photos," he ordered. "Anytime that priest and the lady meet, I want a picture. Discreetly, OK? So they don't notice. You have two rolls of high-speed film in there in case there's not much light, so don't think of using a flash."

They stopped under a streetlight and Don Ibrahim peered inside the bag. "That would be difficult," he said. "There is no flash here."

Peregil, lighting a cigarette, shrugged. "Are you kidding? The cheapest was 25,000 pesetas."

La Albahaca was situated in a seventeenth-century mansion. The proprietors lived on the second floor, and three of the rooms on the ground floor were given over to the restaurant. Although the place was full, the head waiter – Macarena Bruner addressed him as Diego – had reserved for them a table next to the large fireplace in the best room, by a leaded window looking out on the Plaza de Santa Cruz. They made quite an entrance. She looked very beautiful in a black suit with a short skirt, escorted by the slim, dark figure of Lorenzo Quart. La Albahaca was where a certain class of Sevillian brought guests from out of town, to show them off and to be seen, and the arrival of the daughter of the duchess of El Nuevo Extremo with a priest didn't go unnoticed. Macarena exchanged a couple of greetings as she entered, and people at nearby tables were fascinated. Heads bowed, voices whispered and jewels sparkled in the candlelight. The whole of Seville will know about this tomorrow, Quart thought.

"I haven't been to Rome since my honeymoon," she was saying over her appetiser, apparently unaware of the stir they had caused. "The Pope gave us a special audience. I was in black, with a comb and mantilla. Very Spanish . . . Why are you looking at me like that?"

Quart slowly chewed his last piece of goose liver and put his knife and fork on his plate. Above the candle flame, Macarena Bruner's eyes followed his every movement. "You don't seem like a married woman," he said.

She laughed, and the flame enhanced the glints of honey in her eyes. "Do you think the life I lead isn't suitable for a married woman?"

He rested an elbow on the table and tilted his head a little to one side, evasively. "I don't pass judgement on that kind of thing," he said.

"But you wore your collar, instead of a tie as you promised."

They regarded each other unhurriedly. The shadow from the candle hid the lower half of her face, but Quart guessed she was smiling from the glow in her eyes.

"I make no secret of the life I lead," said Macarena. "I left the marital home. I have a boyfriend who's a bullfighter. And before him I had another boyfriend." Her pause was calculated, perfect. In spite of himself, he admired her nerve. "Does that shock you?"

Quart put his finger on the handle of his knife. It wasn't his job to be shocked by such things, he said gently. That was a matter for her confessor, Father Ferro. Priests, too, had their specialities.

"And what's yours? Scalp hunter, as the archbishop says?"

She put out her hand and moved the candle to one side. Now he could see her ample mouth with its heart-shaped upper lip. Under her jacket she wore a low-cut raw silk shirt. Her short skirt was edged with lace. She wore black tights and pumps, also black. The outfit showed off legs that were too long and too shapely for the peace of mind of any priest, including Quart. Although he had more experience of the world than most priests. Not that that guaranteed anything.

"We were talking about you," he said, enjoying the strange instinct that made him stand crabwise, like a dueller.

Macarena Bruner now looked disingenuous. "Me? What else do you want to know?" she asked. "I'm one metre seventy-four centimetres tall, I'm thirty-five but don't look it, I have a university degree, I belong to the Sisters of the Virgin of El Rocio, and at the Seville *feria* I never go in for flounces, I wear a short dress and Cordobes hat." She stopped, as if trying to remember if there was anything else. She fingered the gold bracelet on her left wrist. "When I got married, my mother ceded the dukedom of Azahara to me, a title I don't use. When she dies, I'll inherit another thirty or so titles, twelve grandeeships, the Casa del Postigo with some furniture and paintings, and just enough money to keep me in the manner to which I am accustomed. I'm in charge of preserving what remains and sorting out the family archives. I'm now working on a book about the dukes of El Nuevo Extremo under the Hapsburgs . . . I don't need to tell you the rest." She drank some of her wine. "You can read about it in any gossip magazine."

"The gossip doesn't seem to bother you."

She held her wine glass. "That's true," she said. "It doesn't. Shall I confide in you?"

Quart shook his head. "Maybe you shouldn't." He was being honest. He felt relaxed but also expectant, amused, strangely lucid. He put it down to the wine, although he'd had little. "I don't even know why you invited me to dinner here this evening."

Macarena Bruner took another sip of wine, slowly. "I can think of several reasons," she said at last, putting down her glass. "You're extremely courteous, for one. Nothing like some priests with their unctuous manners . . . In you, courtesy seems to be a way of keeping people at a distance." She glanced quickly at his face – his mouth perhaps – and then at his hands on the table. "You're also very quiet. You don't chatter people into a daze. In that respect you remind me of Don Priamo . . ." As the waiter cleared away the plates, she smiled at Quart. "And then your hair's grey and very short, like a soldier's, like one of my favourite characters: Sir Marhalt, the quiet knight in Steinbeck's *Acts of King Arthur and his Noble Knights*. When I read it as a young girl, I fell madly in love with Marhalt. Are those enough reasons? And anyway, as Gris said, for a priest you certainly know how to wear your clothes. You're the most interesting priest I've ever seen, if that's any use to you."

"Not much use, in my line of work."

Macarena nodded, approving of his tranquil answer. "You also remind me of the chaplain at my convent school," she went on. "You could tell for days beforehand that he was coming to say Mass, because all the nuns were in a flutter. In the end he ran off with one of them, the plumpest, who used to teach us chemistry. Did you know that nuns sometimes fall for priests? That's what happened to Gris. She was the head of a college in Santa Barbara, California, and one day she discovered to her horror that she was in love with the bishop of her diocese. He was due to visit the college, and there she was in front of the mirror, plucking her eyebrows and debating about eyeshadow . . . What do you think of that?"

She looked to see Quart's reaction, but he remained impassive. If she was trying to shock him, she hadn't even come close. She would have been surprised to know how many loves of priests and nuns had been distorted by the IEA.

"So what did she do?" he asked.

Macarena made a sweeping gesture in the air and her bracelet glinted as it slid up her arm. At nearby tables, eyes were following her every move. "Well, she broke the mirror and with a piece of glass cut a vein. Then she went to see her mother superior and asked for a period of freedom to reflect. That was a few years ago."

The head waiter was standing by her side, expressionless, as if he hadn't heard a word. He hoped everything was to their satisfaction, and what would madam like for dinner? She ordered only a salad, and Quart didn't have a main course either, and they both declined the dessert that they were offered on the house, as the management was sorry that her ladyship and the reverend father had so little appetite. They decided to go on with the wine while they waited for their coffee.

"Have you known Sister Marsala long?" Quart asked.

"That sounds so strange. Sister Marsala . . . I've never thought of her like that."

She had almost finished her wine. Quart took the bottle and poured her another glass. His own was barely touched.

"Gris is older than I am," she said. "We bumped into each other in Seville several times a few years back. She came here quite often with her American students on summer courses in fine art . . . I met her when they came to do practice restoration on the summer dining room in my house. I introduced her to Father Ferro and got her accepted on the church restoration project, when relations with the archbishop were still cordial."

"Why are you so interested in that church?"

She looked at him as if he'd asked a strange question. Her family had built it. Her ancestors were buried there.

"Your husband doesn't seem to care much about it."

"Of course he doesn't. Pencho has his mind on other things."

The candlelight made the wine glow red as she lifted her glass to her lips. This time she took a long swallow, and Quart felt obliged to drink a little of his.

"And is it true," he said, wiping his mouth with his napkin, "that you no longer live together although you're still married?"

She blinked. She didn't seem to have expected two questions in a row about her marriage that evening. There was amusement in her eyes. "Yes," she said. "We no longer live together. And yet neither of us has asked for a divorce, or a separation, or anything. Maybe he hopes to get me back. By marrying me, to everyone's applause, he has ensured himself a place in society."

Quart glanced round at the people at the neighbouring tables and then leaned towards her a little. "I'm sorry," he said. "Who do you mean by everyone?"

"Haven't you met my godfather? Don Octavio Machuca was a friend of my father, and he's particularly fond of my mother and me. As he says, I'm the daughter he never had. He wanted my future to be secure, so he encouraged my marriage to the brightest young talent at the Cartujano Bank – who's destined to be his successor now that he's about to retire."

"Is that why you got married? For security?"

Macarena's hair slid forward over her face, and she brushed it back. She was assessing, trying to work out how interested he really was in her.

"Well, Pencho is an attractive man. And he has a very good brain, as they say. And a virtue: he's brave. He's one of the few men I've met who's prepared to risk everything, either for a dream or an ambition. In the case of my husband – ex-husband, or whatever you want to call him – it's ambition." She smiled slightly. "I suppose I was even in love with him when we got married."

"So what happened?"

"Nothing, really. I kept my side of the bargain, he kept his. But he made a mistake. Or several. He should have left our church alone."

"Your church?"

"Mine. Father Ferro's. The duchess's. The church of the people who attend Mass there every day."

Quart laughed. "Do you always refer to your mother as the duchess?"

"When I'm talking to other people about her, yes." She smiled, with a tenderness now that Quart hadn't seen in her before. "She likes it. She also likes geraniums, Mozart, old-fashioned priests, and Coca-Cola. Rather unusual, don't you think, for a woman of seventy who sleeps in her pearl necklace once a week and still insists on calling her chauffeur a coachman? You haven't met her yet? Come and have coffee with us tomorrow afternoon, if you like. Don Priamo visits us every afternoon to recite the rosary."

"I doubt that Father Ferro will want to see me. He doesn't like me much."

"I'll sort it out. Or my mother will. She and Don Priamo get on very well. Maybe it would be a good opportunity for you and him to have a talk, man to man . . . Does one say 'man to man' when talking about priests?"

Quart was thinking of something else, "As for your husband . . ."

"You do ask a lot of questions. I suppose that's the reason you're here."

She seemed sorry that that was the reason. She was looking at his hands again, just as she had when they first met in the hotel lobby. Embarrassed, he'd removed them from the table a couple of times. At last he decided to keep them on the tablecloth.

"What do you want to know about Pencho?" she asked. "That he was wrong to think he could buy me? That the church was why I declared war on him? That he can sometimes be an absolute bastard?"

She spoke matter-of-factly. The people at a nearby table were leaving and a few of them greeted her. They all stared at Quart, particularly the women. Blonde and tanned, the women had the air of upper-class Andalusians who hadn't known a day's hardship in their lives. Macarena responded with a nod and a smile. Quart watched her closely.

"Why don't you ask for a divorce?" he asked.

"Because I'm Catholic."

He couldn't tell if she was serious or not. They said nothing for a moment, and he settled back in his chair, still watching her. In the candlelight, her skin was dark in contrast to her ivory necklace and silk shirt. Her large dark eyes looked back into his. He realised then that his soul was in peril. Had it been a share on the stockmarket, its value would have plunged.

He opened his mouth and spoke, to fill the silence. Something appropriate, no doubt, but five seconds later he forgot what it had been. Now she was saying something, and Quart thought of Spada. Prayer and cold showers, he had said to the Mastiff on the steps of the Piazza di Spagna.

"There are things I'd like to explain to you," she said. "But I don't know how . . ." She stared past him. He nodded, not quite sure why. The main thing was to pay attention to her words again. "In life, you pay very dearly for certain luxuries, and now it's Pencho's turn to pay. He's the type who asks for the bill without flinching, rapping on the bar with his knuckles for service. He's so macho," she said sardonically. "But he's having a hard time now. He may not show it, but I know, and he knows that I know. Seville is like a village; we love gossip. Every whisper, every smile behind his back is a blow to his pride." She gestured round the restaurant. "Imagine what they'll say now they know I'm having dinner with you."

"Was that what you wanted?" Quart was in control of himself again. "To show me off like a trophy?"

She looked at him wearily, knowingly. "Perhaps," she said. "Women are so much more complicated. Men are so straightforward in their lies, so childish in their contradictions . . . So consistent in their vileness." The head waiter brought the coffee; with milk for her, black for him. Macarena added one lump of sugar and smiled thoughtfully. "You can be sure that Pencho will know all about this tomorrow morning. God, some things have to be paid for very slowly." She sipped her coffee and looked at Quart. "Maybe I shouldn't have said 'God'. It sounded like an oath. Thou shalt not take the Lord's name in vain after all."

Quart placed his spoon carefully on his saucer. "I sometimes do it too," he said.

"It's strange." She leaned forward on her elbows, and her silk shirt brushed the edge of the table. Quart could sense what was inside: heavy, brown, soft. He needed more than a cold shower. "I've known Don Priamo for ten years, since he first came to the parish, but I can't imagine a priest's life from the inside. I'd never thought about it until now, looking at you." She gazed again at his hands and then up at his dog collar. "How do priests manage with the three vows?"

If ever there had been an untimely question. He stared at his wine glass and summoned all his composure. "Each of us gets by as he can," he replied. "Some think of it as negotiated obedience, shared chastity, and liquid poverty." He raised his glass as if to make a toast, but put it down untouched and sipped his coffee instead. Macarena laughed. Her laugh was so open and contagious that Quart almost laughed too.

"And you?" she asked, still smiling. "Do you observe your vows?"

"I tend to." He put down his cup, wiped his mouth, folded his napkin carefully and placed it on the table. "I make sure I think through the implications, but I always follow the rules. Some things don't function without obedience, and the firm I work for is one of them."

"Do you mean Don Priamo?"

Quart arched his eyebrows with calculated indifference. He hadn't been alluding to anyone in particular, he said. But yes, now that she mentioned it, Father Ferro wasn't exactly an exemplary priest. He did his own thing, to put it charitably. Deadly sin number one.

"You don't know anything about his life, so you can't judge him."

"I'm not judging. I just want to understand."

"No you don't," she insisted. "For most of his life he was the parish priest in a tiny village up in the Pyrenees. It was cut off by snow for weeks at a time, and sometimes he had to trudge eight or ten kilometres to give a dying man extreme unction. His parishioners were all old and died off one by one. He buried them with his own hands, until there was nobody left. The experience gave him a certain view on life and death, and on the role you priests have in the world. To him, this church is terribly important. He believes it's needed, and that every church closed or lost is a piece of heaven that disappears. Nobody takes any notice, but instead of giving in, he fights. He says he lost enough battles up there, in the mountains."

That was all very well, said Quart. Very moving. He'd even seen a couple of films like that. But Father Ferro was still subject to Church discipline. We priests, he said, can't go through life proclaiming independent republics where we please. Not with things as they are now.

She shook her head. "You don't know him well enough."

"He won't let me get to know him."

"We'll fix that tomorrow. I promise." She pointed. "You obviously meant what you said about liquid poverty. You've barely touched your wine. But you don't look so poor in other respects. You dress well. I know expensive clothes when I see them, even on a priest."

"It's because of my work. I have to deal with people. And have dinner with attractive duchesses in Seville." They looked into each other's eyes, and neither of them smiled this time. "This is my uniform."

There was a brief silence.

"Do you have a cassock?" she asked.

"Of course. But I don't often wear it."

The waiter brought the bill. Macarena wouldn't let Quart pay. She invited him, she said firmly. So he just watched while she took out a gold American Express card. She always let her husband pay the bills, she said mischievously when the waiter had gone. It worked out cheaper than alimony.

"We haven't discussed the last of your three vows," she said then. "Do you also practise shared celibacy?"

"I'm afraid I'm celibate, period."

She nodded slowly and looked round the restaurant before turning to him again. She stared at him, assessing him. "Don't tell me you've never been with a woman."

There are some questions that can't be answered at eleven at night in a restaurant in Seville, by candlelight. But she didn't seem to expect an answer. She carefully took a pack of cigarettes from her bag, put one in her mouth, and then, with a brazenness both calculated and natural, she took a plastic lighter from beneath her bra strap. Quart watched her light the cigarette, forcing himself to think of nothing. Only later did he allow himself to wonder what the hell he was getting himself into.

In a closed world governed by the concept of sin, where contact with women was forbidden, the only even unofficially accepted solution to sex was masturbation or a clandestine liaison later atoned for through the sacrament of penance. For Quart, life as a diplomat and his work for the Institute of External Affairs facilitated what Spada – always good at euphemism – referred to as tactical alibis. But in fact, as a result of his education in Rome and his work over the past ten years, Quart's attitude to sex had become different from that of other priests, who were dominated by the sordid gossip of the seminary and the ways of the Church. The general good of the Church, considered as an end in itself, sometimes justified certain sins; so the success of a handsome nunciature secretary with the wives of ministers, financiers and ambassadors, women who yielded readily to the temptation to adopt an interesting young priest, opened many doors that were barred to older, more leathery monsignors or eminences. Spada called it the Stendhal Syndrome, after two of that writer's characters, Fabrice del Dongo and Julien Sorel. When Quart joined the IEA, Spada recommended that he read the novels. For the Mastiff, culture wasn't at odds with duty. It was left to the moral discretion and intelligence of each priest, God's soldier on a battlefield where the only weapons were prayer and common sense. Risks accompanied the advantages gained from confidences given at receptions, or during private conversations or confession. Women came to priests, seeking a substitute for unavailable men or indifferent husbands. And nothing was more troubling to Old Adam, who lurked beneath most cassocks, than the innocence of a young girl or the pleas of a frustrated woman. Ultimately, the unofficial permission of superiors was more or less assured – the Church of Peter in its wisdom had thus survived for centuries – as long as there was no scandal and results were achieved.

Quart's faith, on the other hand, was that of a professional soldier, and his celibacy was a question of pride – and therefore a sin rather than a virtue. But sin or not, it was a rule that governed his life. Like some of the ghosts he saw when he stared into the darkness, the Knight Templar whose sword was his only weapon beneath a godless sky needed such rules if he was to face with dignity the thunder of Saracen cavalry roaring down from the hill of Hattin.

He returned to the present with difficulty. Macarena was smoking, one elbow on the table, supporting her chin with the hand that held her cigarette. Somehow he could feel the troubling proximity of her legs. She was very close. He could have reached out and brushed her skin with his fingers. But with the same hand that tingled with the desire to touch her he took the postcard to Captain Xaloc from his jacket pocket instead and placed it on the table.

"Tell me about Carlota Bruner," he said.

Instantly the atmosphere changed. She stubbed out her cigarette and looked at him sharply. The gold flecks in her eyes were gone. "Where did you get that postcard?"

"Somebody put it in my room."

Macarena stared at the yellowed photo of the church. She shook her head. "It's mine. From Carlota's trunk. You can't possibly have it."

"Well, I do." Quart turned the postcard over. "Why isn't there a postmark?" he asked.

Her anxious eyes went from Quart to the postcard and back. He repeated the question. She nodded but didn't answer immediately. She picked up the card and examined it. "Because it was never posted," she said. "Carlota was my great-aunt. She was in love with Manuel Xaloc, a poor sailor. Gris said she told you the story . . ." Macarena shook her head, as if denying something or overcome by sadness. "When Captain Xaloc emigrated to America, she wrote him a card or letter almost every week for years. But her father the duke, my great-grandfather Luis Bruner, prevented the letters from getting through. He bribed the post office employees. In six years she didn't receive a single letter, and we believe he didn't either. When Xaloc came back for her, Carlota had lost her mind. She spent days at the window, watching the river. She didn't recognise him."

Quart pointed at the card. "And what happened to the letters?"

"Nobody dared destroy them. They ended up in the trunk where all Carlota's things were stored after she died in 1910. I was fascinated by the trunk when I was a child: I'd try on the dresses, the jet necklaces . . ." Quart saw the beginnings of a smile on her lips, but her eyes returned to the postcard and the smile vanished. "In her youth, Carlota went with my great-grandparents to the Universal Exposition in Paris, and to the ruins of Carthage in Tunisia. She brought back old coins. There are also boat timetables and hotel brochures, old lace and muslins. A whole life. Imagine the effect it all had on me when I was ten or eleven. I read every single letter. My great-aunt seemed such a romantic character. She still fascinates me."

She was running a fingernail on the tablecloth, around the postcard. She stopped, thoughtful.

"A moving love story," she said, looking up at Quart. "And like all moving love stories it had an unhappy ending."

Quart said nothing, wanting her to go on with the story. But she was interrupted by the waiter, who brought her credit card receipt. Quart noticed her signature: nervous, full of angles as sharp as daggers. She gazed at the cigarette stub in the ashtray, lost in thought.

"There's a beautiful song," she went on after a moment, "sung by Carlos Cano, with lyrics by Antonio Burgos: 'I still remember that girl and her piano in Seville . . .' It makes me want to cry every time I hear it . . . Do you know there's a legend surrounding the story of Carlota and Manuel Xaloc?" Her smile was uncharacteristically shy and indecisive. Quart realised that she believed in the legend. "On moonlit nights, Carlota reappears at her window while her lover's ghostly schooner sails down the Guadalquivir." She leaned forward, and again Quart once again felt she was too close. "When I was little, I spent whole nights looking out for them. And once I saw them. She was a pale shadow at the window. And down on the river, in the mist, the sails of an old ship slid slowly out of sight."

Macarena fell silent and leaned back in her chair. The distance between them returned. "After Sir Marhalt," she said, "my second love was Captain Xaloc . . ." Her look was provocative. "Do you think it's an absurd story?"

"Not at all. Everyone has ghosts."

"And what haunts you?"

Quart smiled with a distant look in his eye. Wind and sun, and rain. The taste of salt in his mouth. Memories of a poor childhood, of knees always dirty, and him watching the sea for hours. His youth had been intellectually confined, dominated by discipline, with some happy memories of companionship and brief moments of satisfied ambition. Solitude at airports, over a book, in a hotel room. And fear and hatred in the eyes of other men: the banker Lupara, Nelson Corona, Priamo Ferro. Corpses – real and imaginary, past and future.

"Nothing special," he said coolly. "Like you, ships that set sail never to return. And a man. A Knight Templar in chain mail leaning on his sword, in a desert."

She looked at him strangely, as if seeing him for the first time. She said nothing.

"But ghosts," added Quart, "don't leave postcards in hotel rooms."

Macarena touched the card still lying on the table with the writing face up: I come here to pray for you every day . . . Her lips moved silently as she read the words that never reached Captain Xaloc. "I don't understand," she said finally. "The card was at my house, in the trunk with the rest of Carlota's things. Somebody must have taken it from there."

"Who?"

"I have no idea."

"How many people know about the letters?"

She thought hard. "No," she said after a while. "It's too absurd."

Quart reached with his hand and saw Macarena shift back in her chair, almost as if in fear. He turned over the card and showed her the photograph of the church. "There's nothing absurd about it," he said. "This is the place where Carlota Bruner is buried, near Captain Xaloc's pearls. The church that your husband wants to demolish and that you're defending. It's the reason for my presence in Seville, because two people have died there." He looked up at her. "A church that, according to a mysterious computer hacker we've called Vespers, kills to defend itself."

She began to smile, but the smile faded to preoccupation. When she spoke, surprisingly, the tone was more annoyed than anxious. "Don't say that. It scares me."

Quart watched her turn the plastic lighter over in her fingers. He felt that Macarena Bruner was lying. She wasn't the kind of woman who scared easily.

Since Vespers' appearance a week ago, Father Ignacio Arregui and his team of Jesuits – all computer experts – had been watching the central Vatican system in twelve-hour shifts. It was now ten minutes to one in the morning, and Arregui went to get coffee from the vending machine in the corridor. The machine accepted his hundred-lire coin but returned only an empty cup and a little heap of sugar. The Jesuit cursed, glancing out of the window at the Belvedere Palace. He searched his pockets for more coins and made a second attempt. This time he got a coffee but no sugar. Luckily the previous cup had remained upright in the dustbin so he used the sugar from that to sweeten his drink. He went back to the computer room.

"Here he is again, Father."

Cooey, the Irishman, was staring excitedly at a screen. Another young Jesuit, an Italian called Garofi, was desperately typing at a second terminal.

"Is it Vespers?" asked Father Arregui. He stared over Cooey's shoulder, fascinated by the blinking of the red and blue icons and the vertiginous speed with which the files checked by the hacker scrolled past on the screen. The hacker's movements were shown on one monitor while, on another, Father Garofi tried to track him down.

"I think so," answered the Irishman. "He knows the way and he's going really fast."

"Has he got to the SSs?"

"Some of them. But he's clever: he's not falling into them."

Father Arregui took a sip of coffee. It scalded his tongue. "Damn him," he said.

The SSs – Sadducean Snares, as the team had nicknamed them – were like nets at the mouth of a river, in which hackers were snared or at least revealed information that made it possible to track them. The traps that had been laid for Vespers were sophisticated electronic labyrinths that forced an intruder to show his hand.

"He's looking for INMAVAT," said Cooey.

There was again a hint of admiration in his voice. Frowning, Father Arregui glanced at the young man. It was to be expected, he thought as drank his coffee. He couldn't help feeling professional excitement himself, when he saw a member of the computer fraternity doing his stuff so stealthily and cleanly. Even if Vespers was a criminal who was giving them all sleepless nights.

"He's in," said Cooey.

Garofi stopped typing and simply watched. INMAVAT, the restricted file for high-ranking members of the Curia, was there on screen for all to see.

"Yes, it's Vespers," said the Irishman, as if he'd recognised an old friend.

Garofi watched the cursor of the scanner connected to the police and the Vatican telephone system. "He's doing the same as before," said the Italian. "Hiding his entry point by jumping from one phone network to another."

Father Arregui's eyes were riveted to the scrolling list of eighty-four INMAVAT users. They'd spent several days installing a Sadducean Snare for anyone who tried to get into V01A, the Holy Father's personal computer. The trap would be activated if anyone tried to get in without using the password: once the hacker was inside INMAVAT, he would unwittingly trail a hidden code after himself. When he reached V01A, the signal would switch him to another file, V01ATS, where he couldn't cause any harm and where he'd leave his new message, thinking he was leaving it for the Pope.

The cursor blinked beside V01A. Ten long seconds passed, during which the three Jesuits held their breath, watching the second computer screen. At last the cursor gave a double blink, and a clock appeared.

"He's getting in," said Cooey in a whisper, as if Vespers might hear.

Father Arregui bit his lower lip and undid a button on his cassock. If Vespers realised there was a trap, he might get angry. And who could tell what an angry hacker might do inside a file as delicate as INMAVAT? But the team of Vatican experts had a final trick up its sleeve: with just one keystroke, INMAVAT could be taken out of the system. The problem was that if that happened, Vespers would know they were on to him and disappear. Worse, he might return on another occasion with a new tactic. A killer virus, for instance, infecting and destroying everything it touched.

The clock disappeared, and a new window opened on the screen.

"There he goes," said Garofi.

Vespers was inside V01A, and for one agonising moment the three Jesuits watched anxiously to see which of the two files, the real or the fake, he'd entered. Cooey read out in a tense voice as the code appeared on the screen:

"Vee-Zero-One-A-T-S."

He smiled proudly. Vespers had stepped into the Sadducean Snare. The Pope's personal computer was out of his reach.

"Thank God," said Father Arregui.

He'd pulled the button off his cassock. Holding it in his hand, he leaned over to read the message:

> Lift up thy feet unto the perpetual desolations; even all
> that the enemy hath done wickedly in the sanctuary.
> Thine enemies roar in the midst of thy congregations;
> they set up their ensigns for signs.
> But now they break down the carved work thereof at
> once with axes and hammers.
> They have cast fire into thy sanctuary; they have
> defiled by casting down the dwelling place of thy
> name to the ground.
> O God, how long shall the adversary reproach? Shall
> the enemy blaspheme thy name for ever?

After that Vespers disappeared.

"There's no way we can follow him," said Garofi, mouse clicking hopelessly. "As he switches phone networks, he leaves behind a kind of explosive charge that erases any trace of his route. This hacker certainly knows what he's doing."

"And he knows the Psalms," said Father Cooey, switching on the printer to get a copy of the text. "It's sixty-four, isn't it?"

Father Arregui shook his head. "Seventy-four. Psalm seventy-four," he said, still staring anxiously at Garofi's screen.

"Now we know one more thing about him," said Cooey suddenly. "The man has a sense of humour."

The other two priests looked at the screen. Little spheres bounced like ping-pong balls, multiplying at every bounce. When two of them collided there was an explosion and a small mushroom cloud with the word BOOM in the middle.

Arregui was indignant. "The swine," he said. "The heretic."

He became aware that he was still holding the button from his cassock. He threw it in the bin. Still watching the screen, Fathers Cooey and Garofi chuckled quietly.

VII
The Bottle of Anis del Mono

In the distant past when, studying the sublime Science, we would lean over the mystery replete with heavy enigmas . . .
Fulcanelli, *The Mystery of Cathedrals*

It was a little after eight in the morning when Quart walked across the square towards Our Lady of the Tears. The sun shone on the faded belfry but had not yet risen above the line of eaves of the houses, painted red-ochre and white, and the orange trees were still in shade. Their fragrance accompanied him to the door of the church, where a beggar sat on the ground, his crutches against the wall. Quart gave him a coin and went inside, stopping for a moment beside the figure of Jesus surrounded by ex-votos. The Mass hadn't yet reached the offertory.

He sat at the back. About twenty of the faithful sat in the pews in front, occupying half the nave. The rest of the pews were still piled up against the wall, amongst the scaffolding. The altarpiece light was on, and beneath the motley ensemble of carvings and images, at the foot of the Virgin of the Tears, Don Priamo Ferro performed Mass assisted by Father Oscar. The congregation consisted mostly of women and old people; people of modest means, pensioners, housewives, office workers on their way to work. Some of the women had baskets or shopping trolleys. Two or three elderly women were dressed in black, and one of them, kneeling not far from Quart, had a veil over her head, the kind women wore to Mass twenty years ago.

Father Ferro came forward to read the Gospel. His vestments were white, and, beneath the chasuble and stole, Quart could see that he wore an amice – the strip of linen that, until the second Vatican Council, priests had worn over their shoulders while performing

Mass, in memory of the cloth that covered Christ's face. Only very traditional or very elderly priests continued to wear the vestment, but it wasn't the only anachronism. Father Ferro's old chasuble, for instance, was bell-shaped, a style that had been replaced by one lighter and more comfortable.

"And Jesus said to his disciples . . ."

The old priest had read the text hundreds of times during his life and hardly needed the book open on the lectern. His gaze was fixed on some vague point in space before the congregation. He didn't have a microphone, and he didn't need one in such a small church; his loud, flat voice rang out authoritatively in the silence of the nave. It left no room for argument or doubt; nothing but those words, pronounced in the name of the Other, had significance or value. This was the Word.

Verily, verily, I say unto you, That ye shall weep and lament, but the world shall rejoice: and ye shall be sorrowful, but your sorrow shall be turned into joy.

And ye now therefore have sorrow: but I will see you again, and your heart shall rejoice, and your joy no man taketh from you . . .

"Word of God," he said, returning behind the altar, and the congregation recited the Creed. With little surprise, Quart caught sight of Macarena Bruner. She sat three rows in front of him, her head bowed in prayer. She wore dark glasses and jeans, her hair was tied in a ponytail, and her jacket was draped over her shoulders. Quart looked back at the altar and met Father Oscar's eyes. He was watching Quart inscrutably while Father Ferro continued to celebrate Mass, aware of nothing but the ritual of his words and gestures:

"Benedictus est, Domine, deus universi, quia de tua largitate accepimus panem . . ."

Quart listened. Father Ferro was pronouncing those sections of the Mass not directly addressed to the congregation or not recited collectively, in the ancient canonical language of the Church. It wasn't a serious offence. Certain churches had a special right to do this, and in Rome the Pontiff himself often celebrated Mass in Latin. But since Paul VI, ecclesiastical regulations stipulated that Mass be said in the language of the parish, so that congregations find it easier to comprehend and participate. Father Ferro had not accepted all the modern reforms of the Church.

"Per huius aquae et vini mysterium . . ."

Quart watched him closely during the offertory. Having placed the liturgical objects on the corporal, the priest raised to heaven the Host on the communion plate and then, mixing a few drops of water with the wine brought in cruets by Father Oscar, he also raised the chalice. He then turned to his assistant, who held out a small basin and a silver pitcher, and washed his hands.

"Lava me, Domine, ab iniquitate mea."

Quart followed the movement of Father Ferro's lips as he whispered the words in Latin. The lavabo was another custom that was almost extinct, although it was still part of the common order of Mass. Quart noticed other anachronisms, rituals that had rarely been performed since he was an altar boy of ten or eleven assisting his parish priest. Father Ferro placed his fingers against one another, beneath the stream of water poured by his assistant, and then, when he dried his hands, he kept his thumbs and index fingers together, in a circle, so that they shouldn't come into contact with anything else. He even turned the pages of the missal with the other three fingers, held rigid. He was observing, to the letter, the usage of old clerics who refused to accept change. All that remained was for him to officiate facing the altarpiece and the image of the Virgin, his back to the congregation, as was the practice thirty years ago. And Quart suspected it wouldn't have bothered Don Priamo Ferro in the slightest to do so, as he recited the canon, his stubborn head bowed with its uneven, bristly hair: *Te igitur, clementissime Pater.* His unshaven chin sunk into the collar of his chasuble, he whispered – the words perfectly audible in the absolute silence of the church – the prayers of the sacrifice of Mass, exactly as they had been pronounced for the past thirteen hundred years:

"Per ipsum, et cum ipso, et in ipso, est tibi Deo Patri omnipotenti . . ."

Despite his doubts about such anachronism and his disdain for Father Ferro, the priest in Lorenzo Quart could not but feel moved by the strange solemnity that the ritual conferred upon the old priest. As if the symbolic transformation being acted out at the altar turned the rough provincial priest into a figure of authority, giving him a spiritual power that made one forget the stained cassock and scuffed shoes, the threadbare chasuble. God – if there was a God behind all the gilded baroque carvings that surrounded the Virgin of the Tears – had without a doubt laid His hand, for a moment, on the shoulder of the grumpy old man bowed over the Host and chalice, performing a symbolic re-enactment of the mystery of the incarnation and death of the Son. At that moment, Quart thought as he observed the faces of the people around him – including Macarena Bruner – it mattered little whether there was a God prepared to punish or reward, to damn or grant eternal life. What mattered, in the silence filled by Father Ferro's harsh voice intoning the liturgy, were the people, their grave, calm faces intent on his hands and voice, whispering with him, whether they understood or not, a text that could be summed up in a single word: solace. It was a friendly hand in the darkness, a warmth to keep out the cold. And Quart, kneeling like them, his elbows on the back of the pew in front, repeated the words of the Consecration. He was uneasy, because he knew he had taken a first step towards understanding this church, its priest, the message sent by Vespers, and the reason he himself was here. It was easier, he realised, to despise Father Ferro than to see him, small and uncouth in his old-fashioned chasuble, creating with the words of the ancient mystery a humble haven where the twenty or so faces, most of them tired or bowed with age, watched – with fear, respect, hope – the piece of bread that the old priest held in his proud hands. He raised the chalice containing the wine, fruit of the vine and of man's labours, and then lowered it, transformed into the blood of Jesus, who Himself gave food and drink to His disciples at the Last Supper with the exact same words that Father Ferro now intoned, unchanged, twenty centuries later, beneath the tears of Carlota Bruner and Captain Xaloc: *Hoc facite in meam commemorationem.* Do this in my memory.

Mass was over. The church was deserted. Quart remained seated, motionless, after Don Priamo Ferro said *Ite, missa est* and walked away from the altar without glancing once in his direction. The congregation left one by one, including Macarena. She gave no sign of noticing Quart from behind her dark glasses as she passed. For a time, the old woman in the veil was the only other person there. While she prayed, Father Oscar emerged from the door to the vestry and extinguished the candles and the altarpiece light. He left again without looking round. The old woman then departed too, and the IEA agent was alone in the gloom of the empty church.

Despite his views and rigid adherence to the rules, Quart was a clear-minded man. His lucidity was like a silent curse. It prevented him from accepting totally the natural order of things but gave him nothing in return to make such clarity of mind bearable. For a priest, as in any other walk of life that required a belief in the myth that man held a privileged position in the universe, such lucidity was awkward and dangerous, for it said that human life was totally insignificant. In Quart's case, only willpower, expressed as self-discipline, offered protection from the naked truth that gave rise to weakness or apathy or despair. Maybe that was why he remained sitting there beneath the blackened vault that smelled of wax and cold, ancient stone. He looked round at the scaffolding, at the figure of Christ with dirty hair surrounded by ex-votos, the altarpiece in gloom, the flagstones worn by the footsteps of people long dead. He could still see Father Ferro's unshaven, frowning face at the altar pronouncing the mysterious words, and twenty faces looking back at him, momentarily relieved of their human condition by the hope that there was an all-powerful father and a better life where the just were rewarded and the heathens punished. This modest church was far removed from the vulgarity of Technicolour religions where anything went – open-air arenas, giant television screens, Goebbels' methods, rock concerts, the dialectic of the World Cup, and electronic sprinklers for holy water. Like the forgotten pawns who didn't know whether there was still a king to fight for, some pieces chose their square – a place where they could die. Father Ferro had chosen his, and Lorenzo Quart, experienced scalp hunter for the Roman Curia, didn't find it difficult to understand. Perhaps for that reason he now had doubts, sitting in the small, dilapidated, lonely church that the old priest had made into his tower: a refuge where he could defend the last of his flock from the prowling wolves outside.

Quart sat turning this over for some time. At last he stood and walked up the aisle to the high altar, his steps echoing beneath the elliptical dome of the transept. He stopped in front of the altarpiece and beheld the carved figures of Macarena's ancestors at prayer on either side of the Virgin of the Tears. Beneath her regal baldachin, accompanied by cherubs and saints, surrounded by leaves and flourishes of gilded wood, Martínez Montañes's carving was visible in the semidarkness, with light from the windows filtering through the rational, geometrical structure of the scaffolding. She looked very beautiful and very sad, her face turned upwards almost reproachfully, her palms empty, open, held out as if she were asking why her son had been taken from her. Captain Xaloc's twenty pearls gleamed gently on her cheeks, her crown of stars and her blue tunic. Beneath the tunic her bare foot rested on a crescent moon crushing a serpent's head.

". . . And I will put enmity between thee and the woman, and between thy seed and her seed . . ."

The voice came from behind him. Quart turned and saw Gris Marsala. She had come in noiselessly in her trainers.

"You creep like a cat," said Quart.

She laughed. As usual her hair was tied in a plait, and she wore a baggy sweatshirt and jeans spattered with paint and plaster. Quart pictured her applying makeup in front of a mirror before the bishop's visit, then her cold eyes multiplying in the fragments of shattered mirror. He looked for the scar. There it was: a pale line three centimetres long on the inside of her right wrist. He wondered if she'd meant to kill herself.

"Don't tell me you came to Mass," she said.

Quart nodded. She smiled indefinably. She noticed that he was looking at her scar, and turned her arm to hide it.

"That priest," said Quart.

He was about to add something but didn't – those two words said it all. After a moment she smiled again, as if at a private thought. "Yes," she said quietly, "that's exactly it." She seemed relieved and stopped hiding her wrist. She asked if he'd seen Macarena. Quart nodded.

"She comes here every morning, at eight," she said. "With her mother on Thursdays and Sundays."

"I would never have imagined she was so devout."

He hadn't intended it to sound sarcastic, but Gris Marsala stiffened and said, "Look, I really don't like your tone."

He took a few steps towards the altarpiece, regarded the Virgin, then turned to the woman again: "I'm sorry. But I had dinner with her last night, and she confuses me."

"I know you had dinner." Her blue eyes were fixed on him. "Macarena woke me at one in the morning and kept me on the phone for almost half an hour. One of the many things she said was that you would come to Mass."

"That's impossible," said Quart. "I came on impulse."

"Well, she was sure. She said that you would come, and would begin to understand." She stopped and looked at him with curiosity. "And have you?"

"What else did she tell you?" He tried to sound casual, ironic, but was afraid it was obvious that he wanted to know what Macarena had told her friend the nun. He was annoyed with himself.

Gris Marsala pursed her lips thoughtfully. "She said lots of things. That she likes you, for instance. And that you're not as different from Don Priamo as you think. She also said you're the sexiest priest she's ever seen." She smiled mischievously. "That was exactly how she put it."

"Why are you telling me this?"

"Because you asked."

"Please, don't make fun of me. I'm too old for that. Look, my hair's grey, like yours."

"I like your hair that short. So does Macarena."

"You haven't answered my question, Sister Marsala."

She laughed, and her eyes crinkled.

"Drop the title, please." She pointed to her dirty jeans and the scaffolding against the walls. "I don't know if any of this is appropriate for a nun."

It wasn't, thought Quart. Nor was her part in the strange triangle formed by the two of them and Macarena Bruner. And maybe a fourth, Father Ferro, should be included. Quart couldn't picture Gris Marsala in a convent, in a nun's habit. She had come a long way since Santa Barbara.

"Will you ever go back?"

She took a moment to answer, looking down the nave at the pews piled up by the door. She hooked her thumbs in the back pockets of her jeans, and Quart wondered how many nuns could have worn jeans like that – she was as slim as a young girl. Only her face and hair showed age. There was still something very attractive about her, about the way she moved.

"I don't know," she said thoughtfully. "Maybe it depends on this church, on what happens here. I think that's why I haven't left." She spoke without looking at Quart, squinting at the sunlight in the doorway. "Have you ever suddenly felt a void where you thought your heart was? The feeling lasts only a moment, then everything goes on as before, but you know that things aren't the same and you wonder what's wrong."

"And do you think you'll find the answer here?"

"I have no idea. But we search in places that may have answers."

Quart shifted uneasily from one leg to the other. He didn't like this sort of conversation, but he had to persevere – it might yield clues.

"I think," he said, "we spend our whole lives roaming round our tombs. Maybe that's the answer."

To make it sound less important, he smiled, but she wasn't fooled by the smile.

"I was right. You're not like other priests."

Quart didn't ask what that meant. They were both silent as they walked up the nave, past the walls with flaking paint and the cornices with tarnished gilding. At last she spoke again.

"There are things," she said, "places, people that leave their mark on you. Do you know what I mean? No, I don't think you do yet. I mean this town. This church. And Don Priamo, and Macarena." She stopped and smiled mockingly. "You need to know what you're getting into."

"Maybe I have nothing to lose."

"It's strange to hear you say that. Macarena says that's the most interesting thing about you. The impression you give." They were by the door now. "As if, like Don Priamo, you have nothing to lose."

The waiter turned the handle of the awning until Pencho Gavira and Octavio Machuca's table was shaded. A bootblack sat at the old banker's feet, polishing his shoes.

"Could I have the other foot now, sir?"

Machuca obediently placed his other foot on top of the box decorated with gold tacks and little mirrors. The bootblack positioned the guards so as not to stain Machuca's socks and then proceeded conscientiously with his task. He looked like a Gypsy and was very thin, with tattoos all over his arms and lottery tickets sticking out of his shirt pocket. He must have been over fifty. The chairman of the Cartujano Bank had his shoes polished every day at 300 pesetas a time, while he watched the world go by from his table on the corner of La Campana.

"Some heat," said the bootblack.

He wiped the sweat running down his nose with a hand blackened with polish. Gavira lit a cigarette and offered him one. The bootblack placed it behind his ear without stopping the brushing of Machuca's shoes. With a cup of coffee and the *ABC* on the table in front of him, the old man looked down with satisfaction at the job the bootblack was doing. When the bootblack finished, Machuca handed him a thousand-peseta note. The bootblack scratched the back of his neck, confused.

"I don't have any change, sir."

The chairman of the Cartujano smiled and crossed his legs. "Well, charge me tomorrow, Rafita," he said. "When you get some change."

The bootblack returned the note, raising his hand in something that vaguely resembled a military salute, and headed off towards the Plaza Duque de la Victoria, his little seat and box under his arm. Gavira saw him pass Peregil, who was waiting at a respectful distance outside a shoe shop, a few steps away from the dark-blue Mercedes at the kerb. Machuca's secretary was going through some papers at a nearby table, quiet and efficient as always.

"How's that business with the church going, Pencho?"

It was a routine question, like asking after the health of a relative. Old Machuca picked up the newspaper and leafed through it vaguely, until he came to the obituaries, which he read with great interest. Gavira leaned back in his wicker chair and watched the patches of sun gaining ground at his feet and moving slowly towards the Calle Sierpes.

"We're working on it," he said.

Machuca was engrossed in the obituaries. At his age it was comforting to see how many acquaintances had died before him. "The members of the board are losing patience," he said without looking up. "Or, to be more exact, some of them are. Others are hoping you'll fall flat on your face." He turned a page, smiling wryly at the long list of relations praying for the soul of Mr Luis Jorquera de la Sintacha, illustrious son of Seville, Commander of the Order of Mañara, who passed on after having received extreme unction, etc. Machuca and all Seville knew that the deceased had been a complete crook who'd made his fortune smuggling penicillin in the years after the Civil War. "There are only a few days left before the board meets to discuss your plans for the church."

Gavira nodded, his cigarette in his mouth. The Saudis of Sun Qafer Alley would be landing in Seville twenty-four hours before the meeting to purchase Puerto Targa at last. And with a signed contract on the table, nobody would dare say a word.

"I'm putting the final touches on it," he said.

Machuca nodded slowly a couple of times. He looked up from his newspaper to stare at the passers-by.

"The priest," he said. "The old one."

Gavira paid attention. But Machuca was silent for a moment, as if trying to find the right words. Or maybe he simply wanted to needle his successor. Whatever the old man's reasons, Gavira said nothing.

"He's the key," said Machuca. "Unless he gives in, the mayor won't sell, the archibishop won't secularise the land, and your wife and her mother won't back down. That Thursday Mass will really screw things up."

He insisted on referring to Macarena as Gavira's wife. Although technically it was true, it made Gavira very uncomfortable. Machuca refused to accept the end of the marriage he'd brokered. It was also a kind of warning: Gavira's succession wasn't assured while his marital situation remained equivocal and while Macarena went around publicising that fact. High society in Seville never forgave certain things. It had accepted Gavira when he married the daughter of the dukes of El Nuevo Extremo. Whatever Macarena did with bullfighters or priests, she was high society. Gavira wasn't. Without his wife, he was just a parvenu.

"Once I've dealt with the church," he said, "I'll sort things out with her."

Machuca looked sceptical as he turned the pages of his newspaper. "Don't be too sure you'll be able to. I've known her since she was a child." He leaned forward and sipped his coffee. "You might manage to get the priest out of the way and level his church, but the other battle you'll lose. Macarena has taken it personally."

"What about the duchess?"

The banker gave a hint of a smile. "Cruz respects her daughter's decisions. And she's in complete agreement with her over the church."

"Have you seen her recently? The duchess, I mean."

"Of course. On Wednesday, as usual."

One afternoon a week, Octavio Machuca sent his car to collect Cruz Bruner while he waited for her at the Parque de Maria Luisa, where they took a stroll. They could be seen there, under the willow trees or sitting on a bench in the Glorieta de Becquer on sunny afternoons.

"But you know what your mother-in-law is like." Machuca's smile widened. "We just chat about the weather, and the plants and flowers in her garden, or Campoamor's poetry . . . And every time I recite that bit, 'The daughters of the women I so loved kiss me now as one kisses a saint,' she laughs like a young girl. It would be vulgar to mention her son-in-law, or the church, or her daughter's failed marriage." He motioned at the defunct Levante Bank, on the corner of the Calle de Santa Maria de Gracia. "I bet you that building that she doesn't even know you're separated."

"You mustn't exaggerate, Don Octavio."

"I'm not exaggerating."

Gavira sipped his beer and said nothing. It was an exaggeration, of course. But it summed up the personality of the old lady. She lived cloistered like a nun in the Casa del Postigo – among shadows and memories in an old mansion now far too large for her and her daughter, at the heart of a historic district that was all marble, tiles, wrought-iron gates, and flower-filled courtyards complete with rocking chairs, canaries, piano music, and siesta. She was unaware of what went on outside her house, except on her weekly walks full of nostalgia with her late husband's friend.

"I'm not trying to interfere in your private life, Pencho." The old man watched him from beneath half-lowered lids. "But I often wonder what happened between you and Macarena."

Gavira shook his head stoically.

"Nothing in particular, I can assure you," he said. "It was just that life, my work, all created tensions, I suppose . . ." He took a drag on his cigarette and exhaled smoke through his nose and mouth. "And, you know, she wanted a child right away." He hesitated a moment. "I'm in the middle of a battle to secure my position, Don Octavio, I don't have time for nappies. So I asked her to wait . . ." He took another sip of beer, because his mouth suddenly felt very dry. "To wait a little, that's all. I thought I'd managed to convince her and that everything would be fine. Then suddenly one day, that was it. She left, slamming the door behind her, and declared war on me. Maybe it coincided with our disagreement over the church." He frowned. "I don't know, maybe everything coincided."

Machuca stared at him coldly, curiously. "The business with the bullfighter," he suggested, "was a low blow."

"A very low blow." So was mentioning it, but Gavira kept that observation to himself. "And there were a few others, after she left me. Men she knew before she was married, and that Curro Maestral, who was already hanging around." He threw his cigarette down and ground it out viciously with the heel of his shoe. "It's as if she wanted to make up for the time she wasted on me."

"Or to get her revenge."

"Maybe."

"You must have done something wrong, Pencho." The old banker shook his head with conviction. "Macarena was in love with you when she married you."

Gavira looked around without seeing anything. "I swear to you I don't understand," he said. "Revenge for what? I didn't have my first affair until a good month after she left me, by which time she'd been seen with that winemaker from Jerez, Villalta. By the way, with your permission, Don Octavio, I've just refused him credit."

Machuca raised one of his bony, claw-like hands, brushing it all aside. He knew of his successor's recent liaison with a well-known model. No, Macarena had too much class to create a scandal over her husband's skirt-chasing. If all wives did that, Seville would be in a real mess.

Gavira fiddled with his tie. "Well, we're in the same boat, Don Octavio. The godfather and the husband both in the dark."

"With one difference," said Machuca, and a smile appeared again beneath his sharp, cruel nose. "The church and your marriage are both your business, aren't they? I'm just an onlooker."

Gavira glanced over at Peregil, who was still standing by the Mercedes. His jaw tensed. "I'll step up the pressure."

"On your wife?"

"On the priest."

The old banker's rasping laugh rang out. "Which one? They've been multiplying like rabbits lately."

"The parish priest. Father Ferro."

"Right." Machuca too glanced at Peregil out of the corner of his eye. He sighed deeply. "I hope you'll have the good taste to spare me the details."

Some Japanese tourists passed, carrying huge rucksacks and looking very hot. Machuca put the newspaper down and said nothing for a moment, reclining in the wicker chair. At last he turned to Gavira. "It's hard walking a tightrope, isn't it?" he said, the predatory eyes mocking. "That's how I spent years, Pencho. From the time I smuggled the first consignment from Gibraltar after the war. And then when I bought the bank, wondering what the hell I was getting myself into. Anxious, sleepless nights . . ." He shook his head. "Suddenly one day you find you've crossed the finishing line and you don't give a damn anymore. No one can touch you, however hard they try. Only then do you start enjoying life, or what's left of it."

He smiled wearily.

"I hope you get there, Pencho," he said. "Until then, you must pay the price without complaining."

Gavira motioned to the waiter and ordered another beer and another coffee. He ran a hand over his hair and glanced absent-mindedly at the legs of a passing woman. "I've never complained, Don Octavio," he said.

"I know. That's why you have an office on the main floor on the Arenal and a chair beside me here, at this table. While I read the paper and watch you."

The waiter brought the coffee and the beer. Machuca put a lump of sugar in his coffee and stirred it as two nuns from Sor Angela de la Cruz walked by in their brown habits and white veils.

"By the way," the old banker asked suddenly, "what's happening with that other priest?" He stared after the nuns. "The one who had dinner with your wife last night."

It was at moments such as these that Pencho Gavira showed his mettle. He forced himself to watch a car turn into the street and then disappear around the corner, while he tried to still the pounding in his ears. He took about ten seconds before he arched an eyebrow and said, "Nothing. According to my information, he's still carrying out his investigation on behalf of Rome. Everything's under control."

"So I hope, Pencho." Machuca raised his cup to his lips with a slight grunt of satisfaction. "Nice place, La Albahaca." He took another sip. "I haven't been there for some time."

"I'll get Macarena back. I promise."

Machuca turned to face him, "You have a brain. There could be no better future for Macarena than with you. That's how I saw it from the start . . ." He laid a hand lightly on Gavira's arm; the hand felt bony and dry. "I appreciate your qualities, Pencho. Maybe you're the best thing that could happen to the bank now. But the fact is, at this point I couldn't care less about the bank. It's your wife I care about. And her mother."

Gavira felt trapped. He had to keep pedalling, he told himself, or else he'd fall off the bicycle. "The church," he said bitterly, "is their future."

"And yours, Pencho." Machuca shot him a malicious glance. "Would you sacrifice the church deal and the Puerto Targa operation to get your wife back?"

Gavira didn't answer immediately. This was the crux of the matter, and he knew it better than anyone.

"If I lose this chance," he said evasively, "I lose everything."

"Not everything. Only your prestige. And my backing."

Calm, Gavira allowed himself a smile. "You're a hard man, Don Octavio."

"Possibly." The old man stared at the PEÑA BÉTICA sign opposite. "But I'm just. The church deal was your idea, and so was your marriage. Although I may have helped things along a little."

"Then I'd like to ask you something," Gavira said, putting his hands on the table. "Why won't you help me now, if you're so fond of Macarena and her mother? You could make them see reason."

"Maybe, maybe not," Machuca said, narrowing his eyes. "But if I helped you, you see, it would mean that I'd allowed Macarena to marry a fool. Let's understand each other, Pencho: for me this is like owning a racehorse or a boxer or a good fighting cock. I enjoy watching you fight."

He made a sign to his secretary. The audience was over.

Gavira stood up, buttoning his jacket. "Do you know something, Don Octavio?" He put on his Italian designer sunglasses and stood by the table, cool, immaculate. "Sometimes I think you don't want a definite outcome . . . As if deep down you don't care about any of it: Macarena, the bank, me."

Across the street, a young woman with long legs and a very short skirt came out of a clothes shop with a bucket and started washing down the shop window. Old Machuca watched the girl thoughtfully. At last he said: "Pencho, did you ever wonder why I come here every day?"

Gavira stared at him, surprised, not knowing what to answer. What did this have to do with anything? he thought. Damn the old man.

There was a glint of mockery in the banker's eyes. "Once, a long time ago," he said "I was sitting at this very table when a woman walked by. She was beautiful, the kind of woman that takes your breath away . . . I watched her go by, and our eyes met. I thought of getting up, stopping her. But I didn't. Social convention carried more weight. I was known in Seville . . . She continued on her way. I told myself I'd see her another day. But she never walked past here again."

His voice was flat as he told the story. The secretary approached, briefcase in hand. With a nod in Gavira's direction, Canovas sat down in the chair that Gavira had just vacated. Settling back into his own chair, Machuca smiled coldly at the young vice-chairman of the Cartujano. "I'm a very old man, Pencho," he said. "In my lifetime, I've won some battles and lost others. But now I don't feel involved in any of it." He took one of the documents his assistant handed him. "What I have now, more than a desire for victory, is a sense of curiosity. Like someone who puts a scorpion and a spider in a bottle and waits to see what happens. With no sympathy for either of them."

He turned his attention to the document, and Gavira muttered a goodbye before going to his car. He had a deep vertical line on his forehead, and the ground felt shaky beneath his feet. Peregil, smoothing his hair over his bald head, looked away as Gavira approached.

Sunlight bounced off the corner of the white-and-red-ochre Hospital de los Venerables. Across the street, beneath a poster for that Sunday's bullfight at the Maestranza bullring, two pale-skinned tourists, looking on the verge of sunstroke, sat outside the Bar Román, recovering. Inside, Simeon Navajo carefully peeled himself a prawn and then looked at Quart.

"The Computer Crime Department didn't come up with anything," he said. "No previous records."

He ate the prawn and gulped down half his beer. He was always having extra breakfasts, snacks, sandwiches, and Quart wondered where the skinny deputy superintendent put it all. Even the .357 magnum was so bulky on his slight frame that he carried it in a strong-smelling, fringed leather bag over his shoulder. With his ponytail and baggy flower-print shirt, Simeon Navajo made a sharp contrast with the tall, soberly dressed priest.

"We have nothing on our files," the policeman went on, "on any of the persons you asked me to check . . . We've got young students playing pranks on their computers, a pile of people selling pirated copies of computer programs, and a couple of guys who get into systems they shouldn't from time to time. But there's no sign of what you're looking for."

They were standing at the bar, beneath rows of cured hams hanging from the ceiling. The policeman took another prawn, tore off its head and sucked it with relish, and then began expertly peeling the rest. Quart's own glass of beer was almost untouched.

"Did you make the enquiry I asked you to? Those companies, and Telefonica?"

"I did," said Navajo with his mouth full. "Nobody on your list bought any computer equipment from them, at least not using their real name. As for Telefonica, the head of security there is a friend of mine. According to him, your Vespers isn't the only one who gets on the network illegally and makes calls abroad, to the Vatican or wherever. All the hackers do that. Some get caught, some don't. Yours seems pretty sharp. Apparently he uses a complicated loop system to get on and off the Internet. He leaves behind programs that wipe any trace of him and make detection systems go bananas." He ate another prawn and ordered another beer. A piece of prawn shell had got caught in his moustache. "That's all I can tell you."

Quart smiled at the policeman: "It's not much, but thanks anyway."

"You don't have to thank me," Navajo said, eating. A pile of prawn shells was growing at his feet. "I wish I could do more. But my bosses made it very clear: I can only help you unofficially. On a personal basis, between you and me. For old times' sake. They don't want to get involved with churches, priests, Rome and all that. It would be another story if someone had committed a crime, within my jurisdiction. But the two deaths were ruled to be accidental . . . The fact that a hacker from Seville is pestering the Pope isn't something we can get too excited about," he said and noisily sucked a prawn head.

The sun slid slowly over the Guadalquivir, and there wasn't a breath of air. On the bank opposite, the palm trees looked like sentries guarding La Maestranza. El Potro del Mantelete was at the window against the glare from the river, a cigarette in his mouth, as motionless as the bronze figure of his hero Juan Belmonte. Don Ibrahim sat at the table. The smell of fried eggs with morcilla wafted from the kitchen, along with La Niña Puñales's song:

Why do I wake trembling and shaking
and look out onto the dark, deserted street?
Why do I have the feeling
that you're going to tell me it's over?

The former bogus lawyer nodded approvingly, moving his lips to the words that La Niña sang in her husky voice. An apron over her polka-dot dress, spatula in hand, she was frying eggs, making them nice and crispy, just as Don Ibrahim liked them. When the three partners didn't get by on tapas from the bars in Triana, they ate at La Niña's place on the Calle Betis. It was a modest apartment on the third floor, but it had a view of Seville – with the Arenal a stone's throw away, and the

Torre del Oro and La Giralda – that kings and millionaires and film stars with all their cash would have killed for. La Niña's window facing the Guadalquivir was the only asset she owned. She bought the apartment years before, with the meagre profits from her momentary fame, and that was one thing at least, as she often said to cheer herself up, that hadn't gone to rack and ruin. She lived there with a few pieces of old furniture, a gleaming brass bed, a print of the Virgen de la Esperanza, a signed photo of Miguel de Molina, and a chest of drawers where the embroidered bedcovers, tablecloths and sheets of her trousseau lay yellowing. With no rent to pay, she could afford the monthly instalments she'd sent for the last twenty years to El Ocaso, S. A., that went towards a humble plot and stone in the San Fernando Cemetery, in the sunniest corner. Because La Niña really felt the cold. She sang:

You looked at me
and your love flowed
through my veins
on a river of song . . .

Don Ibrahim muttered *olé* automatically and went on with the task at hand. His hat, jacket and walking stick were on the chair beside him, and elastic bands held his shirtsleeves up over his elbows. There were patches of sweat under his plump arms and around his neck, and he'd loosened his blue-and-red-striped tie. He claimed that the tall Englishman, Graham Greene, had given him the tie in exchange for a copy of the New Testament and a bottle of Four Roses when he was in Havana writing a spy novel. The tie, in addition to being of sentimental value, was a genuine Oxford tie.

Unlike La Niña, neither Don Ibrahim nor El Potro del Mantelete owned his own place. El Potro lived nearby in a houseboat, a dilapidated tourist boat that a friend from his bullfighting and army days sublet to him. Don Ibrahim lodged in a modest boarding house in El Altozano; it was run by the widow of a civil guard who'd been shot by ETA in the north. The other residents were a travelling salesman who sold combs and a mature lady of faded beauty and dubious employment.

Can't you see how
loving you like crazy
from my soul to my mouth
turns my heart upside down . . .

No one, not even Concha Piquer or Pastora Imperio, could sing like that, thought Don Ibrahim as he listened to La Niña finish her song with the style and verve that the rabble of critics and impresarios and idlers had refused to recognise. It was a stab to his heart to hear her in Holy Week, when, on any street corner where the fancy took her, she started singing a *saeta* to the Virgen de la Esperanza or her son, the Cachorro de Triana. It silenced the drums and gave everyone goose bumps. Because La Niña Puñales embodied the *cante* and the *copla*, and Spain itself. Not the Spain of cheap flamenco for tourists but the other Spain, the real Spain. The legend that smelled of smoky bars, green eyes, and the sweat of a lifetime. The dramatic memory of a people that sang to relieve its sorrows, and exorcised its demons by desperately clutching knives. Knives gleaming like the slices of moon that lit El Potro's way as he jumped over fences at night, naked so as not to tear his only shirt, convinced that he would conquer the world and pave his path with banknotes – before the bulls beat him and left him with a look of defeat in his eyes. The same Spain that ripped down posters of La Niña Puñales, the best flamenco voice of Andalusia, of the century, and didn't even give her a pension to get by on. The distant motherland of which Don Ibrahim dreamed during the nights of his youth in Cuba and to which he planned to return some day like the émigrés of the past, with a Cadillac convertible and a cigar, but she greeted him with nothing but incomprehension, derision and abuse after the wretched business of his bogus law degree. But even sons of bitches owed a debt to their mothers, Don Ibrahim reasoned. And loved them. And ungrateful Spain did have places like Seville, districts like Triana, bars like Casa Cuesta, faithful souls like El Potro, and beautiful, tragic voices like La Niña's. And even if things didn't turn out well, the three of them would dedicate their Temple to that voice. On nights of fino, Manzanilla, cigarette smoke and conversation, they could picture it: formal, solemn, with wicker chairs and silent old waiters – the impassive El Potro would be usher – bottles on the tables, a spotlight on the stage, and a guitar strumming real tunes for La Niña, now returned to her public with even more talent and more feeling. They would admit who they wanted, allow no tourist parties or bores with mobile phones. All Don Ibrahim asked for was a dark table at the back, where he could sit slowly sipping a drink, a smouldering Montecristo in his hand, listening to La Niña with a lump in his throat. And that the takings should be good. It didn't hurt to dream.

Very carefully he poured more petrol into the bottle, making sure not to spill any. He'd laid sheets of newspaper on the table to protect the varnish, and he wiped any petrol dripping down the neck of the Anis del Mono bottle with a cloth. The petrol was unleaded and the best, 97-octane, because, as La Niña had so sensibly pointed out, you shouldn't use cheap stuff to set fire to a consecrated church. So they dispatched El Potro with an empty olive-oil can to the nearest petrol station to bring back a litre. A litre would be plenty, Don Ibrahim said. He claimed he had acquired expertise in these matters when Ernesto "Che" Guevara explained to him, as they drank *mojitos* in Santa Clara, how to make a Molotov cocktail, a Russian invention of Karl Marx's.

The petrol bubbled and spilled down the side of the bottle. Don Ibrahim mopped it with the already soaked cloth and then put the cloth in an ashtray on the table. The incendiary bomb was intended to function with a somewhat primitive, but effective, device of which Don Ibrahim was the proud inventor: a candle, matches, a wind-up alarm clock and two metres of twine to make the bottle topple. Ignition was to take place once the three partners were sitting in a bar with witnesses, because it didn't do to overlook one's alibi. The pews piled against the wall and the old roof beams would take care of the rest. They didn't need to destroy the church totally, Peregil had said when he gave them their instructions. Substantial damage would do, although if the whole place went up, so much the better. The main thing was – he had said, staring anxiously at each of them – it had to seem like an accident.

Don Ibrahim poured in more, and for a moment the smell of petrol smothered the smell of fried eggs. He would have loved to light a cigar, but you couldn't be too careful with all that petrol about and the cloth soaked with it in the ashtray. La Niña had been dead set against the plan at first, the church being a holy place. They convinced her only by reminding her that with all the money they'd get from the deal she'd be able to order a truckload of Masses to atone for it. Anyway, according to the ancient principle of *ad auctores redit sceleris coacti tamarindus pulpa*, or something like that, they were committing a crime on someone else's behalf. The causal party was Peregil. Even after such a legal explanation, La Niña still refused to have anything to do with the incendiary act and agreed to perform only backup tasks, such as providing fried eggs with morcilla. Don Ibrahim respected her views, since he was all for freedom of worship. As for El Potro, his thought processes were hard to fathom. If he had any. He just nodded impassively, fatalistic, ever loyal, always waiting for the bell or bugle to make him spring from his corner or emerge from behind the barrier like an automaton. He didn't object when Don Ibrahim mentioned setting fire to the church. Although he'd been a bullfighter – and, as far as Don Ibrahim knew, all bullfighters believed in God – El Potro wasn't devout. But on Good Friday he donned the navy blue suit he had worn for his ill-fated wedding and a white shirt buttoned to the neck but without a tie, slicked back his hair with eau de Cologne, and joined La Niña amid the candles and drums in the procession behind the Virgen de la Esperanza. As a freethinker, Don Ibrahim could not take part in obscurantist rites, so he just watched them file past behind the Virgin, La Niña in a black mantilla, praying, and El Potro, holding her arm, silent and upright.

Don Ibrahim smiled to himself, with fatherly tenderness, as he watched El Potro's hard profile at the window. He was proud of El Potro's loyalty. Many of the earth's powerful men could not have purchased such devotion. But maybe some day, when he was on his last legs, Don Ibrahim would be asked if he had done anything worthwhile in his life. And he would answer, with his head held high, that he had had a faithful friend in El Potro del Mantelete, and that he had heard La Niña Puñales sing "Cape of Red and Gold".

"Come and get it," said La Niña at the kitchen door, wiping her hands on her apron. Her black kiss-curl, fake beauty spot and blood-red lipstick were all immaculate but her eyeliner was somewhat smudged, because she'd been chopping onion for the salad. Don

Ibrahim noticed that she cast a critical glance at the bottle of Anis del Mono. She still didn't approve of what they were doing.

"You can't make an omelette," he said in a conciliatory tone, "without breaking a few eggs."

"Well, the ones I've just fried are getting cold," answered La Niña, setting her jaw stubbornly.

Don Ibrahim sighed resignedly and poured the last few drops of petrol into the bottle. He mopped up the spillage and put the cloth back in the ashtray. Then he placed both his hands on the table and levered himself with effort out of his chair.

"Trust me, my dear. Trust me."

"Churches shouldn't be burned down," she insisted, frowning. "That's for heretics and communists."

El Potro, silent as ever, moved away from the window and raised his hand to the cigarette in his mouth. I must tell him not to come near the petrol, Don Ibrahim thought fleetingly, still concerned with La Niña.

"God works in mysterious ways," he said, to say something.

"Well, this way doesn't look good at all."

La Niña's failure to understand pained Don Ibrahim. He wasn't the kind of leader who imposed decisions on his troops. He preferred to reason with them instead. They were his tribe, his clan. His family. He was searching for an argument that would settle the matter, at least until after their fried eggs, when out of the corner of his eye he saw El Potro head past the table on his way to the kitchen, and instinctively go to stub out his cigarette in the ashtray. Just where the petrol-soaked cloth was lying.

Ridiculous, Don Ibrahim thought. Of course El Potro wouldn't do such a thing. But he turned to him anxiously anyway.

"Hey, Potro," he said.

But El Potro had already thrown his cigarette end into the ashtray. Don Ibrahim, trying to stop him, knocked over the bottle of Anis del Mono with his elbow.

VIII
An Andalusian Lady

"Can you smell the jasmine?"
"What jasmine? There isn't any."
"The jasmine that used to be here in the old days."
Antonio Burgos, *Seville*

If there was such a thing as blue blood, then the blood coursing through the veins of Macarena Bruner's mother, María Cruz Eugenia Bruner de Lebrija y Álvarez de Córdoba, Duchess of El Nuevo Extremo and twelve times grandee of Spain, must have been navy blue. Her ancestors had taken part in the siege of Granada and the conquest of America, and only two ancient houses of the Spanish aristocracy, Alba and Medina-Sidonia, could claim longer histories. The wealth that went with her titles, however, had long since disappeared. The estates and assets were gradually swallowed up over time and history, so that the tangled lines of her family tree were like strings of shells washed up empty on the seashore. The lady who sat sipping Coca-Cola opposite Lorenzo Quart in the courtyard of the Casa del Postigo was one month and seven days away from her seventieth birthday. Her ancestors could travel all the way from Seville to Cadiz without leaving their own land. King Alfonso XIII and Queen Victoria Eugenia held her over the baptismal font. And after the Spanish Civil War, General Franco himself, despite his dislike of the old Spanish aristocracy, couldn't avoid kissing her hand in that very same Andalusian courtyard, bowing reluctantly over the Roman mosaics that had paved the patio since they were brought straight from the ruins of Italica four centuries earlier. But time moves on relentlessly. So read the motto on the English clock in the gallery of mudéjar columns and arches decorated with rugs from the Alpujarras and with sixteenth-century bureaux that would have ended up in Seville auctions had it not been for the generosity of the banker and family friend, Octavio Machuca. Of past splendours there remained only the fragrant courtyard full of geraniums, aspidistras and ferns, the plateresque railings, the garden, the summer dining room with its Roman busts, a few pieces of furniture and some paintings on the walls. And in the midst of it all, with only a maid, a gardener and a cook in the house where she'd grown up with a staff of twenty, lived the white-haired lady with a string of pearls round her neck, a tranquil shadow leaning over its past. She offered Quart more coffee and cooled herself with an old fan decorated, with a personal dedication, by Julio Romero de Torres.

Quart poured coffee into the slightly cracked cup. He was in his shirtsleeves. The duchess had been so insistent that he remove his jacket because of the heat that he'd had no choice but to obey, hanging it over the back of his chair. He wore a black, short-sleeved shirt that showed his strong, tanned forearms. Clean-cut, good-looking and wholesome, he looked like a missionary, in sharp contrast with the small, hard figure of Father Ferro sitting beside him in his stained, threadbare cassock. On the low table set out next to the central fountain there was coffee, hot chocolate, and, rather eccentrically, a bottle of Coca-Cola. The old duchess remarked that she hated drinking Coke from a can. It tasted different, metallic that way. Even the bubbles felt different.

"More chocolate, Father Ferro?"

The parish priest nodded briefly without looking at Quart and held out his cup. Macarena filled it under her mother's approving gaze. The duchess seemed pleased to have two priests in her house. For years Father Ferro had arrived on the dot of five every afternoon except Wednesdays, to recite the rosary with the old lady. Afterwards he stayed for coffee, in the courtyard if the weather was good, in the summer dining room if it was raining.

"How lucky you are to live in Rome," the duchess said, opening and shutting her fan. "So near His Holiness."

She was remarkably bright and vivacious for her age. Her hair was white with slight hints of blue, and there were liver spots on her arms, hands and forehead. She was slim, slight, had angular features, and skin that was as wrinkled as a raisin. Her almost non-existent lips were outlined with lipstick, and from her ears hung small pearls identical to those of her necklace. Her eyes were dark like her daughter's, though age had turned them watery, red-rimmed. But there was still resolve and intelligence in them, and a light that often turned inwards, as if memories were moving across them like passing clouds. She had been fair-haired in her youth, as Quart saw in a portrait of her by Zuloaga in a room off the hall. So Macarena must have got her black hair from her father, a handsome gentleman in a framed photograph near the Zuloaga portrait. The duke consort was dark, with white teeth, a thin moustache, hair combed back, and a gold tie pin fastening down the points of his collar. Had one fed all these details into a computer along with the words "Andalusian gentleman", thought Quart, exactly that photograph would have come up on the screen. He had found out enough about Macarena's family history to know that in his day Rafael Guardiola Fernández-Garvey had been the most handsome man in Seville. He was also cosmopolitan, elegant, and in fifteen years of marriage had managed to squander the remainder of his wife's already reduced fortune. If Cruz Bruner was a consequence of history, the duke consort was a consequence of the worst vices of Sevillian aristocracy. All the businesses he embarked upon ended in resounding failure, and only his friendship with the banker Octavio Machuca, who always faithfully bailed him out, saved the duke consort of El Nuevo Extremo from winding up in jail. Ruined by his final project, a stud farm, he ended up penniless, his health destroyed by flamenco parties till dawn and several litres of Manzanilla, forty cigarettes and three cigars a day. At the end, he shouted for a confessor, just as in old films or romantic novels. He was buried, having confessed and received the sacraments, in the uniform of a gentleman of the Real Maestranza of Seville, with his sabre and plume. All of Seville high society was present at the funeral. Half of those attending, a gossip columnist said maliciously, were cuckolded husbands there to make sure that the duke had truly been laid to rest. The other half were creditors.

"His Holiness once granted me an audience," the old duchess told Quart. "And to Macarena too, after her wedding."

She bowed her head slightly as she reminisced. Over a third of a century and the reigns of several popes must have elapsed between her visit to Rome and her daughter's, but she referred to His Holiness as if it was the same man. Quart reflected that in some ways this was logical. At seventy, things either changed too fast or not at all.

Father Ferro still stared sullenly into his cup, and Macarena watched Quart. The duchess of El Nuevo Extremo's daughter was in jeans and a blue checked shirt. Her hair was in a ponytail and she wore no makeup. She looked relaxed and sure of herself as she poured the hot chocolate and coffee, attentive to her mother and the guests, Quart in particular. She seemed amused by the situation.

"What do you think of our church, Father?" asked Cruz Bruner as she sipped her Coca-Cola and smiled affably, her fan in her lap. Her voice, despite her age, was firm and serene. She waited for his answer. Quart smiled politely, aware also of Macarena's gaze.

"It is much loved," he said non-committally. Out of the corner of his eye he saw the dark, silent figure of Father Ferro. Here, in the presence of the duchess and her daughter, they were on neutral ground. On arriving, they had exchanged conventional greetings, but the rest of the time they were careful not to say a word to each other. Quart sensed, however, that this was the prelude to something. Nobody invites a scalp hunter and his supposed victim for coffee without having a purpose in mind.

"Don't you think it would be a shame to lose it?" insisted the duchess.

"I hope that will never happen," Quart said reassuringly.

"We had thought that was why you came to Seville," said Macarena Bruner pointedly.

Quart could see the ivory necklace round her neck and wondered if this afternoon too the plastic cigarette lighter was tucked under her bra strap. He would have willingly spent two months in Purgatory to see Father Ferro's expression as she used it to light a cigarette.

"No," he said. "I'm here because my superiors want a precise picture of the situation." He sipped his coffee and carefully placed the cup back on the inlaid table. "Nobody's trying to remove Father Ferro from his parish."

Father Ferro stiffened. "Aren't they?" He raised his scarred face to the galleries above them, as if somebody were about to appear there. "I can think of several people and institutions. The archbishop, for instance. The Cartujano Bank. The duchess's son-in-law . . ." He shot a suspicious glance at Quart. "And don't tell me that Rome's losing sleep now over a small church and its priest."

I have your measure, his look said. So don't give me all your fine words. Quart, sensing Macarena's eyes on him, tried to conciliate. "Rome cares about all churches and all priests."

"You must be joking," said Father Ferro, and he laughed coldly.

Cruz Bruner tapped the priest's arm affectionately with her fan. "I'm sure Father Quart isn't joking, Don Priamo," she said and looked at Quart for confirmation. "He seems a fine, upright priest. I think his mission is important. And since he's here to gather information, we ought to co-operate." She glanced quickly at her daughter and then fanned herself wearily. "The truth never harmed anyone."

Father Ferro inclined his head, respectful but stubborn. "I wish I shared your innocence, madam." He drank his hot chocolate, and it dripped down his badly shaven chin. He wiped it with a huge, filthy handkerchief which he pulled from the pocket of his cassock. "But I fear that in the Church, as in the rest of life, almost all truths are lies."

"You shouldn't say such things." The duchess was half-shocked, half-jesting. "You'll be damned." She opened and closed her fan.

Then, Quart saw Father Ferro smile properly for the first time. A good-natured, sceptical expression – a bear pestered by its cubs. It softened his features, making his face look unexpectedly gentle – as in the photograph, taken in that same courtyard, that was back at Quart's hotel. Quart thought of Spada, his boss at the IEA. The archbishop and Father Ferro had the same smile, like veteran gladiators. Quart wondered if his smile would ever become like theirs.

"Father," the duchess said after a glance at her daughter and a moment's thought, "this church is very important to my family. Not only because of its historical significance but also because, as Don Priamo says, whenever a church is demolished, a piece of heaven is removed. And I would hate to see the place I hope to end up in reduced in size." She drank some more Coca-Cola, half shutting her eyes with pleasure as the fizzing tickled her nose. "I'm putting my faith in our parish priest that he'll get me there before too long."

Father Ferro blew his nose. "You will get there, madam," he said, blowing his nose again. "You have my word." He put the handkerchief away and glared at Quart, as if defying him to question his ability to keep such a promise.

Cruz Bruner clapped her fan against her hand, delighted. "You see?" she said to Quart. "That's the advantage of having a priest to tea six days a week . . . It gives one certain privileges." She looked gratefully at Father Ferro. The expression in her watery eyes was both serious and mocking.

The old priest shifted in his chair, made uneasy by Quart's silence. "You'd get there just the same without me," he said sullenly.

"Maybe, maybe not. But I know that if they don't let me in, you'll give them what for up there." The old lady considered the jet rosary beads lying next to a prayer book on the table covered with magazines and newspapers. She sighed. "At my age, I find that reassuring."

In the garden, beyond the open gate, blackbirds could be heard singing. A gentle chirrup that ended in two sharp trills. The duchess turned to listen. May was their mating season, she explained. They often perched on the wall of the convent next door and could be heard singing at the same time as the nuns. Her father the duke, Macarena's grandfather, had spent the last few years of his life recording the blackbirds' song. The tapes and records were still in the house somewhere. Through the recorded birdsong you could hear the sound of the duke's footsteps on the gravel paths.

"My father was an old-fashioned gentleman," continued the duchess. "He wouldn't have liked the way the world's changed." From the tilt of her head, it was obvious she didn't like it either. "In a book published before the Civil War, *The Large Estates of Spain*, my family is mentioned as being one of the wealthiest in Andalusia, though even then the wealth was only on paper. Money's in different hands now. Banks and financiers own the big country estates and surround them with electric fences. They have expensive cars, and they're buying up all the wineries in Jerez. Sharp people who've made their money overnight, as my son-in-law would like to do."

"Mother."

The duchess raised her hand. "Let me say what I have to say. Don Priamo never liked Pencho, but I did. And the fact that you're separated changes nothing." She fanned herself again, with unexpected vigour. "I admit that in this business over the church he's not behaving like a gentleman."

Macarena shrugged. "Pencho was never a gentleman," she said. She took a lump of sugar and sucked it thoughtfully. Quart watched her, until she suddenly looked up at him. "And he's never tried to pass himself off as one."

"No, of course not," said the old lady, suddenly sarcastic. "Your father, now he was a gentleman. A real Andalusian gentleman." Then she was lost in thought, touching the tiles around the fountain with her fingertips. The tiles, she explained to Quart, dated from the sixteenth century and had been laid throughout the house in strict accordance with the rules of heraldry. "An Andalusian gentleman," she repeated after a moment's silence. The line of lipstick on her thin, faded lips contorted – a bitter, private smile.

Macarena Bruner shook her head: "The church means nothing to Pencho." She seemed to address Quart rather than her mother. "He sees it only in terms of square metres ripe for development. We can't expect him to see things our way."

"Of course not," the duchess said. "Maybe someone from your own class would have."

"You married someone from your own class," replied Macarena, annoyed.

"You're right." The old lady smiled sadly. "At least your husband is a man. Courageous, with the insolence that comes from relying on oneself alone . . ." She looked quickly at Father Ferro. "Whether we like what he's doing to our church or not."

"He hasn't done it yet," said Macarena. "And he won't, not if I can help it."

Cruz Bruner frowned. "Well, you're making him pay, dear," she said.

They had strayed into an area that seemed to make the old lady uneasy. Her manner towards her daughter was discreetly reproving. Macarena stared into space beyond Quart's shoulder. "He hasn't finished paying," she said quietly.

"He'll always be your husband," said her mother, "whether you live with him or not. Isn't that so, Don Priamo?" The expression in her watery eyes was mischievous again when she turned to Quart.

"Father Priamo doesn't like my son-in-law, but he maintains that a marriage – any marriage – is indissoluble."

"That's true," said the priest. He had spilled more hot chocolate and was brushing it from his cassock angrily. "God Himself cannot undo what a priest has united on earth."

How difficult it was, thought Quart, to distinguish between pride and virtue. Between truth and error. Determined to remain on the sidelines, he lowered his eyes to the Roman mosaic at his feet, brought here by Macarena's ancestors: a ship surrounded by fish, and something that looked like an island with trees, and a woman on the shore carrying a jug or amphora. There was also a dog with the inscription CAVE CANEM, and a woman and a man touching each other. Some pieces were loose and he nudged them back into place with his foot.

"What does that banker, Octavio Machuca, have to say about all this?" he asked, and noticed the duchess's expression instantly soften.

"Octavio is a very old and dear friend. The best I ever had," she said.

"He's in love with the duchess," said Macarena.

"Don't be ridiculous." The old lady fanned herself, staring disapprovingly at her daughter. Laughing, Macarena insisted it was true. The duchess was forced to admit that Machuca, when he first arrived in Seville, had indeed wooed her for a time before she married. But such a marriage would have been inconceivable at the time. He never married, and never made any advances to her while her husband, his friend Rafael Guardiola, was alive. She sounded sorry, but Quart couldn't tell what she regretted.

"He asked you to marry him," said Macarena.

"That was later. I was a widow by then. But I thought it best to leave things as they were. Now we take a stroll in the park every Wednesday. We're very good, old friends."

"What do you talk about?" asked Quart, smiling to make his question seem less intrusive.

"Nothing," said Macarena. "I've spied on them, and all they do is flirt quietly."

"Ignore her. I take his arm, and we chat about our own things. Of times gone by. Of when he was a young adventurer, before he settled down."

"Don Octavio recites *The Express Train* by Campoamor to her."

"How do you know?"

"He told me."

Cruz Bruner straightened, touching her pearl necklace with a hint of past coquettishness. "Well, yes, it's true. He knows I like it. 'My letter, rejoicing as it goes to meet you, will tell you of my memory . . .'" Her smile was melancholy. "We also talk about Macarena. He loves her like a daughter and he gave her away at her wedding . . . Look at Father Ferro's face. He doesn't like Octavio."

The old priest scowled defiantly. It was almost as if he were jealous of their walks in the park. On Wednesdays he didn't take coffee with the duchess of El Nuevo Extremo and she recited the rosary without him.

"I neither like nor dislike him, madam," he said, uncomfortable. "But I find his attitude to the problem of Our Lady of the Tears highly reprehensible. Pencho Gavira is his subordinate. Don Octavio could stop Gavira from proceeding with this sacrilege." His anger made his face look hard. "In that respect he has not served you or your daughter well."

"Octavio has an extraordinarily pragmatic approach to life," said Cruz Bruner. "He couldn't care less about the church. He respects our deep affection for it, but he believes that my son-in-law has made the right decision." She gazed at the escutcheons carved in the spandrels above the courtyard arches. "Macarena's future, he'd say, is not in clinging to the wreckage but in climbing aboard a brand-new yacht. Which my son-in-law can provide."

"It has to be said, Don Octavio isn't taking sides," agreed her daughter. "He's neutral."

Don Priamo raised an apocalyptic finger. "One cannot be neutral about the house of God."

"Please, Father," Macarena said to him with a tender smile, "try to stay calm. Have more chocolate."

The old priest refused a third cup and stared sullenly at the tips of his scuffed shoes. I know who he reminds me of, thought Quart. Jock, the grumpy, aggressive little fox terrier in *Lady and the Tramp*. Except that Father Ferro was more truculent. Quart said to the old duchess,

"Earlier you mentioned your father the duke . . . Was he Carlota Bruner's brother?"

The old lady was taken aback. "You know the story?" She played for a moment with her fan, glancing at her daughter and then at Quart. "Carlota was my aunt, my father's older sister. A sad family tale . . . Macarena has been obsessed with the story since she was a child. She would spend hours with her trunk, reading those unhappy letters that never reached their destination and trying on old dresses at the window where they say Carlota sat waiting."

There was something new in the atmosphere. Father Ferro looked away, embarrassed. The subject seemed to make him uncomfortable.

"Father Quart," Macarena said, "has one of Carlota's cards."

"That's not possible," said the duchess. "They're in the trunk up in the pigeon loft."

"Well, he has. It's a picture of the church. Somebody put it in his hotel room."

"How ridiculous. Who would do such a thing?" The old lady looked suspiciously at Quart. "Has he returned it to you?" she asked her daughter.

Macarena shook her head slowly. "I've let him keep it. For the time being."

The duchess was confused. "I don't understand. Only you ever go up to the pigeon loft, or the servants."

"Yes," said Macarena, turning to the old priest, "and Don Priamo."

Father Ferro almost jumped out of his seat. "For the love of God, madam. You're surely not insinuating that I . . ."

"I was joking, Father," said Macarena. Although Quart couldn't tell from her expression whether she was or not. "But the fact is, the card got to the Doña Maria Hotel and it's a mystery how."

"What's the pigeon loft?" asked Quart.

"You can't see it from here, only from the garden," explained Cruz Bruner. "It's what we call the house's tower. There was once a pigeon loft up there. My grandfather Luis, Carlota's father, studied astronomy and set up an observatory. Eventually it became the room where my poor aunt spent her last years, as a recluse . . . Now Don Priamo uses it."

Quart looked at the old priest in evident surprise. This explained the books he'd found in his quarters. "I didn't know you were interested in astronomy," he said.

"Well, I am." The priest was uneasy. "There's no reason you should know. It's none of your business, or Rome's. The duchess is kind enough to let me use the observatory."

"That's right," said Cruz Bruner, pleased. "The instruments are all very old, but Father Ferro keeps them clean, and in use. And he tells me about what he sees. He won't make any discoveries with that equipment, but it's a pleasant pastime." She tapped her legs with her fan, smiling. "I don't have the strength to climb up there, but Macarena goes up sometimes."

One surprise after another, thought Quart. This was a strange little club that Father Ferro had here. An insubordinate astronomer priest.

"You didn't mention your interest in astronomy either," Quart said, looking into her dark eyes, wondering what other secrets were hidden there.

"I'm interested in tranquillity," said Macarena simply. "You can find it up there, among the stars. Father Ferro lets me stay while he works. I read or watch him."

Quart looked at the sky above their heads – a rectangle of blue framed by the eaves of the Andalusian courtyard. There was a single cloud, high up. Small, solitary and motionless, like Father Ferro. "In the past," he said, "astronomy was forbidden to clerics. It was considered too rational and therefore a threat to the soul." He smiled in a friendly way at the old priest. "The Inquisition would have imprisoned you for it."

Father Ferro looked down, bad-tempered, unyielding.

"The Inquisition," he muttered, "would have imprisoned me for a lot of things, not just astronomy."

"But not anymore," said Quart, thinking of Cardinal Iwaszkiewicz. "Not that they wouldn't like to."

For the first time they all laughed, even Father Ferro, reluctantly at first, then with good humour. Talking of astronomy seemed to have narrowed a little the gulf between him and Quart. Macarena sensed it and looked pleased, glancing first at one and then the other. Bright glints once again shone in her eyes, and she laughed her frank, open laugh, like a boy's. She suggested that the old priest show Quart the pigeon loft.

The brass telescope gleamed beneath the mudéjar arches open on all four sides of the tower. It looked out over the rooftops of Santa Cruz. In the distance, among television aerials and flocks of pigeons flying in all directions, were La Giralda, the Torre del Oro and a stretch of the Guadalquivir with jacarandas in flower like blue splashes along its banks. The rest of the landscape before which Carlota Bruner had languished a century earlier was now a mass of modern concrete, steel and glass buildings. There was not a single white sail in sight, nor boats bobbing on the current, and the four pinnacles of the Archivo de Indias looked like forgotten sentinels atop the Lonja building, guarding the paper, dust and memories of a time long past within it.

"What a wonderful place," said Quart.

Father Ferro didn't answer. He took his dirty handkerchief from his pocket and wiped the tube of the telescope, breathing on it. It was an ancient model, almost two metres long, with an altazimuth mounting. The long brass tube and all the metal parts had been carefully polished. The telescope shone in the sunlight, and the sun was moving slowly towards the far bank, over Triana. There was little else in the pigeon loft: a couple of old torn leather armchairs, a desk with numerous drawers, a lamp, a print of seventeenth-century Seville on the wall, and a few leather-bound books: Tolstoy, Dostoyevsky, Quevedo, Heine, Galdós, Blasco Ibáñez, Valle-Inclán, together with some treatises on cosmography, celestial mechanics and astrophysics. Quart went to take a closer look at them: Ptolemy, Porta, Alfonso de Córdoba. Some were very old editions.

"I would never have imagined it," Quart said. "I mean, that you'd be interested in this sort of thing."

His tone was sincere, conciliatory. In the last few hours his view of Father Ferro had undergone considerable change. The old priest was rubbing the telescope, as if a genie with all the answers were asleep inside. He shrugged. His cassock was so stained and threadbare that it looked more grey than black. Strange contrast, thought Quart: the small, dingy priest beside the gleaming telescope.

"I like watching the sky at night," Father Ferro said at last. "The duchess and her daughter allow me to spend a couple of hours a day up here, after dinner. There's direct access from the courtyard, so I don't bother anyone."

Quart touched the spine of one of the books, *Della celeste fisionomia*, 1616. Next to it were some volumes he'd never heard of, *Tabulae Astronomicae*. A rough village priest, His Grace Aquilino Corvo had said. The thought made Quart smile to himself as he leafed through the astronomical tables.

"When did you become interested in all this?"

Apparently satisfied with the condition of the telescope, Father Ferro put the handkerchief away in his pocket, turned to Quart, took the book from him, and put it back in its place. "I spent many years living on a mountain," he said. "At night, when I sat outside the church, there was nothing to do but look at the sky."

He fell silent, as if he'd said more than he had needed to. It wasn't difficult to picture him sitting at nightfall beneath the stone portico of his village church, staring up at the vault of heaven, where no human light could disturb the harmony of the spheres revolving through the universe. Quart picked up a copy of Heine's *Travel Pictures* and opened it at a page marked by a red ribbon:

Life and the world are the dream of a drunken god, who steals away from the banquet of the gods and falls asleep on a solitary star, unaware that he creates what he dreams of . . . And the images of his dreams appear, at times with a motley extravagance, at others harmonious and rational . . . The *Iliad*, Plato, the battle of Marathon, the Venus de Medici, the French Revolution, Hegel, steamships, all are thoughts that emerge from his long dream. But one day the god will wake, rubbing his sleepy eyes, he will smile, and our world will sink into oblivion and none of it will ever have existed . . .

There was a warm, gentle breeze. Muffled sounds reached the pigeon loft from the courtyards and streets below. Through the windows of a nearby school came a chorus of children's voices reciting a lesson or poem. Quart listened – something about nests and birds. Suddenly the recitation stopped and the chorus burst into cries of laughter.

Over towards the Reales Alcázares, a clock struck three times. It was a quarter to six.

"Why the stars?" asked Quart.

Father Ferro took a small dented tin from his pocket, and from the tin he took a filterless cigarette. He moistened the end with his tongue and put it in his mouth.

"They're pure," he said.

He lit the cigarette in the hollow of his hand, inclining his head as he did so. His forehead and scarred face became even more creased. The smoke floated out through the arched windows while the smell, strong and acrid, reached Quart.

"I understand," Quart said, and Father Ferro turned to look at him with a flicker of interest. The man almost smiled. Unsure whether to regret this or congratulate himself, Quart realised that something had changed. The pigeon loft was a neutral space between heaven and earth where their mutual distrust seemed to diminish, as if, according to the old custom, they could both take sanctuary here. Quart felt the impulse towards comradeship that was often – although in his case not too often – established between one cleric and another. Solitary, lost soldiers encountering each other on the battlefield.

"How long did you spend up there?"

The old priest said, the cigarette smoking in his mouth, "Over twenty years."

"It must have been a small parish."

"Very small. Forty-two people when I arrived. None by the time I left. They either died or moved. My last parishioner was over eighty – she didn't survive the snow that last winter."

A pigeon wandered up and down one of the ledges of the gallery, near the priest. He stared at it intently, as if it might have a message tied to its leg. But when it flew off with a flapping of wings, his gaze remained fixed on the same spot. His clumsy movements, his slovenliness still reminded Quart of the old priest he hated as a child, but now he could see significant differences between that priest and this. He had thought that Father Ferro's roughness sprang from a primitive state. That he was just a grey cleric who, like the priest from Quart's distant past, had not been able to rise above his own mediocrity and ignorance. But here in the pigeon loft Quart found a different kind of priest: consciously reactionary, fully aware that he was renouncing a brilliant career in the Church. It was quite clear that Father Ferro had once been – and in some ways continued to be, almost in secret – more than a coarse village priest, more than the surly, stubborn parish priest who ignored the reforms of the second Vatican Council by celebrating Mass in Latin at Our Lady of the Tears. It was not done from a lack of education or because of age; it was done out of firm conviction. In Quart's terms, Don Priamo Ferro had chosen his flag.

There was a notebook open on the desk, with pencil diagrams of a constellation. Quart thought of the old priest peering through his telescope at night, absorbed in the silence of the firmament revolving slowly beyond the lens, while Macarena Bruner sat reading *Anna Karenina* or the *Sonatas* in one of the old armchairs, moths fluttering around the lamp. He suddenly wanted to laugh at himself. It made him feel terribly jealous.

He saw that Father Ferro was watching him, as if the look on Quart's face had set him thinking.

"Orion," Father Ferro said, and Quart, disconcerted, took a moment to realise that the priest meant the diagram in the notebook. "At this time of year you can see only the topmost star of the Hunter's left shoulder. It's called Betelgeuse and appears over there." He pointed at a section of the sky, still light, on the horizon. "West by northwest." He still had the cigarette in his mouth, and ash dropped on to his cassock.

Quart turned the pages of the book, which were full of notes, diagrams, and figures. He could identify only the constellation of Leo, his own sign. According to legend, the javelins of Hercules had bounced off Leo's body of metal.

"Do you believe," Quart asked, "that everything is written in the stars?"

Father Ferro grimaced. "Three or four centuries ago," he said, "that kind of question would have cost a priest his life."

"I've told you, I've come in peace."

Father Ferro's laughter was sarcastic. A harsh, grating sound. "You're referring to astrology," he said at last. "I'm interested in astronomy. I hope you'll underline the subtle difference in your report to Rome." He fell silent, but went on looking at Quart curiously, as if reappraising him. "I have no idea where things are written," he added after a while. "Although I can tell at a glance that you and I aren't even using the same alphabet."

"Please explain."

"There's not much to explain. You work for a multinational organisation that is based on all the demagogy Christian humanism and the Enlightenment filled our heads with: that man evolves to higher states through suffering, that humanity is destined to reform itself, that goodwill begets more goodwill . . ." He turned to the window, again dropping ash down his cassock. "Or that Truth with a capital T exists, and is enough in itself."

Quart was shaking his head.

"You don't know me," he said. "You don't know anything about me."

"I know who you work for. That's enough." He turned back to the telescope, checking again for dust. He put his hands in his pocket. "What do you or your bosses in Rome know, with your bureaucrats' mentality? All you know of love or hate are their theological definitions, or whispers in the confessional. . . . I can tell at glance, just by the way you talk and move, that you're a man whose sins are those of omission. You're one of the TV preachers, pastors of a soulless church, who speak of the faithful the way companies speak of their customers."

"You're wrong about me, Father. My work . . ."

The old priest again made the grating sound that was his laughter. "Your work!" He turned abruptly to Quart. "Now you're going to tell me that you get your hands dirty, aren't you? Even though you're always so well groomed. I'm sure you have plenty of justifications and alibis. You're young, strong, your superiors give you room and board, they think for you and throw you bones to gnaw. You're the perfect policeman working for a powerful corporation that serves God. You've probably never loved a woman, or hated a man, or felt sympathy for a miserable wretch. No poor have blessed you for their bread, no sick for their solace, no sinners for their hope of salvation. . . . You follow orders, nothing more."

"I follow the rules," said Quart, and instantly regretted it.

"Do you?" The old priest looked at him with intense irony. "Well, my congratulations. You'll save your soul. Those who follow the rules always go to heaven." His mouth twisted as he took a last drag on his cigarette. "To rejoice in God's presence." He threw the cigarette end out of the window and watched it fall.

"I wonder," said Quart, "if you still have faith."

These were strange words, coming from Quart, and Quart knew it. Quite apart from the fact that such questions – more appropriate to the hounds of the Holy Office – were not within the jurisdiction of his mission. As Spada would have said, at the IEA we deal not with people's hearts but with their actions. Let's stick to being good centurions and leave the dangerous task of probing the human soul to His Eminence Jerzy Iwaszkiewicz.

And yet Quart waited for an answer in the long silence that followed his remark. As the old priest moved slowly round the telescope, his reflection slid along the polished brass tube.

"Still is an adverb of time," Father Ferro said at last, frowning, possibly reflecting on time, or adverbs. "But I forgive sins," he added. "I help people die in peace."

"It's not your office to forgive," Quart said. "Only God can do that."

The priest looked at him, as if he'd forgotten that Quart was there. "When I was young," he said suddenly, "I read all the philosophers of Antiquity, from Socrates to Saint Augustine. And I forgot them. The only thing that remained of them was bittersweet melancholy and disillusionment. Now I'm sixty-four, and all I know about people is that they remember, they're afraid, and they die."

Quart must have looked surprised and embarrassed, because Father Ferro nodded, his hard dark eyes fixing him for a moment. He looked up at the sky. The solitary cloud – maybe no longer the same one – had gone to meet the setting sun, and a reddish glow now spread over the distant buildings.

"I searched for Him up in the mountains for a long time," Father Ferro went on. "I wanted to have it out with Him, a kind of settling of scores, one to one. I'd seen so many people suffer and die . . . Forgotten by my bishop and his aides, I lived in atrocious solitude. I emerged only to say Mass every Sunday in a small, almost empty church, or to trudge through rain or snow to give extreme unction to a soul who waited for my arrival to die. For twenty-five years, sitting at the bedside of those who gripped my hands because I was their only comfort in the face of death, I prayed to Him. But I never received an answer."

He broke off. It was Quart who spoke now: "Either we live and die according to a plan, or merely by accident." It was neither a question nor an answer. He was just prompting Father Ferro to continue. For the first time, Quart had some understanding of the man before him; and he knew that Father Ferro could sense this.

The old priest's face softened. "How to preserve, then," he said, "the message of life in a world that bears the seal of death? Man dies, he knows he will die, and he also knows that, unlike kings, popes and generals, he'll leave no trace. He tells himself there must be something more. Otherwise, the universe is simply a joke in very poor taste; senseless chaos. So faith becomes a kind of hope, a solace. Maybe that's why not even the Holy Father believes in God anymore."

Quart burst out laughing, startling the pigeons. "That's why you're defending your church tooth and nail," he said.

"Of course." Father Ferro frowned. "What does it matter whether I have faith or not? Those who come to me have faith. That's justification enough for the existence of Our Lady of the Tears. And it's no coincidence that it's a church of the baroque, which was the art of the Counter-Reformation, which declared, 'Don't think. Leave that to the theologians. Admire the carvings, the gilding, the sumptuous altars, the passion plays that have been the essential means of entrancing the masses since the time of Aristotle . . . Be dazzled by the glory of God. Too much analysis robs you of hope. See us as the solid rock on which to take refuge from the roaring torrent. The truth kills you before your time.'"

Quart raised a hand: "There's a moral objection to all this, Father. What you describe is alienation. Your church, presented like that, is the seventeenth-century equivalent of television."

"So what?" said Father Ferro with a shrug. "What was religious baroque art but an attempt to win the audience away from Luther and Calvin? Anyway, where would the modern papacy be without television? Naked faith can't be sustained. People need symbols to wrap around themselves, because it's cold outside. We're responsible for our last innocent faithful, those who followed us believing that we'd lead them to the sea, lead them home, as in the *Anabasis.* At least my old stones, my altarpiece, and my Latin are more dignified than all that amplified singing and the huge screens that have turned services into a spectacle for the masses, dazzling them with electronic gimmicks. The Church leaders think that's the way to keep their customers. But they're wrong, they only degrade us. The battle's been lost, and now the time has come for false prophets."

He shut his mouth and bowed his head, morose. The conversation was over. He leaned on the window ledge and looked out over the river. Quart didn't know what to do or say. After a moment he went and leaned on the ledge beside Father Ferro. He had never been so near the priest. Father Ferro's head came up to his shoulder. They stood like that, without speaking, until long after the clocks on the towers of Seville struck six. The solitary cloud had dissolved and the sun was sinking. To the west, the sky was slowly turning gold. Don Priamo Ferro spoke again.

"I know only one thing: when the seduction is over we'll be finished too. Logic and reason will mean the end. But as long as some poor woman needs to kneel in my small church in search of comfort, the church must remain standing." He took his dirty handkerchief from his pocket and noisily blew his nose. The light from the setting sun lit the white stubble on his chin. "Burdened as we are by our miserable condition, priests like me are still needed . . . We're the old, patched drum skin on which the glory of God still thunders. And only a madman would envy our secret. We know," said the old priest darkly, "the angel who holds the key to the abyss."

IX
It's a Small World

Worthy of being dark and Sevillian.
Campoamor, *The Express Train*

The floodlights illuminating the cathedral created an area of unreal brightness in the night. Confused by the light, pigeons flew in all directions, suddenly appearing and then disappearing into the darkness among the huge mountain of cupolas, pinnacles and flying buttresses, on top of which perched the tower of La Giralda. It was almost fantastical, thought Quart, a backdrop as extraordinary as old Hollywood movie sets made of canvas and papier-mâché. The difference was that the Plaza Virgen de los Reyes was real, built of bricks over the centuries – the oldest part dated from the twelfth century – and no film studio could have reproduced such an incredible place, however much money and talent they threw at the project. It was unique, a perfect stage. Particularly when Macarena Bruner walked across it and stopped beneath the huge lamppost in the centre of the square. She stood against the golden glow of the floodlit stone façades, tall and slender, her dark eyes calmly fixed on Quart.

"There are very few sights like this," she said.

It was true, but the man from Rome was also aware of how much the woman's presence added to the fascination of the place. The daughter of the duchess of El Nuevo Extremo was dressed as she had been that afternoon in the courtyard of the Casa del Postigo, but she now had a light jacket around her shoulders and carried a small leather rucksack. They had hardly spoken as they walked here. Quart had left Father Ferro in his observatory and taken leave of the duchess. Come back to see us, the elderly lady said pleasantly, and as a souvenir she gave him a small mudéjar tile of a bird. It once decorated the courtyard but it fell from the wall in the bombardments of 1843 and spent a century and a half amongst several dozen broken and damaged tiles in a cellar near the old stables. As Quart was leaving the house with the tile in his pocket, Macarena stopped him at the gate. She suggested they take a walk and then eat tapas in a bar in Santa Cruz. Unless you have another appointment, she added, giving him a look. With an archbishop or something. Quart laughed, buttoning his jacket. And now here they were, the two of them, in the plaza with the illuminated cathedral. Looking at each other. And none of this, Quart thought with clarity, was doing much for the spiritual tranquillity that the ordinances of the Church recommended for the eternal salvation of a priest's soul.

"I'd like to thank you," she said.

"What for?"

"For Don Priamo."

More pigeons flew into the darkness. Quart and Macarena walked towards the Reales Alcázares and the arch in the wall, she turning to him occasionally, a faint smile on her lips. "You got close to him," she said. "Maybe now you understand."

Quart said he could understand certain things. Father Ferro's attitude, his stubbornness about the church, his resistance to Quart's mission there. But was that only part of the problem. Quart's task in Seville was to make a general report on the situation, including, if possible, the identity of Vespers. But he still had no information on the hacker. Father Oscar was about to leave, and Quart hadn't been able to determine whether he had anything to do with the matter or not. And Quart had yet to go through the police reports and review the investigation of the archbishop's palace into the deaths of the two men at the church. In addition – he indicated the jacket pocket where he'd put Carlota Bruner's postcard – he had yet to solve the mystery of the card and the page marked in the New Testament.

"Whom do you suspect?" Macarena asked.

They now stood in the archway by the small baroque altar to the Virgin, which was enclosed in glass, and Quart's laughter echoed dry and humourless in the vault. "Everybody," he said. "Don Priamo Ferro, Father Oscar, your friend Gris Marsala . . . Even you. Everyone here is a suspect, whether suspected of the deed or of keeping silent."

He glanced to the left and right as they entered the courtyard of the Alcázares, as if he expected to find culprits there, lying in wait. "I'm sure you're all covering up for one another. It would take only one of you to talk openly for thirty seconds, and my investigation would be closed."

Macarena stood beside him, looking at him intently, holding her rucksack to her chest. "Is that what you think?" she asked.

Quart inhaled the fragrance of the orange trees in the courtyard. "I'm certain of it," he said. "Vespers is one of you, and he sent the message to attract Rome's attention and help Father Ferro save his church . . . He believes, in his simplicity, that appealing to the Pope will mean the truth will out. That the truth cannot harm a just cause. Then I come to Seville, ready to uncover the truth that Rome wants, which possibly is not the truth as you all see it. Maybe that's why nobody's helping me, why instead I am presented with mystery after mystery, including the riddle of the postcard."

They walked on, crossing the square. Sometimes their steps brought them closer to each other, and Quart was aware of her perfume, like jasmine, with hints of orange blossom. Her smell was the smell of the city.

"Maybe the point is not to help you," she said, "but to help others. Perhaps it's all about making you see what's happening."

"I understand Father Ferro's attitude. But my understanding is of no use. You sent your message, hoping for a good cleric full of sympathy, and what they sent is a soldier wielding Joshua's sword." He shook his head. "Because that's what I am, a soldier, like that Sir Marhalt you were so keen on as a young girl. My job is to report the facts and find those responsible. It's up to others to show understanding and find solutions, if there are any." He paused and then smiled slightly. "It's no use seducing the messenger."

They came to the curving passageway that led into Santa Cruz. As they walked, their shadows joined along the whitewashed walls. It was strangely intimate, and Quart felt relieved when they emerged at the other end, into the night.

"Is that what you think?" she asked. "That I'm trying to seduce you?"

Quart didn't answer. They went on in silence by the wall, then turned down a narrow street that took them into the old Jewish quarter.

"Sir Marhalt also championed just causes," she said.

"Those were different times. Anyway, your Sir Marhalt was only a creation of John Steinbeck's. There are no just causes left. Even mine isn't one." He paused, as if reflecting on the truth of his words. "But it's my cause."

"You forget Father Ferro."

"His isn't a just cause. It's a personal choice. Everyone gets by as they can."

"Oh, please. I've seen *Casablanca* about twenty times. That's all I need, a priest playing the disillusioned hero. A priest who thinks he's Humphrey Bogart."

"I don't. I'm taller. Anyway, you're wrong. You know nothing about me." She walked on ahead, staring straight in front of her, as if she didn't want to hear. He wanted to take her by the arm and hold her back, but he stopped himself. "You don't know why I'm a priest, or why I'm here, or what I've done to be here," he said. "You don't know how many Priamo Ferros I've known in my life, nor how I dealt with them when I received orders." He spoke bitterly, knowing his words were useless. How could she understand?

She turned to face him and said, "It sounds as if you're sorry you don't have a head to send back to Rome in the next post." She moved towards him. "You thought it would be easy, didn't you? But I knew that things would be different once you got to know the victim."

"You're wrong," said Quart, holding her gaze. "My getting to know Father Ferro makes no difference, at least not on an official level."

"And what about unofficially?" She tapped her forehead. "You must have your own thoughts."

"That's my business. Anyway, I've known lots of my 'victims', as you put it. And it made no difference."

Her sigh was contemptuous. "I suppose not. I suppose that's why you get to buy custom-made suits from smart tailors, wear expensive shoes and carry credit cards and a fantastic watch." She looked him up and down, provoking, hostile. "They must be your thirty pieces of silver."

She was angry, and Quart began to wonder how far she intended to go. They stood facing each other in a narrow street. Overhead, loaded with flowerpots, the balconies on either side almost touched.

"These clothes," Quart said, holding his lapel between two fingers, showing it to her, "and these shoes, and these credit cards, and this watch are very useful when you're trying to impress a Serbian general or an American diplomat. There are worker priests, married priests, priests who say Mass every morning, and priests like me. And I couldn't tell you who makes it possible for whom to exist." He smiled ironically, but his attention was elsewhere – Macarena was too near him, the street too narrow. "Although your Father Ferro and I agree on one thing: neither of us has any illusions about his job."

He stopped, suddenly afraid of his need to justify himself to her. They were alone in the street, lit by a distant streetlight. She looked lovely, her parted lips showing her white teeth. She breathed slowly, with the serenity of a woman who is beautiful and knows it. Her expression was no longer contemptuous. Quart felt a very real, physical, male fear, similar to vertigo. He had to make an effort not to step backward and rest against the wall. "Why won't you tell me what you know?" he asked.

She looked at him as if she'd expected something else. Her eyes moved to his dog collar. "You may not believe this, but I know very little," she answered finally. "I can guess at certain things. But I won't be the one to speak. You do your job, while others do theirs."

Quart set off up the narrow street. She followed in silence, clasping her leather rucksack to her chest.

Inside Las Teresas, hams hung among bottles of La Guita, old posters for Holy Week and the April *feria*, and faded photographs of slender, serious, long-dead bullfighters. At the bar, waiters wrote down customers' orders while Pepe, the manager, cut thin slices of Jabugo ham with a long razor-sharp knife, singing softly:

How pleased I am,
dear cousin,
how pleased I am
to eat Serrano ham.

He addressed Quart's companion as Doña Macarena and, without either of them ordering anything, brought them tapas of pork in tomato sauce, pork sausage, grilled mushrooms, and two tall-stemmed glasses of fragrant, golden Manzanilla. By the door, leaning on the bar beside Quart, a regular with a red face was conscientiously downing one glass of wine after another. Pepe stopped singing occasionally and, still slicing ham, exchanged a few words with him about a football match soon to be played between Sevilla and Betis.

"Fantastic," the red-faced man said with drunken regularity. Pepe nodded and started singing again, and the man went back to his wine. A grey mouse poked its head from his jacket pocket. From time to time the man gave it little pieces of cheese from the plate beside him on the bar. The rodent diligently nibbled the cheese and nobody seemed in the least surprised.

Macarena sipped her Manzanilla. She rested an elbow on the bar confidently, as if she were at home. In fact, she moved through all of Santa Cruz as if it were part of her home; and in a way it was, or had been for centuries – every corner recorded in her genetic memory, known to her territorial instinct. Quart realised, and the realisation did nothing to calm the IEA agent, that he couldn't conceive of the district or the city without her presence, her black hair, her white teeth, her dark eyes. Once again he thought of the paintings of Romero de Torres, and the old tobacco factory that now housed the university. Carmen the cigarette girl, the damp tobacco leaves rolled against a tanned thigh. He looked up, and his eyes met hers, intent upon him.

"Do you like Seville?" Macarena asked.

"Very much," he said, wondering if she could guess his thoughts.

"It's a special place." She picked at their tapas. "The past and the present live here quite happily side by side. Gris says that we Sevillians are old and wise. We accept anything, and anything's possible." She glanced briefly at their neighbour with the red face and smiled. "Even sharing one's cheese in a bar with a mouse."

"Is your friend any good with computers?"

The look she gave him was almost admiring. "You never give up, do you?" she said, spearing a mushroom with a cocktail stick and eating it. "You have a one-track mind. Why don't you ask her?"

"I did. She was evasive, as you all are."

A man came in. He was fat, about fifty, and dressed in white. For a moment Quart thought he'd seen him somewhere before. The fat man raised his hat as he passed, looked around as if searching for someone, peered at his watch, then left by the other door, swinging a silver-handled walking stick. Quart noticed that the man's left cheek was red and covered with ointment, and that his moustache looked peculiar, as if it had been singed.

"What about the postcard?" Quart asked Macarena. "Does Gris Marsala have access to your great-aunt Carlota's trunk?"

She smiled, amused at his persistence. "She knows where it is, if that's what you mean. But it could just as easily have been Don Priamo. Or Father Oscar, or even me. Or my mother . . . Can you picture the duchess with her Coca-Cola, wearing a baseball cap back-to-front, hacking into the Vatican computer system in the wee hours?" She speared a piece of meat in tomato sauce and offered it to Quart. "I'm afraid your investigation may become absurd."

As Quart took the cocktail stick from Macarena, his fingers brushed hers. "I'd like to have a look at that trunk," he said.

She watched him as he ate the tapa. "Now? You and I, alone?" She smiled. "That's rather risky, isn't it? Although I suspect your real purpose is to see what kind of computer I have." Pepe put a plate of ham in front of them and she looked absent-mindedly at the red slices streaked with fragrant fat. "Well, why not? It'll give me something to tell my friends. And I'd love to see the archbishop's face when he finds out." She tilted her head to one side thoughtfully. "Or my husband's."

Quart looked at the silver hoops in her ears. "I don't want to cause you any trouble," he said.

She laughed. "Trouble? I hope it makes Pencho green with envy and seethe with rage. If he hears that not only is his deal for the church falling through, but there's also a rather interesting priest hanging around me, he'll go insane." She looked intently at Quart. "And become dangerous."

"Sounds worrying." Quart finished his glass of Manzanilla, not looking in the least bit worried.

"Anyway," said Macarena after a moment's thought, "it would be good for you to see Carlota's trunk. You'd gain a better idea of what Our Lady of the Tears means."

"Your friend Gris," said Quart, taking a slice of ham, "complains that the money for the restoration work has run out . . ."

"It's true. The duchess and I have only just enough to live on, and the parish has no money. Don Priamo has a small salary, and the Sunday collection isn't enough even to pay for candles. Sometimes we feel like explorers in the movies, with the vultures circling. On Thursdays, in particular, a strange scene takes place."

With a couple of Manzanillas in front of them, she told Quart how Our Lady of the Tears couldn't be touched as long as Mass was held there for the soul of her ancestor Gaspar Bruner de Lebrija, at eight in the morning every Thursday. He died on a Thursday in 1709. So an envoy from the archbishop and a notary hired by Pencho Gavira were present in church every Thursday, in a pew at the back, waiting for the slightest error or irregularity.

Quart said he couldn't believe it, and they both laughed. But Macarena was soon serious again. "It sounds childish, doesn't it? Everything depending on such a little thing." She raised her glass to her lips but stopped and put it down. "All it would take to condemn the church is for the priest not to celebrate the Thursday Mass or to deviate from the set formula. The archbishop of Seville and the Cartujano Bank would then win . . . That's why I'm worried that once Father Oscar is out of the way, they'll try something against Don Priamo."

She actually seemed frightened. Quart didn't know what to think. "That's hard to believe," he said at last. "I don't much like Monsignor Corvo, but I'm sure he'd never allow . . ."

She raised a hand, as if to place it on his lips. "I'm not talking about the archbishop," she said. Then she drew back, turned to the bar, and played with the stem of Quart's glass.

You're trying to muddle me, he thought. He didn't know whether she was acting on her own initiative or for others, or whether the aim was to seduce the messenger or neutralise the enemy. The fact was that between them all, under the pretext of making him see the other side of the story, they were confusing him thoroughly. You need something solid to hold on to, he told himself. Your work, the investigation, the church, anything. Data and facts, questions and answers. A clear mind, a serenity like hers. Woman as instrument of the devil, beacon of perdition, enemy of humanity and the immortal soul. Keep a distance or you're finished, Lorenzo Quart. What was it Monsignor Spada said? If a cleric kept money out of his pocket and his legs out of a woman's bed, he stood a chance of saving his soul. Or something like that.

"About the money," he said. He had to keep asking questions. He was here to carry out an investigation, not to have Carmen of the Tobacco Factory place her fingers on his lips. "Have you thought of selling the pictures in the vestry to fund restoration work?"

"They're not worth anything. The Murillo isn't even genuine."

"What about the pearls?"

She looked at him as if he'd just said something incredibly stupid. "Why doesn't the Vatican sell off its art collection and give the money to the poor?" she replied. She finished her drink, took out her wallet, and asked for the bill. Quart insisted on paying but she wouldn't hear of it. The manager was apologetic: I'm sorry, Father, Doña Macarena's a regular, etc.

They went out into the street. Their shadows lengthened in the light of the streetlamps. In the stretches without lights, the moon took over, white and almost full between the shadows of the eaves and the balconies above their heads. After a moment she spoke. "You still don't understand," she said, sardonic. "The pearls are Carlota's tears. Captain Xaloc's legacy."

Footsteps echoed loudly in the narrow streets, so the three villains kept at a healthy distance from the pair, and they took turns passing them so as not to arouse suspicion: sometimes Don Ibrahim and La Niña Puñales, with El Potro del Mantelete staying behind; at others El Potro on his own, or with La Niña on his arm – the arm that wasn't burned and in a sling – but always keeping the priest and the young duchess in sight. It wasn't easy, because the streets of Santa Cruz twisted and turned, and had many dead ends. On one occasion, the three colleagues had to reverse in a hurry, tiptoeing panic-stricken into the shadows, when Quart and Macarena came to a closed square and returned the way they'd come after standing and talking for a few minutes.

Now everything was all right again. The pair were walking along a street with gentle turns and wide doorways, so they could be followed without much risk. More relaxed, Don Ibrahim – a large pale form in the darkness – took out a cigar and put it in his mouth, twirling it voluptuously in his fingers. El Potro and La Niña walked nine or ten paces ahead, keeping a close eye on the priest and the young duchess. The former bogus lawyer felt a wave of affection as he watched his companions. They were carrying out their mission very conscientiously. In the quiet stretches, La Niña removed her high-heeled shoes to make less noise. She walked with a grace that the years hadn't taken from her in spite of everything, carrying her shoes and the handbag that contained her crocheting, Peregil's camera, and the newspaper clipping allegedly about a man with green eyes who had killed for her love. Eternal Niña in her polka-dot dress, with her dyed hair, the kiss-curl like Estrellita Castro's: a flamenco singer heading for an imaginary *tablao*. At her side, serious, manly, El Potro gave her his good arm, knowing that it was the most precious homage he could pay to a woman like her.

His walking stick under his arm, Don Ibrahim lit his cigar. He pocketed the dented silver cigarette lighter – a keepsake from Gabriel García Márquez, whom Don Ibrahim knew, he said, when the author of *No One Visits Colonel Paramo* was a humble reporter in Cartagena de Indias – and felt the tickets for Sunday's bullfight, purchased that very afternoon by El Potro. In his spare time, the former bullfighter and boxer worked with gangs of thimblerig players near Triana Bridge. He was a shield for the guy who handled the three cups and the little ball: Now you see it, now you don't, come along, sir, lay down twenty-five thousand pesetas. And all around, accomplices crowed about their winnings, and a couple of men on the corner watched out for the police. Looking grave and responsible, in a checked jacket that was too small, El Potro inspired confidence. Thanks to his performance, he and his colleagues had relieved a Puerto Rican tourist of a good wad of dollars. So to make up for his blunder with the Anis del Mono bottle, El Potro presented Don Ibrahim and La Niña with expensive tickets for the bullfight. He'd invested his entire morning's earnings in the three tickets, because there were some really big names on the bill: Curro Romero, Espartaco, and Enrique Ponce (Curro Maestral had been taken off at the last minute with no explanation) and six – six! – Cardenal y Murube bulls.

Don Ibrahim expelled a cloud of smoke and touched the tender skin on his cheek that had been carefully covered with ointment. His moustache and eyebrows had been singed, but he really couldn't complain: it had very nearly been a catastrophe, but they had got away with superficial burns, a ruined table, a blackened ceiling, and a big fright. Particularly when they saw El Potro running around the room with his arm on fire, as in the film with Vincent Price in the wax museum. With great presence of mind and invoking the Virgin Mary, La Niña had given Don Ibrahim a good squirt with the soda siphon and thrown a blanket over the table to put out the fire. After that, it was all smoke, explanations, neighbours banging at the door, and a rather uncomfortable moment when the firemen arrived and found no fire, just the three red-faced partners. By tacit agreement none of them ever referred to the unfortunate incident again. For, as Don Ibrahim put it, raising a learned finger after La Niña got back from the pharmacy with a tube of ointment and plenty of gauze, there are painful episodes in life that are best put out of one's mind.

The priest and the young duchess must have stopped to talk, because La Niña and El Potro were waiting discreetly at the corner, standing against the wall. Don Ibrahim was grateful for the pause – propelling his considerable bulk over long stretches was no easy task. He gazed up at the moon and savoured his cigar, its smoke spiralling gently upwards in the silvery moonlight. Not even the smell of urine and garbage that hung around some of the bars in the darkest streets could entirely obliterate the fragrance of the orange blossom, the jasmine, and the flowers that spilled over the balconies. From behind the blinds one could hear, as one passed, muffled music, snatches of conversation, dialogue from a film or applause on a TV quiz show. From a nearby house came a few bars of a bolero that reminded Don Ibrahim of other moonlit nights on different streets, and he wallowed in nostalgia for his two pasts: the real and the imaginary, which in his memory merged into a series of elegant evenings on the warm beaches of San Juan, long walks through Old Havana, aperitifs in Los Portales de Veracruz with mariachis singing "Divine Women", by his friend Vicente, or "Pretty Maria", a song in whose composition he played such a part. Or perhaps, he said to himself as he took another long drag on his cigar, it was only his youth that he missed. And the dreams that life always destroys.

Anyway, he thought as El Potro and La Niña moved on and he set off after them, he would always have Seville; parts of it reminded him so strongly of places from his past. For at certain corners, in the colour and light, the city retained, as no other city, the gentle hum of time slowly extinguishing itself – or of himself being extinguished. Don Ibrahim took another puff of his cigar and nodded sadly: a beggar was asleep in a doorway, covered with newspapers and cardboard, an empty plate beside him. Instinctively, he put his hand in his pocket and found a coin, beneath the tickets to the bullfight and García Márquez's lighter. He bent down with difficulty and placed the coin next to the sleeping figure. Ten paces further on, he realised that he no longer had change for his phone call to Peregil. He considered turning back and retrieving the coin, but stopped himself. El Potro or La Niña might have some coins. A gesture was a profession of faith. And it wouldn't have been an honourable thing to undo it.

It's a small world, but after that night Celestino Peregil often wondered if the encounter between his boss and the young duchess and the priest from Rome happened by chance, or if she'd promenaded the priest under Gavira's nose on purpose, knowing that at that hour her husband, or ex-husband, or whatever he was technically at that stage, always had a drink at the Loco de la Colina Bar. Gavira was sitting on the crowded terrace with a girlfriend, while Peregil was inside, at the bar, near the door, playing the bodyguard. Gavira had ordered Scotch on the rocks and was savouring his first sip, admiring his companion, an attractive Sevillian model who, despite her notorious deficit in the intellectual department, or maybe because of it, had achieved fame because of a line in a TV ad about a certain make of bra. The sentence was "This is all mine", and Penelope Heidegger, the model – who, anatomically, had every right to make such a claim – said it with devastating effect. Gavira was obviously preparing to enjoy what was all Penelope's in the next few hours. As good a way as any, thought Peregil, for his boss to take his mind off the Cartujano Bank, the church and all the stuff that was making life hell.

The henchman smoothed his hair and glanced around. From his lookout by the door he could see up to the corner of the Calle Placentines. He also had a good view of Penelope's legs, her tiny Lycra miniskirt revealing a generous expanse of thigh, next to Gavira's crossed legs. The temperature was pleasant, and Gavira was in shirt-sleeves, his tie loosened and his jacket hanging over the chair. In spite of his problems, Gavira was looking good, with his hair slicked back, and he exuded wealth, his gold watch gleaming on his strong tanned wrist. Santana's "Europa" was playing. A happy, peaceful, almost domestic scene, thought Peregil. Everything seemed to be going smoothly. There was no sign of the Gypsy Mairena or El Pollo Muelas, and the itching in Peregil's urethra had disappeared thanks to a bottle of Blenox. At that moment, just when he was most relaxed, with high hopes for both himself and his boss – he had his sights on a couple of good-looking chicks sitting at the back, in fact he'd already established eye contact – and as he ordered another whisky ("a twelf-year-old", he told the waiter with cosmopolitan aplomb), he suddenly wondered how things were going for Don Ibrahim, El Potro and La Niña and where they might be at this time of night. When they last checked in, they were about to set fire to part of the church, just enough to close it down and prevent Thursday Mass; but he had not heard from them since. He'd probably find a message on his phone when he got home. Such were Peregil's thoughts as he sipped his whisky. Then he saw the young duchess and the priest from Rome turn the corner, and he nearly choked on an ice cube.

He moved closer to the door but stayed inside. He sensed catastrophe. It was no secret that Gavira was insanely jealous of his still lawfully wedded wife. And even if he hadn't been, the front cover of *Q&S* and those photographs with the bullfighter were reason enough for the banker to be furious. To cap it all, the priest was handsome, well dressed, classy. Like Richard Chamberlain in *The Thorn Birds* but more manly. Peregil started trembling, especially when he saw El Potro, with La Niña on his arm, poke his head discreetly round the corner. After a moment Don Ibrahim joined them, and the three associates stood there, disconcerted and doing a very poor job of looking casual. Peregil wished the earth would swallow him up.

With the blood throbbing at his temples, Pencho Gavira stood up slowly, trying to keep control. "Good evening, Macarena," he said.

Never act on your first impulse, old Machuca had told Gavira when he was starting out. Dilute the adrenaline, do something with your hands, and leave your mind free. Play for time. So he put on his jacket and buttoned it carefully as he stared into his wife's eyes, which were as cold as ice.

"Hello, Pencho," she said, with barely a glance at his companion, an almost imperceptible sneer at the tight skirt and the neckline revealing the bosom that had become a part of the national heritage. For a moment, Gavira wasn't sure who was reproaching whom. Everyone on that terrace, in the bar, in the whole street, was staring at them.

"Would you like a drink?"

Whatever else his enemies might say, they could not deny that he had nerves of steel. He smiled politely, even though every muscle was taut and a red veil blurred his vision as the throbbing increased. He adjusted his tie and stared at the priest, waiting to be introduced. The cleric was pretty elegantly turned out, in a black custom-made suit, black silk shirt, and round collar. On top of that, he was tall. Gavira hated tall men. Particularly when they were quite openly walking through Seville in the evening with his wife. He wondered whether people would disapprove if he punched a priest in the face outside a bar.

"Pencho Gavira. Father Lorenzo Quart."

They continued to stand. Penelope was still sitting, forgotten for the moment, on the margins. Gavira shook Quart's hand, gripping it hard, and the priest responded with equal strength. The priest's eyes were calm, and the banker told himself that there was no reason to think the priest was involved. But when Gavira turned to look at his wife, Macarena's eyes were like daggers. His anger was starting to get the better of him. He sensed that everyone was staring at him. They'd be talking about this for a week.

"You go out with priests now, do you?"

He hadn't wanted it to come out like that. He hadn't wanted to say it at all, but it was too late. There was the hint of a triumphant smile on Macarena's lips and he knew he'd fallen into the trap. It made him even more furious.

"That's extremely rude, Pencho," she said.

It was clear how she felt, and anything he said or did would be noted and used against him. And on that terrace all Seville was a witness. She might even present the priest as her father confessor. Meanwhile, the tall priest was waiting, watching them both without a word. He obviously wanted to avoid trouble, but he didn't look uneasy. He even seemed rather friendly, standing there silently, with his sporty look, like a basketball player in mourning clothes by Armani.

"How's the celibacy going, Father?"

It was as if another Pencho Gavira was taking charge, and the banker had no choice but to go along with it. Resigned to his fate, he smiled after he'd said it. A broad smile. Damn all women, the smile implied. It's their fault that we're standing here, you and I, face to face.

"Fine, thanks." The priest sounded calm, in control, but Gavira noticed that he'd turned slightly to one side. He'd also taken his left hand out of his pocket. This priest's been in a fight before, thought the banker.

"I've been trying to speak to you for days," Gavira said, turning to Macarena but without taking his eye off the priest. "You never answer the phone."

She shrugged contemptuously. "There's nothing for us to talk about." She said it very slowly and clearly. "Anyway, I've been busy."

"So I see."

In her chair, La Heidegger was crossing and uncrossing her legs for the benefit of passers-by, customers and waiters. Accustomed to being the centre of attention, she was rather put out. "Aren't you going to introduce me?" she asked Gavira.

"Shut up." The banker faced the priest again. "As for you . . ." Out of the corner of his eye he could see that Peregil had moved nearer the door, in case he needed him. Just then, a man in a checked jacket and with his arm in a sling passed by. He had a squashed nose, like a boxer's, and he glanced briefly at Peregil, as if expecting a signal from him. When he got none, he continued on down the street and disappeared around the corner.

"As for me," said the priest. He was infuriatingly tranquil, and Gavira wondered how he was going to get out of this without either losing face or causing a scandal. Macarena stood between them, enjoying the situation.

"Seville is very misleading, Father," said Gavira. "You'd be surprised how dangerous she can be when you don't know the rules."

"The rules?" The priest looked at him coolly. "You surprise me, Moncho."

"Pencho."

"Ah."

The banker felt he was losing his composure: "I don't like priests who aren't in cassocks," he said, setting his jaw. "Seems like they're ashamed of being priests."

The cleric stared at Gavira impassively: "You don't like them," he repeated, as if mulling it over.

"Not one bit." The banker shook his head. "And here, married women are sacred."

"Don't be an idiot," said Macarena.

The priest looked at La Heidegger's thighs and then back at Gavira. "I see," he said.

Gavira pointed a finger at the priest's chest. "No," he said, his voice slow, thick, menacing. He regretted every word almost as soon as it was out of his mouth, but he couldn't help himself. It was like a nightmare. "You don't see."

The priest considered Gavira's finger. The red veil before Gavira's eyes was getting thicker. He sensed rather than saw Peregil move closer still, a good subordinate ready to protect his boss. Macarena now looked worried, as if things had gone further than she'd expected. Gavira felt a strong urge to slap both her and the priest, venting all the rage accumulated during the last few weeks over the break-up of his marriage, the church, Puerto Targa, the board of directors that in a few days would decide his future at the Cartujano. His whole life passed before his eyes – the battle to get ahead, the complicated manoeuvring with Don Octavio, his marriage to Macarena, the countless times he'd risked his neck and won. And now that he'd almost made it, Our Lady of the Tears stood there in the middle of Santa Cruz like some dangerous reef. It was all or nothing: you either sail round it or sink. The day you stop pedalling, you'll fall off, as the old banker told him.

Gavira made a tremendous effort not to punch the priest, who'd picked up a glass from the table. It was Gavira's glass. The priest held it casually but like a weapon. Gavira realised that Quart wasn't the kind of priest who turned the other cheek. That calmed him suddenly, and made him look at the man with curiosity. Even with a kind of perverse respect.

"That's my glass, Father," he said.

The priest apologised with a quiet smile. He put the glass back on the table, where Penelope was impatiently drumming her lacquered nails, and then, nodding briefly, he and Macarena went on their way without another word. Gavira took a long gulp of whisky. He watched them thoughtfully, while Peregil, behind him, breathed a sigh of relief.

"Take me home," pouted Penelope.

Gavira, watching his wife and the priest disappear around the corner, didn't even turn. He emptied his glass and only just stopped himself from smashing it on the ground. "Fuck you," he said.

He handed the glass to Peregil, with a look that was as good as an order. Peregil, with another resigned sigh, shattered the glass on the ground as discreetly as he could. As he did so, he startled an eccentric-looking couple just then passing the bar: a fat man dressed in white, with a hat and walking stick, and, on his arm, a woman in a polka-dot dress, with a kiss-curl like Estrellita Castro's, carrying a camera.

The three of them met up just around the corner, beneath the Arab portico of the mosque, on the steps that smelled of horse manure and old Seville. Don Ibrahim seated himself with difficulty, ash from his cigar dropping onto his paunch.

"We were lucky," he said. "There was enough light to take the photos."

They deserved a few minutes' rest. He was in a good mood, feeling satisfied with a job well done. *Audaces fortuna llevat*, and all that; although he wasn't too sure that *llevat* was the right verb.

La Niña sat down next to him with a jangling of bracelets and earrings, the camera in her lap. "I'll say," she agreed in her husky voice. She put her shoes down and rubbed her bony legs, which were covered with varicose veins. "Peregil can't complain this time. By God he can't."

Don Ibrahim fanned himself with his panama and stroked his singed moustache. In this moment of success, his cigar smelled glorious. "No," he said festively. "He can't. He saw himself how it was all carried out with impeccable, almost military precision. Isn't that right, Potro? Like commandos in the movies."

Since no one had told him to sit down, El Potro stood, as if on duty, and nodded. "Exactly," he said.

"Which way did the lovebirds go?" asked Don Ibrahim, placing the panama on his head.

El Potro glanced down the street and said they were heading toward the Arenal; plenty of time to catch up with them.

Don Ibrahim took the camera from La Niña's lap and handed it to him. "Go on, take out the film before it spoils."

Obediently, manoeuvring with both his good arm and the one in the sling, El Potro opened the camera while Don Ibrahim searched for the other roll of film. At last he found it, took it out of its box, and handed it to his associate. "You did rewind it, didn't you?" he asked casually. "Before opening the camera?"

El Potro, very still, stared at Don Ibrahim. Suddenly he snapped shut the camera. "What was it I was supposed to rewind?" he asked suspiciously, arching an eyebrow.

Holding the new film in one hand and his cigar in the other, Don Ibrahim looked at him for some time. "Shit," he said.

They walked in silence to the Arenal. Macarena turned to look at Quart from time to time, but neither of them spoke. There wasn't much to say, and he couldn't ask whether the encounter with her husband had been an accident or planned by her. He would probably never know, he thought.

"This is the way he went," Macarena said at last, when they came to the river.

They descended wide steps that led to the quays of the Guadalquivir, at the foot of the ancient Arab tower named Torre del Oro. There wasn't the slightest breeze, and the shadows of the palms, jacarandas, and bougainvilleas were motionless in the moonlight.

"Who?" he asked.

"Captain Xaloc."

Dark and still, tourist boats were moored to pontoons along the deserted bank. The black water reflected the lights of Triana on the opposite side, bounded by strings of car headlights on the Isabel II and San Telmo bridges.

"This was Seville's old port," said Macarena. She wore her jacket round her shoulders and still clutched her leather bag to her chest. "Only a century ago, there would have been ships docking here . . . The remains of the great trade with America. Ships sailed down the river to Sanlucar, then Cadiz, before crossing the Atlantic." She walked forward and stopped by a flight of steps leading down to the dark water. "Old photographs show all kinds of vessels – brigantines, schooners, skiffs – moored on both banks . . . Over there were the fishermen's boats, and boats with white awnings that brought the cigarette girls over from Triana to the tobacco factory. All the cranes and the warehouses were here on this quay."

She fell silent, turning towards the Paseo del Arenal, the dome of the Maestranza Theatre, the modern buildings that stood between them and the tower of La Giralda, lit up in the distance, and Santa Cruz, hidden from view.

"It was a forest of masts and sails," she added. "That was what Carlota saw from the pigeon loft."

They walked along the quay in the shadows cast by the trees in the moonlight. A young couple was kissing in the light of a street-lamp, and Quart saw Macarena watching them with a thoughtful smile.

"You are nostalgic," he said, "for a Seville you've never known."

Her smile widened, then her face was again in shadow. "That's not true," she said. "I knew it well, and still do. I've read and dreamed a lot about this city. Some things my grandfather and mother told me. Others I simply knew instinctively." She touched her wrist, where her pulse beat. "I feel them here."

"Why did you choose Carlota Bruner?"

Macarena took a moment to answer. "She chose me." She turned to Quart. "Do priests believe in ghosts?"

"Not really. Ghosts don't stand up to electric light or nuclear power . . . Or to computers."

"Maybe that's their charm. I believe in them, or at least in a certain type of ghost. Carlota was a romantic young woman who read novels. She lived wrapped in cotton wool in an artificial world, protected from everything. One day she met a man. A real man. It was as if she'd been struck by lightning. Unfortunately, Manuel Xaloc fell in love with her too."

Occasionally they passed the motionless shadow of someone fishing from the quay, the ember of a cigarette, a glint of light at the end of a rod and line, a splash in the calm waters. A fish flapped on the paving stones of the quay, gleaming in the moonlight until a hand returned it to the bucket.

"Tell me about Xaloc," said Quart.

"He was thirty years old and poor, a second officer on one of the steamers that sailed between Seville and Sanlucar. They met when Carlota took a journey downriver with her parents. They say that he was also handsome, and I imagine that his uniform added to his looks. You know that's often true of sailors, soldiers . . ."

She seemed about to add something but left the sentence unfinished. They passed a tourist boat moored to the quay, black and silent. Quart managed to make out its name in the moonlight: *LOVELY*.

Macarena went on. "Xaloc was caught lurking by the railings of the Casa del Postigo, and my great-grandfather Luis had him fired. He also used all his influence, and it was considerable, to make sure that the man didn't get a job anywhere else. Desperate, Xaloc decided to go to America to seek his fortune. Carlota promised she would wait for him. It's the perfect plot for a romantic novel, don't you think?"

They walked side by side, and once again their steps occasionally brought them so close together that they almost touched. Suddenly Macarena stepped around an iron bollard in the darkness, and she was right next to Quart, brushing his side for the first time. She seemed to take an age to move away.

"Xaloc boarded his ship here," she said. "A schooner called the *Nausicaä.* Carlota wasn't even allowed to come and say goodbye. From the pigeon loft she watched the ship sail down the river; it wouldn't have been possible for her to see him from so far away, but she claimed he was on deck, waving a handkerchief until the boat was out of sight."

"How did things go for Xaloc?"

"Well. After a time he was given command of a ship and smuggled goods between Mexico, Florida and Cuba." There was a hint of admiration in her voice. Quart could picture Manuel Xaloc on the bridge of a ship, a column of smoke on the horizon. "They say he wasn't exactly a saint, that he also did some pirating. Some of the ships that crossed his path sank without trace, or were found mysteriously adrift, plundered. I suppose he was in a hurry to make his fortune and return . . . For six years he sailed the Caribbean and he acquired quite a reputation. The Americans put a price on his head. One day, out of the blue, he landed in Seville with a fortune in banknotes and gold coins and a velvet bag that contained twenty wonderful pearls for their wedding."

"Even though he'd never heard from her?"

"Yes. I suppose Xaloc was a romantic too. He assumed that my great-grandfather had prevented Carlota from writing and he had faith in her love, and in a way he was right. She told him she'd wait for him, and she was still waiting in the tower, watching the river." Macarena stared at the black current. "She had gone mad two years before his return."

"Did they get to see each other?"

"Yes. My great-grandfather was devastated. At first he refused. He was an arrogant man and blamed Xaloc for the misfortune. In the end, on the advice of doctors and his wife's pleas, he agreed to a meeting. The captain came one afternoon to the courtyard that you know, in his merchant navy uniform: navy blue, gilt buttons . . . You can picture the scene, can't you? His skin was weathered by the sun, and his moustache and sideburns had turned grey. They say he looked twenty years older than he was. Carlota didn't recognise him. After ten minutes a clock struck and she said, 'I must go to the tower. He may return at any time.' And she left."

"What did Xaloc do?"

"He didn't say a word. My great-grandmother was weeping and my great-grandfather was plunged into despair. Xaloc picked up his cap and left. He went to the church where he'd hoped to be married and gave the priest the pearls he'd brought for Carlota. He spent the night wandering around Santa Cruz, and at dawn he left on the first ship that set sail. This time nobody was there to watch him wave his handkerchief."

There was an empty beer can on the ground. Macarena nudged it into the water with her foot. They heard a faint splash and both watched the small black shape float away.

"You can read the rest of the story," she said, "in newspapers of the time. While Xaloc was on his way back to the Caribbean in 1898, the *Maine* was blown up in the port of Havana. The Spanish government authorised privateering against North America, and Xaloc immediately got hold of a letter of marque. His ship was a very fast cutter, the *Manigua*, armed and with a crew recruited from riffraff in the West Indies. He sailed around probing the blockade. In June 1898, he attacked and sank two merchant ships in the Gulf of Mexico, and had a nighttime encounter with a gunboat, the *Sheridan*, in which both ships were badly damaged . . ."

"You sound as if you're proud of him."

Macarena laughed. He was right. She said she was proud of the man who might have been her great-uncle had the stupidity and blindness of the family not interfered. Manuel Xaloc was a real man, to the end. Did Quart know that he went down in history as the last Spanish pirate, and the only one in the Spanish-American War. His great achievement was breaking the blockade of Santiago. He entered the port at night with messages and supplies for Admiral Cervera, and then on the morning of the third of July he headed out to sea with the other ships. He could have stayed in port since he was a merchant seaman and wasn't under the orders of the squadron, which everyone knew was doomed. It consisted of old and poorly armed ships that didn't stand a chance against the American battleships and cruisers. But he set sail. He went last, after all the Spanish ships, having gone forth one after the other, had been sunk or torched. He didn't think of escape. Instead, he headed for the enemy ships at full steam, with a black flag hoisted alongside the Spanish one. When he was sunk, he was still trying to ram the battleship *Indiana*. There were no survivors."

The lights of Triana, reflected in the river, flickered softly on Macarena's face.

"You know the story well," said Quart.

She smiled slowly. "Of course I do. I've read accounts of the battle a hundred times. I've even kept the newspaper clippings in the trunk."

"Carlota never knew?"

"No." Macarena sat on a stone bench and searched in her bag for her cigarettes. "She waited another twelve years at that window, staring at the Guadalquivir. Gradually the port declined and there were fewer and fewer boats. The schooners no longer plied up and down the river. And one day she too disappeared, from the window." She put a cigarette in her mouth and pulled out her lighter. "By then, the story of Carlota and Captain Xaloc had become a legend. As I said, there were even songs about them. She was buried in the crypt of the church where she would have been married. And by order of my grandfather Pedro, who was the new head of the family after the death of Carlota's father, the twenty pearls were used to represent tears on the face of the Virgin."

She lit her cigarette, shielding the flame of the lighter with her hand. She waited for the lighter to cool and then tucked it back under her bra strap, apparently unaware that Quart was watching her every move. She was engrossed in the memory of Captain Xaloc.

"That was my grandfather's homage," Macarena went on, "to the memory of his sister and the man who might have been his brother-in-law. The church is all that's left of them now. That, and Carlota's things, the letters and all the rest of it." She glanced at Quart, as if she'd just remembered he was there. "Including that postcard."

"There's also you, and your memories."

There was no joy in Macarena's moonlit smile. "I'll die, just like the others," she said quietly. "And the trunk and its contents will end up in an auction, surrounded by other dusty objects, just like everything else." She drew on her cigarette and exhaled the smoke abruptly, almost scornfully.

Quart sat beside her. Their shoulders touched, but he made no effort to move away. The fragrance of jasmine, blended with the smell of tobacco, reached him. "That's why you're fighting your battle," he said.

She nodded. "Yes. My battle, not Father Ferro's. A battle against time and oblivion." She spoke so quietly that Quart could hardly make out her words. "I belong to a breed that's dying out, and I'm fully aware of it. It's lucky, really, because there's no longer a place for people like me and my family, or for memories like mine . . . Or for beautiful, tragic stories like that of Carlota Bruner and Captain Xaloc." The ember of her cigarette glowed. "I'm just waging my own personal war, defending my space." She spoke louder and addressed her words directly to Quart. "When the time comes for me to die, I'll accept my end is near with a clear conscience. Like a soldier who surrenders only when he's fired his last bullet. Having done my duty to the name I bear and to the things I love. That includes Our Lady of the Tears and Carlota's memory."

"Why must it all end like that?" Quart asked gently. "You could have children."

Something flashed across the woman's face. There was a long silence before she spoke again. "Don't make me laugh. My children would become little aliens sitting in front of computer screens, dressed like the kids in American sitcoms. To them Captain Xaloc's name would sound like something out of a cartoon." She threw her cigarette into the river. "So I'll pass on that ending. Whatever there is will die with me."

"And your husband?"

"I don't know. For the time being, he's in good company, as you've seen." She laughed contemptuously. "Let's make him pay all his debts . . . After all, Pencho's the kind of man who likes to rap on the bar for his bill and leave with his head held high." She bowed her head, and that gesture seemed an omen or a threat. "But this time the price will be high. Very high."

"Does he still have a chance?"

She turned to him, surprised, mocking. "With whom? With what? The church deal? With that little tramp with the big tits? With me?" As she moved in the darkness, her eyes reflected distant lights and the pale glow of the moon. "Any man would have a better chance with me. Even you."

"Please, leave me out of it," said Quart. His tone must have been too emphatic, because she paused, interested.

"Why should I leave you out? It would be a wonderful way of taking my revenge. And very pleasant. At least I hope so."

"Revenge against whom?"

"Against Pencho. Against Seville. Against everything."

The shadow of a tug, silent and flat-bottomed, moved down river. After a while, the muffled rumble of motors reached them, as if unrelated to the boat itself, which seemed to move unaided on the current.

"It looks like a ghost ship," she said. "Like the schooner Captain Xaloc sailed away on."

The only light on the vessel, the solitary port-side light, cast a red glow on her face. She followed the boat with her eyes until it took the bend in the river and the green light on the other side showed. The red gradually disappeared, and there remained only a tiny green dot that receded into the distance until it too faded completely.

"He appears on nights like this," she added. "When there's a full moon. And Carlota looks out of her window. Would you like to go and see her?"

"Who?"

"Carlota. We could go into the garden and wait. As when I was a child. Wouldn't you like to come with me?"

"No."

She looked at him for a time in silence. "I wonder," she said, "where you get your damned composure from."

"I'm not as composed as you think." And Quart laughed quietly. "At the moment my hands are trembling."

It was true. He had to stop himself from reaching out and clasping her head, under her ponytail, and pulling her to him. Dear God. From some deep recess of his mind came the memory of Spada laughing. Abominable creatures, Salome, Jezebel. The devil's creation. She put out her hand and linked fingers with Quart, and found that he really was trembling. Her hand was warm. It was the first time they had touched other than in greeting. Quart released his hand carefully, and punched the stone bench hard with his fist. The pain shot up into his shoulder.

"I think it's time for us to go back," he said, standing.

She looked at his hand and then up at his face, disconcerted. Without a word they walked slowly towards the Arenal, avoiding contact. Quart chewed his lip so as not to make a sound of pain. He could feel the blood trickling down his fingers from his wounded knuckles.

Some nights are just too long, and this one wasn't over yet. Quart had just returned to his hotel and taken his key from the sleepy concierge when he saw Honorato Bonafé waiting in the lobby. Among the man's many unpleasant traits was the habit of appearing at the most inconvenient times.

"Could I have a word, Father?"

"No."

With his injured hand in his pocket and holding his key in the other, Quart started towards the lift, but Bonafé stood in the way, smiling in the same unctuous manner as at their earlier meeting. He also wore exactly the same crumpled beige suit and carried the same small bag with a wrist strap. Quart looked down on the journalist's plastered hair, flabby jowls, and cunning, watchful little eyes. Nothing good could have brought the man here.

"I've been investigating," said Bonafé.

"Go away," said Quart, about to ask the concierge to throw him out.

"Aren't you curious to know what I've learned?"

"I'm not interested in anything you have to say."

Bonafé looked hurt. "Pity," he said, puckering his moist lips. "We could come to an agreement. And my offer is generous." He moved his thick waist, swaying slightly. "You tell me a couple of things about that church and the parish priest that I could use in an article, and in exchange I give you a nice little piece of information you don't have." His smile broadened. "And while we're at it, we won't mention your little evening strolls."

Quart stopped dead, not believing his ears. "What do you mean?"

The journalist seemed satisfied that he'd aroused the priest's interest. "Something I know about Father Ferro," he said.

"No, I mean what you said about evening strolls." Quart fixed him with his eyes.

Bonafé waved a small manicured hand dismissively. "Oh, well, what can I tell you? You know . . ." He winked. "Your busy social life here in Seville."

Quart gripped the key in his good hand and considered using it against the man. But that was inconceivable. No priest – not even one as devoid of Christian meekness and with an unusual speciality such as Lorenzo Quart – could fight a journalist over a woman, at night, only twenty metres from the archbishop's palace and a few hours after a public scene with a jealous husband. Even though he belonged to the IEA, they'd post him to Antarctica. So he made a great effort to control himself. Vengeance is mine, saith the Lord.

"I suggest a pact," said Bonafé. "We tell each other a couple of things, I leave you out of all this and we keep it all very friendly. You can trust me. Just because I'm a journalist doesn't mean I don't have principles." He struck his chest theatrically at heart level, his little eyes gleaming cynically between their puffy lids. "My religion is the truth."

"The truth," repeated Quart.

"That's right."

"And what truth do you want to tell me about Father Ferro?"

The man's smile broadened again. A servile, conspiratorial grimace. "Well." He checked his nails. "He's had some problems."

"We all have."

Bonafé clicked his tongue with a worldly look. "Not that kind," he said, lowering his voice lest the concierge overhear. "Apparently, in his previous parish he was short of money. So he sold a few things: a valuable icon, a couple of paintings . . . He didn't tend the Lord's vine as he should." He laughed, amused at his own joke. "He drank the wine."

Quart remained impassive. He'd been trained to take in information and analyse it later. Anyway, he felt a stab to his pride. If this was true, he should have known about it. But nobody had informed him. "And what does this have to do with Our Lady of the Tears?"

Bonafé pursed his lips. "Nothing, in theory. But you have to agree that it would cause a nice little scandal." The odious smile became roguish. "That's journalism for you, Father: a bit of this, a bit of that . . . All we need is a grain of truth somewhere, and voilà, a front-page story. It can be denied later, or we can get more information, or whatever. Meanwhile, two hundred thousand copies have been sold."

Quart looked at him with disgust. "A moment ago, you said the truth was your religion."

"Did I say that?" Bonafé replied, impervious to Quart's contempt. "I must have meant the truth with a small t, Father."

"Get out."

"I'm sorry?" Bonafé was no longer smiling. He glanced warily at the key that Quart was gripping in his left hand. And now Quart took the other hand out of his pocket, its knuckles swollen and covered with dried blood, and the journalist's anxious eyes went from one hand to the other.

"I said get out, or I'll have you thrown out. I might even forget that I'm a priest and throw you out myself." He took a step towards Bonafé, who took two steps back.

"You wouldn't dare . . ." the journalist protested feebly. But he said no more. There were evangelical precedents: the merchants in the temple and all that. There was actually a very expressive relief on the theme only a few metres away, above the door of the mosque.

Quart grabbed Bonafé and dragged his small podgy person towards the door, to the astonishment of the concierge. Bonafé tried to readjust his clothing before receiving one last push that sent him through the door and into the street. His bag fell to the ground.

Quart picked it up and threw it out after him. "I don't want to see you again," he said.

Under the streetlight, the journalist was trying to recover his dignity. His hands were trembling and his hair was dishevelled. He was white with humiliation and fury. "I haven't finished with you," he managed to say at last. His voice cracked in an almost feminine sob. "You son of a bitch."

Quart shrugged; it wasn't the first time he'd been called that. He returned to the lobby. Behind the reception desk, one hand still on the telephone receiver – he'd begun to call the police – the concierge gaped, his eyes popping with astonishment and respect. Some priest.

Despite the cuts on his knuckles and the swelling, Quart could move the joints of his right hand without too much difficulty. Cursing his stupidity aloud, he took off his jacket and went to the bathroom to wash and disinfect the wound. Then he filled a handkerchief with all the ice he could find in the minibar and applied it to his hand. He stood for a while at the window, looking out at the illuminated Plaza Virgen de los Reyes and the cathedral beyond the eaves of the archbishop's palace. He couldn't get the encounter with Bonafé out of his head.

By the time the ice had all melted, his hand didn't feel too bad. He went over to his jacket and emptied the pockets. He placed their contents neatly on the sideboard – wallet, fountain pen, cards for making notes, loose change. The faded postcard to Captain Xaloc showed the church, and the water carrier with his donkey disappearing like a ghost into the white halo surrounding the picture. And the image, voice, smell of Macarena Bruner suddenly flooded Quart; the dam holding it all back burst. The church, his mission in Seville, Bonafé all turned as pale as the vanishing water carrier, and nothing remained but Macarena: her half smile in the darkness on the quay of the Guadalquivir, the glints of honey-coloured light in her dark eyes, the warm smell of her closeness. Carmen the cigarette girl rolling damp tobacco leaves against her thigh. Macarena naked on a hot afternoon, her tanned skin against white sheets and the sun filtering in horizontal stripes through the blinds. Beads of sweat at the forehead edge of her black hair, and in her dark triangle, and on her eyelashes.

It was still very hot. It was almost one in the morning when he went to take a shower. Slowly he undressed, dropping his clothes at his feet. As he did so, it seemed as if a stranger were staring back at him from the wardrobe mirror. A tall, grave man removing shoes, socks and shirt, and then leaning over to undo his belt and drop his black trousers to the floor. Then slipping his underpants down his thighs, uncovering his penis, which was stiff with the memory of Macarena. Quart stood looking at the stranger in the mirror. Slim, with a flat stomach, narrow hips, the pectorals firm and well defined, like the curve of the muscles on his arms and shoulders. Like a soldier, ageless and timeless, devoid of his chain mail and weapons, the silent man regarding Quart looked good. And what, he wondered, was the bloody point of looking so good?

The sound of running water and the awareness of his own body brought the memory of another woman. It was in Sarajevo, August 1992, during a short, dangerous trip to mediate in the evacuation of Monsignor Franjo Pavelić, a Croat archbishop highly regarded by the Pope. Pavelić was under threat from both the Bosnian Muslims and the Serbs. It took 100,000 German marks for them to agree for the prelate to go to Zagreb and not be shot at a checkpoint, which had happened to his assistant, Monsignor Ješić, killed by a sniper. Quart arrived in a United Nations helicopter with an armed escort, the money in a briefcase chained to his wrist. This was Sarajevo in its most brutal period, the shelling of bread lines, twenty or thirty dead every day and hundreds of wounded piling up in the corridors of the hospital, without electricity or medicine; no room in the cemeteries, victims buried in football pitches. Jasmina wasn't exactly a prostitute. There were women who survived by offering their services as interpreters to journalists and diplomats at the Holiday Inn, and they often exchanged more than that for a can of food, a packet of cigarettes. Encouraged by his ecclesiastical garb, Jasmina approached Quart and told him the kind of story that was all too common in the besieged city: an invalid father, the war, the hunger, no cigarettes. Quart promised to get hold of cigarettes and food, and she returned that evening, dressed in black to avoid the snipers. For a handful of marks, Quart got her a packet of Marlboros and some military rations. That night there was running water in the rooms, and she asked if she could take a shower, her first in a month. She undressed by the light of a candle and stood under the water while he watched, fascinated. She was blonde, with pale skin and large firm breasts. With the water running down her body, she turned to look at Quart with a smile of gratitude and invitation. He didn't move, his back against the door frame, he just smiled. That time it hadn't been a question of rules. It was simply that you couldn't receive certain things in exchange for merely food and cigarettes. So when she was dressed, they went down to the hotel bar, and in the light of another candle they drank half a bottle of brandy, while outside, Serbian bombs fell. Afterwards, Jasmina kissed the priest quickly on the mouth and ran off into the shadows.

Shadows and women's faces. The cold water running down his face and body made Quart feel better. He held his injured hand out of the water, rested it against the tiled wall. He stood there for a while, his skin tingling, then got out and dripped on the tiled floor. He dried himself lightly with a towel and lay down on the bed, face up. His naked body left a damp outline on the sheets. He put his wounded hand between his thighs and felt his flesh grow strong and hard, from his thoughts and memories. He could make out a man walking alone between two lights, a solitary Knight Templar on a high plateau beneath a godless sky. He closed his eyes in anguish. He tried to pray, challenging the void behind every word. He felt immense solitude. A quiet, desperate sadness.

X
In Ictu Oculi

Look at that house. It was built by a holy spirit. Magic barriers protect it.
The Book of the Dead

Quart arrived at the church mid-morning, after a brief visit to the archbishop's palace and another to Deputy Superintendent Navajo. Our Lady of the Tears was deserted. The only sign of life was the candle burning at the altar. He sat in a pew and for a long time looked at the scaffolding against the walls, the blackened ceiling, the gilded reliefs of the altarpiece in shadow. When Father Oscar came out of the vestry and saw Quart, he didn't seem surprised. The assistant priest was wearing a grey clerical shirt, jeans, and trainers. He looked older than at their last meeting. His fair hair was unkempt, and he had dark rings under his eyes, visible behind his glasses. His face was greasy, as if he'd woken very early or had a sleepless night.

"Vespers strikes again," Quart told him, showing him the message that had been forwarded by fax from Rome. It had come at around one in the morning, about the time Quart had been dealing with Bonafé in the hotel lobby. The IEA agent didn't mention this to Father Oscar, however. Nor did he tell him that Arregui's team had again managed to divert the hacker to a parallel file, where the hacker left his message in the belief that he was communicating directly with the Holy Father. Father Garofi traced Vespers' signal to the telephone line of El Corte Inglés department store, in the centre of Seville, where the hacker made a loop to hide his trace.

The temple of the Lord is God's place, God's building. If any man defile the temple of God, him shall God destroy; for the temple of God is holy.

* * *

"One Corinthians," said Father Oscar, handing the paper back to Quart.

"Do you know anything about this?"

The young priest seemed about to speak, but instead shook his head dejectedly and sat down beside Quart. "You're still casting about blindly," he said, and added, "You're not as good as they said you were."

"When do you leave?" Quart asked, putting Vespers' message back in his pocket.

"Tomorrow afternoon."

"The place you're going is unpleasant."

"Worse than unpleasant," he said with a sad smile. "It rains about once a year. They might as well send me to the Gobi Desert." He gave Quart a look.

Quart raised a hand. "I had nothing to do with it," he said.

"I know." Oscar Lobato ran his fingers through his hair and stared a while at the candle on the altar. "Monsignor Corvo himself is getting even with me. He thinks I betrayed him." He laughed bitterly. "You know. I was trustworthy, a young priest with a brilliant future. That's why he decided to appoint me as Don Priamo's assistant. But instead of acting as the archbishop's mole, I went over to the enemy."

"High treason," said Quart.

"Yes. And there are certain things the Church will never forgive."

Quart nodded. He could testify to that. "Why did you do it?" he asked. "You knew better than anyone that it was a lost cause."

The assistant priest crossed his legs, resting his feet on the kneeler. "I think I answered that question during our last conversation." His glasses slid down his nose, making him look even more vulnerable. "Sooner or later Don Priamo will be made to leave the parish, and then the era of the merchants will have arrived . . . The church will be demolished and they'll cast lots for her garments." He laughed bitterly, staring straight ahead. "But I'm not so sure that the battle's been lost."

There was silence beneath the vault. The two priests sat motionless.

"Until only a few months ago, I was a promising young cleric," Father Oscar said at last. "All I had to do was sit at the archbishop's feet and keep my mouth shut. But I found my dignity here, both as a man and as a priest. Paradoxical, isn't it? That I should have learned dignity from an old priest with such an unpleasant manner and rough appearance; an Aragonese priest who's as stubborn as a mule, says Mass in Latin and dabbles in astronomy." He leaned back and folded his arms. "Life's strange. The fate that awaits me would once have seemed a tragedy. Now I see it differently. God can be anywhere, in any corner, because He goes with us. Jesus fasted for forty days in the desert. Monsignor Corvo doesn't know it, but now I feel like a real priest, with something to fight for. By sending me into exile, they only make me stronger and more determined. All they've accomplished is to make my faith rock-solid."

"Are you Vespers?"

Father Oscar took off his glasses and wiped them on his shirt. He squinted warily at Quart. "That's all that matters, isn't it? The church, Father Ferro, me – you don't really care about any of it." He clicked his tongue. "You have your mission." Absently, he cleaned one lens, then the other. "Who Vespers is," he said, "isn't important. The message is a warning. Or an appeal to whatever there is that's still noble in the firm that you and I work for." He put on his glasses. "A reminder that honesty and decency still exist."

Quart made a sour face. "How old are you?" he asked. "Twenty-six? With age you'll find you get over that nonsense."

Father Oscar raised an eyebrow. "Did you acquire your cynicism in Rome," he asked, "or was it something you already had? Don't be foolish. Father Ferro is an honest man."

Quart shook his head. An hour before, he had been at the archbishop's palace leafing through Father Ferro's file. Monsignor Corvo confirmed the main points during a brief conversation with Quart in the Gallery of the Prelates, beneath portraits of their graces Gaspar Borja (1645) and Agustin Spinola (1640). Ten years ago, Father Ferro was the subject of an ecclesiastical inquiry in the diocese of Huesca as a result of an unauthorised sale of church property. Towards the end of his time as parish priest in Cillas de Ansó in the Pyrenees, a panel and a figure of Christ on the Cross disappeared. The figure of Christ was nothing special, but the panel dated from the early fourteen-hundreds and was attributed to the Master of Retascón. The local bishop was very concerned when he found out it was missing. The parish was a poor one, and that kind of episode was common at the time, when a parish priest was almost entirely free to dispose as he wished of the heritage entrusted to him. Father Ferro escaped lightly, with only a reprimand from his ordinary.

It certainly bore out what Bonafé had hinted at. Quart sensed that Corvo, uncharacteristically open on this occasion, was probably quite happy that this murky area of Father Ferro's past was becoming public knowledge. Quart suspected even that the journalist's source had been, directly or indirectly, the archbishop himself. In any case, the story about Cillas de Ansó was true; Quart got the next instalment at police headquarters, when Navajo made a couple of calls to his colleague in Madrid, Chief Inspector Feijoo, head of investigations into thefts of works of art. An altarpiece by the Master of Retascón, identical to the one that disappeared from Cillas de Ansó, was acquired with a receipt in due form by Claymore's Auctioneers in Madrid. Francisco Montegrifo, director of Claymore's and a well-known art dealer, confirmed that a certain sum was paid to the priest Don Priamo Ferro Ordás. A pittance compared to what the picture fetched at auction, but it was a question of supply and demand, Montegrifo pointed out to Chief Inspector Feijoo, who then passed the information on to Navajo.

"As for Father Ferro's honesty," Quart said to Father Oscar, "perhaps he hasn't always been so upright."

"I don't know what you're insinuating," said the the young priest. "And I don't care. I respect the man that I know. Go look for your Judas elsewhere."

"Is that your last word? It may not be too late."

Father Oscar glared at him. "Not too late? Is that a hint that I might yet be pardoned? As long as I co-operate?" Shaking his head in disbelief, he stood up. "It's funny. Yesterday Don Priamo mentioned that he'd had a conversation with you at the duchess's and that maybe now you were beginning to understand. But whether you understand or not is irrelevant. Killing the messenger is what matters, isn't it? To you and your bosses, it's not the fact that there's a problem but that someone has dared to bring the problem into the open."

With a last dismissive look he headed towards the vestry. He stopped suddenly, as if he'd thought of something, and half-turned to Quart.

"Maybe Vespers was wrong after all," he said, his voice echoing in the vault. "Maybe the Holy Father wasn't worthy of his messages."

A shaft of sunlight shifted slowly from left to right across the worn flagstones at the foot of the high altar. Quart looked up at the window through which the light streamed: it depicted the Descent from the Cross. The stained glass from Christ's torso, head, and legs was missing, making it seem as if Saint John and Mary were bringing only two arms down from the Cross. The lead around Christ's missing figure formed a ghostly outline, a blurred presence making the mother's and the disciple's suffering and effort appear futile.

Quart walked to the high altar and the entrance to the crypt. He stopped beside the iron gate at the top of steps descending into darkness and touched the skull carved in the lintel; as before, the stone chilled his hand. Trying to suppress his uneasiness at the silence of the church, the gloomy staircase, and the musty air rising from the crypt, he made himself stand there. From the Greek *kryptos*, hidden, he whispered. Where stone held the key to other times, other lives. Where the bones of fourteen dukes of El Nuevo Extremo lay, and the shadow of Carlota Bruner.

The patch of sun on the ground had moved a whole flagstone to the right and was shrinking when the IEA agent proceeded to the middle of the nave. He looked up at the gap where the chunk of cornice had come away, fatally injuring the archbishop's secretary. He went over to the scaffolding supporting the cornice and shook it, but it seemed firmly anchored. He stood at the approximate spot where Father Urbizu had stood when he was killed. There was enough room for someone to stand on the scaffolding under the cornice and dislodge a chunk, but the police report discounted the possibility. That, and the account of the municipal architect's fall – this time with witnesses present – seemed to rule out human intervention in both deaths, attributing them, as Vespers and Father Ferro claimed, to the wrath of God. Or to fate, which in Quart's view was a cosmic watchmaker who seemed to wake up every morning with a taste for practical jokes.

Or to the clumsiness of sleepy Rabelaisian gods. When they dropped a slice of their morning toast, it always fell to earth butter side down.

Vespers' motive was clear. His computer messages were an appeal to common sense, an appeal for justice, to vindicate an old priest fighting his last battle in a forgotten corner of the board. But Father Oscar was right when he said that Vespers had made a mistake in sending his messages. Rome couldn't understand them, and Spada had sent the wrong man. The world and the ideas to which the hacker had made his appeal had long ceased to exist.

Quart took a few steps back and examined the scaffolding and damaged windows on the left-hand side of the church. When he turned again to the nave, Gris Marsala was behind him, watching.

The exhibition Religious Art in Baroque Seville was declared open, and applause filled the rooms of the Cartujano Bank Arts Foundation. Afterwards, waiters brought round trays of drinks and canapés while guests admired the works that would be on display in the Arenal building for the next three weeks. Between *Christ of the Good Death* by Juan de Mesa, on loan from the university, and a *Saint Leandro* by Murillo from the cathedral vestry, Pencho Gavira greeted the gentlemen and kissed the hands of the ladies, smiling to left and right. He wore an immaculate charcoal-grey suit and the parting in his gelled hair was as perfect as the white collar and cuffs of his shirt.

"A very good speech, Mayor."

The banker and Manolo Almanzor, mayor of Seville, exchanged slaps on the back. The mayor was chubby, with a moustache. He had an honest face that had won him the popular vote and a re-election, but a scandal concerning improper contracts, a brother-in-law grown wealthy in dubious circumstances, and accusations of sexual harassment by three of the mayor's secretaries at the town hall all meant that now, less than a month away from the municipal elections, he was certain to lose.

"Thanks, Pencho. But this'll be my last public function."

The banker smiled consolingly and said, "Things will improve."

The mayor shook his head doubtfully. At least Gavira was going to sweeten his departure from office. In return for reclassifying the land of Our Lady of the Tears, providing a precontract of sale and withdrawing any obstacle to the urban development of Santa Cruz, Almanzor would have a certain loan cancelled, a hefty sum with which he'd purchased a luxurious house in the most expensive and exclusive district of Seville. Cool as a poker player, the general manager of the Cartujano had summed it up neatly a few days earlier, over dinner at the Becerra Restaurant, when he suggested the deal: Bread consoles, Mayor.

A waiter passed, and Gavira took a glass of chilled sherry from the tray. He sipped and looked around. Among the ladies in evening dresses and gentlemen in suits and ties – Gavira always stipulated formal attire for such occasions – the second front, the clerics, was also circulating. His Grace the archbishop of Seville and Octavio Machuca progressed slowly through the room, apparently exchanging impressions on the Valdés Leal loaned to the exhibition by the church of the Hospital de la Caridad. *In Ictu Oculi*: Death snuffing out a candle before the crown and tiaras of an emperor, a bishop, and a pope. But Gavira was sure that the picture wasn't the subject of their conversation.

"Bastards," the mayor said, beside him.

Almanzor wasn't referring to the archbishop or the banker; he meant the other guests, who were giving him the cold shoulder. All Seville knew that he would be out in another month. His likely successor, a politician from Andalucismo Andaluz, Almanzor's own party, was walking round and receiving advance congratulations with a prudent smile.

"Have a drink, Mayor," said Gavira with an encouraging wink. He grabbed him a whisky from the tray and the mayor gulped down half of it. A beaten dog, he gave the banker a grateful look. It was amazing, thought Gavira, how the walking dead created a vacuum around them. People used to toady to Manolo Almanzor; now nobody came near for fear of contamination. Those were the rules of the game. In Almanzor's world there was no mercy for the defeated, only a drink on the eve of execution. Gavira stood there offering him whisky on behalf of the Cartujano after getting him to open the exhibition, partly because he still needed the man and partly because, buying the mayor, he felt a certain responsibility towards him. Gavira wondered if someone would be offering him drinks one day.

"Smash that church, Pencho," the mayor said and drained his glass bitterly. "Build whatever the hell you want there and fuck the lot of them."

Gavira nodded absent-mindedly, his attention on the two men chatting by the Valdés Leal. He excused himself and moved closer, making sure his approach looked casual. On his way, he smiled in the appropriate directions, shook hands, and kissed a few powdered cheeks. Polite, confident, he felt the envy of the men and the admiration of the women who came up to him the moment he moved away from the mayor. He heard Macarena's name whispered behind him a couple of times, but he didn't let it dent his smile. He put his glass on a tray, checked his tie, and a moment later stood next to Monsignor Corvo and Don Octavio Machuca.

"Nice picture," he said.

The archbishop and the old banker looked at the painting as if they'd only just noticed it. Death held a scythe and carried a coffin under his emaciated arm. At his feet, a map of the world, a sword and books and parchments symbolised his victory over life, glory, science and worldly pleasures. With his other bony hand he was snuffing out a candle. The skull's empty eye sockets fixed the viewer. *In Ictu Oculi*. Gavira didn't have any Latin, but the picture was well known in Seville and its meaning was obvious.

"Nice?" The archbishop exchanged a glance with old Machuca. "Only a young man would say that about such a terrible scene. Death seems distant to you, my dear Gavira. But for us, this picture is somewhat closer to home. Isn't that so, Don Octavio?"

The banker nodded, his predatory eyes alert. In fact Corvo was almost twenty years younger than Machuca, but the archbishop liked to affect the bearing of a venerable old man, as if it went with his office.

"Pencho's a winner," said Machuca. "He's not afraid his candle will be snuffed out."

The old man's eyes glinted mockingly between half-closed lids. He had one hand in the pocket of his old-fashioned double-breasted jacket; the other hung by his side, almost as skeletal as the hand of

Death in the painting. The archbishop smiled conspiratorially. "We're all subject to God's will," he said, with a professional air.

Gavira agreed vaguely, but gave the banker a pointed look. Machuca understood his intention. "We were talking about your church, Pencho," he said.

Gavira took it to be a good sign that Aquilino Corvo, his smile unwavering, ignored Machuca's use of the possessive. After all, the archbishopric would be receiving substantial compensation, as well as the Cartujano's promise to build another church in a different location. Not to mention the foundation for community work among the Gypsies that the archbishop had cleverly slipped into the package.

"It's still Your Grace's church," Gavira observed dutifully.

Monsignor Corvo gratefully acknowledged the remark. Since they were talking about churches, he felt obliged to comment in an official capacity. "A painful conflict," he said, after searching for the right phrase.

"But unavoidable," added Gavira, looking regretful.

Out of the corner of his eye he saw Machuca's grin. He remembered that the old man knew, alongside the offers made by the Cartujano to His Grace, about an unpublished report concerning half a dozen clerics in the diocese who had broken the rules on celibacy. The priests were all popular with their parishioners, and the publication of such information, with photographs and sworn statements, would cause quite a stir. Corvo had neither the resources nor the authority to deal with the problem, and a scandal would force him to make decisions that he, more than anyone, was unwilling to make. The priests were good men; and in times of change and with few candidates for the priesthood, a hasty decision would be regrettable. So Monsignor Corvo had accepted with relief Gavira's compromise solution of buying the report to prevent its publication. In the Catholic Church, a problem postponed was a problem solved.

Gavira wondered uneasily how Machuca had found out about the stratagem. Gavira himself had masterminded the operation, paying the private investigators to do the research and then using his influence with the press to hush up, for the archbishop, what was in effect a classic example of blackmail.

"His Grace guarantees his neutrality," said Machuca, closely watching Gavira. "But he was telling me a moment ago that disciplinary proceedings against Father Ferro are going rather slowly. Apparently" – he narrowed his eyes – "the priest from Rome hasn't been able to gather sufficient evidence against him."

Corvo raised a hand. Beneath his pastoral calm he looked uncomfortable. It wasn't exactly a question of that, he said in a grave voice made for the pulpit. Father Quart hadn't come to Seville to act *against* the parish priest of Our Lady of the Tears but, rather, to provide *Rome* with detailed information. The prelate reminded the two men that an ecclesiastical formality prevented the See of Seville from taking direct action. He went on to describe the sad situation: a priest getting on in years, a question of discipline, and so on. He agreed with Rome on the general principles, but he had reservations. As he said this, Corvo avoided Gavira's eyes and glanced at Machuca, checking to see whether it was appropriate to continue. The old man remained inscrutable, so His Grace went on to say that Father Quart's investigation wasn't proceeding with the desired diligence. The archbishop had alerted his superiors, but in a matter such as this he could do no more.

"Do you mean," Gavira said with a frown of irritation, "that you don't expect Father Ferro's imminent removal from his post?"

The archbishop raised both hands, as if to say *Ite, missa est.* "More or less. It will happen eventually, of course. But not in two or three days. A couple of weeks maybe." He cleared his throat. "A month at the most. As I've said, the matter's out of my hands. You have all my sympathy, of course."

Gavira, regarding the Valdés Leal, suppressed the urge to say something rude. He felt like punching the archbishop. He counted to ten, staring at Death's empty eyes, and then managed a smile.

Machuca had his eyes fixed on him. "That's too long, isn't it?" the old banker asked.

Corvo, thinking that the remark was addressed to him – though, in fact, Machuca's narrowed eyes hadn't left Gavira's face – pointed out that he could do nothing without an order from Rome, nothing while Father Ferro continued to celebrate Mass every Thursday.

Gavira couldn't keep in his anger. "Your Grace shouldn't have referred the matter to Rome," he said sharply. "It should have been taken care of under your jurisdiction, while there was still time."

The archbishop went white. He straightened. "Maybe," he said. "But we prelates also have a conscience, Mr Gavira. Now if you'll excuse me." He nodded and walked away, tight-lipped.

"You've offended him," said Machuca, wrinkling his nose.

Gavira had made another mistake. He shrugged, impatiently. "Monsignor's dignity has a price, like everything else. A price that I can pay." He hesitated for a moment, gauging the old banker's reaction. "That the Cartujano can pay."

"But for the time being there's still that priest," Machuca said malevolently. "The old priest, I mean." He watched Gavira closely. The younger man, well aware of the scrutiny, touched his tie and cuffs and looked round. A beautiful woman passed, and he smiled at her. Machuca went on, watching the woman walk away, "And that means that Macarena and your mother-in-law will go on fighting for the church. For the time being."

It didn't work. Gavira had recovered his composure. "Don't worry," he said. "I'll sort it out."

"I hope so, because you're running out of time. How many days do you have until the meeting? A week?"

"You know how long," said Gavira. "Eight days."

Machuca nodded slowly. "You know something, Pencho? I'm curious to see how you handle this. On the board they really want your head." He smiled slyly. "But if you pull it off, congratulations."

Machuca went to greet some acquaintances, and Gavira was left alone beside the Valdés Leal. A flabby little man, with lacquered hair and a double chin that looked like a continuation of his cheeks, stood nearby. As soon as he met Gavira's eye, he came up and said, "My name's Honorato Bonafé, from *Q&S* magazine." He held out his hand. "Could we talk for a moment?"

Gavira ignored the outstretched hand, frowning, wondering who'd let the man in.

"I'll only take a minute of your time."

"Ring my secretary," the banker said coldly, turning his back. He moved away, but to his surprise Bonafé followed. Both obsequious and smug, the man was pursing his lips and peering at Gavira out of the corner of his eye. An odious character, thought Gavira, stopping at last.

"I'm doing a story," Bonafé said, "on that church you're so interested in."

"What do you mean?"

Bonafé raised a podgy hand. "Well," he said with an ingratiating grin, "if we consider that the Cartujano Bank is the main party that wants to have Our Lady of the Tears demolished, I think that a conversation, or a statement, would be . . . You understand."

Gavira remained impassive. "I don't."

Unctuously, patiently, Bonafé put the banker in the picture: the Cartujano, the church and the reclassifying of the land. The parish priest, a somewhat dubious individual, clashing with the archbishop of Seville and subject to disciplinary action or something similar. Two accidental deaths, or who knows what. A special envoy from Rome. And, well, a beautiful wife, or ex-wife, daughter of the duchess of El Nuevo Extremo. And she and that priest from Rome . . .

He stopped, seeing Gavira's expression. The banker took a step towards him, glaring.

"Right, well, you understand," said Bonafé. "I'm telling you this so you get the idea: headlines, the cover, and so on. We're publishing the story next week. So naturally your comments would carry a lot of weight."

The banker remained still, saying not a word. Bonafé smiled vaguely, waiting for an answer. At last Gavira said, "You want me to tell you all about it."

"That's right."

Peregil passed close by. Gavira thought he saw a look of alarm on his face when he caught sight of Bonafé, and he was tempted to call Peregil over and ask him if he was responsible for the journalist's presence. But this wasn't the right moment for a confrontation. What he really wanted to do was to kick the fat little man out.

"And what do I get from talking to you?"

Bonafé's smile was insolent. "Well. You would have control over the information. You'd be giving your side of things." Bonafé paused meaningfully. "You could get us on your side, if you see what I mean."

"And if I don't talk?"

"Ah, well, that's different. We'll run the article anyway. You'll have missed a good opportunity."

Now it was Gavira's turn to smile menacingly, with the smile that had earned him his nickname. "That sounds like a threat."

Bonafé shook his head, oblivious to the meaning of Gavira's smile. "Good God, no. I'm just letting you know how things stand." His puffy little eyes shone with greed. "I'm playing fair with you, Mr Gavira."

"And why are you doing that?"

"Well . . . I don't know." Bonafé smoothed his crumpled jacket. "I suppose it's because you have a good public image. You know, 'Young Banker Imposes New Style', and so on. You look good in photos, you're popular with the ladies. In other words: you sell papers. You're in fashion, and my magazine can help make sure you stay in fashion. Think of it as a way of boosting your image. Now, your wife . . ."

"What about my wife?"

Gavira spat out the words, but Bonafé didn't seem to notice the danger signs. "She looks good in photos too," he said, meeting Gavira's eye calmly. "Though I think that that bullfighter . . . But that's all over. Now, the priest from Rome . . . You know the one I mean, don't you?"

Gavira thought fast. He needed only a week; after that, nothing would matter. "Yes, I see," he said. "And how much might this boost to my image cost?"

Bonafé lifted both hands, placing his fingers together as if in prayer. "Oh, well," he said, relaxed, pleased. "I thought maybe an in-depth interview about that church. An exchange of views. Beyond that, I don't know." He gave the banker a wink. "Maybe you'd like to invest in the press."

Peregil passed again. Gavira noticed that his assistant looked more and more worried. The banker smiled. "I've been investing in the press for some time," he said. "But I haven't had to deal with someone like you before."

The journalist looked smug, conspiratorial. And Gavira thought to himself that Honorato Bonafé was just the kind of oily little man who turned up dead in the movies.

"What fascinates me about Europe," said Gris Marsala, "is its long history. You come to a place like this, look at a landscape, or lean against an old wall, and it's all there. Your past, your memories. You yourself."

"Is that why you're obsessed with this church?" asked Quart.

"Not just with this church."

They were inside the portico, before the figure of Jesus with the real hair and dusty ex-votos hanging on the wall.

"Maybe you have to be American to understand," said the nun after a while. "Over there you sometimes get the feeling that all this was built by strange, alien people. Then one day you come here and you understand that it's part of your own history. That, through your ancestors, you placed these stones one on top of the other. Maybe that's why many of my countrymen are so fascinated by Europe." She smiled at Quart. "You turn a corner, and suddenly you remember. You thought you were orphaned, but it turns out you're not. That's why I don't want to go back."

She leaned against the wall, next to the stoup. As usual, her grey hair was plaited and she wore an old blue turtleneck that smelled slightly of sweat. She hooked her thumbs in the back pockets of her stained jeans.

"I was orphaned several times," she said. "And being an orphan means being a slave. Memories give you some security; you know who you are and where you're going. Or where you're not going. Without them you're at the mercy of the first person who comes along and calls you daughter. Don't you agree?" She waited for him to nod, and he nodded. "To defend one's memories is to defend one's freedom. Only angels have the luxury of being spectators."

Quart was thinking about the report on Gris Marsala that he'd received from Rome and that was now lying on his hotel desk, with certain paragraphs underlined in red. She had joined a religious order at eighteen. Studied architecture and fine art, at the University of California in Los Angeles, taking specialised courses in Seville, Madrid and Rome. A brilliant academic record. Seven years teaching art. Four years as director of a religious university college in Santa Barbara. A personal crisis, with health complications. Indefinite provisional dispensation from her order. Three years in Seville, where she earned her living teaching art students from the USA. Discreet, nothing special to report. She barely kept in contact with a local residence of the order to which she belonged. Living in private accommodation. She hadn't requested to leave the order. The report didn't say whether she'd taken any computer courses.

Quart looked at the nun. Outside, in the square, the light was growing more intense and it was getting hot. He was grateful for the cool of the church. "So it's your recovered memories that keep you here."

"More or less." Gris Marsala smiled sadly, looking at the military medal tied to a wedding bouquet among the ex-votos, as if wondering who once held those flowers. "The Futurists," she said, "thought Venice should be blown up, in order to destroy the model. What seemed like a pretentious paradox then has now become a reality in architecture, literature . . . And in theology. Razing cities to the ground is an extreme example, a brutal way of hurrying things up. There are subtler methods."

"You and the others can't win this battle," Quart said gently.

"I and the others?" The nun was surprised. "We're not some kind of clan or sect. We're just people who have gathered around this church, each for their own personal reasons." She shook her head – it was obvious. "Take Father Oscar. He's young and has found a cause to fall in love with. It could just as easily have been a woman, or liberation theology. As for Don Priamo, he makes me think of that wonderful book, *The Equinoctial Adventure of Lope de Aguirre* by Ramon Sender, whom I heard lecture at the university. It's the story of a small, hard conquistador who limps from old wounds and is always in armour despite the heat because he trusts no one. Like him, Father Ferro is rebelling against an ungrateful, distant king and fighting his own personal battle. Isn't it amusing? Kings sent men like you to imprison or execute men like Aguirre." She sighed and was silent a moment. "I suppose it's inevitable."

"Tell me about Macarena."

On hearing the name, Gris Marsala looked closely at Quart. He bore her scrutiny. "Macarena," she said, "is defending her own memories: a few mementoes, her great-aunt's trunk, and the books she read as a child that marked her deeply. She's struggling with what she herself, in moments of humour, calls the Buddenbrooks effect: the awareness of a dying world, the temptation to side with the parvenus in order to survive. The desperation of intelligence."

"Please go on."

"There's not much more to tell. It's all there for you to see." Gris Marsala pointed out of the door at the sun-filled square. "She inherited a world that no longer exists, that's all. She's another orphan clinging to the wreckage."

"And what part do I play in all of this?" He regretted it as soon as he'd said it, but she didn't seem to find it odd.

"I don't know," she said with a shrug. "You've become a witness." She thought a moment. "They're all so alone. I think they want you to understand, or, rather, they want those who sent you to understand. Just like Aguirre, who deep down wanted his king to understand him."

"What about Macarena?"

Gris Marsala considered the wounds on Quart's knuckles. "She likes you," she said simply. "As a man, I mean. I'm not surprised. I don't know if you're aware of it, but your presence in Seville gives everything a special quality. I imagine that she's trying to seduce you, in her own way." She smiled like a mischievous little boy. "I don't mean in the physical sense."

"Does that bother you?"

The nun glanced at him with curiosity. "Why should it? I'm not a lesbian, Father Quart. I say that in case you're concerned about the nature of my friendship with Macarena." She laughed. "As for men in general and good-looking priests in particular, I'm a virgin by vow and by choice."

Embarrassed, Quart glanced out at the square beyond the woman's shoulder. "What's going on between Macarena and her husband?" he asked.

"She loves him." She looked surprised, as if it was so obvious it needed no explanation. She smiled ironically at Quart. "Don't look like that, Father. It's obvious you don't spend much time in a confessional. You know nothing about women."

Quart went outside and the sun fell on his shoulders like a heavy cloak. Gris Marsala followed, skirting round a pile of sand and gravel, and stopped by the cement mixer. The priest looked up at the belfry covered with scaffolding, and his gaze stopped at the headless Virgin above the door. "I'd like to see your apartment, Sister Marsala."

"You surprise me."

"I don't think so."

There was a silence.

"I hate being called Sister Marsala. Or is that a way of making your request sound official? After all, you are proposing to visit the apartment of a nun who lives alone. Aren't you worried about what people will say? Monsignor Corvo, for instance. Or your bosses in Rome. Although of course you keep your bosses in Rome informed."

Quart didn't know whether to frown or laugh. In the end, he laughed. "It's only a suggestion," he said. "An idea. I'm trying to piece together the puzzle. Seeing how you live might help." He looked straight into her eyes. She realised that he meant it.

"I see. You're looking for clues."

"I am."

"Computers connected to Rome. That sort of thing."

"Yes."

"And if I refuse, will you get in anyway, as you did with Don Priamo's quarters?"

"How do you know about that?"

"Father Oscar told me."

There was too much information circulating, thought Quart, annoyed. They all told one another everything in that strange little club. The only person who had to struggle for information was he. With the sun beating down mercilessly, he suddenly felt very tired; he was tempted to loosen his dog collar and take off his jacket. But he didn't.

Gris Marsala walked slowly round the cement mixer. "Why not?" she said at last with a thoughtful smile. "There hasn't been a man in my apartment in the three years I've lived there. It'll be interesting to see how it feels. I'll try not to throw myself at you the minute I shut the door. Will you defend yourself like Saint Maria Goretti, or will I have a chance with you? Although at my age I don't think I'd be much of a test of anyone's resolve. It's hard, you know, for any woman to realise that she's lost her looks for good." Her expression became harder now. "Especially for a nun."

* * *

"Make yourself comfortable," she said.

The irony was thick. There was little of comfort in the small sitting room of her apartment, on the third floor. The narrow balcony looked out on to the Calle San José near the Puerta de la Carne. It took them only ten minutes to get there from Our Lady of the Tears. With the sun beating down, the streets were like furnaces and the whitewashed walls dazzled. Seville was all light. White walls and light in every variation, thought Quart as he had walked with Gris Marsala, zigzagging in search of shade. It reminded him of when he and Monsignor Pavelić ran from shelter to shelter down the streets of Sarajevo, avoiding the snipers.

As he put his sunglasses away, he looked around the room. Everything was immaculately clean and tidy. There was a sofa with crocheted antimacassars, a television, a small bookcase containing books and tapes, a desk with papers, folders and pots of pens. And a personal computer. Sensing Gris Marsala's eyes on him, he went to the PC: a 486 with a printer. Powerful enough to be Vespers', but it didn't have a modem, and the telephone was across the room. The telephone, also, had an old-fashioned fixed plug.

He ran an eye over the books and tapes. She had mainly baroque music, but there was also quite a lot of flamenco, both classical and modern, and all of Camarón's albums. The books were treatises on art and restoration, and studies of Seville. Two of them, *The Baroque Architecture of Seville* by Sancho Corbacho and *Guide to the Art of Seville and Surrounding Provinces*, were full of slips of paper covered with notes. The only religious work was a worn, leather-bound bible. On the wall hung a framed reproduction of *The Chess Game* by Pieter Van Huys.

"Guilty or innocent?" asked Gris Marsala.

"Innocent, for the moment," he answered. "Due to lack of evidence."

She laughed. As he turned to face her, smiling, he saw his reflection in a mirror on the wall opposite. With an old, beautiful frame of very dark wood, the mirror stood out in the modest apartment.

The nun followed the direction of his gaze. "Do you like it?" she asked.

"Very much."

"I lived on sandwiches for several months to save up for it." She looked at herself in the mirror, then went to the kitchen for two glasses of water.

"What's so special about it?" asked Quart when he'd drunk his water.

"The mirror?" Gris Marsala hesitated. "You could say it's a kind of personal revenge. A symbol. It's the only luxury I've allowed myself here." She gave Quart a sardonic look. "That, and letting a man into my apartment, even if he is a priest. I haven't weakened too many times in three years, have I? We nuns are very strict." She made a theatrical sigh, and they both grinned. She gestured around the room. "From the beginning, as a novice, you're taught that in a nun's cell mirrors are dangerous," she said. "According to the rules, your image can be reflected only in the rosary and in the prayer book. You own nothing: you receive your habit, your underwear, even your sanitary towels from the hands of the community. If you're to save your soul, there must be no show of individuality or personal choice."

She went over to the window and opened the blind a little. Sunlight flooded in, making Quart squint.

"I've followed the rules all my life," she said. "And I've continued to do so here in Seville, despite this minor infringement of my vow of poverty. I had a problem. Macarena said she told you. A disease of the spirit more than of the flesh. I was the director of a university college for girls. I never exchanged a word with the archbishop of my diocese about anything but professional matters. Yet I fell in love with him, or thought I did, which is the same thing . . . And the day I found myself, aged forty, applying makeup in front of the mirror because he was coming, I realised what had happened." She showed the scar on her wrist to Quart. "It wasn't attempted suicide, as my colleagues suspected, but a fit of rage. Of desperation. When I came out of hospital and asked my superiors for advice, all they recommended was prayer, discipline and the example of our sister Saint Thérèse of Lisieux."

She was silent a moment, rubbing her wrist as if trying to erase the scar. "Do you remember Saint Thérèse, Father?" she asked. The priest nodded. "She had tuberculosis and slept in a freezing cell but never complained and never asked for a blanket. The good Lord rewarded her for her suffering by taking her unto Him at the age of twenty-four!"

She laughed quietly, wrinkling up her eyes. She must have been attractive once, thought Quart. In a way she still was. He wondered how many members of a religious order, male or female, could have done what she did.

Gris Marsala took a seat in the armchair while Quart remained standing. She smiled at him bitterly. "Have you ever visited a nuns' cemetery, Father Quart? Rows of small, identical headstones. And engraved on them, their adopted names, not the ones they were baptised with. They were members of an order; nothing else counts before God. They're the saddest tombs you'll ever see. Like a war cemetery with thousands of crosses with the inscription 'unknown'. They are so unbearably lonely, and seem to ask, what was it all for?"

Quart spoke cautiously, a hunter trying not to scare his prey. "Those are the rules. You knew them when you took your vows."

"When I took my vows, I didn't know the meaning of words like 'repression', 'intolerance', and 'ignorance'. Those are the true rules. It's like Orwell's *1984*: Big Sister's watching you. And the younger and more attractive you are, the worse it is. The gossiping, the cliques, best friends, envy, jealousy . . . You know the old saying: they come together without knowing one another, they live without loving one another, they die without mourning one another . . . If I ever stop believing in God, I hope at least I'll go on believing in the Last Judgement. I'd love to find some of my fellow nuns and all my superiors there!"

"Why did you become a nun?"

"This is turning into a confession. I didn't bring you here to unload my conscience. Why did you become a priest? Was it the usual story: a repressive father and over-affectionate mother?"

Quart shook his head. This wasn't the way he wanted the conversation to go. "My father died when I was very young," he said.

"Right. Another case of oedipal transference, as dirty old Freud would have said."

"I don't think so. I also considered joining the army."

"How literary. The scarlet and black." She played with the antimacassar. "My father was a jealous, domineering man. I was afraid of disappointing him. If you take a close look at many women's vocations, especially those of pretty girls, you'll often find long-term anxiety caused by the continual warnings of their fathers: all men want only one thing, and so on. From childhood lots of nuns are taught, as I was, to be careful with men and not lose control in front of them. You'd be surprised how many nuns' sexual fantasies involve beauty and the beast."

They regarded each other in silence for some time. Quart felt there was now fellow feeling between them based on awareness that they were in the same job. The strange and painful solidarity that arose between clerics in a difficult world.

"What can a nun do when she realises, at the age of forty, that she's still that little girl dominated by her father?" Gris Marsala went on. "A child who, out of the intense desire not to displease him, not to commit any sin, has committed the even greater sin of not really living her own life. Is it wise, or is it stupid and irresponsible, at eighteen, to renounce worldly love, and with it trust, surrender, sex? What is a woman to do when these feelings come too late?"

"I don't know," Quart said. He was friendly, sincere now. "I'm only a low-ranking priest. I don't have many answers." He considered the room, the modest furniture and the computer. "Break a mirror, perhaps, and then buy another. That takes courage."

"Perhaps," replied Gris Marsala. "But the woman in the mirror isn't the same." There was pain in her eyes when she looked up at Quart. "There are few things in life as tragic as awakening to the truth too late."

They were waiting for him at the Casa Cuesta Bar, punctual as always, sitting at a table under the sign for the Seville-Sanlucar-Coast steam train, around a bottle of La Ina sherry.

"You're a disaster," said Celestino Peregil. "You're making me look really bad."

Don Ibrahim frowned at the embers of his cigar, which were about to drop on to his white waistcoat. He pulled nervously on the ends of his singed moustache while Peregil let rip. Beside him, El Potro del Mantelete stared intently at his left hand, still bandaged, resting on the table. La Niña Puñales seemed to be the only one indifferent to their common shame, her vacant eyes fixed on a yellowed poster on the wall – LINARES BULLRING, 1947, GITANILLO DE TRIANA, DOMINGUIN AND MANOLETE. Her long, emaciated brown hands had nails as red as her lips and coral earrings, and her silver bracelets jangled every time she filled her glass. She'd drunk half the bottle herself.

"It was really stupid of me to give you this job," said Peregil. He was furious, felt sick, and his tie was crooked. His face looked greasy, and his elaborate comb-over hairdo was in disarray. Just an hour ago, Gavira had hauled him over the coals. Results, imbecile. I pay you to get results, and for a week you've just been messing around. I gave you six million for this job, and we haven't got anywhere. Now, on top of that, there's this journalist, Bonafé, sticking his nose in things. Oh, and by the way, Peregil, when we get a moment, you can tell me what your business is with that creep. You can explain it to me really slowly, because I think there's something I don't know about. Now, you have till Wednesday. Understand? Wednesday. Because on Thursday I want no one in that church, not even God. Otherwise you're going to be shitting out the six million, bit by bit. You're a cretin, Peregil, a complete cretin."

"Dealing with priests brings bad luck," said Don Ibrahim.

Peregil, glaring at him, said, "You're the ones who bring bad luck."

"The business with the petrol," remarked La Niña, "was a warning from God. The flames of hell." She was reading the poster for Manolete's last bullfight. Don Ibrahim looked tenderly at her Gypsy profile and smudged makeup, and once again felt the weight of responsibility. El Potro was waiting like a faithful dog. Peregil's comment that they brought bad luck had probably only just sunk in. Don Ibrahim gave El Potro a reassuring look. "A warning from God," he said, echoing La Niña, out of respect and from lack of anything better to say.

"*Othu.*"

"Does that mean you're backing out?" asked Peregil.

"Nobody's backing out," Don Ibrahim said with dignity, placing his hand on his chest. As he did so, ash dropped on to his paunch.

"Nobody," repeated El Potro.

"So what are you going to do?" asked Peregil. "We're running out of time. There must be no Mass in that church this Thursday."

The former bogus lawyer raised a hand. "Let us weigh and consider," he said. "Though we may, for reasons of conscience, have decided not to strike at a sacred building, there's nothing to prevent or impede us from dealing with the human element." He drew on his cigar and watched a ring of Cuban smoke float away. "I refer to the priest."

"Which of the three?"

"The parish priest." Don Ibrahim smiled confidently. "According to intelligence gathered by La Niña around the neighbourhood and among the parishioners, the assistant priest is leaving tomorrow – Tuesday – so the parish priest will be alone." His sad, red eyes, lacking lashes since the petrol incident, rested on Pencho Gavira's henchman. "Do you follow, my friend?"

"Yes," said Peregil, shifting in his chair. "But I'm not sure where this is leading."

"You don't want a Mass there on Thursday, right?"

"Right."

"No priest, no Mass."

"Yes. But the other day you told me your conscience didn't allow you to break the old guy's legs. And while we're on the subject, I'm sick of your conscience."

Don Ibrahim looked round and lowered his voice cautiously. "We don't have to go that far. Imagine that this priest, this venerable minister of the Lord, disappears for two or three days without suffering any physical damage."

A faintly hopeful smile broke on the henchman's face. "Could you see to that?"

"Of course." Don Ibrahim drew on his cigar. "A clean operation. No blood, no broken bones. But it'll cost you a little more."

"How much more?" asked Peregil, suspicious.

"Oh, not much." Don Ibrahim shot a glance at his companions and hazarded a sum. "Half a million each for accommodation and food."

Four and a half million was nothing at this point, so Peregil agreed. His financial situation was dire, but if this worked, Gavira wouldn't quibble at the extra sum.

"What have you got in mind?" asked Peregil.

Don Ibrahim looked out of the window at the narrow white arch of the Callejón de la Inquisición, reluctant to give details. Feeling very hot despite the chilled wine, he picked up La Niña's fan and fanned himself. "There's a place on the river," he said. "The boat where El Potro lives. We could keep the priest there till Friday, if you like."

Peregil glanced at El Potro's vacant face and arched his eyebrows. "Will it work?"

Don Ibrahim nodded, gravely. "It'll work."

Like all men desperate to be reassured, Peregil calmed down. He took out a packet of American cigarettes and lit one. "Sure you won't harm the priest?" he asked. "What if he puts up a fight?"

"Please." Don Ibrahim glanced anxiously at La Niña and placed his hand on El Potro's shoulder. "An elderly priest. A man of God."

Peregil nodded. They had to make sure to keep an eye on the priest from Rome, and, er, the lady, he reminded them. And photographs. Above all, they mustn't forget the photographs. "It's not a bad plan," added Peregil. "How did you get the idea?"

Stroking what was left of his moustache, Don Ibrahim smiled, looking both gratified and modest. "From a film they showed on TV last night: *The Prisoner of Zenda*."

"I think I've seen it," said Peregil, readjusting his hair to hide his bald patch. He signalled for the waiter to bring a second bottle. "Is that the one where the guy is put in prison by his friends, then he finds treasure and gets his revenge?"

Don Ibrahim shook his head as the waiter poured the fino. "No," he said. "That's *The Count of Monte Cristo*. The one I mean is where the evil brother kidnaps the king, so he can be king himself. But then Stewart Granger comes along and saves him."

"Well, isn't that something." Peregil nodded, pleased. "It's a real education watching TV."

It wasn't only in his personality that Honorato Bonafé possessed certain pig-like qualities. By the time he reached the portico, sweat poured down his pink double chin, soaking his collar. He mopped his face with his handkerchief as he took in the ex-votos hanging on the wall, the pews piled up to one side of the nave, and the scaffolding.

It was late afternoon in Santa Cruz. The light filtering through the damaged windows was gold and red, bathing the chipped and dusty carvings in a strange haze. Two angels stared into space, and the shadowy figures of the dukes of El Nuevo Extremo, kneeling in prayer, seemed alive.

Bonafé walked forward uncertainly, looking round at the vault, the pulpit and the confessional, whose door was open. There was no one there or in the vestry. He went up to the gate of the crypt and looked down the steps into the darkness. He turned to the altar. The figure of the Virgin was there in her niche, surrounded by scaffolding. Bonafé stood looking at her for a moment and then, with the determined air of one who has planned his move, he climbed the ladder to the figure, some five metres above the ground. The reddish light from the windows illuminated the foreshortened baroque carving, the heart pierced with daggers, the eyes of our Lady of Sorrows raised to heaven. And on her cheeks, blue mantle and crown of stars gleamed Captain Xaloc's pearls.

Bonafé took out his handkerchief, again mopped the sweat on his brow and neck, and dusted the pearls. He peered at them closely. He took a small penknife from his pocket. He gently scraped one of the pearls set into the mantle and stared at it thoughtfully. Then he carefully prised it out. It was about the size of a chickpea. He held it in his palm for a moment, then put it in his jacket pocket with a satisfied smile.

In the deserted nave, the evening light filtered in past the torsoless Christ on the damaged window, reddening the drops of sweat on Bonafé's flabby face. He mopped it yet again with his handkerchief. At that moment he heard a gentle rustle behind him and felt the scaffolding move very slightly.

XI
Carlota Bruner's Trunk

All the wisdom in the world is in the eyes of those wax dolls.
Valéry Larbaud, *Poems*

The English clock struck ten as they were finishing dessert, and Cruz Bruner suggested they take their coffee out into the cool courtyard. Quart gave the duchess his arm and they left the summer dining room, where they had dined among marble busts brought, together with the mosaic laid in the main courtyard, four centuries ago from the ruins of Italica. In the surrounding gallery with its coffered mudéjar ceiling, ancestors in white ruffs and dark clothes stared gravely from their frames as Quart and the duchess passed. Leaning on his arm, the old lady, in a black silk dress with small white flowers at her neck and wrists, pointed them out: an admiral, a general, a governor of the Low Countries, a viceroy of the West Indies. As they passed the lamps from Cordoba, the slim shadow of the priest was visible beside the small, stooping shadow of the duchess, between the arches of the gallery. And behind them, in a black ankle-length dress and sandals and carrying a cushion for her mother, walked Macarena Bruner, smiling.

Quart sat between the two women, beside the tiled fountain. The courtyard, full of flowers, smelled of jasmine. Macarena dismissed the maid, after the maid put down the tray, and she served the coffee herself on the marquetry table. Black for Quart, with milk for her. Coca-Cola – not too cold – for her mother.

"It's my drug, as you know," said the old lady. "My doctors don't allow me coffee."

"My mother sleeps very little," Macarena told Quart, "if she goes to bed early, she wakes up at three or four in the morning. This keeps her awake. We all tell her it can't be good for her, but she takes no notice."

"Why should I?" asked Cruz Bruner. "This drink is the only thing from the USA I like."

"You like Gris, mother."

"That's true," conceded the old lady between sips. "But she's from California: she's almost Spanish."

Macarena turned to Quart. "The duchess thinks that in California the landowners still wear *charro* outfits covered with silver buttons, Brother Junipero's still preaching, and Zorro's still riding around fighting for the poor."

"You mean they aren't?" asked Quart, amused.

Cruz Bruner nodded energetically. "That's how it should be," she said. "After all, Macarena, your great-great-great-grandfather Fernando was governor of California before they took it from us."

She spoke with all the assurance of her lineage – as if California had been snatched directly from her or her family. There was something singular in the mixture of familiarity and courteous if somewhat haughty tolerance with which the duchess addressed people. Quart looked at her wrinkled hands and face covered with liver spots, at her withered skin and the pale line of lipstick on her lips, at her white hair, pearl necklace and fan decorated by Romero de Torres. There were few women like her left. He had met some – lonely old ladies dragging their lost youth and nostalgia around the Côte d'Azur, matrons of the ancient Italian nobility, shrivelled central-European relics with Austro-Hungarian surnames, devout Spanish ladies. Cruz Bruner was one of the last. Their sons and daughters were either penniless layabouts, fodder for the tabloids, or else they worked from nine to five in offices and banks, or ran wineries, shops, and fashionable nightclubs, dealing with the financiers and politicians on whom their livelihoods depended. They studied in America, visited New York rather than Paris or Venice, couldn't speak French, and married divorcés, or models, or parvenus. Cruz Bruner had spoken of this with a mocking smile during dinner. Like a whale or a seal, she said, I belong to an endangered species – the aristocracy.

"Some worlds don't end with an earthquake or a great crash," the old lady now said, looking doubtfully at Quart, wondering if he understood. "They expire quietly, with a discreet sigh." She adjusted the cushion behind her back and for a few moments listened to the crickets in the garden. A soft glow in the sky announced the moon's arrival. "Quietly," she repeated.

Quart looked at Macarena, who had her back to the light from the gallery, half her face in shadow. Her hair had slipped over her shoulder. Her legs were crossed, and her bare feet in sandals showed below her black dress. The ivory necklace gleamed at her neck. "Not Our Lady of the Tears," he said. "Her departure from this world is anything but quiet."

Macarena said nothing.

"Not all worlds disappear willingly," the old duchess whispered.

"You have no grandchildren," said Quart. He tried to sound neutral, casual, yet it came out sounding provocative, even rude.

"True. I don't," replied Cruz Bruner, and she turned to her daughter.

Macarena sat forward then, and in the moonlight Quart saw her anger. "It's none of your business," she said at last, evenly, to him.

"Maybe it's none of my business either," said the duchess, coming to her guest's aid. "But it's a pity."

"Why?" Macarena asked sharply. She addressed her mother but was looking at Quart. "Sometimes it's better not to leave anything behind." She pushed her hair back, exasperated. "Soldiers who go to war leaving nothing behind are lucky. They have no one to worry or suffer over."

"Like some priests," said Quart, his eyes fixed on her.

"Perhaps." Macarena laughed. It was bitter; nothing like her usual, open laugh. "It must be wonderful to have no responsibilities, to be so selfish. To choose a cause that you love or that suits you, as Gris has done. Or as you have. Instead of inheriting a cause or having one imposed upon you."

Cruz Bruner wrapped her fingers round her fan. "Nobody forced you to get involved with the church, my dear," she said. "Or to turn it into a personal battle."

"Please. You know better than anyone that sometimes a person has no choice. That if you open a trunk, you may have to pay for it . . . Some lives are ruled by ghosts."

The duchess snapped open her fan. "You heard her, Father. Who said romantic heroines have disappeared?" She fanned herself, looking absently at Quart's injured knuckles. "But only the young are troubled by ghosts. True, ghosts multiply over time, but they bother you less: the pain turns to melancholy. Mine just float about gently now." She gestured at the mudéjar arches of the courtyard, the tiled fountain and the rising moon. "They don't cause me sadness any more." She looked at her daughter. "Only you do. A little."

The old lady tilted her head to one side, just as Macarena did, and Quart suddenly recognised her daughter's features in her face. He had a glimpse of what the beautiful woman beside him would look like in thirty or forty years. Everything comes to pass, thought Quart. And everything ends.

"For a time my daughter's marriage gave me hope," Cruz Bruner went on. "It consoled me, for sooner or later I would be leaving her. Octavio Machuca and I agreed that Pencho was ideal: clever, handsome, with a great future . . . He seemed very much in love with Macarena, and I'm sure he still is, despite all that's happened." She pursed her almost non-existent lips. "Suddenly everything changed. My daughter left the marital home and came back to live with me."

Quart finished his coffee and put his cup on the table. He felt he was continually brushing against the truth but not quite grasping it. "I don't dare ask why," he said.

"You don't." The duchess fanned herself, looking at him teasingly. "Nor do I. At any other time, I would have considered it a great misfortune, but I don't know what's best any more . . . I'm the last-but-one of my line, I'm almost three-quarters of a century old, and I have a gallery full of portraits of ancestors whom no one fears, respects or even remembers."

The moon was now centred in the rectangle of sky above their heads. Cruz Bruner asked for the lamps to be turned off. The light became silvery blue with accents of white – the patterns on the tiles, the chairs, and the mosaic on the floor standing out as clearly as if it were day.

"It's like crossing a line," she said. "The world looks different from the other side."

"And what's on the other side?" he asked.

The old lady looked at him with mock surprise. "That's a worrying question coming from a priest. Women of my generation always thought priests had the answer to everything. When I asked my old confessor how to deal with my husband's infidelities, he always told me to accept them, to pray and to offer my anguish to Jesus. According to him, Raphael's private life and my salvation were entirely separate matters. One had nothing to do with the other."

Quart wondered what advice Father Ferro had given Macarena about her marriage.

"As we approach the line," continued Cruz Bruner, "we feel a certain dispassionate curiosity. A tender tolerance towards those who will get here sooner or later, but don't know it."

"Such as your daughter?"

The old lady thought a moment. "For example," she agreed. She peered at Quart, interested. "Or you. You won't always be a handsome priest who attracts his female parishioners."

Quart ignored her last remark. The truth still seemed just out of reach. "And what's Father Ferro's view from the other side?" he asked.

The old lady shrugged. The conversation was starting to bore her. "You'll have to ask him. I don't think Don Priamo is either tender or tolerant. But he's an honest priest, and I believe in priests. I believe in the Holy Roman Catholic and Apostolic Church, and I hope to save my soul for eternity." She tapped her chin with her closed fan. "I even believe in priests like you who don't conduct Mass or anything; or priests who wear jeans and trainers, like Father Oscar . . . In the lost world I come from, a priest meant something." She smiled at her daughter. "Macarena is very fond of Don Priamo, and I believe in Macarena too. I like to see her fight her personal battles, even though I don't always understand them. They are battles that would have been impossible when I was her age."

It was the second time in two days that someone had proclaimed Father Ferro's honesty. But that contradicted the report about Cillas de Ansó. Quart glanced at his watch. "Is Father Ferro up in the observatory?" he asked.

"It's too early," answered Cruz Bruner. "He usually arrives a bit later, around eleven. Would you like to wait?"

"Yes. There are a couple of things I want to talk to him about."

"Good. We can enjoy your company a little longer." The crickets were chirping again, and the old lady listened, her face towards the garden. "Have you found out who put our postcard in your room?"

Quart took the card from his pocket and placed it on the table. "No," he said, feeling Macarena's eyes on him. "But at least now I know what it means."

"Do you really?" Cruz Bruner opened and shut her fan, then tapped the postcard with it. "In that case, while you wait for Don Priamo, maybe it would be a good time for us to put the card back in Carlota's trunk."

Quart looked at the two women, undecided. Macarena stood up and waited, holding the card, with the moon behind her. He got to his feet and followed her through the courtyard and garden.

From the pigeon loft they could see clouds brushing the moon. The city below looked unreal. Like an old stage set, the roofs of Santa Cruz stretched away in terraces, with planes of shadow interrupted here and there by a light in a window, a distant street lamp, a terrace hung with washing – shrouds in the darkness. Illuminated, La Giralda rose up in the background as if painted on a dark backdrop. Seen through the long white net curtains billowing gently in the breeze, the belfry of Our Lady of the Tears appeared very near, almost within reach.

"The breeze doesn't come from the river but from the sea," said Macarena. "It comes up at night, from Sanlucar." She took the lighter from under her bra strap and lit a cigarette. The smoke floated out through the windows. Insects fluttered round the lamp. "This is all that's left of Carlota Bruner," she said, indicating the open trunk in the lamplight.

It was full of objects: lacquer boxes, beads of jet, a porcelain figurine, broken fans, a very old and threadbare lace mantilla, hatpins, whalebone stays, a fine silver-link handbag, opera glasses, faded fabric flowers from a hat, albums of photographs and postcards, old illustrated newspapers, boxes made of leather and cardboard, a strange pair of long red chamois gloves, tattered old books of poetry and school exercise books, wooden bobbins for lace-making, a very long braid of light chestnut hair, a catalogue for the Universal Exposition in Paris, a piece of coral, a model of a gondola, an old tourist guide to the ruins of Carthage, a tortoiseshell comb, a glass paperweight containing a little seahorse, Roman coins, and several other silver coins bearing the likenesses of Isabel II and Alfonso XII. And there were the letters – a thick packet tied with ribbon. Macarena untied the bow and handed them to Quart. There must have been about fifty: almost two-thirds were letters; the rest were postcards. The ink had faded on the brittle, yellow paper and in places was almost illegible. None bore a postmark. They were all written in Carlota's fine, sloping hand and addressed to Captain Manuel Xaloc, Port of Havana, Cuba.

"There aren't any from him?"

"No." Kneeling by the trunk, Macarena took some of the letters and glanced over them, her cigarette between her fingers. "My great-grandfather burned them when they arrived. It's a pity. We have her letters but not his."

Sitting in one of the old armchairs, with shelves of books behind him, Quart looked through the postcards. They were all popular views of Seville, like the one left in his hotel room: Triana Bridge, the port with the Torre del Oro and a schooner moored in front of it, a poster for the *feria*, a reproduction of a painting of the cathedral. I'm waiting for you, I'll always wait for you, with all my love, always yours, I wait to hear from you, all my love, Carlota. He took a letter from an envelope. It was dated the eleventh of April, 1896.

Dear Manuel,

I can't resign myself to not hearing from you. I am certain that my family is intercepting your letters as I know that you have not forgotten me. Something in my heart, like the quiet ticking of your watch, tells me that my letters and hopes do reach their destination. I will give this letter to a maid whom I believe to be trustworthy, and hope that my words will reach you. With them I repeat my message of love and my promise to wait for you always, until you return at last.

How long it seems since you left, my love! Time passes and I still wait for one of the ships sailing upriver to bring you to me. Life must, I'm sure, prove generous to those who suffer so much as a result of trusting in her.

At times my courage fails me and I weep in despair, sure that you will never return. That you have forgotten me, despite your promise. See how unfair and silly I can be?

I wait for you always, each day, in the tower from which I watched you leave. At siesta time, when all are asleep and the house is silent, I come up here and sit in the rocking chair, and watch the river. It is very hot, and yesterday I thought I saw the galleons move in the paintings on the stairs. I dreamed, too, of children playing on a beach. I think these are good omens. Perhaps at this very moment you are on your way back to me.

Return soon, my love. I need to hear your laugh, to see your white teeth, and your strong, brown hands. And to see you look at me as you do. And to have you kiss me as you once did. Please return. I beg you. Return or I will die. I feel that I am already dying inside.

All my love,
Carlota

"Manuel Xaloc never read this letter," said Macarena. "Or any of the others. She kept her sanity another six months, and then everything went dark. She wasn't exaggerating: she was dying inside. When at last he came to see her and sat in the courtyard in his blue uniform with gold buttons, Carlota was already dead. She didn't recognise him. She was just a shadow."

Quart put the letter back in its envelope. He felt embarrassment for having intruded on the intimacy of the letter's words of love that were never answered.

"Would you like to read more?" asked Macarena.

He shook his head. The curtains billowed still in the breeze that came up the Guadalquivir from Sanlucar, and through them he caught a glimpse of the church tower. Macarena sat on the floor, leaning against the trunk, rereading some of the letters. Her black hair shone in the lamplight. Quart admired the curve of her neck, her tanned skin, her bare feet in the leather sandals. She exuded such an intense warmth that he had to stop himself from reaching out and touching her neck.

"Look at this," she said.

She held out a piece of paper. It was a sketch of a ship beneath the words: ARMED CUTTER, THE *MANIGUA*. Below the sketch was a list of the specifications of the ship, obviously copied from a periodical of the time, all in Carlota's hand.

1886	Year of construction, England
341	Tons of displacement
47	Length
2.2	Draft
1,800	H.P. Moving power
22	Knots
Range	1,800 miles at 10 knots
Armaments	2 of 47 (to stern)
	1 of 75 (in the centre)
Crew	27 men (3 x 4 gunners)

Macarena handed him a folder tied with ribbon. "This dates from later on. My grandfather put it in the trunk after Carlota died. It's an epilogue to the story."

Quart opened the folder. It contained several cuttings from newspapers and illustrated magazines, all dealing with the end of the Spanish-American war and the naval defeat of July 3, 1898. A front page from *La Ilustración* showed an engraving of the destruction of Admiral Cervera's squadron. There was also a page with an account of the battle, a map of the coast of Santiago de Cuba, and pictures of the principal chiefs of staff and officers killed in the battle. Amongst them Quart found the one he was looking for. The engraving was of poor quality, and a note from the illustrator stated that it had been "drawn based on reliable accounts". It showed a good-looking man with sad eyes, his jacket buttoned to the neck. He had short hair, a large moustache and sideburns. He was the only officer dressed in civilian clothes, and it seemed as if the illustrator had tried to emphasise that this man wasn't a proper member of Cervera's squadron. Captain of the Merchant Navy Mr Manuel Xaloc Ortega, commander of the *Manigua*. Xaloc stared into space, as if indifferent to being listed among the heroes of Cuba. Below, on the same page, was the text:

The Infanta María Teresa, *having withstood the concentrated fire of the American squadron for almost an hour, ran aground in flames on the*

11 de Abril de 1896

Querido Manuel:

No me resigno a vivir sin noticias tuyas. Tengo la seguridad de que mi familia interviene tu correo, pues sé que no me has olvidado. Hay algo en mi corazón, un pequeño tic-tac como el de tu reloj, que dice que mis cartas y mi esperanza no viajan al vacío. Voy a enviarte esta con una doncella, que creo segura, y espero que mis palabras lleguen a ti. Con ellas te renuevo mi mensaje de amor y mi promesa de aguardarte siempre, hasta que regreses por fin.

¡Qué larga es la espera, corazón! Pasa el tiempo y sigo aguardando que una de las velas blancas que vienen río arriba te traiga contigo. La vida tiene forzosamente que ser, al final, generosa con los que tanto sufren por confiar en ella. A veces me faltan las fuerzas, y lloro, y me desespero, llego a creer que no volverás nunca.

Que me has olvidado, a pesar de tu juramento. ¿Ves qué injusta y estúpida puedo llegar a ser?

Te espero siempre, cada día, en la torre desde la que te vi marchar. A la hora de la siesta, cuando todos duermen y la casa está en silencio, vengo aquí arriba y me siento en la mecedora a mirar el río por el que volverás. Hace mucho calor, y ayer me pareció ver moverse, navegando, los galeones que hay pintados en los cuadros de la escalera. También he soñado con niños que jugaban en una playa. Creo que son buenas señales. Quizás en este momento estés ya de camino hacia mí.

Vuelve pronto, amor mío. Necesito oír tu risa, y ver tus dientes blancos, y tus manos morenas y fuertes. Y verte mirarme como me miras. Y renovar ese beso que una vez me diste. Vuelve, por favor. Te lo suplico. Vuelve o me moriré. Siento que por dentro ya me estoy muriendo.

Mi amor

Carlota

coast. Meanwhile, the other Spanish ships set sail from the Port of Santiago, between the forts of El Morro and Socapa, and were immediately greeted by artillery fire from Sampson's battleships and cruisers, whose strength was overwhelming. The Oquendo, *its entire port-side ablaze, guns unfired, bridges and superstructure almost destroyed and with a large number of dead and wounded on board, passed before its flagship, which had run aground. Unable to continue, its commander (Commodore Lazaga) fallen, the* Oquendo *ran aground one mile to the west so as not to fall into enemy hands.*

Pushing their engines to the limit, the Vizcaya *and the* Cristóbal Colón *sailed parallel to the coast, pressed against it by a barrage of North American fire. They passed their destroyed companions, whose survivors were trying to swim to shore. Being faster, the* Colón *moved ahead, while the unfortunate* Vizcaya *suffered the full force of the enemy fire. Its commander, Commodore Eulate, made futile attempts to ram the battleship* Brooklyn, *but the* Vizcaya *was in flames and ran aground under the intense fire of the* Iowa *and the* Oregon. *It was then the turn of the* Colón *(Commodore Díaz Moreu). At one in the afternoon, pursued by four American ships, defenceless, as it had no heavy artillery, it was forced against the coast and was scuttled by its crew. Meanwhile, without hope of surviving, the light units of the squadron, the destroyers* Plutón *and* Furor, *left port one after the other. They were joined in the last few hours by the armed cutter* Manigua, *whose commander, Captain of the Merchant Navy Xaloc, refused to remain in port. His ship would have remained unharmed and been captured with the town, which was about to fall. Aware that escape was impossible, the* Plutón *and the* Furor *headed straight for the American battleships and cruisers. The* Plutón *(Lieutenant Vázquez) ran aground after it was split in two by a heavy shell from the* Indiana, *and the* Furor *was sunk by fire from the* Indiana *and the* Gloucester. *As for the fast, light* Manigua, *it left the Port of Santiago last, when the coast was littered with Spanish ships run aground and in flames. It hoisted a black flag alongside the Spanish flag and, under enemy fire, headed straight for the nearest American ship, the cruiser* Indiana. *The* Manigua *sailed for three miles in a zigzag towards the cruiser, under intense fire, and sank at twenty past one in the afternoon, its deck devastated and in flames from bow to stern, still attempting to ram the enemy . . .*

Quart put the cutting back in the folder and returned it to the trunk with the rest of the papers. Now he knew what Captain Xaloc was looking at in the picture: the cannons of the battleship *Indiana*. He pictured Xaloc on the bridge, surrounded by cannon fire and smoke, resolved to end his long journey to nowhere.

"Did Carlota ever find out about this?" Quart asked.

Macarena was leafing through an old photograph album. "I don't know," she said. "By July 1898 she had completely lost her mind, so we have no idea how she might have reacted to the news. Anyway, I think they kept it from her. She came up here to wait, until the day she died." She showed him a page of the album. There was an old photograph, with the stamp of the photographer's studio in a corner, of a young woman in light summer clothes, holding a parasol and wearing a wide-brimmed hat covered with flowers, a hat like those in the trunk. The photograph was very faded, but he could distinguish slender hands holding gloves and a fan, light-brown hair gathered in a bun, and a pale face with a sad smile and vacant eyes. She wasn't beautiful, but her face was pleasing: sweet, serene. She looked about twenty. "Maybe she had this taken for him," said Macarena.

A stronger breeze moved the curtains, and through them Quart once again saw the belfry of Our Lady of the Tears. To dispel his uneasiness, he went over to one of the arched windows. He took off his jacket and stood contemplating the outline of the church in the darkness. He felt bereft, as Manuel Xaloc must have felt when he left the Casa del Postigo for the last time and went to the church to leave Carlota's pearls there. "I'm sorry," he murmured, not quite knowing why. He remembered the cold against his hand of the entrance to the crypt, the hiss of burning candles during Father Ferro's Mass, the odour of a barren past rising from the trunk.

Macarena came and stood beside him, and she too looked out at the tower of Our Lady of the Tears. "Now you know all you need to know," she said.

She was right. Quart knew more than enough, and Vespers had achieved his futile purpose. But none of it could be translated into the official prose of a report for the IEA. Monsignor Spada, and His Eminence Jerzy Iwaszkiewicz, and His Holiness the Pope were concerned only with the identity of the hacker and the likelihood of

Yate armado "MANIGUA"
Capitán don Manuel Xaloc

1886 Año de construccion. Ynglaterra

327 Toneladas de desplazamiento

47 Eslora

2,2 Calado

1.800 H. P Fuerza Motriz

22 Nudos

Autonomia 1.800 millas a 10 nudos

Armamento 2 de 47 (a popa)
1 de 75 (en el centro)

Dotación 27 hombres (3×4 artillería)

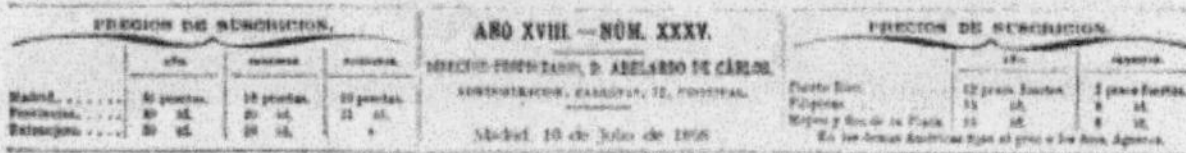
PRECIOS DE SUSCRICION.

	[illegible]	[illegible]	[illegible]
Madrid	[illegible]	[illegible]	[illegible]
Provincias	[illegible]	[illegible]	[illegible]
Extranjero	[illegible]	[illegible]	[illegible]

AÑO XVIII.—NÚM. XXXV.

DIRECTOR-PROPIETARIO, D. ABELARDO DE CÁRLOS.

Madrid 10 de Julio de 1898

PRECIOS DE SUSCRICION.

	[illegible]	[illegible]
Puerto Rico	[illegible]	[illegible]
Filipinas	[illegible]	[illegible]
Méjico y Rio de la Plata	[illegible]	[illegible]

SANTIAGO DE CUBA.- TRAGICA DESTRUCCION DE LA ESCUADRA DEL ALMIRANTE CERVERA.

a scandal in a small Seville parish. The rest – the lives and stories contained within the walls of the church – was of no consequence. As Father Oscar had said, Our Lady of the Tears was too far from Rome. Like Captain Xaloc's doomed *Manigua*, it was just a small ship heading unsteadily towards the implacable steel mass of a destroyer.

Macarena placed her hand on his arm. He didn't pull away, but she must have felt him tense. "I'm leaving Seville," he said.

She said nothing for a moment, then turned to look at him. "Do you think they'll understand in Rome?" she asked.

"I don't know. But whether they do or not isn't important." He gestured at the trunk, the bell-tower, the city in darkness below. "They haven't been here. The hacker drew their attention for a moment, but to them this is just a tiny point on a map. My report will be filed the minute it's been read."

"It's not fair," said Macarena. "This is a special place."

"You're wrong. The world is full of places like this. With a Carlota waiting at the window, a stubborn old priest, a dilapidated church . . . The Pope isn't going to lose sleep over Our Lady of the Tears. You people aren't important enough."

"What about you?"

"It doesn't matter. I don't sleep that much anyway."

"I see." She moved her hand away. "You don't like to get involved, do you? You just have your orders." She pushed her hair back abruptly and moved so that he had no choice but to look her in the face. "Aren't you going to ask me why I left my husband?"

"No, I'm not. That's not necessary for my report."

She laughed quietly, contemptuously. "Your report," she said. "You came here and asked questions. You can't leave without hearing all the answers. You've pried into everybody's lives, so here's the rest of mine." Her eyes were fixed on Quart. "I wanted to have a child, so there would be something between me and the abyss. I wanted a child, but Pencho didn't." Her voice became sarcastic. "You can imagine his objections – too soon, a bad time, a crucial period in our lives, we need to concentrate our efforts and energies, we can have one later . . . I ignored him and became pregnant. Why do you look away, Father Quart? Are you shocked? Pretend this is confession. Part of your job."

Quart shook his head, suddenly firm. His job was the one thing he was still clear about. "You're wrong again," he said gently. "It's not my job. I told you before that I didn't want to hear your confession."

"You can't get out of this, Father." Her voice was harsh. "Think of me as a soul in torment that can't be turned away. Anyway, I'm not asking for absolution."

He shrugged, as if that released him. But intent on the moon, she seemed not to notice. "I got pregnant," she went on, "and Pencho felt as if the bottom had fallen out of his world. He insisted it was too soon. He put pressure on me to get rid of the baby."

So that was it. Things were falling into place.

"So you did," Quart couldn't help saying.

She smiled with a bitterness he'd never seen in her before. "Yes. I'm Catholic, and I refused for as long as I could. But I loved my husband. Against Don Priamo's advice, I checked into a clinic and got rid of the baby. There were complications – a perforation of the uterus, haemorrhaging, and I had to have an emergency hysterectomy. Do you know what that means? Now I can never be a mother." Her face was towards the moon. "Never."

"What did Father Ferro say?"

"Nothing. He's old, he's seen too much. He still gives me communion when I ask."

"Does your mother know?"

"No."

"And your husband?"

Her laugh was dry, brief. "He doesn't either." She slid her hand along the windowsill, towards Quart's arm, but didn't touch it this time. "Only Father Ferro and Gris know. And now you." She hesitated a moment, as if to add another name.

"Did Sister Marsala approve your decision to have an abortion?" asked Quart.

"On the contrary. It nearly cost me her friendship. But when I had the complications at the clinic, she came to see me. I didn't let Pencho come with me, so he thought everything went smoothly. I went home to convalesce, and seemed fine to him."

She turned to the priest. "There's a journalist," she said. "A man called Bonafé. The one who published some photographs last week . . ."

She paused, as if expecting him to say something, but Quart was silent. The photographs were the least of his worries, but he was concerned to hear Macarena mention Honorato Bonafé.

"An unpleasant little man," she went on. "You wouldn't want to shake his hand. It would probably be clammy."

"I know who you mean," said Quart.

Macarena looked at him with curiosity. She lowered her head and her face was hidden by her hair. "He came to see me this morning," she said. "Actually, he stopped me at the door. I would never have asked him into the house. I told him to go away, but before he left, he hinted at something about the clinic. He had been there asking questions."

Dear God. Quart wished he'd been more forceful with Bonafé at their last meeting. He hoped he'd find the journalist in the hotel lobby again when he got back, so he could wipe the smile off his greasy face.

"I'm worried," Macarena admitted.

"It's no longer illegal to have an abortion in Spain," Quart said.

"Yes. But that man and his magazine feed on scandal." She crossed her arms, suddenly cold. "Do you know how an abortion is done, Father Quart? No, I don't imagine you do. Not the details. The bright light, the white ceiling, a woman's legs wide open. You feel you want to die. And the endless, cold, terrifying loneliness . . ." She moved away from the window. "Damn all men, including you. Damn every last one of them."

A deep sigh. The play of light and shadow on her face aged her; or perhaps it was the bitterness.

"I didn't let myself think about what had happened," she continued. "It was like a nightmare I desperately wanted to wake up from. One day, three months after I left the clinic, I went into the bathroom while Pencho was taking a shower. We'd just made love for the first time. I sat on the edge of the bath watching him. He smiled at me, and suddenly he wasn't the man I loved but a stranger. A man who'd made me lose my chance of having children. I felt then worse than I had at the clinic. I packed my things and came back here. Pencho didn't understand. He still doesn't."

Quart breathed in slowly. "That's why you're hurting him," he said.

"Nobody can hurt him. His selfishness and his obsessions are like armour. But I can make him pay: through that church I can strike at his prestige as a financier, and at his pride as a man. Seville can turn on you very quickly. *My* Seville, I mean. The Seville whose recognition Pencho wants."

"Your friend Gris claims you still love him."

"Sometimes she talks too much." She tried to laugh but couldn't. "Maybe that's the problem, that I love him. Anyway, it makes no difference."

"And me? Why are you telling me all this?"

"I don't know. You told me you're leaving, and suddenly that bothers me." She was now so near that when the breeze blew, her hair brushed Quart's face. "Maybe it's because by your side I don't feel so alone. As if, despite yourself, you embody the old ideal of a priest that so many women have always cherished: someone strong and wise to trust and confide in. Maybe it's your black suit and your collar, or the fact that you're also an attractive man. Perhaps your arrival from Rome and all that it represents has impressed me. Maybe I'm Vespers. Maybe I'm trying to win you over to my side, or simply trying in a twisted way to humiliate Pencho. It might be some of these things or all of them. In what my life has become, you and Father Ferro stand at opposite edges of reassuring terrain."

"That's why you're defending that church," said Quart. "You need it as much as the others do."

She gathered her hair and lifted it, exposing the lovely curve of her neck. "Maybe you too need it, and more than you think," she said. She let go of her hair, and it fell about her shoulders again. "As for me, I don't know what I need. Maybe the church, as you say. Maybe a handsome silent man who'll make me forget. Or at least stop the pain. And another man, old and wise, who absolves me of blame for seeking oblivion. Do you know something? A couple of centuries ago it was wonderful to be Catholic. It solved everything: you just told the priest the truth, and waited. Now even you priests don't believe. There's a film called *Portrait of Jennie*. Do you know it? At one point Joseph

Cotten, who's a painter, says to Jennifer Jones: 'Without you I'm lost.' And she answers, 'Don't say that, we can't both be lost.' Are you as lost as you appear, Father Quart?"

He turned to her, but he had no answer. He wondered how a woman's mouth could be both mocking and tender at the same time, so shameless and so timid, and so near. He was about to say something, though he didn't quite know what, when a nearby clock struck eleven. The Holy Spirit must have just ended his shift, thought Quart. He lifted his hand, the injured one, to the woman's face, but managed to stop himself halfway. Unsure if he was disappointed or relieved, he caught sight of Don Priamo standing in the doorway, watching them.

"The moon's too bright," said Father Ferro, a small dark figure by the telescope, looking up. "It's not a good night for watching the stars."

Macarena had gone downstairs, leaving the two priests in the pigeon loft. Quart was standing by Carlota's trunk, which he had just closed.

"Turn off the light," said Father Ferro.

Quart obeyed. The books, Carlota's trunk, the engraving of seventeenth-century Seville, all melted into the darkness. Now the man at the window looked more compact. "I wanted to speak to you," said Quart. "I'm leaving Seville."

"Berenice," Father Ferro said after a while. "I can see Berenice's hair."

Quart went to the window, the telescope between him and Father Ferro.

"Those thirteen stars there," said Father Ferro. "To the northwest. She sacrificed her hair to achieve victory for her armies."

Quart looked not at the sky but at the priest's dark profile. The lights illuminating La Giralda went out, and the tower vanished suddenly, but as Quart's eyes adjusted, he could again distinguish its shape in the moonlight.

"And there, further away," the old priest continued, "almost at the zenith, you can see the Hunting Dogs." He said the name with disdain: intruders invading beloved territory.

This time Quart looked up, and he could make out, in the north, two stars, one big, one smaller, that seemed to be travelling together through space. "You don't like them much," he said.

"No. I despise hunters. Even more so when they hunt on others' behalf. In this case, they're the dogs of adulation. The bigger of the two stars was named Cor Caroli by Halley, because it shone more brightly the day Charles II returned to London."

"So it's not the dogs' fault."

The older priest laughed his grating laugh. In the moonlight his untidy hair almost looked clean. "You're a very suspicious man, Father Quart. And I'm the one who's known for being suspicious. No, I was referring only to the stars." He reached into the pocket of his cassock and brought out his cigarettes. His wrinkled, scarred face and unshaven chin were visible as he lit one, cupping the flame in his hand. "Why are you leaving?" he asked. The ember of his cigarette was now a point of light in the darkness. "Have you found Vespers?"

"Vespers' identity is the least of it, Father. He could be any of you, all of you, or none of you. It makes no difference."

"I'd like to know what you're going to put in your report to Rome."

Quart told him: the two deaths had been regrettable accidents, and Quart's investigation supported police findings. As an entirely separate matter, an elderly priest was waging his own personal battle, with the support of several of his parishioners. It was a story as old as Saint Paul, so Quart didn't think anyone in the Curia would be shocked. If the hacker hadn't sent the message to His Holiness, the matter would have gone no further than the ordinary of Seville.

"What will happen to me?" asked Father Ferro.

"Oh, nothing special. Monsignor Corvo has already drawn up a document summarising the disciplinary proceedings against you, and it'll be attached to my report, so I should imagine you'll be discreetly pushed into early retirement. You may possibly be given the chaplaincy of a convent, but I think it more likely that you'll be sent to a rest home for elderly priests."

The ember of the cigarette moved in the darkness. "What about the church?"

"That's outside my jurisdiction," Quart said. "But as things stand,

I don't see much of a future for it. There are too many churches in Seville and not enough priests. Anyway, Corvo has already said a requiescat."

"For the church or for me?"

"Both."

The priest's grating laugh rang out again. "You have all the answers," he said.

"To tell you the truth, there's one I'm missing. About something in your file. I don't want to put it in my report without hearing your version. You had some trouble when you were a parish priest in Aragon. A certain Montegrifo, if you remember."

"I remember Mr Montegrifo perfectly."

"He says he bought an altarpiece from your parish, from you."

"It was a small Romanesque church," Father Ferro said after a long silence. "The beams were rotting, the walls were cracked, and it was full of crows' nests and rats. The parish was very poor; sometimes I didn't even have the money to buy communion wine. My parishioners were spread out over several kilometres. Humble people – shepherds, peasants. They were old, sick, uneducated, without future. I said Mass every day beneath an altarpiece in danger of collapse from woodworm and damp. On weekdays the church was completely empty. There were places like that all over the country, with works of art that were stolen by dealers or that disappeared when the church roof caved in, or that just remained open to the elements. One day a man came to see me. I'd seen him before. He was with another, very well-dressed man; he said he was the head of an auction house in Madrid. They made an offer for the Christ and the small altarpiece."

"It was very valuable," said Quart. "Fifteenth-century."

"What does it matter?" snapped the old priest. "They were willing to pay. Not a great sum, but enough for a new roof and, above all, enough to help my parishioners."

"So you did sell it?"

"Of course I did. Without a moment's hesitation. I had the roof fixed, bought medicine for the sick, repaired some of the frost-damage, and saved some livestock. I helped people to live, and to die."

Quart gestured towards the church "But now you're defending this church. A contradiction."

"Why? The artistic worth of Our Lady of the Tears matters as little to me as it does to you and the archbishop. I leave all that to Sister Marsala. My parishioners, though few in number, are more important than any painting."

"So you don't believe . . ." began Quart.

"In what? In fifteenth-century altarpieces? In baroque churches? In the Supreme Watchmaker up there turning the cogs one by one?" The ember of Father Ferro's cigarette glowed more brightly as he took his last drag, then he threw it out of the window. "It doesn't matter," he said. "They believe."

"That business of the altarpiece left a black mark on your file," said Quart.

"I know." The old priest swivelled the telescope. "I had a very unpleasant meeting with my bishop. If somebody had done the same thing in Rome, I told him, it would have been a different matter. But here, we're all dancing to Saint Peter's tune. It's all tears and Quo Vadis Domine and crucify me. Meanwhile we stand outside, suppressing our conscience while the beatings go on in the hall of judgement."

"I see you don't think much of Saint Peter either."

The old priest laughed. "No. He should have let himself be killed in Gethsemane, when he drew his sword to defend his Master."

It was Quart's turn to laugh. "If that had happened, we wouldn't have had our first pope."

"That's what you think." The old priest shook his head. "In this business there are plenty of popes. But none with balls." He looked through the eyepiece. He turned the wheels, and slowly the tube of the telescope moved up and left. "When you look at the sky," he said, "things occupy a different place in the universe. Did you know that our little Earth is only a hundred and fifty million kilometres from the Sun, whereas Pluto is almost six billion kilometres away? And that the Sun is a tiny dot compared to an average star like Arcturus? Not to mention Aldebaran, which is thirty-six million kilometres across, or Betelgeuse, which is ten times bigger than that." He moved the telescope to the right. He pointed out a star to Quart. "Look. That's Altair. At three hundred thousand kilometres per second, its light takes sixteen years to reach us. It might have exploded in the meantime, and we could be seeing light from a star that no longer exists.

Sometimes, when I look towards Rome, I feel as if I'm looking at Altair. Are you sure everything will still be there when you get back?"

At Father Ferro's invitation, Quart looked through the eyepiece. As he moved away from the brightness of the moon, between the stars appeared myriad points of light, clusters and nebulae that were red, blue, white, flickering or still. One of them gradually moved and then disappeared in the glare of another – a shooting star or maybe a man-made satellite. Quart looked for the Great Bear, following the line through Merak and Dubhe upwards, four times the distance, if he remembered correctly. There was the Pole Star, large, bright, confident.

"That's Polaris," said Father Ferro, who had followed the movement of the telescope. "The tip of the Little Bear, which always indicates the Earth's zero latitude. Always but not immutable." He told Quart to point the telescope to his left. "Five thousand years ago the Egyptians venerated another one, the Dragon, as the guardian of the north. It has a 25,800-year cycle, of which only three thousand have passed. So in another two hundred and twenty-eight centuries the Dragon will be the pole star again." He drummed his fingers on the brass tube. "I wonder if there will be anyone on Earth then to notice."

"It gives one vertigo," said Quart, taking his eye away from the lens.

The old priest clicked his tongue, nodding in agreement. He seemed to enjoy Quart's vertigo, like an experienced surgeon seeing medical students go white during an autopsy. "Funny, isn't it? The universe is amusing. Polaris, the star you were looking at a moment ago, is four hundred and seventy light-years away. That means we're orientating ourselves by light that comes from the beginning of the sixteenth century." He pointed at another spot. "And over there, in the Cat's Eye Nebula, concentric shells of gas are all that's left of a star that died a thousand years ago." He walked over to another window and his features were more visible in the moonlight. "What are we?" he asked. "What part do we play in this great scene spread out above our heads? What do our miserable little lives and desires mean? Your report to Rome, the church, the Holy Father, you and I, what does all this matter to those lights?" His grating laugh rang out again.

"Supernovas will shine, stars will fade, planets will be born and die, and it will go on rotating when we are no more."

Quart again felt the instinctive solidarity between priests. Exhausted warriors, each standing in his own square on the board, isolated, far from the kings and princes. He would have liked to put his hand on the old man's shoulder, but he didn't. "I don't think I like astronomy," he said slowly. "It borders on despair."

The old man looked at him with surprise. "Despair? On the contrary, Father Quart. It gives one serenity. Because it's only the serious, valuable, significant things that cause us pain if we lose them. Little withstands the awareness that one is a tiny drop in an ocean, in the red twilight of the universe." He paused, resting his eyes on the church tower, visible through the gently moving curtains. "Perhaps only the offer of a friendly hand, before our stars go out one by one and it turns very, very cold."

After that, Father Ferro said nothing. Quart switched on the lamp, and the stars disappeared.

He went down into the garden with his jacket over his shoulder and breathed in the night air. She was waiting. The moonlight cast the shadows of leaves over her face and shoulders.

"I don't want you to leave," she said. "Yet."

Her eyes shone, the teeth between her parted lips gleamed white, and the ivory necklace was a line of white around her tanned neck. The day was very hot. Thin slits of afternoon sun filtered through a blind on to the naked body of a woman. Carmen the cigarette girl rolled tobacco leaves on her thigh, tiny drops of sweat beading a dark triangle. There was a soft breeze. The leaves of the orange trees and bougainvilleas moved over Macarena Bruner's face, and the moonlight slid down the priest's shoulders like a coat of mail sliding off and falling to his feet. The weary Knight Templar stood straight and looked round, listening to the rumble of the Saracen cavalry heading towards the hill of Hattin. He heard the stormy sea thundering against the breakwater as the fragile little boats struggled to return to port. And a woman dressed in mourning held a child's hand. Soup boiled while an old priest sat by a fireplace declining *rosa, rosae*. And, lost in a world that guided itself by starlight five centuries old, the little boy's shadow was cast on the wall that protected him from the bitter cold outside. His shadow moved closer to the other shadow waiting beneath bougainvilleas and orange trees, until he could breathe in her fragrance and her warmth, and her breath. But a second before he ran his fingers through her hair to escape loneliness for one night, the shadow, the boy, the man watching the naked body in the sunlight filtered through the blind, the exhausted Knight Templar, they all turned to look up at the dimly lit window of the pigeon loft, where an old priest, unsociable, sceptical and brave, deciphered the terrible secret of a cruel sky, in the company of a ghost searching the horizon for a white sail.

XII
The Wrath of God

He has disappeared before our very eyes and we have no idea how.
Gaston Leroux, *The Phantom of the Opera*

Through the pipe smoke, the archbishop of Seville looked exultant. "So Rome's giving in," he said.

Quart put down his cup and wiped his mouth with a napkin embroidered by a local order of nuns. He smiled and sighed. "That's one way of looking at it, Your Grace."

Monsignor Corvo blew out another cloud of smoke. The two men sat facing each other across a coffee table. It was the archbishop's custom to have breakfast with his first visitor of the morning. The coffee and toast before them had been intended for the dean of the cathedral, but the archbishop offered it to Quart instead when Quart arrived unexpectedly to take his leave, disrupting the schedule. The archbishop hated his coffee to get cold.

"I told you, didn't I, that this business wouldn't be easy to resolve," said His Grace.

Quart leaned back in his armchair. He would have preferred to deprive the archbishop of this opportunity for sarcastic remarks and smiles wreathed in pipe smoke; but form required that he pay his respects before leaving. "I would remind Your Grace," he said, "that I didn't come here to resolve anything. I came simply to inform Rome of the situation. And that's exactly what I will do now."

Corvo was delighted. "You never learned who Vespers was," he said.

Quart glanced at his watch. "No. But Vespers is not really the problem. The hacker getting through to the Pope is a trivial matter; they'll find out who he is sooner or later. The important thing is Father Ferro and Our Lady of the Tears. With my report, whatever decision is made will be made with full knowledge of the situation."

The yellow stone in the archbishop's ring glinted as he raised his hand. "Don't give me your jesuitical waffle, Father Quart. You've failed." The pipe smoke could not hide his glee. "Vespers has made fun of both you and Rome."

"Neither I nor Rome would have intervened," Quart said coldly, "had Your Grace nipped things in the bud. Father Ferro and Our Lady of the Tears are in your diocese. And you know the saying: straying sheep, shepherd asleep."

Corvo clenched his teeth over his pipe, indignant. "Listen, Quart," he said, his voice hard. "The only straying sheep here is you. Do you take me for a fool? I know about your little visits to the Casa del Postigo. And all the rest of it, the walks and the dinners."

His Grace, whose talents in the pulpit were well appreciated by the diocese, proceeded to vent all his scorn and spleen in a harsh homily that lasted several minutes. His main point was that the IEA agent had allowed himself to be taken in by the priest of Our Lady of the Tears and his own personal pressure group made up of nuns, aristocrats and devout old ladies. Quart had lost his sense of perspective and betrayed his mission in Seville. And the daughter of the duchess of El Nuevo Extremo – who was still, by the way, Gavira's wife – had played no small part in the seduction.

Quart listened impassively to the tirade but stiffened at this last remark. "I'd be most grateful if Your Grace would put any allegations concerning this last matter in writing."

"I will indeed." Corvo was delighted to have touched a raw nerve at last. "I'll send it to your bosses in the Vatican. To the nuncio. To all and sundry. I'll do so by letter, by telephone, by fax, and to the accompaniment of a guitar." He took the pipe from his mouth and leered. You'll lose your reputation just as I lost my secretary."

That was that. Quart folded his napkin, dropped it on the tray and stood up. "If there's nothing more, Your Grace . . ."

"Nothing more." The archbishop looked at him mockingly. "My son." He remained seated, regarding his own hand, wondering whether to deal a final blow and require that Quart kiss his ring. But at that moment the telephone rang, so he simply dismissed the priest with a wave and went to answer it.

Quart buttoned his jacket and went out into the corridor. His steps echoed beneath the painted ceiling of the Gallery of the Prelates, and then on the marble steps of the main staircase. Through the windows he could see the courtyard where the prison La Parra once stood, in which the bishops of Seville placed unruly priests. A few centuries earlier, Quart thought, Father Ferro, and maybe Quart himself, would have ended up in there, while Monsignor Corvo sent his version of events to Rome by the slowest means possible. Quart was on the bottom flight of steps, reflecting on the advantages of modern technology, when he heard someone call his name. He stopped and turned. It was the archbishop himself, and no longer looking so pleased.

"If you could come back up, Father Quart. There's something we need to discuss."

Quart retraced his steps, intrigued. As he mounted the steps, he noticed that His Grace was extremely pale. "You can't leave," Monsignor Corvo said when Quart came level with him. "There's been another unfortunate incident at the church."

He made his way past the cement mixer and two police cars. Our Lady of the Tears was thronging with policemen. He counted at least twelve – one at the door, the others inside taking photographs, lifting fingerprints, and searching the floor, pews and scaffolding for clues. The church echoed with their whispered conversations.

Gris Marsala sat alone on the steps of the high altar. Quart walked towards her up the central aisle. Simeon Navajo came to meet him halfway. As usual, the deputy superintendent had his hair in a ponytail and was wearing his round glasses and a loud shirt. The leather bag – with the .357 magnum inside, Quart assumed – was slung over his shoulder. It struck Quart that Navajo looked very out of place in the church. They shook hands. Navajo was pleased to see him.

"This makes three, Padre," he said jovially. He leaned casually against a pew, and Quart, peering past him, saw a pair of feet sticking out of the confessional.

He approached without a word, closely followed by Navajo. The door of the confessional was open. Quart thought the position of the feet strange. He could see crumpled beige trouser legs. The rest of the body was covered by a piece of blue canvas, although a yellowish, waxen hand was visible, palm up. A wound ran from wrist to index finger.

"Strange place to die, isn't it?" the policeman remarked.

"Who is it?" asked Quart hoarsely.

The question was unnecessary. He recognised the shoes, the beige trousers, the small flabby hand.

Navajo stroked his moustache. "The man's name is Honorato Bonafé. He's a journalist. Was. He was well known around Seville."

Quart nodded.

"You knew him, didn't you? I thought so. People tell me he's been rooting around here these last few days. Do you want to take a look at him, Padre?"

Navajo reached into the confessional, his ponytail shaking like the tail of a diligent squirrel. He lifted the canvas that covered the body. Bonafé was very still and very yellow, slumped on a corner of the wooden seat inside the confessional, his chin sunk into thick folds. There was a big bruise on the left side of his face, and his eyes were closed. He looked peaceful, or possibly tired. Blood had run from his nose and mouth, spreading out over his neck and shirt. It was dried.

"The forensic pathologist has just looked him over," Navajo said, pointing to a young man who was sitting in a pew making notes. "He says he died from massive internal injuries. A blow, maybe, or a fall. What we don't know is how he ended up in the confessional."

Out of duty, overcoming the revulsion he felt for the man while he was alive, Quart muttered a brief prayer and made the sign of the Cross.

Navajo watched with interest. "I wouldn't bother if I were you, Padre. He's been dead quite a while. So wherever he was going" – with his hands he imitated two flapping wings – "he'll be there by now."

"What was the time of death?"

"We don't know yet. But at a guess, our expert says twelve or fourteen hours ago."

A couple of policemen up on the scaffolding by the Virgin were having an animated conversation, and their voices rang in the vault.

Navajo told them to keep it down. They obeyed, embarrassed. Quart saw that Gris Marsala was still on the altar steps. She was watching him. For the first time, she appeared fragile. As Navajo covered Bonafé again, he told Quart that the nun had found the body early that morning.

"I'd like to talk to her," said Quart.

"Of course, Padre," Navajo said with an understanding smile. "But if you don't mind, before you do, I'd like you to tell me briefly how you knew the deceased. So we don't get the statements mixed up." He looked at Quart over his glasses.

"As you like. But the first person you ought to talk to is the parish priest."

The policeman held his gaze for a moment, without answering. Then he nodded and said, "Yes. That's what I think. The problem is, no one can find Don Priamo this morning. Strange, don't you think?"

"Have you been to his quarters?" asked Quart.

Navajo looked disappointed, as if he'd expected more than that from Quart. "From what I hear," he said, "he's disappeared off the face of the earth. In the prophet Elijah's chariot."

Quart told the deputy superintendent about his encounters with Honorato Bonafé in the hotel lobby. His description was interrupted twice by Navajo's mobile phone. Navajo extracted it from his leather bag, apologising both times. The first call was the report that there was still no sign of Father Ferro. The priest had spent the evening as usual, in the pigeon loft at the Casa del Postigo – which Quart was able to confirm, giving the hour at which he left him – and then disappeared without a trace. Father Ferro's cleaning lady said that his bed hadn't been slept in. Father Lobato had set off for his new parish late the day before, by bus. The journey was a long one, with several possible connections. Both the police and the civil guard were trying to find him. Were the priests suspects? asked Quart. Navajo put his phone away after the second call and said that until the cause of death was established, nobody was a suspect. Or to put it another way, everybody was – he peered over his glasses apologetically – although he had cause to suspect some more than others.

"What kind of probability are we talking about this time?" asked Quart.

Navajo scratched the bridge of his nose. "Well," he said, "between you and me, Padre, I'd say this time somebody gave the church a helping hand."

Quart wasn't surprised. He was no expert on corpses, although he'd seen a few, but one look at Bonafé was enough. "Murdered?" he asked, hoping to hear more.

"Your colleague the parish priest is a likely candidate," said Navajo.

"Because of his disappearance?"

"Of course. Unless the forensic guy tells us something else."

Navajo excused himself, summoned by one of his officers. Quart made his way to the altar steps, where Gris Marsala still sat.

"How are you?" he asked.

She had her arms round her legs and her chin resting on her knees. "A little in shock," she said, her American accent stronger than usual. "But I'm all right."

"Have the police bothered you much?"

The nun thought a moment. "No," she said. "They've been quite pleasant." In the church overrun with police, she looked alone and vulnerable.

"They're looking for Father Ferro," said Quart, taking a seat beside her. Then added, thinking that sounded too serious, "And for Father Lobato."

She was deep in thought, blinking from time to time as if in disbelief. She sighed and nodded. "It's possible," she said at last, "that Oscar stopped to see his parents, who live in a little village near Malaga, before going on to Almeria. That may be why they haven't found him yet."

They were both dazzled by a camera flash. One of the policemen had taken a photograph of something on the floor behind them. Quart leaned forward. "What about Don Priamo?" he asked.

She was expecting the question. No doubt she'd been asked it before. "I don't know. I arrived this morning as usual, at nine. I found the church locked. One of them always opened it at seven thirty, for Mass at eight. Nobody said Mass today."

"I was told you found the body."

"Yes. First I went to their quarters, but there was no one there. So I came in through the vestry door, using my own key." She shrugged, seemed perplexed. "At first I didn't notice anything. I went over to the scaffolding in front of the window. I turned on the lights, prepared my things. But it all seemed rather odd, so I went to phone Macarena to ask her if Don Priamo was in the pigeon loft last night. And on my way to the vestry I saw that man in the confessional."

"Did you know him?"

The expression in her blue eyes hardened. "Yes," she said, "I was standing outside with Oscar one day, and he – the journalist – came and asked us questions about Don Priamo and the work on the church. Oscar told him to go to hell."

Quart looked at her trainers, her pale ankles, the scar on her wrist. She was still hugging her legs. Quart had so many things to do – he hadn't yet managed to get through to Rome – but he couldn't leave her like this. He gestured to Navajo, who was checking on his men. "I'm afraid the police will continue bothering you," Quart said. "Three dead people is a lot. And this time it seems unlikely that it was an accident. Would you like me to phone your consul?"

She smiled. "I don't think that'll be necessary," she said. "The police have been fine."

"Did you get through to Macarena?"

Quart felt agitation when he said her name. Until this moment he'd managed to avoid thinking of her. He could drift away, with no effort at all, on those four syllables. Only a few hours before, he'd repeated that name on her lips, inside her mouth. And suddenly all was darkness again, the gleam of ivory, the warm flesh whose fragrance still lingered on his skin, his hands, his lips that she had bitten until they bled. Her tanned body rising up from his dreams, bars of light and shade on the white expanse of sheet on which they lay, a desert of sand or salt. She, tense, slender, struggling to escape her desire for him, to leave while wanting to stay, her head thrown back, her beautiful face absent, transformed, a selfish mask, moaning as his hard arms anchored her firmly, moaning as she was pinned by his man's body, her naked thighs around his waist. Catching her breath in the heat, saliva on her moist skin, sex, mouth, and the curve of her breasts, and warm neck, and chin, and again her mouth, moaning, and again her thighs open, a challenge or a refuge. Long, intense hours of struggle that passed in an instant, for at each moment he knew that what was happening had a limit and an end. And the end came with dawn and the last climax, long and fierce in the grey light filtering through the windows of the Casa del Postigo. And suddenly Quart was alone once more, in the deserted streets of Santa Cruz, not knowing whether he was damned for all eternity, or saved.

He shook his head to dispel the memory. Desperation was the exact word. So as not to give in to it, he focused on the church, the scaffolding, the figure of the Virgin, the police officers chatting animatedly by Honorato Bonafé's corpse. Later, he thought with an effort of will. Maybe later.

"We haven't spoken this morning."

Gris Marsala was looking at him intently, and it took Quart a moment to realise that she was answering his question. He wondered how much she knew about what had happened in the last few hours, both at the church and between Macarena and him.

"But the police have been to see her," added the nun. "I think they're at the Casa del Postigo now."

The priest frowned; Navajo hadn't wasted any time. And now Quart must hurry too. Half an hour earlier, at the archbishop's palace, Corvo had been unequivocal: whether Vespers was involved or not, the matter concerned only Rome, or – which came to the same – only Lorenzo Quart, and His Grace washed his hands of the whole affair. This had nothing to do with him as ordinary of Seville. Of course, Quart and the IEA could count on his support and his prayers, etc.

"Where's Father Ferro?"

Without waiting for Gris Marsala to answer, Quart started to analyse the situation. Navajo had a head start at the moment, but Quart ought to be able to catch up. They wouldn't take it very well in Rome if a priest was arrested before Quart had had the chance to brief them. Ideally the Church itself should take the initiative in the investigation. That meant finding the old priest a good lawyer and defending him until there was evidence of guilt. And if the guilt became obvious, aiding the process of secular justice. The main thing, as usual, was to keep up appearances. It remained to be seen where Quart's conscience fitted in all this; but that could wait until a better time.

"I don't know where Don Priamo is any more than you do," the nun said, surprised at how little attention he seemed to be paying to her answers. "I saw him briefly yesterday afternoon. Everything seemed normal."

Everything seemed normal too when Quart saw him at midnight, but in the meantime Bonafé had died. Quart glanced anxiously at his watch. Navajo had more resources at his disposal. With no autopsy result and no leads to follow, Quart would have to act on instinct. "Who locks up the church?" he asked.

"The main door or the vestry door?" Gris Marsala asked hesitantly.

"The main door."

"I always do. At this time of year, I work while there's daylight, until about seven or seven thirty. That's what I did yesterday. Oscar or Don Priamo usually locks the vestry door, at nine."

Quart couldn't get hold of Father Oscar, so he'd have to wait for Navajo to give him information about the assistant priest. Meanwhile he had to phone Rome immediately, go to the Casa del Postigo, keep an eye on Gris Marsala, and, above all, find the old priest. He pointed at the confessional. "Did you see this man here yesterday?"

"Before seven thirty I'm positive he wasn't in the church. I was here all the time." The nun thought a moment. "He must have come in later through the vestry."

"Between seven thirty and nine," prompted Quart.

"I suppose so."

"Who locked the vestry? Father Oscar?"

"I don't think so. Oscar came to say goodbye to me in the afternoon. His bus was leaving at nine, so it couldn't have been he who locked the vestry door. It must have been Father Ferro. But I don't know when."

"He must have seen Bonafé in the confessional."

"It's quite possible he didn't. This morning I didn't notice him myself at first. Maybe Don Priamo didn't come into the church but just locked the door from the corridor leading to his quarters."

Quart tried to piece things together. As an alibi it was somewhat weak, but it was the only one at the moment: if the autopsy established that Bonafé had died between seven thirty and nine, a greater number of possibilities opened up, considering that the parish priest could have locked up without looking inside the church. But if the time of death was later, the question of the locked door complicated things. Especially since Father Ferro's disappearance made him a suspect.

"Where will you be?" murmured Gris Marsala. In her confusion and anxiety her American accent was coming through her Spanish.

Quart raised both hands, powerless, not knowing what to say, his thoughts elsewhere. His mind worked like a clock moving backwards and forwards, establishing times and alibis. Twelve or fourteen hours, Navajo had said. In theory there were many imponderables, unknown people who might be implicated; but in the immediate vicinity the list of suspects was neither long nor difficult to draw up. Every one of them could be included on it, even Father Oscar – he could have murdered Bonafé before he left. Father Ferro too would have had plenty of time to kill Bonafé, lock the vestry door, and go to the pigeon loft, where he met Quart at eleven that night, before disappearing. And anyway, as Navajo had remarked with his policeman's logic, Father Ferro's disappearance put him at the head of the list. But Gris Marsala was also to be considered, moving around the church like a cat, with the main door locked and the vestry open until nine, and no one to back up her statement. As for Macarena Bruner, when Quart arrived at her house for dinner at nine, she was there with her mother. But the previous hour and a half put her too on the list of suspects. After all, she had been worried that Bonafé might try to blackmail her.

Furious with himself, Quart tried to maintain his concentration. The image of Macarena dispersed his thoughts, tangled the threads of logic that linked the church, the corpse, and the players. At that moment he would have given anything for a calm mind.

The examining magistrate had arrived. The policemen gathered round the confessional, ready to proceed with the removal of the corpse. Navajo talked quietly to the magistrate, glancing from time to time at Quart and Gris Marsala.

"You may have to answer more questions," Quart said to the nun. "From now on, I'd rather you did so in the presence of a lawyer. Until we find Father Ferro and Father Oscar, we have to be cautious. Do you agree?"

"Yes."

Quart wrote a name on a card and handed it to her. "This man is absolutely trustworthy. He specialises in canon and criminal law. His name is Arce, and he's worked for us before. I telephoned him from the archbishop's palace, and he'll be arriving from Madrid at midday. Tell him all you know and follow his instructions to the letter."

Gris Marsala stared at the name on the card. "You're not bringing a lawyer like this here just for me," she said, seeming more sad than frightened. As if her church had already fallen before her eyes.

"Of course not." Quart tried to reassure her with a smile. "It's for all of us. This is a very delicate matter, with civil justice intervening. It's best if we get expert advice."

She folded the card carefully and put it in the back pocket of her jeans. "Where's Don Priamo?" she asked again, her blue eyes reproachful, as if Quart were to blame for the priest's disappearance.

"I have no idea," he said quietly.

"He's not the kind of person who runs away."

Quart looked at the confessional. The police had removed the blue canvas and were bringing out Bonafé's body. Navajo was still talking to the magistrate. "I know he's not," Quart said at last. "And that's precisely the problem."

It took him less than five minutes to get from Our Lady of the Tears to the Casa del Postigo. He usually didn't sweat, but that morning his black shirt was sticking to his back and shoulders, under his jacket, when he rang the bell. The maid answered, and as Quart was asking for Macarena, he caught sight of her in the courtyard talking to two police officers, a man and a woman. When she realised he was there, she came over to him. She was in jeans, a blue checked shirt, and the same sandals as the previous night. She wore no makeup. Her hair was loose and still slightly wet. She smelled of shampoo.

"He didn't do it," she said.

The fragrance of lemon verbena and basil hung in the air, and the morning sun was already casting rectangles of light on the ferns and geraniums in the courtyard. It also put glints of honey in the woman's dark eyes.

"Where is he?" Quart asked.

Macarena stared at him gravely, tilting her head to one side. "I don't know," she said.

They were very far from the night, from the garden below the illuminated window of the pigeon loft, from the shadows of leaves over her face and moonlit shoulders. The ivory necklace didn't look the same against her freshly washed morning skin. There was no longer any mystery, no complicity, no smile. The weary Knight Templar looked around, disconcerted; he felt naked in the sunshine, his sword broken, his chain mail torn. Mortal like the rest of humanity, and as vulnerable and vulgar. Lost, as Macarena had so rightly said just before she worked her dark miracle on his body. Because it was written: She will destroy your heart and your will. The exquisite, innocent, destructive power of a woman always left her lover the lucidity to understand his defeat. Quart was left facing himself, deprived of alibis.

He glanced at his watch without seeing the time, touched his collar, tapped his jacket pocket where he kept his cards for notes, attempting to regain his composure with familiar gestures. Macarena waited patiently. Say something, he told himself. Something that has nothing to do with the garden, her skin, the moon.

"How is your mother?" he asked.

Macarena waved vaguely towards the gallery above. "Upstairs, resting," she said. "She doesn't know."

"What's happening here?"

She shook her head. The ends of her hair left damp marks on her shirt. "I don't know." Her thoughts were on Father Ferro, not Quart. "But Don Priamo would never do something like that."

"Not even for his church?"

"No. The police say that Bonafé died in the evening. You saw Don Priamo last night. Do you think he'd have come here calmly to look at the stars if he'd just killed a man?"

"But he's run away."

Macarena looked doubtful. "I'm not sure. And that's what worries me."

She looked down at the mosaics, lost in thought. Quart gazed at her face, the gentle lines beneath the open shirt. His fingers tingled as he remembered, with a deep sense of loss, the warm, dark path. In the light of day, Macarena was still absolutely beautiful. "The police have been here an hour and I've hardly had time to think," she said. "There's something that doesn't make sense . . . Imagine for a moment that Don Priamo had nothing to do with it. And that that's why he acted so normally last night."

"He didn't sleep at home last night," Quart countered. "And we assume that he locked the church with the corpse inside."

"I can't believe it." Macarena put a hand on his arm. "What if something happened to him too? Maybe he left here, and then . . . I don't know. Things can happen."

Quart pulled his arm away, but she didn't notice. Between them, water splashed in the tiled fountain. "You know something I don't," he said. "Where were you yesterday, before dinner?"

"With my mother." She seemed surprised by the question. "You saw us both here."

"Before that?"

"I went for a walk and looked around the shops . . ." She stopped suddenly, stunned. "Don't tell me you think I'm a suspect."

"What I think doesn't matter. It's the police I'm worried about."

She breathed out. She seemed more confused than angry. "The police are stupid," she muttered, "but not that stupid. At least I hope not."

It was starting to get very hot. Quart unbuttoned his jacket. Being here was his only advantage over Navajo. Maybe they'd already found Oscar Lobato and heard his version of events.

"Tomorrow's Thursday," Macarena said despondently, resting her elbows on the fountain parapet.

Quart understood now what had been worrying her since the police gave her the news: if there was no Mass tomorrow, Our Lady of the Tears was finished. The archbishop of Seville, the city council and the Cartujano Bank would pounce like wolves. "The church is the least of it now," he said. "If Father Ferro appears tomorrow, the chances are he'll be put in prison."

"Unless he had nothing to do with it . . ."

"We have to find him first and ask him. Better we than the police."

Macarena shook her head – that wasn't the point. She bit her thumbnail, lost in thought. "Tomorrow's Thursday," she repeated. But this time there was anger in her voice, and menace.

* * *

The bootblack finished polishing Octavio Machuca's shoes, sold him a lottery ticket and left with his box under his arm, humming a *copla*. The sun was high in the sky, and a waiter at La Campana unfolded the awning to shade the tables on the terrace. Sitting beside Machuca, Pencho Gavira drank his chilled beer with pleasure. The light gleamed on his sunglasses.

The old banker was recounting something – an episode from the last shareholders' meeting – and Gavira nodded distractedly. Machuca's secretary had left, and the chairman of the Cartujano Bank was about to go to Casa Robles for lunch. From time to time Gavira glanced discreetly at his watch. He had an appointment, a business lunch with three of the board members who would be deciding his future next week. Gavira didn't believe in leaving anything to chance, so in the last few hours he'd been doing some delicate manoeuvring. Of the nine board members, he was sure these three could be persuaded. And he was sure he could get a fourth to co-operate – there were some compromising photographs of that board member on a yacht in Sotogrande with a male dancer who had a taste for middle-aged bankers and cocaine. So, unusually, he wasn't paying much attention to what his boss was saying, simply nodding occasionally, as he sipped his beer. He was concentrating, like a samurai before battle, working out the seating arrangements at lunch, and how he would present matters. Gavira knew from experience that bribing a board member wasn't the same as buying any old pen-pusher. He'd have to be careful, and the cost might be high.

Machuca was interrupted by the waiter: there was a telephone call for Mr Fulgencio Gavira. Gavira excused himself and went inside, removing his sunglasses. It was probably Peregil, who hadn't surfaced all morning. He walked to the end of the bar and took the phone from the cashier. It was his secretary calling from the office. Gavira listened in silence for the next few minutes, then hung up.

He took an age to reach the door, touching his tie as if about to loosen it. He needed to order his thoughts, but his mind was sluggish with the heat, the hum of conversations, the traffic noise and the dazzling sunlight. He couldn't decide whether what had happened was good or bad; it threw his plans into disarray and meant he'd have to think again. But Gavira didn't lose his head. By the time he reached the door, he realised he didn't have time to cancel the lunch meeting, cursed Peregil for not being there when he needed him, and worked out at least three arguments why the news he'd just been given was a good thing. He wondered how to present it to Don Octavio. But the old man wasn't alone. He was on his feet, greeting Macarena with two kisses. She was with the tall priest from Rome; and all three stared at Gavira as he emerged from the bar. Gavira swore under his breath, making two elderly ladies turn to look, in shock.

It was Macarena who did the talking. Frowning, she sat on the edge of her seat, facing Machuca, leaning towards him as she spoke.

Quart saw her profile, her hair falling over her shoulders, her shirtsleeves turned up to show her tanned forearms and long, expressive hands. Now and then the old banker took one of her hands in his bony claws, squeezing it gently to calm her. But Macarena would not be calmed.

This was her terrain, her husband, her godfather. Her memories, her wounds. So Quart stayed on the sidelines, listening to and watching the two men who, one way or another, held in their hands the fate of Our Lady of the Tears. At last Macarena finished and sat back with a hostile look at Gavira, who had been smoking in silence, his legs crossed. Impassive, he opened and closed his sunglasses, glancing at Quart from time to time.

Old Machuca spoke first. "What do you know of this, Pencho?"

Gavira put the sunglasses down. "Don't be absurd, Don Octavio," he said. "Why should I know anything?"

A beggar came to their table, but Machuca waved him away.

"We're not talking about the dead man," said Macarena. "But about Don Priamo's disappearance."

Gavira took a drag on his cigarette and exhaled slowly. He glanced again at Quart. "I would think the two things are linked," he said.

Macarena clenched her fists, as if about to strike the table. Or her husband. "You know that they aren't," she said.

"You're wrong. I know nothing." Gavira smirked cruelly. "You're the expert on churches and priests." He pointed at Quart. "I see you don't go anywhere without your father confessor."

"Damn you."

Machuca raised a hand for calm. Quart noticed that the old banker didn't take his eyes off Gavira.

"The truth, Pencho," said Machuca. "I want the truth."

Gavira finished his cigarette and threw it on the ground. He looked his boss in the eye. "Don Octavio. I swear that I know nothing about the dead man in the church, other than that he was a journalist and a creep. And I don't know where the hell the priest is. All I know is what my secretary just told me on the phone: there's a corpse in the church, Father Ferro is a suspect, and the police are looking for him."

Macarena insisted: "You've been interfering with the church, wheeling and dealing around it all this time. I don't believe you know nothing."

"Well, I don't," Gavira said coolly. "I don't deny that I did have somebody look into things." He turned to Machuca, appealing to him. "I'm telling the truth, Don Octavio. I don't mind telling you that I did consider using strong-arm tactics to change the parish priest's mind. I thought about it, but that's all. Now it turns out that Father Ferro is in a mess and the church's privilege is in jeopardy." The Shark's smile widened. "What can I say? I'm sorry about the priest, but for myself I'm as pleased as can be. For myself and for the Cartujano. Nobody will shed any tears over that church."

Macarena glared. "I will," she said.

A flower seller approached, offering jasmine for the lady. Gavira told the woman to get lost. He looked at his wife more directly now. "That's the only thing I regret in all this," he said. "Your tears." For a moment he sounded almost gentle. "I still don't understand what happened between you and me." He glanced coldly at Quart. "Or what's happened since."

Macarena shook her head. "It's too late to talk about us. Father Quart and I have come to ask about Don Priamo."

Gavira's dark eyes glinted. "I'm beginning to get fed up with bumping into Father Quart."

"It's mutual," said Quart, only just maintaining his professional composure. "This is what you get for meddling with the church."

For a moment it seemed the banker might strike Quart. But then he smiled a smooth and dangerous smile. The moment passed.

Gavira said to Macarena, "I assure you I had nothing to do with it."

"No." She leaned forward again, her elbows on the table, grim. "I know you, Pencho. I know you're lying. Even when you're being sincere, you're lying. Some things just don't make sense; they can't be explained without your hand in it. Don Priamo's disappearance, today of all days, bears your stamp. Your style."

Gavira hesitated for a second. "No," he said.

Octavio Machuca narrowed his eyes, watching him curiously. In that instant Quart was certain that Macarena was right.

"Pencho," said Machuca quietly. It was both rebuke and request. But Gavira remained impassive. There was a honking of horns from the street. "If you had anything to do with it, Pencho . . ." said Machuca.

An uncomfortable thought came to Gavira then. "That kind of coincidence just doesn't happen," he muttered. He looked at Macarena and Quart. The traffic lights turned from red to green, the sun reflected off the procession of windscreens was blinding. Gavira blinked, reddening, suddenly overcome by the heat. "You'll have to excuse me," he told them. "I have a business lunch to attend." He clenched his fist and raised it to his chin, as if to punch himself. When he stood, he knocked over his glass of beer.

XIII
The Lovely

"Ah, Watson," said Holmes. "Maybe you would not behave so elegantly yourself if you were at once deprived of both wife and fortune."
A. Conan Doyle, *The Adventures of Sherlock Holmes*

With a *paso doble* playing in the background, the guide's voice could be heard over a loudspeaker – something about the Torre del Oro being eight centuries old. The engine of the tourist boat resounded outside on the river, and after a few moments the swell reached the *Lovely*, rocking the moored vessel. The cabin smelled of stale sweat. As the sound of the engine and the music faded, Don Ibrahim watched a ray of sun that was streaming through the open porthole move slowly to starboard, across the table littered with the remains of a meal. The ray glinted on La Niña Puñales's silver bracelets and then slowly returned to port, coming to a stop on Peregil's poorly disguised bald patch.

"You could have chosen a place that didn't rock," said Peregil. His hair was untidy and he mopped his sweating forehead with a handkerchief. His eyes were dull and he had the unmistakable pallor of the seasick. Tourist boats passed frequently; and the swell of each brought new discomfort.

Don Ibrahim said nothing. His own life had taught him not to judge other men in their misery and shame. He removed the band from a Montecristo and gently stroked the cigar. He pierced it with Orson's penknife and placed it in his mouth, turning it voluptuously as he wetted one end and savoured its aroma.

"How's the priest?" asked Peregil, a little more composed now that the boat had stopped rocking but still waxen.

Unlit cigar in his mouth, Don Ibrahim nodded gravely, as befitted a situation involving a man of the cloth. There was no reason for a kidnapping to be devoid of respect. This was something he'd learned in Latin America, where people shot one another while preserving good manners. "He's fine. Very quiet and composed."

Peregil steadied himself by the table, making sure he didn't look at the food, and smiled faintly. "The old man's tough," he said.

"*Othu*," said La Niña. "Bloody tough." She was crocheting, her fingers moving quickly, her bracelets jangling. From time to time she put the work down and had a swig of her Manzanilla, the half-empty bottle within arm's reach. Her mascara had run in the heat, and her lipstick was smeared. Her long coral earrings swung as the boat rocked.

Don Ibrahim arched his eyebrows approvingly at La Niña's remark. She wasn't exaggerating. They'd gone to nab the old priest after midnight, in the alley leading to the garden gate of the Casa del Postigo, and it took some doing to get a blanket over his head, tie his hands and bundle him into the van – rented for twenty-four hours – waiting on the corner. In the scuffle, Don Ibrahim's walking stick was snapped in two, El Potro received a black eye and La Niña lost two fillings. You wouldn't have believed what a fight the little old man put up.

Peregil was nervous as well as seasick. Manhandling a priest and keeping him out of circulation for a few days wasn't likely to be viewed sympathetically by a judge. Don Ibrahim was having doubts too, but he knew it was too late to go back now. Besides, this was all his idea. Men like him went forward bravely. On top of that, the four and a half million they'd get for the job wasn't to be sniffed at.

Like Don Ibrahim, Peregil had removed his jacket. But unlike Don Ibrahim's white shirt, Peregil's shirt was a lurid combination of blue and white stripes with a sweat-stained salmon-pink collar, and his tie, patterned with green, red and mauve chrysanthemums, looked like a dead bouquet. "I hope you'll stick to the plan," he said.

Don Ibrahim looked offended. He and his colleagues were conducting this operation with razor-sharp precision – if you discounted little episodes like El Potro's contretemps with the petrol, or the unfortunate propensity of film to be ruined by exposure to light. Anyway, the plan was nothing special. It was just a question of holding on to the priest for another day and a half and then letting him go. It was easy, inexpensive, and had a certain elegance. Stewart Granger, James Mason, Ronald Colman and Douglas Fairbanks Jr.

would have approved. Don Ibrahim, El Potro and La Niña had rented videos for research purposes.

"As for renumeration . . ." The former bogus lawyer tactfully left the sentence unfinished, concentrating on lighting his cigar. Men of honour didn't discuss money. Peregil wouldn't know what honour was if it hit him in the face, but that was no reason not to give him the benefit of the doubt. So Don Ibrahim held his lighter to the Montecristo, took the first, delicious draw, and waited for Peregil to speak.

"When you let the priest go," Peregil said, "I'll pay the three of you. A million and a half each, excluding VAT." He laughed quietly at his own joke and mopped his forehead again. La Niña looked up from her crocheting for a moment, and Don Ibrahim squinted at Peregil through the cigar smoke. He didn't like the man or his laugh, and suddenly he had the awful suspicion that Peregil might not have the money to pay them. With a sigh, he pulled his watch from his jacket. It was hard being a leader, he thought. Pretending you were confident, giving orders in a steady voice, hiding your doubts with a gesture, a glance, a smile. Maybe Xenophon – he of the five hundred thousand – or Columbus, or Pizarro when he drew a line in the sand with his sword, maybe they too had experienced this feeling of having the ladder whipped away from under you and being left dangling cartoon-like from the ceiling.

Don Ibrahim looked tenderly at La Niña. The only thing that worried him about going to prison was that they would be apart. Who would look after her then? Without El Potro, without Don Ibrahim to go *olé* when she sang, to praise her cooking, to take her to the Maestranza bullring, to give her his arm when she'd had a bit too much to drink, the poor thing would die like a bird out of its cage. And what about the *tablao* they wanted to set up for her?

"Take over from El Potro, Niña."

She finished her Manzanilla, stood up, smoothed her polka-dot dress and looked through the porthole. Beyond the geraniums planted in old cans – wilting even though El Potro watered them every afternoon – she could see the old quay, a couple of tethered boats and, in the background, the Torre del Oro and San Telmo Bridge. "No Moors in sight," she said.

Taking her crocheting with her, she crossed the cabin, her starched flounces bouncing, and left behind a heady fragrance of Maderas de Oriente, which made Peregil visibly queasy. When she opened the cabin door, Don Ibrahim caught a glimpse of the priest: sitting on a chair, facing away, one of La Niña's silk scarves tied around his eyes, his wrists bound to the back of the chair with thick tape bought the previous afternoon from a pharmacy in the Calle Pureza. He was as they'd left him, unmoving, closed off, not saying a word except when asked if he wanted a sandwich, a little glass of something, or to take a piss. Then he would tell them to go to hell.

La Niña went in and El Potro came out, closing the door behind him.

"How's he doing?" asked Peregil.

"Who?"

El Potro stopped by the table, looking perplexed, his eye the worse for wear after the trouble last night. His lean, hard pectorals, glossy with sweat, were outlined beneath his vest. His left forearm was still bandaged. On his right shoulder, next to the vaccination mark, he had a tattoo of a woman's head, in blue, with an illegible name beneath. Don Ibrahim had never asked if it was the name of the unfaithful one who caused his downfall, and El Potro had never referred to it. Maybe he didn't remember. Anyway, their private lives were their business.

"The priest," said Peregil faintly. "How's he doing?"

Frowning, the former bullfighter and boxer pondered the question. At last he looked at Don Ibrahim, like a hound who, receiving a command from a stranger, seeks confirmation from his master.

"Fine," he answered when he saw no objection in his boss's eyes. "Sits still and doesn't say a word."

"He hasn't asked any questions?"

El Potro rubbed his squashed nose, trying to remember. Perhaps the heat made it hard for him to think. "No," he said. "I unbuttoned his cassock a bit so he could breathe, but he didn't say anything."

"It's to be expected," put in Don Ibrahim. "He's a man of the church. This is an attack on his dignity." He shook ash from his shirt front, while El Potro nodded slowly, staring at the closed door as if he'd just resolved something that had been bothering him.

"I'm going," Peregil said, pale and sweaty. With the cigar smoke and the rocking, he couldn't take it any more. "Stick to my instructions." He started to get up, automatically smoothing his hair over his bald patch. At that moment, the *Lovely* rocked as another tourist boat went by, and Peregil obsessively watched the ray of sun enter the porthole, move from starboard to port, and return. He gasped for air, and turned to Don Ibrahim and El Potro with wild eyes. "Excuse me," he said in a stifled voice, then rushed for the door.

It was the worst lunch of his life. Gavira barely touched the cuttlefish with broad beans and the grilled salmon. He just managed to get to the dessert with his smile intact and without jumping up every five minutes to phone his secretary, who was desperately trying to get hold of Peregil. The banker lost the thread several times right in the middle of a sentence, with the board members of the Cartujano waiting for him to finish an explanation. Only with a tremendous effort of will was he able to get through the ordeal gracefully. He needed time to think, to devise plans and solutions to the problems raised by his henchman's absence; but there was no time. This meeting was crucial to his future; he couldn't neglect his lunch guests. He had to fight on two fronts, like Napoleon against the British and Prussian armies at Waterloo. He smiled, sipped his Rioja, presented his point of view, lit a cigarette, while his mind was working frantically. The board members were gradually coming over to his side, but he was growing seriously worried at the lack of news from Peregil. His assistant must have had something to do with the priest's disappearance and might also be involved in Bonafé's death. The thought made Gavira break into a cold sweat, but he put on a brave face. A lesser man would have sobbed on the tablecloth.

The head waiter made his way between the tables, and it was clear from his face that he was coming to tell Gavira something. Suppressing the urge to jump up from his chair, Gavira finished his sentence, stubbed out his cigarette, took a sip of water, wiped his mouth with a napkin, and only then stood up, saying to the board members with a smile, "Would you excuse me a moment?"

He went to the lobby, his hands in his pockets to stop their trembling. His stomach lurched when he caught sight of Peregil, whose hair was in disarray and who was wearing a horrendous tie.

"I've got good news," said the henchman.

They were alone. Gavira hustled him into the gents, locking the door behind them when he was sure there was no one else there. "Where have you been? he said.

"Making sure there's no Mass tomorrow," said Peregil, with a smug smile.

Gavira could have killed his assistant then and there, with his bare hands. "What have you done, you bastard?"

Peregil's smile faded. He blinked. "What do you think?" he stammered. "I did what you told me. I neutralised the priest."

"The priest?"

In the neon light, Peregil's bald head shone beneath the scraggly strands of hair. "Yes," he said. "Some friends of mine have put him out of circulation until the day after tomorrow. He's perfectly safe." He stared at his boss, bewildered.

"When was this?" Gavira asked.

"Last night," Peregil answered, hazarding a timid smile. "He's in a safe place and being treated well. They'll let him go on Friday, and that'll be that."

"What about the other one?"

"What other one?"

"Bonafé. The journalist."

"Oh, that one." Peregil flushed, and looked shaken. "Look, I can explain. It's a complicated story, but I can explain everything, I swear."

Gavira felt a wave of panic. If his assistant was involved in Honorato Bonafé's death, Gavira's problems were only just beginning. He paced about, trying to think. But the white tiles made his mind go blank. He turned to Peregil and said, "Well, it had better be good. The police are looking for the priest."

Oddly, Peregil didn't seem particularly surprised. In fact, he looked relieved. "They're quick," he said. "But don't you worry."

Gavira couldn't believe what he'd just heard. "Not worry?"

"No. It'll only cost five or six million more."

Gavira pushed his henchman against the washbasin. He didn't know whether to punch his face or ask him another question. Controlling himself, he said, "Are you serious, Peregil?"

"Yes. You have nothing to worry about."

"You're joking, aren't you?"

"I wouldn't joke with you, boss. I'd never do that."

Gavira closed his eyes. "You come and tell me that you've kidnapped a priest who's wanted for murder and I'm not to worry?"

"What do you mean, wanted for murder?" asked Peregil, suddenly quiet.

"Just what I said."

The henchman looked around and checked that the door was locked. Again he asked Gavira, "What murder?"

"A murder in the church, and your damn priest is the prime suspect."

Peregil gave a short, desperate laugh. "Don't joke like that, boss."

Gavira came so close that Peregil almost had to sit in the washbasin. "Look at me. Do I look like I'm joking?"

Peregil was now as white as the tiles. "A murder?" he asked.

"That's right. And they think the priest did it."

"Before or after we nabbed him?"

"How the hell should I know? Before, I suppose."

Peregil swallowed with difficulty. "I haven't quite got this clear, boss. Who was murdered?"

Gavira left Peregil throwing up in the gents. He took his leave of the board members and climbed into his Mercedes. He told the chauffeur to turn on the air-conditioning and go and get himself a drink. Cellular phone in hand, he tried to think. He was sure his assistant had told him the truth. Now that his initial panic was over, he could see new problems. He didn't know if it was a series of coincidences or whether Peregil's people had really happened to kidnap the priest shortly after he did away with the journalist. The fact that the police had established that the hour of death had been early evening and that the priest hadn't been kidnapped – according to Macarena and the priest from Rome – until after midnight left Priamo Ferro without an alibi. This changed everything. Guilty or not, the priest was a suspect, and the police were looking for him. Holding on to him, therefore, was risky. Gavira was sure the priest could be set free without jeopardising his own plans. In fact, it suited him rather well: Father Ferro would be kept pretty busy with the interrogation. If Gavira's men let him go this evening, it was a sure thing there wouldn't be Mass at Our Lady of the Tears the following day. The trick would be returning the priest to public life cleanly, without a scandal. Whether the priest fled or turned himself in after that, Gavira didn't care. One way or another, Priamo Ferro would be out of circulation for a while. An anonymous call might help. The archbishop of Seville wouldn't be in a hurry to find a replacement. As for Don Octavio, it would be all the same to him.

The question of Macarena still had to be resolved, but Gavira could benefit from the new situation. It would be perfect if he could convince her that he'd had the priest set free as a favour to her, that Peregil had got a bit carried away in kidnapping the old man but that Gavira himself had had nothing to do with it. With the matter of Bonafé hanging over them all, and in particular over her dear Don Priamo, she would be careful to be discreet. There might even be some sort of reconciliation between them. Macarena and the priest from Rome could take charge of the parish priest with or without the police. Gavira didn't really have anything against the old man, but with a bit of luck, he was now as doomed as his church.

With the air-conditioning on, the temperature inside the Mercedes was perfect. More relaxed now, Gavira sank back in the black leather seat and considered himself in the rear-view mirror. Maybe it hadn't been such a bad day after all. The Shark smiled as he dialled the number of the Casa del Postigo.

Macarena looked at Quart as she hung up the phone. She fell into thought, resting an elbow on the table covered with books and papers in a corner of the room she used as a study. They were on the top floor. There were tiles decorated with flowers, leaves and Maltese crosses, dark beams on the ceiling, and a large black marble fireplace. Signs of Macarena were everywhere: a television, a VCR, a small hi-fi, books on art and history, ancient bronze ashtrays, comfortable armchairs upholstered in dark corduroy, embroidered cushions. A large cupboard contained a jumble of ancient manuscripts, volumes with yellow parchment bindings and video tapes, and a couple of good paintings were hung on the walls: a Saint Peter by Alonso Vázquez, and a painting of the Battle of Lepanto by an unknown artist. Near the window, under a bell jar, a frowning archangel held his sword aloft.

"That's it," said Macarena.

Quart stood up, but she didn't move.

"There's been a mistake, and he apologises," she said. "He swears he had nothing to do with it. The people who work for him did it on their own initiative."

Quart didn't care. There would be time later to establish who was responsible. The main thing was to get to Father Ferro before the police did. Guilty or not, he was still a priest: the Church couldn't stand by with hands folded.

"Where are they holding him?" he asked.

"He's safe, on a boat moored to the old quay by the Arenal. Pencho will call when he's sorted it out." She crossed the room, picked up a cigarette from her desk, and took her lighter from under her bra strap. "He offers to return him to me rather than to the police, in exchange for a truce. Although his mentioning the police is just a bluff."

Quart exhaled, relieved. At least that part of the problem was solved. "Will you tell your mother?" he asked.

"No. It's better if she doesn't find out until everything's settled. This news could kill her." She was upset. She had forgotten to light her cigarette. "You should have heard Pencho," she added. "Attentive, charming, at my disposal. He knows he's about to win and he's selling us a non-existent alternative. Don Priamo can't escape when they let him go."

She said it coldly, and the coldness filled Quart. Each time one of her gestures awakened a recent memory, he felt a great sadness. Having got so close to him and taken him to a place where the edges were blurred and solitude and tenderness were shared, she had moved away again. It was too soon to know what the priest would be losing and gaining in the woman's warm flesh; but the image of the betrayed Knight Templar tormented him. Seville had taken too much from Quart in too short a time, giving him nothing in return save a painful self-awareness. He wished for a call to battle; it would restore his tranquillity.

Macarena's dark eyes were on him, but she wasn't thinking about him. There were no honey-coloured glints, no moon casting shadows of bougainvillea and orange tree leaves. For an instant, the IEA agent wondered what the hell he was doing there. "I don't see why Father Ferro should run," he said, with effort. "If he disappeared because he was kidnapped, then he's less of a suspect."

She wasn't reassured. "That changes nothing. They'll say he locked the church with the dead man inside."

"Yes. But maybe, as Gris said, he can prove he didn't see Bonafé. It would be good for everyone if he explained himself at last. Good for you and me. And for him."

She shook her head and said, "I must talk to Don Priamo before the police do." She went over to the window and leaned against the frame, looking down at the courtyard.

"So must I," said Quart, moving closer. "It would be better if he turned himself in, with me and the lawyer I've summoned from Madrid." He looked at his watch. "Who must now be with Gris at police headquarters."

"She'd never accuse Don Priamo."

"Of course not."

Macarena turned to Quart, anxiety in her eyes. "They're going to arrest him, aren't they?"

How absurd to be jealous of a small, dishevelled old priest, but Quart couldn't deny it. "I don't know," he said. In a rocking chair beside the tiled fountain in the courtyard below, oblivious to all that was going on around her, Cruz Bruner sat fanning herself and reading peacefully. "But from what I saw at the church, I'm afraid they will."

"You think he did it, don't you?" Macarena looked very sad, contemplating her mother. "Even though he didn't disappear of his own free will, you still believe he did it."

"I don't believe anything," snapped Quart. "It's not my job to believe." He thought of Uzzah in the Bible, who "put forth his hand to the ark of God, and took hold of it . . . And the anger of the Lord was kindled against Uzzah; and God smote him there for his error; and there he died by the ark of God."

Macarena crumbled the unlit cigarette between her fingers, and shreds of tobacco fell at her feet. "Don Priamo is no murderer."

Quart said nothing. He thought of Honorato Bonafé lying dead in the confessional, struck down by the implacable fury of the Almighty. He could see Father Ferro as a murderer.

* * *

A quarter to eleven. Leaning against a lamppost beneath Triana Bridge, Celestino Peregil heard the clock strike as he watched glittering reflections in the black waters of the river. The headlights of cars crossing the bridge slid along the iron railing, above the arches and stone pillars, and also beyond the parapet of gardens and terraces rising from the Paseo de Cristóbal Colón, by the Maestranza. But below, all was still.

He set off along the esplanade beneath the bridge, towards the old quays of the Arenal. The breeze from Sanlucar rose, gently rippling the dark surface of the Guadalquivir and lifting the henchman's spirits. After the high emotion of the last few hours, everything was returning to normal. Even his ulcer was letting up. The appointment was for eleven o'clock by the boat, where Don Ibrahim and his colleagues would be waiting. Gavira had given Peregil full instructions so that no mistakes would be made: the lady and the tall priest would arrive to collect Father Ferro, and all Peregil had to do was make sure that everything went without a hitch. The parish priest was to be led off the boat and the handover would take place in one of the old warehouses on the quay. Peregil had the key to the warehouse in his pocket. As for the money for the three scoundrels, the assistant had had a lot of trouble convincing his boss to pay; but the urgency of the situation and the banker's desire to rid himself of the parish priest helped things along. Peregil patted his belly lovingly: he was carrying the four and a half million in notes of ten thousand hidden under his shirt, tucked into the waistband of his shorts. He had another five hundred thousand at home that he got out of his boss at the last minute, under the pretext of expenses vital to the successful completion of the operation. All that cash in his pants made him walk stiffly, as if he were wearing a corset.

He began to whistle optimistically. Other than a few fishermen or dating couples, the place was deserted. Peregil listened with pleasure to the frogs croaking among the reeds. The moon was rising over Triana and all was right with the world. Five minutes to eleven. He quickened his pace. He was dying to get this over with so he could head straight for the Casino, to see if the half a million yielded anything good. Making sure he kept twenty-five thousand back for an encounter with Dolores la Negra.

"Ah, Peregil, this is a surprise."

He stopped dead. Two figures rose from a stone bench as he passed. One was tall, thin, menacing: the Gypsy Mairena. The other was slim, elegant, with the precise movements of a dancer: El Pollo Muelas. The moon was hidden by a cloud, or maybe it was Peregil's eyes that clouded. His ulcer gave a stab. He went weak at the knees.

"Guess what day it is."

"Wednesday," said Peregil in a faint, plaintive voice. "I've got one day left."

The two shadows moved closer. Their cigarettes glowed, one higher than the other. "You haven't worked it out right," said the Gypsy Mairena. "You've got one hour left. Thursday begins on the dot of midnight." He struck a match, and the flame lit up his hand, lit up the stump of his little finger. "One hour and five minutes."

"I'll pay," said Peregil. "I swear."

El Pollo Muelas's laugh was friendly. "Of course you will. That's why we're going to sit down here together on this bench, all three of us. To keep you company until it's Thursday."

Peregil looked around in a blind panic. The river offered no protection, and he didn't have a chance if he ran along the deserted quay. He could temporarily solve things by handing over what he had on him, but there were two drawbacks to this: the amount didn't cover his entire debt to the moneylender, and he wouldn't be able to justify the loss to Gavira, to whom he now owed the sum of eleven million. Without even considering the kidnapped priest hanging like a heavy burden from a rope around Peregil's neck. The lady and the tall priest would show up, and he could just imagine the look on the faces of Don Ibrahim, El Potro del Mantelete and La Niña Puñales if he left them holding the baby. Added to that, there was the dead man in the church, the police, and all the other trouble. He looked again at the black river. Maybe it would be cheaper if he just jumped in and drowned.

He sighed deeply and took out a pack of cigarettes. He glanced at the two shadows in turn. Why worry, he thought resignedly, there are plenty of hospitals. "Either of you got a light?"

The Gypsy Mairena was just about to strike a match when Peregil tore off along the quay towards Triana Bridge, as if his life depended on it. Which it did.

For a while he thought he was safe. His breathing was measured – one, two, one, two – blood throbbed at his temples, his heart pounded and his lungs burned as if they were being ripped from his chest and turned inside out. He ran almost blindly in the darkness. He could hear the two men behind him, the curses of the Gypsy Mairena, the wheezing of El Pollo Muelas. A couple of times Peregil thought he felt them touch his back or legs, and in a frenzy of terror he ran faster and believed he was getting away. He could see the car lights approaching rapidly up ahead, on the bridge. Steps, he thought incoherently, befuddled by his exertions. There were steps somewhere to the left, and up there – streets, lights, people. He veered, something hit his back, and he speeded up again, crying out. There were the steps: he sensed rather than saw them in the shadows. He made a last effort, but he was finding it more and more difficult to get his legs to obey him. He lurched forward, his lungs were a searing wound, he couldn't breathe. He reached the foot of the steps and thought that maybe he would make it after all. Then his strength failed, and he fell to his knees, as if he'd been shot.

He was done in. Under his shirt, the notes were stuck to him with sweat. He rolled over on his back, lying against the bottom step, and the stars above revolved like fairground lights. Where's all the oxygen gone, he thought, one hand pressing on his heart to keep it from jumping out of his mouth. Beside him, panting, leaning against the wall, the Gypsy Mairena and El Pollo Muelas were trying to catch their breath.

"Son of a bitch," he heard the Gypsy say, spluttering. "Runs like the wind."

El Pollo Muelas was now crouching, heaving like a bellows full of holes, his bared teeth visible in the light of a street lamp. "That was great, Peregil. It really was," he said, gently patting Peregil's face. "We're impressed." He struggled to his feet and, smiling, gave Peregil another couple of friendly pats, then jumped on his right arm and snapped the bone. It was the first of Peregil's bones to be broken that night.

* * *

Macarena glanced at her watch for the hundredth time. It was eleven forty. "Something's wrong," she whispered.

Quart was sure she was right, but he said nothing. They waited in the darkness by the locked gate of a jetty for pedaloes. Above them, beyond the palm trees and bougainvilleas and the deserted terraces of the Arenal, the cupola of the Maestranza and a corner of the Cartujano Bank were visible. Some three hundred metres downriver, the Torre del Oro, all lit up, mounted guard by San Telmo Bridge. Exactly midway, moored to the quay, was the *Lovely*.

With a sweater tied round her shoulders, she watched the place where Gavira's man should have appeared. The boat in which Father Ferro was supposed to be being held looked deserted, silent and dark. They'd arrived early, and after a time Quart thought the banker might have tricked them. But then he rejected the idea – Gavira couldn't afford to play tricks at this stage.

A breeze made the jetty creak. Water lapped gently around the posts of the quay. Something must have happened to alter the plan. Assuming that the old priest was on the boat – and they had no guarantee of that other than Gavira's word – his rescue was going to be more complicated if the intermediary didn't show up. Quart thought of Navajo.

"Maybe we should phone the police," he suggested.

"Absolutely not," she said, not taking her eyes off the boat. "First we have to talk to Don Priamo."

Quart glanced round. "Nobody's coming," he said.

"They will. Pencho knows he's got a lot to lose here."

But nobody appeared. When it was gone twelve, the tension had become unbearable. Macarena paced up and down by the gate to the jetty. She'd forgotten her cigarettes. Quart stayed and watched the *Lovely* while she went to a phone to call her husband. She returned looking grim. The banker had assured her that Peregil promised he would be there at eleven on the dot, with the money for the handover. He had no idea what had happened but would meet them there in fifteen minutes.

Gavira appeared after a time, walking under the acacias towards the jetty. In the darkness he seemed more tanned than usual. "God knows what's happened to Peregil," he said by way of greeting. That was it – no apologies or superfluous remarks. He was clearly worried – and prepared to do anything to deliver Father Ferro from a kidnapping to which he, Gavira, could be linked. Anything, as long as the police weren't involved. Quart admired the man's composure. Gavira had brought cigarettes, and he and Macarena lit up, cupping their hands around the flame. The banker listened more than he spoke, his head tilted, in control. He just wanted everything to be resolved for the best. At last he looked directly at Quart and asked, "What do you think?" It wasn't a challenge or a threat, simply an objective question.

Quart hesitated only a moment. He didn't like the idea of the old priest's going from the hands of the kidnappers straight into the hands of Deputy Superintendent Navajo. Quart had to talk to him first. "We should go in," he said, nodding at the *Lovely.*

"Let's do it, then," said Macarena, resolute.

"One moment," said Quart. "We need to know first what we'll find there."

Gavira told him. According to Peregil's reports, there were three. A fat man of about fifty was the boss. There was also a woman and a former boxer. The boxer might be dangerous.

"Do you know the layout of the boat?"

Gavira didn't, but it was the usual type of tourist boat: an upper deck with several rows of seats, a bridge in the bow, and, below deck, half a dozen cabins and an engine room. The boat had obviously been out of service for some time.

The ghosts that had troubled Quart over the last few hours gradually dispersed. The night, the boat in darkness, the imminent confrontation, all filled him with an almost childishly pleasant sense of anticipation. He was in control, back on familiar territory. He even discovered in Pencho Gavira an unexpected comrade in arms, and his dislike of the man diminished. No doubt the dislike would return tomorrow, but for tonight at least, the Knight Templar had an ally. Quart appreciated the fact that Gavira had come on foot, alone, and was now preparing to board the *Lovely* without superfluous words.

"Let's go," said Macarena impatiently. At that moment she couldn't have cared less about either man. Her only concern was the boat.

Gavira looked at Quart. His teeth shone white in the darkness. "After you, Father," he said.

They approached, careful not to make any noise. The boat was tied to the quay with two ropes, one to the bow and one to the stern. Crossing the gangway stealthily, they found a deck littered with coils of rope, old lifebelts, tyres, tables and chairs. Quart switched his wallet to his trouser pocket, removed his jacket, and left it folded on one of the seats. Gavira silently followed suit.

They crossed the upper deck. For a moment they thought they heard movement beneath their feet, and the quay became faintly illuminated, as if someone had opened a porthole to look out. Quart held his breath and trod softly. Blood pounded in his ears; he tried to calm himself so he could hear everything around him. He came to the bridge, where the helm and instruments were under canvas covers. Leaning against the bulkhead, he listened. The place smelled dirty and abandoned. Macarena and Gavira stood tense beside him. The banker looked questioningly at Quart. Macarena frowned; from the determination on her face, you'd have thought she'd been raiding boats in the middle of the night all her life. From behind the door came the muffled sound of a radio.

"If there's trouble, we take a man each," whispered Quart. "Macarena can see to Father Ferro."

"What about the woman?" asked Gavira.

"I don't know. We'll see if she does anything and deal with it then."

They discussed the situation in hushed voices. The banker said he would speak for Peregil and try to resolve things amicably. They quickly weighed pros and cons. The problem, of course, was that the kidnappers were expecting money and Gavira only had his credit cards. Regretting now that they hadn't called the police, Quart reviewed tactics. If they tried the friendly approach, there would be a lot of talking. A raid entailed speed, surprise, violence. The idea was not to give their opponents time to think, to stun them. And should the worst happen, he hoped that God – or whoever was on duty that night – would make sure there weren't any casualties.

"Let's go in."

This is ridiculous, he thought. Then he picked up a heavy metal bar, took a deep breath, and opened the door. He wondered whether he should also have made the sign of the Cross.

Don Ibrahim spilled his coffee down his trousers. The tall priest had materialised in the doorway, in shirtsleeves, with a nasty metal bar in his hand. Don Ibrahim struggled to his feet and now saw another man behind the priest, dark and good-looking, and he recognised the banker Gavira. Then the young duchess appeared.

"Please stay calm," said the tall priest. "We've come to talk."

Still in his vest, the Spanish Legion tattoo on his shoulder glossy with sweat, El Potro del Mantelete sat up in his bunk and put his bare feet on the floor. He looked at Don Ibrahim as if asking whether this visit was scheduled or not.

"Peregil sent us," announced Gavira. "Everything's in order."

If everything was in order, thought Don Ibrahim, they wouldn't have been there, Peregil would be putting four and a half million on the table, and the tall priest wouldn't be holding that metal bar. Something had gone wrong. He glanced over the shoulders of the three new arrivals, expecting the police to appear any moment.

"We need to talk," said the tall priest.

What Don Ibrahim, La Niña, and El Potro needed to do was get the hell out of there. But La Niña was next door with the old priest, and leaving wouldn't be that easy – because, among other things, three people were blocking the exit. Damn his luck, he thought. Damn it and all the Peregils and all the priests in the world. He knew getting involved with cassocks would bring bad luck. He was an idiot – it had been obvious from the start.

"There's been a misunderstanding," Don Ibrahim said, playing for time.

The priest's face was stony; with his dog collar, the metal bar in his hand was as incongruous as a couple of pistols in the hands of Jesus. Don Ibrahim leaned on the table, while El Potro watched him like a dog awaiting orders. If only he could protect La Niña, Don Ibrahim thought. And make sure she wasn't implicated if the worst happened.

Events made his decision for him. The young duchess looked around, her eyes flashing. "Where are you keeping him?" she demanded. Not waiting for an answer, she took a couple of steps to the closed door of the cabin. That young lady was certainly pretty mad, thought Don Ibrahim. Instinctively, El Potro stood up, blocking her way. He looked hesitantly at his colleague, but Don Ibrahim didn't know how to react. At that moment, the banker moved as if to defend the woman, and El Potro, more decisive with regard to an adult male, shot him a left hook that threw him against the bulkhead. After that things became complicated. As if a bell had rung somewhere in his battered memory, El Potro held up his fists and started to bounce around the cabin, striking out in all directions, ready to defend his bantamweight title. Gavira was flung against a cupboard full of tin cups that came crashing down, the young duchess ducked to avoid one of El Potro's right-handers and made for the cabin where the old priest was being held, and Don Ibrahim started shouting for everyone to calm down. Nobody listened.

La Niña, hearing the noise, came out to see what was going on and slammed into the young duchess, while Gavira, no doubt seeking revenge for El Potro's punch, advanced on Don Ibrahim, looking none too friendly. The tall priest looked hesitantly at the metal bar in his hand, threw it to the ground and stepped back to avoid El Potro, who was still striking out at anything that moved, including his own shadow.

"Stop!" pleaded Don Ibrahim. "Stop!"

La Niña became hysterical, pushed the young duchess, and rushed at the banker as if to scratch his eyes out. Gavira stopped her dead with a very ungentlemanly punch that flung her back into the cabin, flounces and polka dots flying, right at the feet of the old priest, who was blindfolded and tied to a chair. At this, Don Ibrahim forgot his conciliatory intentions. The former bogus lawyer overturned the table, lowered his head as Kid Tunero and Don Ernesto Hemingway had taught him in the Floridita Bar in Havana, and yelling "Viva Zapata!" – it was the first thing that entered his head – he flung his hundred and ten kilos at the banker, taking him crashing to the other side of the cabin. Just then, El Potro hit the priest in the face with a left hook, the priest grabbed the lamp to keep himself from falling, the electric cord sparked as it was pulled from the socket, and the boat was plunged into darkness.

"Niña! Potro!" shouted Don Ibrahim, gasping from the struggle and letting go of the banker.

Something shattered. The darkness was filled with cries and blows. Someone, perhaps the tall priest, fell on top of Don Ibrahim and elbowed him in the face so hard that he saw stars. The bastard wasn't turning the other cheek. With blood trickling from his nose, Don Ibrahim crawled away, dragging his belly. It was dreadfully hot and he could hardly breathe. El Potro appeared for a moment as a dark shadow in the doorway, still striking out to left and right, in a world of his own. More blows and curses came from various directions, and something broke with a great splintering of wood. A high-heeled shoe trod on Don Ibrahim's hand, and then a body fell on top of him. He immediately recognised the flouncy dress and fragrance of Maderas de Oriente.

"The door, Niña! Run to the door!"

He struggled to his feet, let loose a punch – missing – at someone who got in his way, grabbed La Niña by the hand, and dragged her up on deck. El Potro was already out there, bouncing around the helm. Don Ibrahim, heart pounding, exhausted, certain he would have a coronary at any moment, took El Potro by the arm and, still gripping La Niña's hand, pulled them both to the ladder and dry land. There, pushing them ahead of him, he managed to steer them along the quay. La Niña was weeping. Beside her, his head down and breathing through his nose – left, right – El Potro del Mantelete did battle with the shadows.

They took Father Ferro up on deck and sat there, enjoying the cool evening air after their skirmish. With the torch they'd found, Quart could see Gavira's swollen cheek and right eye almost closed, Macarena's dirty face with a scratch on her forehead, and the scruffy figure of the old priest, his cassock wrongly buttoned and two days of stubble covering his scarred face. Quart himself wasn't in much better shape: the man who looked like a boxer had got in a good punch just before the lamp went out. Quart's jaw was now stiff, and his ears buzzed. He prodded a tooth with the tip of his tongue and thought he could feel it move.

It was a strange situation: the deck of the *Lovely* littered with broken seats, the lights of the Arenal above the parapet, the Torre del Oro illuminated beyond the acacias downriver. And Gavira, Macarena and he in a semicircle around Father Ferro, who had not said a single word. The old priest stared at the black river, as if he were far away.

Gavira was the first to speak. Precise and calm, he put his jacket round his shoulders. Without denying that he was responsible, he said that Peregil had misunderstood his instructions. That was why he was here now, trying to set things right if he could. He was prepared to offer the old priest compensation, which included tearing Peregil to shreds when he laid hands on him; but he made it clear that this didn't change his attitude towards the church. The two matters were completely separate. He paused to feel his swollen cheek and light a cigarette. "In which case," he added after a moment's thought, "I'm no longer involved in this." That was all he said.

Macarena spoke next, giving the old priest a detailed account of everything that had happened since his disappearance. Father Ferro listened without any sign of emotion, even when she told him that Honorato Bonafé was dead and the police suspected Father Ferro of the murder. This was Quart's area. Father Ferro turned to him and waited.

"The problem is," said Quart, "you have no alibi."

By the light of the torch, the old priest's eyes were sunken and inscrutable. "Why should I need an alibi?" he asked.

"Well," said Quart, leaning forwards, his elbows on his knees, "there's a crucial period, between seven or seven thirty in the evening until about nine o'clock. It depends what time you closed the church. If you had any witnesses to what you were doing during that time, it would be wonderful." He waited for the priest to answer, observing how hard the old man's face looked.

"There are no witnesses," said Father Ferro.

He seemed not to care. Quart and Gavira exchanged a glance. The banker remained silent. Quart sighed.

"This makes things difficult," he said. "Macarena and I can testify that you arrived at the Casa del Postigo shortly after eleven, and that there was absolutely nothing suspicious in your behaviour. Gris Marsala can confirm that everything happened as usual until seven thirty. I assume that the first thing the police will ask you is how you could have failed to notice Bonafé in the confessional. But you didn't go into the church, did you? That's the most logical explanation. We have a lawyer for you, and I assume he'll ask you to confirm that point."

"Why should I?"

Quart looked at him with exasperation. "What can I say? It's the most credible version. It'll be harder to assert your innocence if you tell them you locked the church knowing there was a dead man inside."

Father Ferro remained impassive, as if it had nothing to do with him. Quart went on to remind him that the days were long gone when the authorities accepted the word of a priest as gospel. Particularly when corpses turned up in his church. But the old man paid no attention, glancing at Macarena or staring silently at the black river.

"Tell me. What would suit Rome?" Father Ferro said at last.

This was the last thing Quart expected to hear. He became impatient. "Forget Rome. You're not that important. There will be a scandal anyway. Imagine, a priest accused of murder, and in his own church."

Father Ferro scratched his chin. He seemed almost amused. "Good," he said at last. "Then what has happened suits everyone. You get rid of the church," he said to Gavira, "and you and Rome" – to Quart – "get rid of me."

Macarena stood up. "Please don't say that, Don Priamo," she said. "There are people who need that church, and who need you. I need you. And so does the duchess." She stared defiantly at her husband. "And tomorrow's Thursday."

For a moment Father Ferro's face softened. "I know," he replied. "But things are out of my hands now. Tell me one thing, Father Quart. Do you believe I'm innocent?"

"I do," said Macarena, almost pleading. But the old priest's eyes remained fixed on Quart.

"I don't know," Quart said. "I really don't. But that doesn't matter. You're a fellow priest. It's my duty to help you as much as I can."

Father Ferro gave Quart a strange look, a look he had never given him before. For once, there was no hardness in his eyes. Gratitude, perhaps. The old man's chin trembled, but then he blinked, clenched his teeth, and his face was hostile again. "You can't help me," he said.

"No one can. I don't need alibis or proof, because when I locked the vestry door, that man was lying dead in the confessional."

Quart closed his eyes. This left no way out. "How can you be sure?" he asked, guessing and fearing the answer.

"Because I killed him."

Macarena turned abruptly with a cry. Gavira lit another cigarette. Father Ferro stood up, clumsily buttoning his cassock. "You'd better turn me over to the police now," he said to Quart.

The moon slid slowly down the Guadalquivir, meeting the reflection of the Torre del Oro in the distance. Sitting on the bank, with his feet hanging just above the water, Don Ibrahim held a handkerchief to his bleeding nose. His shirt was untucked, showing his fat belly covered with coffee stains and oil from the boat. Beside him, lying face down as if the referee had counted to ten and it no longer mattered, El Potro too stared at the black, silent waters, lost in a dream of bullrings and afternoons of glory, of applause under the spotlights in the boxing ring. He was a tired hound waiting faithfully beside his master.

> And the early risers ask you:
> María Paz, what are you waiting for . . .

At the foot of the stone steps leading down to the river, La Niña dipped the hem of her dress in the water and wiped her forehead, singing softly to herself in a husky voice redolent of Manzanilla and defeat. And the lights of Triana winked from the far bank, while the breeze from Sanlucar and from the sea and – it was said – from America rippled the surface of the river, soothing the three companions:

> He once swore his love,
> but now he sings a different tune.

Don Ibrahim put a hand to his heart and let it drop again. He'd left Don Ernesto Hemingway's watch and García Márquez's cigarette lighter and his panama and the cigars all back on the *Lovely*. Together with the remaining shreds of his dignity and the promised four and a half million they were going to use to set up a *tablao* for La Niña. There had been many bad business ventures in his life, but none as disastrous as this.

He sighed deeply and, leaning on El Potro's shoulder, got to his feet. La Niña came up the steps from the river, gracefully gathering her damp skirts. The former bogus lawyer looked affectionately at the dishevelled kiss-curl, collapsing bun, smudged mascara and withered mouth bare of lipstick. El Potro stood up too and Don Ibrahim caught a whiff of his honest male sweat. And then, invisible in the darkness, a fat round tear ran down Don Ibrahim's cheek.

At least all three of them were safe. And this was Seville. On Sunday, Curro Romero would be fighting at La Maestranza. Triana, all lit up, spread out across the river like a refuge, guarded by the impassive bronze figure of Juan Belmonte. And there were eleven bars within three hundred metres, at the Plaza del Altozano. Somewhere a guitar strummed impatiently, waiting for a voice to start singing. And, after all, none of it mattered that much. One day, Don Ibrahim, El Potro, La Niña, the king of Spain and the Pope in Rome would all be dead. But Seville would still be there, just as it always was, smelling of bitter oranges and jasmine in the spring. Watching the city's reflection in the river that had given and taken so much, good and bad, so many dreams and so many lives, La Niña sang:

> You stopped your horse,
> I gave you a light,
> and your eyes
> were two green stars
> of May for me . . .

As if her singing was a signal, the three companions set off, side by side, without looking back. And the silent moon followed them on the waters of the river, until they disappeared into the shadows and all that remained was a very faint echo of La Niña Puñales's last song.

XIV
Eight O'Clock Mass

> ***There are people – amongst whom I would include myself – who detest happy endings.***
>
> Vladimir Nabokov, *Pnin*

The policeman on duty peered curiously from behind the glass partition at Lorenzo Quart's black suit and dog collar. After a moment he left his post in front of four closed-circuit monitors trained on the exterior of police headquarters and brought the priest a cup of tea. Quart thanked him and watched his receding back with handcuffs on the belt and two bullet clips beside the holstered gun. The policeman's footsteps and then the sound of the door closing echoed in the deserted hallway. The hall was cold, white, sterile in the neon light, with a marble floor. It was three thirty in the morning by the digital clock on the wall.

He had been waiting almost two hours. After they left the *Lovely*, Gavira exchanged a few words with Macarena and then held out a hand to Quart, who shook it in silence. "We're not enemies, Father." He said it without smiling, looking him straight in the eye, and then turned and walked away, towards the steps leading up to the Arenal. Quart couldn't tell whether Gavira meant Father Ferro or Macarena. But the gesture had cost the banker nothing. Having diluted his responsibility for the kidnapping by his last-minute intervention, confident that neither Macarena nor Quart would cause him problems, and worried only about his assistant and the money for the handover, Gavira had had the decency not to crow over the strong position he now occupied with regard to Our Lady of the Tears. After Father Ferro's confession, the vice-chairman of the Cartujano was undoubtedly the victor that night. It was difficult to see how anyone could stand in his way now.

Macarena had seemed to be walking at the edge of a nightmare. On the deck of the *Lovely*, Quart saw her shoulders shake as she watched her dream collapse. She didn't say another word. They took Father Ferro to police headquarters and then Quart took her home in a taxi. He left her sitting in the courtyard by the tiled fountain, in the dark. When he said a soft goodbye, he saw that she was looking up at the pigeon loft. The rectangle of black sky looked like a backdrop painted with tiny luminous dots above the Casa del Postigo.

Quart heard a door open, and voices and footsteps at the other end of the white hall. But no one appeared, and after a moment all was silent again. He got up and paced. He stood at the glass door and smiled with forced friendliness. He went and smiled at the policeman outside, who was walking up and down in a bulletproof vest and with an automatic rifle over his shoulder. The station was in the modern part of the city. At the crossroads, deserted at that time of the night, the traffic lights changed slowly from red to green.

He tried not to think. Or rather, to think only about the technical aspects of the case. Father Ferro's new legal situation, the reports Quart would have to send to Rome first thing in the morning . . . He tried to keep his emotions from taking over. But his old ghosts joined the ranks of the more recent ones, and this time he could feel them drumming against his very skin.

For a long time he stared at his reflection in the dark glass of the door. The good soldier turning grey and in need of a shave. The white collar that could no longer protect him. He had come a long way, only to find himself again on the breakwater pounded by the waves, brine streaming down the cold hand to which the boy clung.

A door opened across the hall, and as Quart turned to look, he saw Simeon Navajo coming towards him, his red shirt vivid in the white, sterile hall. Quart went to meet him. The deputy superintendent was drying his hands on a paper towel. He had just come out of the toilets, and his damp hair was smoothed back into a ponytail. He had bags under his eyes and his glasses had slipped down his nose.

"That's it," he said, throwing the towel into a bin. "He's just signed his statement."

"He claims he killed Bonafé?"

"Yes." Navajo gave an apologetic shrug. These things happen, the shrug said. Neither of us is to blame. "We asked him about the other two deaths, as a formality, and he neither admitted to them nor denied them. It's a nuisance, because those cases were closed, but now we have to reopen the investigation."

He went to the door and stood watching the lights in the empty street, his hands in his pockets. "To tell you the truth," he said, "your colleague isn't very communicative. He only answered yes or no the whole time, or remained silent as the lawyer advised."

"Is that all?"

"Yes. He didn't even bat an eyelid when we confronted him with Miss . . . er . . . Sister Marsala."

Quart glanced at the door. "Is she still in there?" he asked.

"Yes. She's signing the last few forms, with that lawyer you brought. She can go home soon."

"Does she back up Don Priamo's confession?"

Navajo made a face. "On the contrary. She doesn't believe it. She says the priest doesn't have it in him to kill anybody."

"And what does he say?"

"Nothing. Just looks at her and doesn't say a word."

The door at the end of the hall opened again and Arce, the lawyer, walked out. He was a placid-looking man, in a dark suit with the gold badge of the Lawyers' Association on his lapel. He'd been handling legal matters for the Church for years and was renowned for dealing with irregular situations like this. He charged a fortune.

"How's she getting on?" asked Navajo.

"She signed her statement," said Arce. "She's asked for a few minutes alone with Father Ferro, to say goodbye. Your colleagues don't object, so I've left the two to talk for a moment. Under supervision, of course."

The deputy superintendent glanced suspiciously at Quart, then at the lawyer. "They've had over three minutes," he said. "It'd be better if you took her away now."

"Will you be putting Father Ferro in a cell?" asked Quart.

"He'll sleep in the sick bay tonight," Arce answered, with a gesture that said they could thank the deputy superintendent for this concession. "Until the judge decides tomorrow."

The door opened again, and Gris Marsala was led out by a policeman holding some typed sheets of paper. The nun looked forlorn, exhausted. She was in her usual jeans and trainers, with a denim jacket over her blue shirt. In the harsh white light she looked even more vulnerable than she had that morning.

"What did he say?" asked Quart.

She took an age to turn to the priest, as if she didn't recognise him at first. "Nothing," she replied in a flat voice. "He says he killed him, and that's all."

"And you don't believe him?"

From somewhere in the building came the muffled sound of doors opening and closing. Gris Marsala looked at Quart, infinite contempt in her blue eyes.

After the lawyer and the nun left by taxi, Navajo seemed to relax. "I hate those guys," he confided to Quart. "With all their habeas corpus tricks. I can't stand them, Father, and this one of yours has more tricks up his sleeve than a magician." Once Navajo had got this off his chest, he ran an eye over the papers his colleague had handed to him and then passed them to the priest. "Here's a copy of the statement. This is slightly irregular, so please don't tell anyone. But you and I . . ." Navajo smiled. "Well. I wish I could have been more help in all this."

Quart looked at him gratefully. "You have helped."

"I don't mean that. I mean a priest arrested for murder . . ." Navajo fiddled with his ponytail, embarrassed. "You understand. It doesn't make one feel very proud of one's job."

Quart glanced over the photocopied sheets, all written in officialese. Don Priamo Ferro Ordás, from Tormos in the province of Huesca, appears in Seville on such-and-such a date. At the bottom of the last sheet was the priest's signature, a clumsy scrawl. "Tell me how he did it," said Quart.

Navajo pointed at the papers. "Everything he told us is there. And we've guessed the rest from the questions he refused to answer. Bonafé was in the church around eight or eight thirty. He probably came in through the vestry door. Father Ferro went into the church to make his rounds before locking up, and there was Bonafé."

"He was trying to blackmail everybody," said Quart.

"Maybe that was it. Whether Bonafé had an appointment or it was just chance, the parish priest says he killed him, and that's that. He gave no details, only said that afterwards he locked the vestry door, leaving Bonafé inside."

"Inside the confessional?"

Navajo shook his head. "He won't say. But my people pieced together what happened. Bonafé must have been up on the scaffolding in front of the high altar, by the carving of the Virgin. Father Ferro must have gone up there too." Navajo accompanied his account with the usual hand motions. "They argued, struggled, or something. Bonafé fell, or was pushed, from five metres up. He got the wound to his hand when he tried to grab the scaffolding. On the ground, badly hurt but still alive, he dragged himself a few metres and got as far as the confessional. He collapsed inside and died."

The fingers representing Bonafé now lay motionless, on the palm of the other hand, which was the confessional. Quart could picture the scene easily, but the story didn't make sense. He said that to Navajo.

The deputy superintendent returned Quart's gaze without blinking. "I don't agree," he said at last. "As a priest, you would like there to be another explanation. The moral aspect is distasteful to you, I can understand that. But look at it from my point of view." He removed his glasses and held them up to the light. "I'm a policeman, and I have very few doubts: I have a forensic report and a man, even if he's a priest, in full possession of his mental faculties, who confesses to the murder. As we say here: if it's white and in a bottle, it's got to be milk. Skimmed or full cream, however you like it, but it's still milk."

"Fine. You know he did it. But I need to know how and why."

"Well, Father, that's your business. But maybe I can give you a few more details. Bonafé was up on the scaffolding when Father Ferro came upon him." He put on his glasses and took a little plastic bag from his pocket. "Well, look what we found on the corpse."

"It looks like a pearl."

"It is a pearl," said Navajo. "One of the twenty set into the Virgin's face, crown and mantle. And it was in Bonafé's jacket pocket."

Quart stared at the little plastic bag, at a loss. "And?"

"It's a fake. As are the other nineteen."

* * *

In his office, surrounded by empty desks, the deputy superintendent gave Quart the remaining information. He poured the priest a coffee and got himself a bottle of beer. It had taken all afternoon and part of the evening for the necessary tests to be completed, but it was definite that somebody had replaced all the pearls on the carving with fakes. Navajo let Quart read the reports and faxes on the matter. His friend, Chief Inspector Feijoo, had worked till late in Madrid trying to trace the pearls. All the clues pointed to Francisco Montegrifo, the Madrid art dealer who had been Father Ferro's contact for the illegal sale of the altarpiece from Cillas ten years earlier. It was Montegrifo who had put Captain Xaloc's pearls on the market. The description matched that of a set of pearls found in the hands of a fence, a Catalan jeweller who was also a police informer. Montegrifo's role couldn't be proved, but there was evidence. The date the informer gave for the transaction coincided with the resumption of renovation work on the church. Builders' merchants contacted by Navajo's men confirmed that the cost of the goods supplied exceeded the parish priest's salary and the contents of the church collection box.

"So we have a motive," concluded Navajo. "Bonafé's on the trail. He turns up at the church and confirms that the pearls are fake. He tries to blackmail Father Ferro, or maybe the old priest doesn't even give him time." The policeman enacted the scene with his hands. "Maybe he catches him in the middle of what he's doing and kills him. He locks the vestry door and spends a couple of hours at the Casa del Postigo, thinking. Then he disappears for a couple of days." Navajo looked at Quart, as if encouraging him to fill the gaps in his account. Disappointed when Quart said nothing, he continued reluctantly, "Father Ferro won't tell us anything about his disappearance. Strange, don't you think? And you haven't helped much in that area, Padre, if you'll allow me to say so." He took another bottle of beer and a ham sandwich from the small refrigerator behind him and started to eat.

"I'd rather say nothing than lie to you," said Quart. "By talking I'd compromise people who have nothing to do with this. Maybe later, when the whole thing's over . . . But you have my word as a priest: none of it directly affects the case."

Navajo bit into his sandwich, took a swig of beer, and regarded Quart thoughtfully. "A secret from confession, right?"

"You could call it that."

Another bite. "I have no choice but to believe you, Padre. Anyway, I've received instructions from my superiors and, I quote, I'm to proceed with the utmost tact in this affair." He smiled, his mouth full. "Although once the case is resolved, on the surface, I intend to look deeper into it, even if only in a personal capacity. I'm a devilishly curious policeman, if you'll permit the expression." For a moment he became serious. "And I don't like people pulling my leg." He screwed his sandwich wrapper into a ball and threw it in the bin. "I haven't forgotten that I owe you." He raised a finger suddenly: he'd just remembered something. "Oh, by the way. A man was just admitted to the Reina Sofia Hospital in a pretty serious condition. He was found under Triana Bridge a little while ago." Navajo peered at Quart closely. "A small-time private investigator. They say he works for Pencho Gavira, Macarena Bruner's husband. Rather a lot of coincidences for one night, don't you think? I assume you know nothing about this either."

Quart held Navajo's gaze. "No."

Navajo picked his teeth with a fingernail. "I thought not," he said. "The guy's a mess: both arms and his jaw broken. It took him half an hour to get out a couple of words. And when he did, all he said was that he'd fallen down the stairs."

Since Quart was the only Church representative available, Navajo gave him some official documents along with the keys to the church and to the priest's quarters. He also made him sign a brief declaration to the effect that Father Ferro had handed himself in voluntarily.

"You're the one cleric who showed his face. The archbishop telephoned this afternoon, but only to wash his hands of the whole thing." The policeman frowned. "Ah. And to ask us to keep the reporters out of it." He threw his empty beer bottle into the bin, yawned theatrically, and glanced at his watch, a hint that he wanted to go home.

Quart asked to see the parish priest. Navajo, after a moment's thought, said he saw no reason why not if Father Ferro agreed. He went to arrange it, leaving the fake pearl in its little plastic bag on the table.

Quart stared at the pearl, imagining it in Bonafé's pocket. It was large, with some of the sheen scraped off where it had been set into the carving. For the murderer, whoever the murderer was – Father Ferro, the church itself, or any of the people involved with it – the pearl, once out of its setting, had become a deadly object. Unwittingly, Bonafé had been treading at the edge of a secret that went beyond the scope of the police investigation. Do not profane my Father's house. Do not threaten those who seek sanctuary there. Conventional morals offered a poor vantage point for considering these events. One had to go beyond them, to cross that boundary to reach the inhospitable paths that the small, hard parish priest had trodden for years, bearing on his weary shoulders the weight of a cruel sky. Willing to provide peace, shelter, compassion; to forgive sins; and even – as on that night – to take the blame for them.

It wasn't such a mystery after all. Quart smiled sadly, staring at the fake pearl from Our Lady of the Tears. Things fell into place: the pearl, the church, the city itself, the particular point in time and space.

"Whenever you like, Father," announced Navajo, peering round the door.

It didn't matter who pushed Honorato Bonafé off the scaffolding. Quart reached out and touched the plastic bag containing the pearl. Contemplating Our Lady's fake tear, the soldier lost on the hills of Hattin recognised the hoarse voice and clash of steel of a brother waging his own personal battle in the same corner of the board. The man had no friends left to give him a hero's burial in a crypt among recumbent statues of knights in gauntlets with a lion at their feet. The sun was high in the sky, and at the foot of the hills the corpses of men and horses lay spread out at the mercy of jackals and vultures. So, dragging his sword, sweating beneath his chain mail, the tired warrior got to his feet and followed Simeon Navajo down the long white corridor. At the end, in a small room with a guard at the door, Father Ferro sat on a chair, in grey trousers and a white shirt, without his cassock. They hadn't handcuffed him, but he looked very small and defenceless. His black eyes, red-rimmed, stared impassively as Quart entered. With the guard and deputy superintendent watching, stunned, from the door, Quart went and kneeled before the old priest.

"Forgive me, Father, for I have sinned."

For an instant, the old priest looked in astonishment at the man kneeling before him. Then he slowly raised his hand and made the sign of the Cross over Quart's head. The old man's humid eyes shone, and his chin and lips trembled as he pronounced, soundlessly, the ancient formula offering solace and hope. On hearing it, all the Knight Templar's ghosts and dead comrades smiled at last, relieved.

He crossed the deserted square and walked along the avenue towards San Telmo Bridge, in the absolute solitude and silence of dawn. He saw a free taxi but didn't stop; he needed to walk. As he drew closer to the Guadalquivir, the air seemed damp, and he felt cold for the first time since his arrival in Seville. He turned up his jacket collar. By the bridge, unlit at that hour, the Almohad Tower melted into the darkness.

He crossed the bridge. The fountain at the Puerta de Jerez wasn't on as he passed the brick-and-tile façade of the Alfonso XIII Hotel. He walked along the wall of the Reales Alcázares. Near La Juderia he breathed in the fragrance of orange trees and damp earth and then turned down the narrow streets of Santa Cruz, the sound of his footsteps preceding him. He didn't know how long he'd been walking, but he felt he'd travelled a great distance, outside time, as if in a dream. Suddenly he was in the middle of a small square with houses painted red-ochre and white, a square with railings, pots of geraniums, and tiled benches that showed scenes from *Don Quixote.* And at one end, clad in scaffolding, with a dilapidated bell-tower, and guarded by a headless Virgin, stood the church of Our Lady of the Tears: three centuries old and full of memories of the people who had found refuge there.

He sat on a bench and looked at the church for a long time. Nearby, bells rang out; the swifts and pigeons took wing and then settled back on the eaves. The moon had disappeared, but the stars were still visible, twinkling icily. At daybreak it grew colder, and the priest's muscles and back began to ache. At peace now, he watched the light grow in the east. The nearby clock struck again, and once more the birds rose. The pink glow pushing night towards the other side of the city, the clear outline of the belfry, the roof, the eaves around the square – all signalled the arrival of day. Cocks crowed, because Seville was the kind of city where cocks still crowed at dawn. Quart got up, as if waking from a long dream.

At the entrance he took out the key and turned it in the lock. The door creaked as it opened. Sufficient light filtered through the windows for him to see his way between the pews facing the altar, which was still in shadow. At the altar, a candle burned. He stood in the middle of the church, looking at the confessional with its door open, at the scaffolding against the walls, at the worn flagstones and the black mouth of the crypt where Carlota Bruner's remains lay. He kneeled in one of the pews and waited until day had fully dawned. He didn't pray – he didn't know who to pray to – and the accustomed rituals of his old discipline didn't seem appropriate. So he simply waited, his mind empty, comforted by the silent reassurance of the old walls. In the growing light he could make out a bearded prophet, an angel's wings, a cloud or a ghostly figure on the smoke-blackened ceiling. The sun arrived at last, filtering through the window with the lead outline of Christ, and the altarpiece to the glory of God was lit up, all baroque gilding and pale columns. The Holy Mother crushed a serpent's head with her foot, and that, thought Quart, was all that mattered. He went and rang the bell. He sat on the floor beneath the thick rope for a quarter of an hour and then rang the bell again. There was another quarter of an hour to go before eight o'clock Mass.

He switched on the altarpiece light and lit the six candles, three on either side of the altar. He set out the books and the cruets, then went to the vestry and washed his face and hands. He opened the cupboard and drawers, took out the liturgical objects and chose the appropriate vestments. When everything was ready, he put them on in the order and manner that no cleric taught in a seminary ever forgets. He began with the amice, the strip of white cloth still worn only by very traditional or old priests like Father Ferro. Following the ritual, he kissed the Cross at its centre before putting the amice over his shoulders and tying the ribbons behind his back. There were three albs – two of them were too short for him, so he chose the third, probably the one used by Father Lobato. He then took the wide band of white silk known as the stole and, having kissed the Cross at its centre, put it on over the amice. At last he took the old white silk chasuble, with faded gold embroidery, and slipped it over his head. When he was dressed, he stood motionless, his hands resting on the sideboard, staring at the dented old crucifix between the two heavy candelabra. Despite not having slept, he felt clear-headed and peaceful, just as he had when he sat on the bench out in the square. Following the ritual, performed in the same way by others for almost two thousand years, diminished his sense of solitude. It didn't matter that the temple was damaged, that the belfry was covered with scaffolding, that the paintings on the ceiling were faded. Or that on the wall, Mary bowed her head before an angel in a painting full of cracks and stains and darkened varnish. Or that at the end of Father Ferro's old telescope, millions of light-years away, the cold stars mocked it all.

Maybe Heinrich Heine was right and the universe was nothing but the dream of a drunken God who had fallen asleep on a star. But the secret was well guarded. Father Ferro was prepared to go to prison for it, and neither Quart nor anyone else had the right to reveal it to the good people now waiting in the church. Sounds – a cough, foot-steps, a pew creaking as somebody knelt – reached him through the vestry door, beside the confessional where Honorato Bonafé died for touching Tanit's veil.

He looked at his watch. It was time.

XV
Vespers

Using his real name would have contravened the Code.
Clough and Mungo, *Approaching Zero*

Two days after returning to Rome and presenting his report on Our Lady of the Tears, Quart received a visit from Monsignor Paolo Spada at his apartment on the Via del Babuino. It was raining, just as it had been three weeks before, when Quart was ordered to Seville. When the doorbell rang, Quart was at an open window that looked on to the terrace; he was watching the rain fall on the roofs, the ochre walls of the houses, the grey sheen of the paving stones and the steps of the Piazza di Spagna.

Spada stood in the doorway, solid and square in a dripping black raincoat, shaking the rain from his bristly head. "I was passing," he said, "and I thought maybe you could give me a cup of coffee." Without waiting for an answer, he hung his raincoat on a hook, went through to the austere sitting room, and sat in an armchair by the windows. He sat there in silence, staring at the rain, until Quart returned from the kitchen carrying a coffee pot and cups on a tray.

"The Holy Father received your report."

Quart nodded, helping himself to sugar, and then stood while he stirred his coffee. His sleeves were rolled up above the elbow, and his collar was unbuttoned.

The Mastiff peered over his cup, inclining his heavy gladiator's head. "He also received," he said, "a report from the archbishop of Seville in which your name is mentioned."

The rain intensified, and the splashing on the terrace drew the two men's attention for a moment. Quart placed his cup on the tray and smiled, a sad, distant smile. "I'm sorry if I've caused you problems,

Monsignor." Disciplined and respectful, as usual. Though he was in his own apartment, he remained standing, almost lining up his thumbs with his trouser seams.

The director of the IEA gave him an affectionate look and then shrugged. "You haven't caused *me* any problems," he said gently. "On the contrary: you completed your report in record time, carried out a difficult assignment, and made the appropriate decisions with regard to Father Ferro's surrender to the police and his legal defence." He paused, considering his own huge hands. "Everything would have been perfect if you had limited yourself to that."

Quart smiled sadly again. "But I didn't."

The archbishop, his eyes streaked with brown, watched his agent for some time. "No. In the end you decided to take sides," he said with a frown. "To get involved, I suppose that's the word. And you did so at the least appropriate time and in the least appropriate way."

"It didn't seem so to me, Monsignor," said Quart.

The archbishop bowed his head benevolently. "Of course. I know. But it did seem so to the IEA." He put his cup on the tray and looked at Quart curiously. "Your orders were to remain impartial."

"I knew it was futile," said Quart. "A symbolic gesture, nothing more." He was lost in thought for a moment. "But there are times when a gesture seems important."

"Well, in fact, it wasn't entirely futile," said Spada. "According to my information, the nunciature in Madrid and the archbishopric of Seville have this morning received instructions to preserve Our Lady of the Tears and to appoint a new parish priest." He gave Quart an ironic and good-humoured wink. "Those final remarks of yours about a little piece of heaven disappearing, the patched skin of the drum, and all the rest of it certainly had an effect. Very moving and convincing. Had we known about your rhetorical abilities earlier, we would have made greater use of them." The Mastiff fell silent. Your turn to ask the questions, his silence implied. Make things a bit easier for me.

"That's good news, Monsignor," said Quart. "But good news can be given over the phone . . . What's the bad news?"

The prelate sighed. "The bad news is His Eminence Jerzy Iwaszkiewicz." He looked away and sighed again. "Our dear brother in Christ feels that he let the mouse escape, and he wants to get his own back. He's made much of the archbishop of Seville's report. According to which, you exceeded your authority. Iwaszkiewicz has also given credence to certain insinuations made by Monsignor Corvo regarding your personal conduct. The fact is, between the two of them, they're going to make things rather difficult for you."

"And for you, Your Grace?"

"Oh, well." Spada raised a hand dismissively. "I'm less easy to attack, I have files and things like that. And I have the relative backing of the secretary of state. Actually they've offered to leave me in peace for a small price."

"My head."

"More or less." The archbishop stood up and paced the room. His back to Quart, he studied a small framed sketch on the wall. "It's symbolic, of course. Like your Mass last Thursday. It's unfair, I know. But life is unfair. Rome is unfair. That's how it is. Those are the rules of the game, and you've known them all along." He turned to face Quart, hands crossed behind his back. "I'll miss you, Father Quart," he said. "You're still the good soldier. I know you did the best you could. Maybe I placed too many burdens on your shoulders. I hope that the ghost of that Brazilian, Nelson Corona, will rest in peace now."

"What will they do with me?" The question was neutral, objective, with no trace of anxiety.

Spada raised his hands in disgust. "Iwaszkiewicz, always so charitable," he said, "wanted to have you sent to some obscure secretariat." He tutted. "Luckily I held a few good cards. I'm not saying I risked my neck for you, but I took the precaution of getting out your CV, and I reminded them of your excellent record, including the business in Panama and the Croat archbishop you got out of Sarajevo. So in the end Iwaszkiewicz agreed simply that you should be dismissed from the IEA." The Mastiff shrugged his square shoulders. "The Pole will be taking one of my bishops, but the game has ended in a draw."

"And what was the verdict?" asked Quart. He pictured himself far from all of this. Maybe it won't be so difficult, he thought. A bit harder and a bit colder, but it's cold inside too. For a moment he wondered if he'd have the courage to give it all up if the sentence was too harsh. To start over somewhere else, without the black suit to protect him. The problem was that, since Seville, there were fewer places to go.

"My friend Azopardi," Spada was saying, "the secretary of state, has agreed to help. He's promised to deal with your case. The idea is to find you a post as an attaché to a nunciature, in Latin America if possible. After a time, if the situation becomes more favourable and I'm still at the head of the IEA, I'll request your return." He seemed relieved when he saw that Quart remained calm. "Consider it a temporary exile, or a mission that's longer than usual. To sum up, you are to disappear for a time. After all, Peter's work may be eternal, but popes and their teams come and go. Polish cardinals grow old, retire, or get cancer. You know how it is." He smiled crookedly. "And you're young."

Quart went to the window. Rain was still splashing the tiles. Below his feet, it slid in grey sheets across the roofs of the nearby houses. He breathed in the damp air. The Piazza di Spagna shone like a newly varnished oil painting. "What news is there of Father Ferro?" he asked.

The Mastiff arched an eyebrow. That's out of my hands, it meant. "According to the nunciature in Madrid," he said, "the lawyer you found him is doing a good job. They believe Father Ferro will be released on grounds of senility and lack of evidence, or, if the worst comes to the worst, he'll get a lenient sentence under Spanish law. He's getting on in years and there are lots of things that could predispose a judge in his favour. For the time being he's in the prison hospital in Seville, under fairly comfortable conditions. They may request that he's sent to a rest home for retired priests. I don't think he'll care much either way."

"No," said Quart. "I don't think he will."

Spada poured himself another coffee. "Quite a character, that old priest. Do you think he did it?" He looked at Quart, cup in hand. "We haven't heard from Vespers again. It's a pity you didn't find out who it was. If you had, I would have been able to defend you better against Iwaszkiewicz." He sipped his coffee gravely. "That would have been a tasty bone for the Pole to gnaw."

At the window, watching the rain, Quart nodded in silence, and the light made his short hair look even greyer. Drops of rain splashed on his face. "Vespers," he said.

* * *

His last evening in Seville, he went down to the lobby and found her there, just as he had the first time, sitting in the same armchair. Only a week had passed since that first day, but to Quart it seemed as if he'd been in Seville for ever. Like the huge stone nave standing a few metres away, across the square, with its pinnacles and flying buttresses. Like the disorientated pigeons crossing the area of night lit up by the spotlights. Like Santa Cruz, the river, the Almohad Tower, and La Giralda. Like Macarena Bruner, who now watched him approach. When she stood up in the middle of the empty lobby, Quart knew that her presence still moved him to his very core. Luckily, he thought as he walked towards her, she didn't love him.

"I've come to say goodbye," said Macarena. "And to thank you."

They went out into the street. It was indeed a farewell: short sentences, monosyllables, clichés, the kind of polite remarks that passed between strangers, and not a single reference to the two of them. Quart noticed the formality of her tone. She was relaxed yet avoided his eyes. For the first time, she seemed intimidated. They spoke of Father Ferro, of Quart's journey the following day. Of the Mass he had conducted at Our Lady of the Tears.

"I never imagined I'd see you there," said Macarena.

Occasionally, as on the night they had walked around Santa Cruz, their steps happened to bring them into contact, and each time Quart experienced an acute, physical sense of loss. They walked now in silence, as everything between them had been said; to continue talking would have required words that neither wished to say. The light of the street lamps cast their shadows against the Arab Wall, and they stopped there, facing each other. Quart beheld her dark eyes, the ivory necklace against her tanned skin. He felt no bitterness towards her. He knew she had used him – he was as good a weapon as any, and Macarena believed she was fighting for a just cause – and he had let himself be used. His thoughts were beginning to return to some sort of order. Soon, only the emptiness of his loss would remain, duly kept in check by his pride and self-discipline. But neither the woman nor Seville would ever be erased from his memory.

He searched for a sentence, a word, at least, before Macarena disappeared from his life for ever. Something that she would remember, that wouldn't jar with the ancient wall, the iron street lamps, the illuminated tower in the background and the sky where Father Ferro's icy stars shone. But he found only a blank. A long, resigned weariness that could be expressed only by a look or a smile. So he smiled in the darkness. And now she looked him in the face, as if a word she couldn't find hung on her parted lips. Quart turned and walked away, feeling her gaze on him. He thought stupidly that if she had at that moment shouted, "I love you," he would have torn off his dog collar and gone back, taken her in his arms like an officer in an old black-and-white movie throwing away his career for a femme fatale, or like those other poor fools, Samson and Holofernes. The thought amused him. He knew – had always known – that Macarena Bruner would never say those words again to any man.

"Wait!" she said suddenly. "I want to show you something."

Quart stopped. They weren't the magic words, but they were enough for him to turn. She was still standing where he had left her, her shadow on the wall. She threw back her head, shaking back her hair in a defiant gesture directed at herself rather than at him.

"You've earned it," she said with a smile.

The Casa del Postigo was silent. The English clock in the gallery struck twelve as they crossed the courtyard with the tiled fountain, among geraniums and ferns. All the lights were out, and in the moonlight their shadows swept across the mosaics, which were glistening wet after the recent watering of the plants. In the garden, crickets chirped at the foot of the dark tower that housed the pigeon loft.

Macarena led Quart across the gallery, through a small sitting room, and then up a wooden staircase with an iron handrail. They came to the glassed-in gallery on the floor above, surrounding the patio, and proceeded to a closed door at the end of it. Before Macarena opened the door, she stopped and whispered to Quart, "Nobody must ever know about this."

She put a finger to her lips and opened the door. Strains of *The Magic Flute* greeted them. The first room, in darkness, was full of furniture under dustcovers. Moonlight filtered through the window.

The music came from another room. There, through an open glass sliding door, a lamp lit up a desk covered with computer equipment: two big Sony monitors, a laser printer, a modem. And, staring at the screen flashing with icons and letters, with the Romero de Torres fan and two empty bottles of Coca-Cola on top of a pile of copies of *Wired* magazine, absorbed in the journey that provided a nightly escape from the house, Seville, herself, and her past, Vespers travelled silently through boundless cyberspace.

She didn't even seem surprised that they were there. She was typing carefully, her eyes glued to one of the monitors. Quart noticed how she did everything with great attention, as if afraid of pressing a wrong key and ruining something important. He looked at the screen: all the numbers and signs were meaningless to him, but the hacker seemed entirely at ease with them. She wore a dark silk robe, slippers, and, around her neck, the beautiful pearl necklace. Quart shook his head. Suddenly all the signs on the screen were replaced by new ones, and the eyes of Cruz Bruner, duchess of El Nuevo Extremo, shone brightly. "There it is," she said and began typing again. After a moment she pressed Enter and leaned back, satisfied. Her eyes, reddened by staring at the screen, gleamed with malice when at last she looked up at her daughter and the priest. "'For yourselves know perfectly that the day of the Lord so cometh as a thief in the night'," she said to Quart. "Isn't that right, Father? First epistle to the Thessalonians, I think. Five, two."

Her daughter placed a hand on her shoulder and looked at Quart. The old lady tilted her head to her. "If I'd known I'd be getting a visit at this time of night, I'd have done myself up," she said, touching her pearl necklace and sounding gently reproachful. "But as it's Macarena who's brought you, it's all right." She squeezed her daughter's hand. "Now you know my secret."

Quart still couldn't quite believe it. He looked at the empty Coca-Cola bottles, the piles of computer magazines – in both English and Spanish – the manuals filling the desk drawers, the boxes of diskettes. Cruz and Macarena Bruner watched him, one with amusement, the other grave. He couldn't deny the evidence of his senses:

from this desk a seventy-year-old lady had given the Vatican the runaround.

"How did you do it?" he asked.

Cruz Bruner took her hand away from her daughter's and slid it over the keyboard. A piano, thought Quart. Elderly duchesses played the piano, did embroidery or gave themselves up to nostalgia; they didn't turn into computer hackers by night.

"I never would have imagined," said Quart.

"That a little old lady could be comfortable with all this?" She straightened, her expression thoughtful. "Well, I admit it's a little unusual, but there you are. One day I took a look, out of curiosity. I pressed a key and found that things happened on the screen. And that you could travel to incredible places and do things you never dreamed of doing." She smiled, and her face was suddenly younger. "It's more fun than watching Venezuelan soap operas on television."

"How long have you been doing this?"

"Oh, not long. Three, four years." She turned to her daughter, trying to remember exactly. "I've always been very curious; if I see a line of print, I just have to start reading . . . One day Macarena bought a computer for her work. When she went out, I'd sit at it, awestruck. There was a game, a little ping-pong ball – that's how I learned my way around the keyboard. I have trouble sleeping, as you know, so I ended up spending quite a few hours at the computer. I think I became addicted."

"At her age," said Macarena affectionately.

"Yes." The old lady faced Quart, as if inviting him to express his disapproval. "I was so curious that I began to read everything I could find about computers. I learned English when I was a child, so I signed up for correspondence courses and subscribed to computer magazines." She gave a little laugh and covered her mouth with her hand, as if shocked at herself. "My health isn't too good, but luckily my brain's still all right. I became a bit of an expert in quite a short time. And I assure you, at my age, that's exhilarating."

"She even fell in love," said Macarena.

Mother and daughter laughed. Quart wondered if they weren't both slightly crazy; it all seemed like a big joke. Or maybe he was the one who was going mad. This city's gone to your head, he told himself. Just as well that you're leaving now, before it's too late.

"She's exaggerating," said Cruz Bruner. "I had the equipment, the software, so I started to get around. And, well, yes, I did have a virtual love affair. One night I happened to get into a hacker's computer, a young man of sixteen . . . You should see your face, Father. I've never seen anyone look so astonished."

"You can't expect me to find this normal."

"No, I suppose not." The old lady motioned at the modem and the pile of magazines. "Imagine," she said, "what it was for a woman of almost seventy to discover such a world. My friend called himself Mad Mike. I'll never hear Mike's voice or see his face, but he led me all over this fascinating world. There was an electronic bulletin board, and that's how I came into contact with other addicts, often boys who spent hours up in their rooms getting into other people's computers."

She sounded proud, as if talking about a highly exclusive club. Quart needed no explanations, but he must still have been looking puzzled, because Macarena smiled and told her mother to explain to him what an electronic bulletin board was.

The old lady put a hand on the keyboard. "People post messages and talk. There are chat rooms, too. After a while you reach a certain level in the hacker world. When you call the first time, they ask you for your name and telephone number. You don't give them your real name but an alias and a false number. A certain amount of paranoia is a good quality in a hacker."

"What's your alias?"

"Do you really want to know? It's against the rules, but I'll tell you, since you've got this far, thanks to Macarena." She held up her head with mock pride. "I'm Queen of the South."

Things were happening on the monitor, and the duchess broke off to press a few keys. A long text, in small type, appeared on screen. Cruz Bruner went on. "After that," she said, "I started to visit secret Websites on the Internet. I made friends there. It's great fun. You swap useful tips, tricks, games, viruses. Gradually I learned how to get into all the networks, travel abroad, hide my entry and exit points, get into protected systems. My happiest day was breaking into the Ayuntamiento and changing my tax bill."

"Which is a crime," her daughter said, scolding, and obviously not for the first time. "When I found out, I ran to city hall. Our bill was entered as having been paid until 2005! I had to tell them it was an error."

"It may be a crime," conceded the old lady, "but it doesn't seem like a crime from here. Nothing does." She smiled at Quart mischievously. "That's the wonderful thing. Now," she went on, "I keep in frequent touch with Mike as well as twenty or so other hackers. Most of them are probably under twenty. I don't know their ages, genders, or real names, but we have terribly exciting virtual meetings in places like the Galeries Lafayette in Paris, the Imperial War Museum, or branches of the Confederation of Russian Banks . . . Which, by the way, is so vulnerable that even a child could get in and alter the accounts. The Confederation tends to be used as a training route for novice hackers."

She was Vespers, there was no doubt about it. Quart could see her crouched over her computer night after night, travelling through cyberspace, meeting other solitary travellers on her journey. Unexpected meetings, exchanges of information and dreams, the excitement of violating secrets and crossing the boundary into the forbidden – a secret fraternity for whom time, space, memory, solitude, success or failure had no meaning, who had created a virtual world in which everything was possible and nothing was subject to laws. A wonderful escape route of infinite possibilities. In her own way, Cruz Bruner too was rebelling against the Seville embodied by the handsome man in the hall portrait, beside the painting of the fair young girl by Zuloaga.

"How did you get into the Vatican?"

"By chance. A contact in Rome, Deus ex Machina – I suspect he's a seminarian or a young priest – had wandered about the edges of the system, for fun. We became friends, and he gave me a couple of good pathways. That was about six or seven months ago. The situation at Our Lady of the Tears was just then becoming serious. Neither the archbishop of Seville nor the nunciature in Madrid would take any notice of Father Ferro, and it occurred to me that this would be a good way of getting Rome's attention."

"Did you tell Father Ferro?"

"No. I didn't even let my daughter know. She found out later, when the existence of Vespers – as you called him – became known." The old lady pronounced the name with obvious satisfaction. Quart would have liked to see the faces of His Eminence Jerzy Iwaszkiewicz and Monsignor Spada hearing all this. "At first, I thought I'd leave a simple message in the central Vatican system, hoping it would reach the right quarters. It was only later, when I found my way around, that I thought of getting through to the Pope's computer. By chance I came across a well-protected file called INMAVAT and I realised there was something important there. I made a couple of attempts to get in, using some tricks taught me by my hacker friends, and one night I succeeded. For a week I visited INMAVAT until I understood what it was all about. I found what I wanted, gathered my ammunition, and began my attack. You know the rest."

"Who sent me the postcard?"

"Oh that. I did, of course. Since you were here, I thought you ought to see the other side of the problem. I went up to the pigeon loft and found something suitable in Carlota's trunk. It was slightly bizarre, but it had the desired effect."

Despite himself, Quart burst out laughing. "How did you get into my hotel room?"

The old lady looked shocked. "Heavens, I didn't do it myself," she said. "Can you see me tiptoeing along hotel corridors? I used a more dignified method. My maid slipped a waitress some money." She half-turned to her daughter. "When you showed Macarena the postcard, she knew immediately it was I. But she was nice enough not to tell."

Quart found confirmation in Macarena's eyes. He glanced at the computer screen. "Tell me what you're up to now."

"Oh, this. You could call it a final settling of scores. Don't be alarmed. It has nothing to do with Rome this time. Something closer to home. More personal."

Quart took a look. `S&B Confidential`, he read. `Summary of CB internal investigation re PT deal and others`. The names of the Cartujano Bank and Pencho Gavira stood out in the text:

```
Some of the methods used to conceal the true situation were as
follows: frenetic searching for new and expensive sources of funds;
false accounting and infringement of banking regulations; and risk-
```

taking that – should the expected sale of Puerto Targa to Sun Qafer Alley (forecast to fetch some hundred and eighty million dollars) not take place – will deal a serious blow to the Cartujano Bank and cause a public scandal, considerably diminishing the Bank's high standing with its shareholders, most of whom are conservative by nature and have small shareholdings.

As for the irregularities for which the present vice-chairman is directly responsible, the investigation has uncovered a general lack of financial prudence. Considerable sums have been paid to professionals and private individuals without due documentary proof. These include cases of payments to public figures and institutions that can only be described as bribery. The investigation has also discovered ...

He looked at Macarena, then at the duchess. This was a shot straight at the ex-husband's fleet. He remembered the banker the night before on the quay, and the brief sympathy established between them as they joined forces to free the old priest. "What are you intending to do with this?" he asked.

Macarena shrugged. It was Cruz Bruner who answered. "I just want to even things out a little. People have done so much for the church. You yourself gained us another week by conducting Mass yesterday. I suppose that's why Macarena thought you deserved to come here tonight."

"He won't tell anyone," said Macarena.

"Good," the duchess said. She studied her daughter, frowning, then turned again to Quart. "Although I feel the same as Father Ferro. At my age, many things no longer matter, and you fear less." She stroked the keyboard absent-mindedly. "Now, for instance, I'm about to see that justice is done. Not a very Christian action, I know, Father Quart." She sounded harder now, more determined. "After this, I imagine I'll have to go to confession. I'm about to sin against charity."

"Mother."

"Leave me alone, dear, please." She pointed at the text on the screen. "This is a report on an internal audit of the Cartujano Bank. It exposes all Pencho's machinations involving Our Lady of the Tears. Making it public would be slightly damaging to the bank and extremely damaging to my son-in-law." She smiled. "I'm not sure Octavio will ever forgive me for it."

"Will you tell him?" asked Macarena.

"Of course."

"Where did you get this report?" asked Quart.

"From my son-in-law's computer. His password wasn't hard to crack." She shook her head. "I'm sorry, because I always liked Pencho. But it's the church or him."

A light flickered on one of the devices. Cruz Bruner glanced at it, then turned to the priest with all the haughtiness of generations of dukes of El Nuevo Extremo. "It's the modem," she said, her eyes sparkling. Her smile was cruel, contemptuous. "I'm faxing the report to all the newspapers in Seville."

Standing beside her mother, her face in darkness, Macarena had stepped back and was staring into space. The English clock struck downstairs, among the dark paintings mounting guard in the shadows of the Casa del Postigo. Quart felt sure that at that moment Carlota Bruner's ghost was smiling up in the tower, while a schooner glided upriver, its white sails filled by the breeze that rose every night from the sea.

Cruz Bruner died at the beginning of winter. By then Quart had spent five months as third secretary at the apostolic nunciature in Bogota. He read about it in the international edition of *ABC*. The death notice gave the long list of the deceased's titles and included the request of her daughter Macarena, heir to the dukedom, that prayers be said for her soul. A couple of weeks later he received an envelope with a Seville postmark, containing only a small printed card edged with black and showing more or less the same text as the death notice. It was accompanied not by any letter but only by the postcard of Our Lady of the Tears that Carlota Bruner sent to Captain Xaloc.

In time, Quart learned about the fates of several of the players in the story. A letter from Father Oscar, having followed a circuitous route from a little village in Almeria to Rome and then on to Bogota, said that Our Lady of the Tears was still open for worship and functioning as a parish. The assistant priest added that he had radically revised his opinion of Quart.

The only news of Pencho Gavira was a brief item in the financial section of the Latin American edition of *El País*, about Octavio Machuca's retirement from the Cartujano Bank in Seville and the appointment of a new chairman of the board. Quart did not recognise the appointee's name. The article also mentioned Gavira's resignation as vice-chairman and general manager of the bank.

Quart received sporadic information about Father Ferro. The verdict was involuntary manslaughter, and Father Ferro was moved from the prison hospital to a rest home for elderly priests in the diocese of Seville. He was still there, in poor health, at the end of that winter, but according to a brief, courteous note from the director of the home, in response to Quart's enquiry, it was unlikely that the old priest would survive until spring. He spent his days in his room and had nothing to do with anyone; at night, in good weather, he went out into the garden, accompanied by a nurse, and sat in silence on a bench watching the stars.

Of the remaining characters whose paths crossed Quart's during his stay in Seville, Quart heard nothing more. They gradually faded from memory, together with the ghosts of Carlota Bruner and Captain Xaloc, who often accompanied him on his long evening walks through the colonial district of old Bogota. All but one of them disappeared. He caught only a brief glimpse of her and was never absolutely sure it was she. This happened some time later. Quart had just been transferred to another even more obscure secretariat in Cartagena and was leafing through a local paper when he saw a report on the peasant revolt in the Mexican state of Chiapas. The report described life in a small, remote village under guerrilla control. At the local school a group of children were photographed with their teacher. The picture was blurred, and even with a magnifying glass Quart couldn't be sure, but the woman looked very familiar. She was wearing jeans, and her grey hair was gathered in a short plait; her hands were resting on her pupils' shoulders, and she stared defiantly at the camera with cold blue eyes. The eyes that were the last thing Honorato Bonafé saw before he was struck down by the wrath of God.